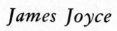

*James Joyce*

# JAMES JOYCE

## BY HERBERT GORMAN
### ILLUSTRATED WITH PHOTOGRAPHS

## OCTAGON BOOKS
A DIVISION OF FARRAR, STRAUS AND GIROUX

New York    1974

*Reprinted 1974*
*by special arrangement with Holt, Rinehart and Winston, Inc.*

OCTAGON BOOKS
A DIVISION OF FARRAR, STRAUS & GIROUX, INC.
19 Union Square West
New York, N. Y. 10003


Library of Congress Cataloging in Publication Data

Gorman, Herbert Sherman, 1893-1954.
    James Joyce.

    Reprint of the ed. published by Rinehart, New York.

    1. Joyce, James, 1882-1941—Biography.
PR6019.09Z547    1974                823'.9'12 [B]                74-12172
ISBN 0-374-93219-0


Manufactured by Braun-Brumfield, Inc.
Ann Arbor, Michigan

Printed in the United States of America

# List of Illustrations

*James Joyce*

# One

A T the junction of Nassau Street and College Green, hard by
the dark wall of Trinity College and in the very heart of
Dublin, one may board the Terenure tram and within fifteen
minutes descend in Rathgar. This pleasant residential suburb of the
city, almost indistinguishable from neighbouring Rathmines, is built
upon the former lands of the Cusack family; and their castle, now
long gone, stood on the ground immediately south of the upper end
of Rathgar Road. It is a district that has witnessed battle and murder. It was over this territory, then sylvan and unadorned by the
brick pillboxes that we call houses, in early August 1649, that the
engagement, one of a series, now known as the Battle of Rathmines
was contested, some two thousand Royalist foot under the command of Lord Inchiquin losing an action in the grove adjoining
Rathgar Castle to Cromwell's Parliamentary troopers.

As for the murder, the *Freeman's Journal* for March 17, 1798,
related: "Yesterday morning about two o'clock, a numerous banditti,
said to be forty in number, attacked the country house [it was called
Rathgar House and stood on Highfield Road] of Charles Farren,
Esq., which is situated near Rathmines Road, adjoining the avenue
that leads to Rathfarnham Road. They first entered the gardener's
lodge, in which was a poor man, in the service of Mr. Farren, named
Daniel Carroll, who giving what resistance he could to the barbari-
ans, they cruelly put him to death, and which we since understand
was the chief purpose for which they came to that place." The murderers were apprehended and publicly hanged at the crossroads of
Terenure, but the "numerous banditti, said to be forty in number,"
dwindled down to three rascals named Kelly, Rooney, and O'Don-
nell. Even in 1798 Irish exaggeration was not to be curbed.

Today Rathgar has the appearance of a thousand other suburbs
that flank the great cities of the world. It is just far enough away
from the congested narrow stone-paved thoroughfares to have detached houses, front lawns shaven or glowing with cultivated flowers

3

in their seasons, trees that shade its well-kept walks, and that pleasant sophisticated serenity that is half-city and half-country-town. There are streaks and lozenges of electric light across its evening ways and the sound of the radio is loud on the air. The thatched cottages and little inns of an earlier day have vanished and ruddy brick has taken the place of weathered timber. But underneath its modern foundations still exists that dark untamed and violent soil that knew battle and murder in the days when the Gael was hammering against the Pale. It is necessary to understand this if one is to understand Dublin. It is necessary to understand that the modern city that we call Dublin and which was once a conglomeration of huts by the Ford of the Hurdles that the Ostmen (Scandinavian rovers) captured and christened Diflyn, or Black Pool, in the ninth century, is builded upon legends, old wives' tales, forgotten horrors and a giant mythos. It exists as a modern metropolis today, but yesterday it was a concentration point for heroic figures that now loom larger than life-size and for gestures, beautiful, savage, gnostic, that become epitomes of all history. In the mythos Howth is more than a hill and the Liffey is more than a river. One does not walk along the pleasant roads of Rathgar and Ranelagh and Rathmines, now pulsing with motorcars and bicycles, without recalling that here were the 'Bloody Fields' where the wild O'Byrnes and O'Tooles swooped down from the Dublin and Wicklow mountains and slaughtered half a thousand Dubliners on a day that was afterwards called Black Monday. From the moment in 836 when the thatched roofs of the squalid little town by the Liffey were supposed to have been ignited by swallows flying with blazing sponges under their wings to the year of dubious grace, 1937, when in the night the equestrian statue of George II was blown up in Stephen's Green by alleged Republican terrorists Dublin has been a focal point of passions and impossibilities, violent controversies, angers, desperate loves, fantastical boastings, and barbarous betrayals. Who can gainsay that there are wild Titanic spirits in the soil?

In 1882 Rathgar was even closer to the febrile mythos of a self-contained Old Ireland than it had ever been. A high anticipation of being master in one's own house permeated the rainy atmosphere that lowered above the Liffey. Men congregated in inns, in public houses, on street corners and violently discussed the dawn of a new era. The spirits in the soil were twitching their long armoured limbs. It was a murky dawn, at best, but the ray of light was there, falling as though through a scarcely-opened door and evident to eyes almost too passionate to see. The battle cry (and Irishmen must always have battle cries) was Home Rule. The Leader (and Irishmen must always have leaders if only to betray them) was Charles Stewart Parnell, a man without a drop of Irish blood in his body. He was a new leader (successor to the impotent Isaac Butt) and at the moment he was incarcerated in Kilmainham Jail, but behind prison bars or out his was the shoulder that was pushing back that scarcely-opened door. On Dublin street corners ragged red-necked ballad singers were bawling:

> Come, all ye gallant Irishmen, and listen to my song,
> Whilst I a story do relate of England's cruel wrong.
> Before this wrong all other wrongs of Ireland do grow pale,
> For they've clapped the pride of Erin's Isle into could Kilmainham Jail.

Already "the pride of Erin's Isle" (and he was but thirty-six years old in 1882) had done much for his country. He was rapidly welding into an impressive political unity a people bewildered, furious, and dislocated from their common goal by purposeless Fenian outrages, cruel famines, Irish-American insistence on unreasonable violence and a scattered energy that constantly dissipated itself on the contemptuous air. Parnell was organizing a trained political army out of a Donnybrook mob. His policy of obstructionism in the English Parliament had already won its fruits. His strategy in creating the policy of the boycott (speedily so named because it was first practised on Captain Boycott, the English agent to Lord Erne) had shaken the selfish complacence of the great landowners who were rackrenting the impoverished Irish. And with the passage of his Land Bill (it became a law on August 22, 1881) Ireland, in the perhaps too-optimistic phraseology of Standish O'Grady, passed from the hands of the landlords to the tenants of the cabins.

All this is put down here to give an idea of the violent impassioned atmosphere that existed in Ireland in 1882 and was to continue to exist until that fatal time in 1890 when Parnell, the Uncrowned King, was toppled from his throne by a hypocritical combination of treacherous lieutenants and the Roman Catholic clergy.

It is also put down to emphasize the fact that whoso is born and bred in Ireland must develop under the influences of a pugnacious ardour that was never disciplined, a priest-ridden and priest-directed civilization, an instability that all too often expresses itself in shameful betrayals, and a subterranean mythos that is pre-Christian in essence. It would be too much, perhaps, to assert that the chaotic eight years extending from 1882 to 1890, years big with hope, marked with struggle and crowned with disaster, could intensively shape the nature of a boy born in the first of those years; and yet the echoes, the violent altercations, the almost savage sense of nationalism, the dim awareness of internecine betrayals, and the atavistic comprehension—an unconscious absorption, say—of the mythos upon which all these quarreling, joking, lying, optimistic, impractical people pulsed must have stamped some mark on such a boy's nature.

And here one must return to Rathgar, a smaller, less built-up Rathgar than it is today, but yet in all essentials quite the same. The small brick houses lined the streets, not too close to each other to be offensive, and flowers bloomed in the front lawns. Instead of the sound of the motor horn there was the clop-clop of horses' hoofs, and oil lamps cast their soft glow across the encroaching darkness. At 41 Brighton Square (really a triangle), in a small modest house, lived Mr. John Stanislaus Joyce and on the morning of February 2, 1882, his wife gave birth to a male child. Mr. John Stanislaus Joyce must have been boisterously pleased. There was ample reason for his pleasure for he had possessed a son before but that son had lived only a fortnight. Now he had another and one that must have seemed like a first son, a re-establishment, so to speak, of the father's perpetuity. And one knowing Mr. John Stanislaus Joyce would readily admit that his large exuberant egotistical Irish nature craved perpetuity. The newly-born son was named James Augustine Joyce (the parish clerk wrote down the middle name as Augusta) and when he was christened in the parish church of Rathgar by Father O'Molloy a ship's chandler named Philip McCann stood as godfather. The godmother was a great-aunt of the boy named Callanan. These two, like most godparents, immediately dissolve into limbo but their shades reappear in books to be published years after the christening. A vivid ghost of Mrs. Callanan is to be found under the name of Aunt Kate in a long short story called "The Dead," and Philip McCann moves cloudily through a portion of *Finnegans Wake*.

To know the son one must know the parents. Who, then, were Mr. and Mrs. John Stanislaus Joyce of 41 Brighton Square, Rathgar?

## II

There are men whose wit, improvidence, and independence develop them into town characters, men to be smilingly pointed out and laughingly welcomed in those urban haunts where time is joyously wasted, but their development is nearly always at the expense of their eclipsed families. Mr. John Stanislaus Joyce, formerly of Cork and afterwards of multitudinous addresses in and near Dublin, was such a man. He was, in his later years at least, an Irish exemplification of Mr. Micawber. Those who remember him in Dublin, and he appears to have left his mark on a city that brimmed with impressive and eccentric personalities, assert—albeit with a tender reminiscential glow—that he was an inebriate and a fop, wore a monocle in one eye, was blessed with a quick natural biting wit, was continuously popular and always notorious for his impecuniousness and improvidence. But those who recall him appear to remember only the last decades of his life. In 1882 he may, perhaps, have been bibulous but he was not impecunious. The money, though from the first it poured like sand through his careless fingers, did not run out until after the Parnell tragedy, say in the early eighteen-nineties. Up to that disastrous period, both for Ireland and for the Joyce family, there were plenty of pounds. Alas, none of them were laid aside for the future. Such thrift was entirely foreign to the expansive nature of John Stanislaus Joyce. He strode through life with a pugnacious relish of it, prodigal in his hospitality to his friends and companions. The fact that his family at home would eventually suffer from this carelessness of living does not appear to have aroused a second serious thought in him. He was an epitome of the Irish "good fellow," a type indigenous and destructive to the old economic and social life of the island. His career may be described as a blithe and unfaltering march downhill from modest affluence to actual cramping poverty.

John Stanislaus Joyce (he had been named James like his father and his grandfather, but the registry clerk who entered his birth into the Cork records was so tipsy at the time that he wrote down 'John' instead) came from an old Cork family that once possessed extensive holdings. The name is obviously of French extraction —Joyeux. There is still in the City of Cork a Joyce's Court, now a slum quarter, which once belonged to the Joyce family. John Stanislaus was the grandson of James Joyce of Fermoy, County Cork, and Ann McCann (apparently no relation to godfather Philip) of Ulster. He was the son of another James Joyce who married Ellen O'Connell, a daughter of Charles O'Connell of Cork, cousin to The Liberator. "Daniel O'Connell was a cousin of my grandfather and a great friend," John Stanislaus once explained to an interviewer, "and I often used to hear my mother say that when he would drive in from his place in Kerry to Cork— there were no trains in those days—he would pull up at my grandfather's shop in Great George's Street, come in to see my grandfather, and then the two of them would walk down the road together arm in arm. Knee breeches were generally worn at the time and of course they wore them. My mother often told me that O'Connell would frequently drive his carriage in from Kerry and back again the same night." So a great ghost was established in the Joyce family annals, the sturdy figure of the Liberator in his knee breeches stamping across the sill of the shop in Great George's Street in the beautiful City of Cork.

John Stanislaus, who was born on July 4, 1849, was the only son of an only son of an only son, but this interesting fact (important as it may be to clairvoyants and seers) does not appear to have had much influence on his life. He seems to have enjoyed an active and ebullient youth if one is to believe the reminiscences he frequently described during those later years when recollection took the place of action. It appears to have been a youth more devoted to movement than to education. "There is not a field in County Cork that I don't know through all the hunts and the jollifications we used to have after the hunts. Oh, but they were great! I was one of the best men after the harriers. I used to hunt with the southern harriers and we had a great pack." The Mr. Flurry Knox of Somerville and Ross's short stories suggests, possibly, the pattern of the young John Stanislaus Joyce.

It must have been before these hunts and jollifications that he passed his three years at St. Coleman's College where he sat under the attentive eye of Dr. Croke, later Archbishop of Cashel. He was the youngest boy in the college (as his son was to be at Clongowes Wood) and possibly it was because of this fact that he sat beside Dr. Croke at dinner in the refectory. He could not have sat there very often nor could he have imbibed much knowledge, for a series of illnesses kept him from his classes a great part of the time. Besides recurrent bouts of rheumatic fever, he was stricken with typhoid and came very near dying. His health had improved by the time he moved on to Queen's College, Cork, where he wasted three years pretending to study medicine and actually winning, according to his own statement, several certificates. The only mark he left on the college, however, was his name carved on one of the desks. The certificates vanished into thin air. "I lost them," he once explained to a friend years later. "I put my portmanteau in pawn one time for ten shillings with a pawnbroker named Cunningham in Marlborough Street. He was a very decent fellow. There was a set of false teeth in the portmanteau too, but, begod, he sold bag, teeth, certificates and all!" John Stanislaus was sixteen when his father died (in 1865) and the entire responsibility of the family fell upon his mother's shoulders. There can be no doubt but what this occupied all her time.

In 1870 the Franco-Prussian War broke out and the young harrier and medical student started immediately for France to join the Imperial Army. He got as far as London where his mother, who was fast on his heels, caught up with him and brought him back to the more peaceful Cork. It must have been shortly after this escapade that the young man moved with his mother into the Dublin area, invested five hundred pounds of the money that came to him from the Cork property of his father and grandfather in a distillery in Chapelizod (later the scene of the short story, "A Painful Case," and of *Finnegans Wake*), one of the environs of Dublin, and became secretary to the business. The whisky was made in an old convent. The distillery proved to be a fiasco and John Stanis-

laus, minus his five hundred pounds and through the influence of
Peter Paul McSwiney, a cousin to his father and Lord Mayor
of Dublin, became secretary to the National Liberal Club at 53
Dawson Street, Dublin. There was no position at that time better calculated to make an active man known amongst the livelier element in the city and from this period began the rapid
evolution of John Stanislaus into that monument of insouciance
that so delighted his friends and acquaintances. He could boast
that he had never tasted the Liffey water except when it was
mixed with whisky or porter. He became a Dubliner, a type that is
as differentiated from an Irishman as a New Yorker is from an
American or a Parisian from a Frenchman. With not too much
education but plenty of mother-wit he saw himself as a wise man
and the sophisticated gloss of the bubbling city gave him a lustre
that must have dazzled his own eyes. He had his political successes
too, ample proof that he was excellently capable of performing the
duties that belonged to his place in the political hierarchy of the
time. Did he not put the last two Conservative members to sit
for Dublin City, Sir Arthur Guinness (afterwards Lord Ardilaun) and Mr. Stirling, out as member of Parliament for the City
of Dublin and Maurice Brooks and Dr. Lyons in and get a hundred pounds for his activities from the grateful victors?

His popularity was enhanced by the qualities of his singing
voice, for in those days Dublin was extremely music-conscious. As
his father before him, he was a talented tenor. In later years the
virtues of his voice when he was a young man were a source of pride
to him. He loved to tell a story about Barton McGuckin, the famous
Irish tenor, and himself. "McGuckin was a tenor in the Carl Rosa
Opera Company," he would declare. "He was the leading tenor. A
most extraordinary thing about McGuckin and myself was this: At
that time I was a young man about twenty-five years of age and I
had a very good tenor voice. I sang at a concert in the Antient Concert Rooms. After this concert when McGuckin would pass me in
the street he used to glance after me. I wondered why he looked so
hard at me, and, by God, I never could make out what it was all
about. It was only after he was dead for some years that I heard the
story. I was in one of my favourite houses in Bachelor's Walk one
evening where a lot of the fellows used to meet for a jollification

and whilst talking about one thing and another singing cropped up. John Phelan said to me, 'You had the best tenor voice in Ireland.' 'Yerra, my God, what put that in your head?' said I. He said, 'I heard it from the very best authority.' 'Who was that?' said I. 'Well,' said he, 'did you ever hear of a gentleman called Barton McGuckin?' 'I did, indeed,' said I. John said, 'Well, that is my authority.' So that accounted why McGuckin used to look so hard at me. When I asked John Phelan what McGuckin knew about me he said, 'McGuckin heard you singing at a concert in the Antient Concert Rooms and said that you had the best tenor voice in Ireland, and, begod, he ought to be a judge.' Anyway, I had a devil of a good tenor voice in those days—and they were great days, my God, they were!"

John Stanislaus should begin to evolve as a personality by now. The jovial young tenor so convinced of his own remarkable attributes is not so far from the older man with the truculent eyebrows who stamped down Grafton Street waving a sharply-worded missive from his bank and declaring loudly to a friend, "If I get another impertinent letter like this I'll remove my overdraft to another bank!" But years were to elapse before that older character was to solidify (there is no other word for it) out of the young tenor. There was work to be done haphazardly when it did not interfere with pleasure, plenty of money to spend recklessly (at one time his income reached a thousand pounds a year), and marriage to be ventured into, a marriage that resulted in sixteen or seventeen children (five of whom died in infancy and youth) in eighteen years.

Before this marriage, however, the Liberal party (pro-Irish, of course) rewarded him for his electioneering activities by appointing him to a permanent position under the Government. At that time there was an office called the Collector General of Rates whose duty it was to collect the rates of the City of Dublin.[1] Appointments to this office were in the gift of the Lord Lieutenant of Ireland and as the duties were easy and remunerative there was always a large number of ambitious young men eagerly awaiting vacancies. John Stanislaus was appointed to a place in this office and there he remained until the Local Government Act abolishing the

[1] The two weirdest shadows in *Ulysses* are probably Wetherup and Macintosh. The former was one of the Castle's Nominees said to have been an ex-waiter. The position was worth about £650 a year, *i.e.,* about £2,500 of our present money.

office of Collector General of Rates and transferring its duties to the
Dublin Corporation was passed. Being well berthed, at least for the
time being, John Stanislaus turned a bold eye on matrimony. On
May 5, 1880, he was married to Miss Mary Jane Murray, originally
of Longford, the daughter of a commercial traveller in wines, at the
Roman Catholic Church, Rathmines. John Stanislaus was thirty-one
years old and his young wife (who was born on May 15, 1859) had
not quite reached her twenty-first year.

It was Mrs. John Stanislaus Joyce who, perforce, had to think
of the morrow but during the first decade of her married life the
problem was far from a vexatious one. The money continued to pour
in and though she may have wondered at the rapidity with which
it poured out again she found no necessity, even if she had dared, to
reorganize the household on a more thrifty basis. If Mrs. Joyce ever
possessed any marked qualities of personality, any flare or unusual
sparkle, they were crushingly obliterated by the swaggering domi-
nancy of her husband's nature. She was, however, a brilliant pianist
and descendant on her mother's side of a family of singers—family name Flynn. She was a shadow to the brightness of John Stanislaus and that is why those in Dublin who remember the couple re-
vert instinctively to John Stanislaus and hardly at all to his wife. In
the retrospect of time she seems like a ghost, a charming ghost, a
pious ghost, a patient ghost slowly drifting into inanition. It was her
portion to keep a disorderly household together, to bear children almost yearly, to see them die and weep over them, and to preserve
peace in an atmosphere that was more often than not strident over
the political crises of the times. She bowed willingly before her two
great masters, John Stanislaus and the Holy Roman Catholic and
Apostolic Church. She meekly accepted where John Stanislaus boldly
scoffed and the delicate precisions of her innate goodness and laborious travail to keep a home together, flashing briefly out of time like
the disappearing wings of a gull in sunlight, must have considerably
ameliorated the taut atmosphere in the various houses in which the
Joyce ménage lived or attempted to live.

Such were the parents of James Augustine Joyce. It is dangerous
to insist too positively on heredity. Were the father and mother of
William Shakespeare the father and mother of the poet of *Hamlet*?
And who were the parents of Dante that their son should have

written the *Divine Comedy?* These are puzzles that no psychology can answer except by suspect assumptions. It is perhaps in those things to which the flesh surrenders that the parents are evident; it is only in the will alone—occasionally, perhaps—that the son acknowledges neither father nor mother. Until his last breath the central figure of the human universe was, for John Stanislaus Joyce, his eldest son James, to the exclusion of all his other children with the exception of his youngest daughter, Mabel, who died at the age of twelve.

III

What was happening in the world on February 2, 1882, while John Stanislaus Joyce was toasting his newly-born son? Many things, of course, of a seeming irrelevancy, but which, considered as a whole, show the colour and temper of the times, give, as it were, a composition of place, and were not without their influence on the future world in which James Joyce was to live. At Eltham Mrs. Katherine O'Shea was big with a child that was delivered on the sixteenth and which Parnell later admitted to be his own. Captain O'Shea was happily announcing that February, 1882, would seal his reconciliation with his wife. Richard Pigott, shabby and down-at-heels, was wandering about the Dublin streets. Parnell sat behind bars in Kilmainham Jail together with Kettle, Davitt, Brennan, and Sexton and planned the Treaty—if a simple understanding can be called a treaty—that was to end the campaign of violence in Ireland. The ballad singers and public-house orators, much against the will of the Leader, were attempting to stir up unrest in the Dublin thoroughfares. The Viceroy, Lord Cowper, weary with the whole business, was considering his resignation, and so, too, was the Right Honourable W. P. Forster, Chief Secretary. Lord Frederick Cavendish, having consulted no clairvoyants, was expressing his willingness to accept the latter's place. The future Invincibles were drinking in a public house near Lower Castle Yard while Charles Dawson, Lord Mayor of Dublin, was presiding at the Mansion House. James Stephens, the poet and novelist, was born in Dublin. Gladstone, heading his Second Administration much to the disapproval of Queen Victoria who regretfully recalled the courtlier days of Dizzy, was pursuing his policy of "clearing out everywhere," Ireland possibly included, much to the disgust of the flag-waving Expansionist middle classes who called him "a cowardly Little Englander." Henry Stanley, sick with jungle fever after his discovery of the lake of brandy-coloured water which he named after his patron, was labouring at the organization of the Congo Free State for Leopold of Belgium. Jules Grévy, President of the French Republic, was conferring with the new ministry headed by Monsieur de Freycinet. Léon Gambetta, out of office at last, was speeding south to Nice to visit his family. Auguste Barbier of the French Academy was gravely ill. Before the Cour d'Assize of the Seine appeared an unfrocked friar of the Dominican Monastery at Flavigny, one Etienne Gruyard, who was accused of flinging vitriol into the face of his mistress, Suzanne Salzac, and then slashing her five times with a knife. The passionate cleric was sentenced to five years' imprisonment. Crowds were pouring into the Théâtre des Nouveautés to witness the one hundredth performance of *Le Jour et la Nuit* and at the Théâtre-Français a faithful group was applauding *Le Demi-Monde* by Alexandre Dumas fils. A boy named Marcel Proust, eleven years old, delicate, asthmatic, sat in his Paris home and dreamed of Illiers, that vast property near Chartres where he passed his summers. A big beardless youth of twenty called Claude-Achille Debussy created his daily disturbance in the class of Professor Guiraud at the Conservatoire. In New York sceptical paterfamilias were unfolding copies of the New York *Times* and reading about a fantastic fellow in knee breeches and velvet jacket named Oscar Wilde who had lectured the night before at Yale College in New Haven on the theories of John Ruskin. Tired of this incomprehensible Irishman, they turned to the new issue of the *Atlantic Monthly* and read the installment of *Two on a Tower*, by an English author named Thomas Hardy. From his cell in the United States Jail at Washington Charles Guiteau, the assassin of President James Garfield, issued a manifesto in which he triumphantly announced: "I am high-toned . . . too high-toned for newspaper devils to notice, and I want them to leave me alone." He went on to speak of "this perverse and crooked generation" that failed to see him as "God's man," a blessed instrument who had saved the Republican party by killing Garfield. A bewildered emergency President named Arthur was doing nothing in the White House while Congress was violently agitating itself over the Star

Route mail frauds. In the Craigie House at Cambridge Henry Wadsworth Longfellow, with less than two months of life before him, sat quietly and listened to the bruit of the new era. And at Bayreuth, while the sullen winter rains dripped in the eaves, Richard Wagner, in his sixty-ninth year, sat at his desk and put the finishing touches to his swan song, *Parsifal,* for the summer festival.

Despite the deaths, births, scandals, discoveries, political coils, wars and rumours of war it was a stuffy world, a world of stuffy furniture and stuffy people, of aspidistras, complacencies, and moral hypocrisies. Although an era was dying and the transitional fin-de-siècle period was at the door, the great bulk of the English and Irish people were dyed-in-the-cotton-wool Victorians. They possessed a way of living and they were loath to relinquish it. It was a social way of living and a social way of thinking and any fantastic braveries of literary or artistic experimentation were left to such volatile and unpredictable peoples as the French. A Huysmans or a Zola was not to be nourished on English roast beef or Irish gammon. Any truant from the established way of thinking or living, blessed and personified in the widespread conception of the practically-invisible Queen Victoria, immediately found some indignant Buchanan barking at his heels. The vital impulse—and stuffy people can have vital impulses—expended itself in the acquisition of lands, properties, peoples, moneys, commercial supremacies, aspidistras, stuffed birds, and an impossible pretension that all races, excepting the Anglo-Saxon, were inferior races and a burden to be carried and conveniently devoured when they became too heavy to carry. Whoso contested this way of thinking and living was flying straight into the face of British respectability. In Ireland a great many people were flying straight into the face of British respectability but it was not for desire of a new philosophy of living or a particularly original way of thinking. It was for an elusive state called Liberty. Excepting for this urge, an urge viewed by British Tories with pity, contempt and anger, the Irish way of living was no more than a replica of the English way of living. It was even smaller to some extent, for it was dominated and directed by the limited minds of the clergy of the Roman Catholic Church. Artistically speaking, Ireland was nonexistent. Its letters, such as they were, were Anglo-Irish and very second-rate Anglo-Irish at that. The Irish language, that rich sea of words from which might have been drawn a National letters, was practically dead. Diarmid O'Cobhthaigh writes: "In the half century from 1840 to 1890 the Irish language was reduced from the general tongue of the people to that of a few peasants in obscure parts of the land." It is true that Douglas Hyde, he of the magnificent walrus moustache, now first President of Eire, had already embarked on his campaign to resuscitate that tongue but his was as yet one of the few faint voices calling to unlistening ears. And William Butler Yeats, who was to be the sole fountain of the Celtic Renascence, was only seventeen years old.

## IV

In such a world and at such a time James Joyce was born. It was neither the sort of world nor the particular environment calculated to create or instigate an æsthetic and creative intellect. That rich incentive towards the finer aspects of living that is afforded by un-vexed satisfaction in one's place in time and the magnetic excitement of ambitious peers was almost completely lacking. The materialism of the time was unadorned and unashamed. What culture there was existed only in the great draughty drawing rooms of the hard-riding, hard-drinking landowners. In James Joyce's particular case there were hardly the rudiments of culture to surround his infancy and fertilize the first blind seeds of incentive towards those finer aspects of living. His father's library, if the few volumes can be so dignified, consisted of *Pelham, or the Adventures of a Gentleman,* by Bulwer-Lytton (John Stanislaus could never make up his mind whether the English author's name was Bulwer-Lytton or Lytton-Bulwer); *Harry Coverdale's Courtship* by Smedley; Jonah Barrington's *Recollections of His Own Times,* and *The House by the Churchyard,* a story about old Chapelizod,[1] by Le Fanu.[2] There was not much there to arouse a tempest in a young mind. John Stanislaus, without any doubt, regarded the excessive exploration of books as ample evidence of a weak mind. It was a sedentary and pusillanimous occupation, fitting enough, perhaps, for Jesuit fathers but no sort of sport for a man who had hunted with the Cork harriers. The mystic Celtic twilight did not envelop John Stanislaus Joyce.

[1] Chapelizod (*Chapelle d'Iseut*) is supposed to be the birthplace of Isolde.
[2] The house by the churchyard is adumbrated in *Finnegans Wake.*

There was, of course, music. Now, that was a different thing and a songbook in the hand was no proof of declining manliness. But it was the music of the voice only, a soaring self-expression in high notes that gratified the ego and produced an attentive admiration in presumably spellbound listeners. John Stanislaus suffered no delusions of inferiority so far as his voice was concerned and his high tenor arrow of sound was often sped in the Rathgar home. His eldest son, therefore, was inducted in infancy to the delight of sturdy expression in song. In those days, so unlike the present deplorable times, Dublin was decidedly music-conscious and no season passed without its bounteous share of opera. The old-fashioned Italian variety maintained its sway over a public that, like John Stanislaus himself, exalted the voice above the instrument. In Michael Gunn's Gaiety Theatre (for his old Theatre Royal on Hawkins Street had burned down in 1880) appeared annually the Carl Rosa Company, Mr. Mapleson's Italian Opera Company, and the D'Oyly Carte Opera Company with its repertoire of Gilbert and Sullivan operettas. Crowded houses applauded the arias of *Fidelio, La Favorita, Maritana, Esmeralda, Mefistofele, Ernani, Lucia di Lammermoor, Il Trovatore,* and that perennial favourite, Balfe's *The Bohemian Girl.* The merits of Marie Rôze, Lillian Nordica, Madame Lablache, Ludwig, McGuckin, Ciampi, and De Anna were almost as eagerly argued as the shifting political phenomena of the day. When Signor Arditi, composer of that beloved melody, "Il Bacio," lifted his baton all Dublin that *was* Dublin leaned back in silent contentment. John Stanislaus, the man whom Barton McGuckin stared after in the street, was a frequent auditor and we may be sure that his vocal cords quivered in sympathy with the old-fashioned tenors when they achieved their famous chest C notes. Jack B. Hall, the Dublin journalist, wrote of the singer with the chest C note: "Its owner would take a few strides toward the back of the stage, accumulating lung-power the while and then return to the footlights to expend it for the benefit of the audience and the glory of himself." This was man's work. And John Stanislaus would do the same thing—according to all accounts, with remarkable success—for the benefit of his family and his friends. His eldest son, therefore, was impregnated with the fireworks of old-fashioned opera and the gentler melodies of Tom Moore, to say nothing of the vast store of come-all-yous and ballads of the type of *Nell Flaherty's Drake* quoted in *Ulysses* and of *Finnegans Wake,* an impregnation sufficiently complete to last all his life.

It was not alone music that made Dublin a lively place throughout the eighties. There was the legitimate theatre as well. It is almost impossible to name a famous actor or actress of the period who failed to visit the Irish capital during those years when Parnell was climbing swiftly to the high place from which he was tumbled so disastrously by his own followers. Across the boards of the Gaiety passed in rapid succession Bernhardt, Modjeska, Ristori, Sálvini, Edwin Booth, Kate Bateman (in *Leah the Forsaken,* of course), Genevieve Ward, Charles Wyndham and Mary Moore, the Kendals, Edmund Tearle, J. L. Toole, Mary Anderson, Kate Vaughan, Nellie Farren, Mrs. Langtry, Osmond Tearle, Ada Rehan, Mrs. Bernard Beere and Henry Irving and Ellen Terry. Barry Sullivan, he who fought so furiously once in the last act of *Richard III* that the frightened Richmond gave up the battle and fled incontinently from the stage, appeared for the last of many visits in 1886. And each year there was the pantomime to delight the hearts of young and old and put them in proper holiday humour, not the sophisticated modernized pantomimes of today but the uproarious slapstick variety represented by such perennials as *Robinson Crusoe, Little Red Ridinghood, Sindbad the Sailor,* and *Dick Whittington.* All this made Dublin in season a lively electrical cosmopolis in miniature.

Against this background, then, a background more often than not snapping and sputtering with electrical waves of excitement, James Joyce passed the first six years of life that preceded his entrance to school. He grew naturally into a small-boned thin nervous lad to an accompaniment of trolling voices, tossed pots, earthy wit, and political argumentation. This last played an important part in the Joyce household, as it did in every Irish household of the day, for the times were heavy with thunder and startled by unexpected flashes of cruel lightning. Parallel with the gaiety of Dublin was the frenzy of Dublin. From one point of view 1882 was an année terrible in the annals of Irish history. On May fifth (when James Joyce was three months and three days old) there was the famous torchlight procession through the streets of the city, a procession celebrating the liberation of Parnell and Michael Davitt from Kilmainham

Jail and loud with optimism for the future. The next day Lord Spencer, the new viceroy, made his state entry into Dublin. And in the twilight of this day (it was a Saturday) Joe Brady and his Invincibles left the public house near the gates of the Lower Castle Yard, drove to the Phoenix Park and there slaughtered the Chief Secretary for Ireland, Lord Frederick Cavendish, and the Permanent Under-Secretary, Thomas Henry Burke. That evening the Carl Rosa Opera Company was singing Wm. Vincent Wallace's *Maritana* at the Gaiety Theatre and as Barton McGuckin had the rôle of Don Cæsar de Bazan it is quite possible that John Stanislaus was in the audience. But whether he was there or not it is easy enough to imagine his excitement, an excitement that shook all Dublin and kept the streets full of people waiting for the midnight edition of the *Evening Telegraph*. James Joyce, sleeping quietly in his crib, was mercifully unconscious of the fact that he had been born in a black period. That he was to find out for himself in the years to come. But Dublin and, naturally, John Stanislaus, who had a way of getting about, knew that Joe Brady, Carey, Kelly, Fagan, and the other Invincibles had changed the history of Ireland in a moment's ferociousness.

It is unnecessary to follow the political consequences of the Phoenix Park murders and the other phenomena of the first six years of James Joyce's life, for the aspect of the period should be clear enough by now. This aspect consciously meant nothing to the infant who grew into the small boy; it was only in its influence on the elders who surrounded him that it coloured the budding mind. Such happenings, agitating all Ireland, as the formation of the National League to take the place of the suppressed Land League, the new Coercion Act, the trial of the Invincibles, the passage of the Reform Act which established household suffrage in Ireland, the fall and return to power of Gladstone, and, in 1886, the first reading of the Bill for the Amendment of the Provision for the Future Government of Ireland, popularly known as the Home Rule Bill, were matters for John Stanislaus and his cronies to discuss over tumblers of Irish whisky; James Joyce was too busy learning to talk and walk and play to pay heed to anything else. What did matter personally to him were the removals of the Joyce family from house to house. Either John Stanislaus was restless or his growing family required larger quarters. Whatever the reason, he provided his eldest son with three houses to live in before that son was six years old. This nomadic existence John Stanislaus was to pursue until the end of his life.

From 41 Brighton Square, Rathgar, after two or three years of residence, the ménage travelled to Castlewood Avenue, Rathmines. James Joyce was too small to understand or care much about this removal; but when, some time later, the yellow van came again, all the furniture was piled in it, the horses strained at the shafts and Castlewood Avenue, Rathmines, was left behind, he was quite old enough to comprehend what it was all about. The new destination was 1 Martello Terrace, Bray. Bray, a fishing village from pre-Norman times, the scene of a skirmish when King James was fleeing from the débâcle of the Battle of the Boyne to the Wicklow Mountains and a once popular haven for smugglers, had undergone a miraculous change during the thirty-odd years before the Joyce family settled there. The extension of the Dublin and Kingstown Railway to the town in 1851 had made it immediately accessible to Dublin as a watering place. Not long after the first trains puffed into the new station the stretch of sandy dunes extending by the shore were covered by an esplanade. Restaurants and boarding houses opened their doors; brassy bands played; and where once the suspicious-eyed smugglers in jackboots and bearing huge pistols rolled their barrels and bags of contraband into the Brandy Hole fashionable Dublin in huge skirts and high hats strolled, drank tea and stronger potions, and gossiped as only Dubliners can gossip. By the mid-eighties Bray had passed its zenith as a resort de luxe but it had yet to degenerate into the vapid third-rate seaside resort that it is today. When the van of the Joyce family rolled up to 1 Martello Terrace the watering place was still a centre of some distinction.

Bray's only importance to the life of James Joyce rests in the fact that it was here he achieved the observant faculties of a naturally-curious boy and it was from here that he first went to school. Unreasoning infancy was left behind at Bray. It was here, too, that the weakness of his eyes became manifest, and glasses, that shameful curse of the small lad, were forced upon him. It was here, again, that the fanatically-bigoted Mrs. Conway came to live with the Joyce family and the boy observed with some interest her lamp of culza oil before the statue of the Immaculate Conception, her green and maroon brushes named for Charles Stewart Parnell and Michael Davitt and her vague attempts to teach him where the Mozambique Channel was and which was the longest river in America. Mrs. Conway, forever famous as the Dante of *A Portrait of the Artist as a Young Man* and the Mrs. Riordan of *Ulysses,* was originally a Miss Hearn from Cork. She had entered a convent in her youth but had ventured back into the world before she had taken her final vows. Being blessed with an excellent income it was not long before an almost painfully polite Mr. Conway cast an admiring eye upon her and persuaded her into matrimony. For some time life proceeded in an auspicious manner. Mr. Conway was punctilious in his attentions and always insisted that Mrs. Conway, lulled, of course, into a purring security, take the choicest morsels at dinner before any other lady was seated. Then one day Mr. Conway abruptly disappeared and with him disappeared Mrs. Conway's money. The result was a fiercely-religious bitter-minded woman forever suspicious of men and intolerant of all departures from the Roman Catholic moral code for middle-class families. Mrs. Conway came to the Joyce family in the early autumn of 1888 as a sort of original governess to James Augustine but by that time John Stanislaus had decided what to do with his eldest son. He would send him to the best Jesuit school for boys in the island. The son, who by this time had discovered the pleasures of pastimes with his young brother (a second John Stanislaus, born on December 17, 1885), who had seen the waves piling up on the shingle and the bathers strolling along the beach, who had lifted his eyes to the cliffs where once the robbers had hid and been guided along the gay Esplanade where the band played and the fashionable Dubliners sauntered, was too young to wonder overmuch about the sudden activity of his mother and why she was mending his garments and providing him with new ones and packing a certain box and sometimes glancing at him with reddened eyes, but he was not too young to understand one early autumn morning that he was on the train rattling along to Clane and that his mother was upset and his father's repartee a little loud and forced. He could see the poles flash past and, perhaps, a jaunting car or two, and a cow that was being driven in through an open gate. And then there was the car that clacked along the browny-yellow road by the green fields and Bodenstown and the farmhouse of the Jolly Farmer and finally up a long drive to a great house that was like a castle out of a book. And finally there he was in the hall of the Castle at Clongowes Wood College being handed over to the charge of the Rector, the Very Reverend John S. Conmee, S.J., while his mother unashamedly burst into tears and his father gave him a handful of pocket money and a manly slap on the back. He could hear the shrill voices of boys raised somewhere in play and he felt very small and lonesome and lost. He could barely restrain his tears when his father and mother went away in the car and he had to peer very hard around the hall, for his eyes were not good and he couldn't see very well when the twilight flowed in through the half-open door.

The life of James Joyce may properly be said to begin here in the Castle at Clongowes Wood when the Rector, a bland and courtly humanist, turned him over to a black-soutaned father who guided him through the corridors to his dormitory.

### v

In the *Ormonde Papers* may be found a passage from a dispatch to England from the Lords Justices at Dublin Castle, dated July 8, 1642, that reads as follows: "Since our despatch of 7th June . . . we afterwards employed Lieutenant-Colonel Monk to two other castles, one of them at a place called Rathcoffey and the other at Clongowes-wood, both some fourteen miles from hence and in the County of Kildare, and sent along with him some two pieces of battery, so to batter and take in those two castles, which exceedingly annoyed the adjoining garrisons and much interrupted our markets at Dublin: which services he well performed, having, after a day's fight at each place, taken both castles, and slain divers persons therein of those that maintained them against him, and took three-score and ten prisoners. And among the rest some priests, whom with the rest he brought hither, to be proceeded with as we should think fit, which was all the quarter he gave them; and we have appointed them to be executed by martial law; and those services so performed, he placed one hundred men to keep the castle of Rathcoffey, which is a place of importance to be kept, and blew up the other castle to make it uninhabitable for the rebels, and so returned hither."

So we return again to that mythos of bloodshed and religious fanaticism that underlies the entire structure and development of Ireland. To keep these dark foundations so mixed with truth and legend always in mind is to understand a little clearer the profundities of a national character often dismissed as a superficial amalgam of eager quarrelsomeness and clownish Handy Andyism. The varying fortunes of Clongowes Wood College before its solemn dedication to Blessed Luigi Gonzaga offer an effective epitome of that Irish progression eternally overshadowed by the two great dark wings of angry struggle and religious domination. Clongowes Wood College (*silva de Clongow*) was originally a medieval castle built on the alluvial plain about a mile north of Clane near Sallins in County Kildare and close to where the Liffey turns from the north and makes for the eastern sea. It was held for generations by the great territorial family of the Eustaces and its importance as a stronghold can only be realized if it be understood that it was one of the outposts of the Pale. In 1494 the Pale, a "double ditch of six feet high above ground at one side or part which mireth next unto Irish men," was completed after six years of indefatigable labour. It wound like a great clumsy snake from Merrion, near Dublin, through Kilteel and its castle where once the Knights Hospitallers of St. John of Jerusalem had their commandery, Ballymore Eustace, Kilcullen, Clane and Athboy to Dundalk. Two sections of this earthen barricade against the wild Irish, those O'Tooles and O'Byrnes who constantly descended in clanking fury out of the mountains, have their ends on the Clongowes demesne and are still travelled as footpaths. From shortly after the time of the Norman invaders to Monk's reduction of the castle the Eustaces, for the most part inflexibly Roman Catholic and increasingly pro-Irish through intermarriage, held this outpost against all marauders. The last vivid glimpse we have of them in connection with Clongowes Castle before its destruction is during the year 1641. It was then that a venerable old Mrs. Eustace, at least ninety years of age, hospitably received a detachment of Cromwellian troopers under one Captain Hues and was barbarously murdered by her ferocious guests. According to the tradition she refused to surrender a key to a supposed secret stronghold, or priest hole, and kept it in her mouth until her jaws were smashed to bits by the soldiers.

After the destruction by Monk's troopers the lands and ruins of Clongowes Wood passed into the possession of Richard Reynell, Chief Justice of Common Pleas under Cromwell, and some while later they were duly confirmed to him by letters patent of Charles II. The Eustaces, who had fought so strenuously for their Faith and guarded the Pale like eager watchdogs, slid abruptly into the long annals of history. Chief Justice Reynell, a busy profiteering man who appears never to have dwelt at Clongowes or nearer there than Dublin, sold the fire-blackened walls of the castle and the neglected lands pertaining to it to Thomas Browne, a Dublin merchant of Kildare origin. This transference took place in 1667. The grandson of the Dublin merchant, one Stephen Fitzwilliam Browne, began the restoration of the castle, an arduous and costly labour which he never completed, and the name of the property was changed to Castle Browne. This Stephen Fitzwilliam married Judith Wogan of the neighbouring demesne of Rathcoffey, that companion castle Monk's troopers battered the same day Clongowes Wood was destroyed.

These are the dry bones of facts from which the living flesh has long departed but as they form a sequence illustrating how a Norman stronghold built for imminent wars was strangely transformed into an Irish Jesuit college they are of some importance here. They speak again of the layer upon layer of conflicting cultures, always with the dark mythos as a foundation, that is the Island of today and the old mother of James Joyce. Even those faraway Brownes were important links in the long chain of Time that was to wind itself so unmistakably about the artist's mind. One must follow them, then, until they cease to be a part of Clongowes Wood.

In the generation after Stephen Fitzwilliam the two families of Browne and Wogan were again connected by marriage, this time a Michael Browne marrying a Catherine Wogan. Their elder daughter, Judith, who lived to the ripe age of ninety-eight and died as late as 1848, was a profoundly religious Roman Catholic, and her good works, especially for the Brigitine nuns at Tullow, among whom she lies buried, were famed throughout Kildare. Judith had two brothers who were successive owners of Castle Browne. The elder, Thomas Wogan Browne, succeeded to the property in 1769; but before we briefly note his career the great ghost story of Clongowes Wood should be summarized.

No ancient keep in Ireland is without its supernatural legend. In this particular case we are concerned with a Browne (the uncle of Judith, perhaps) who became a marshal in the Austrian armies and fell at the Battle of Prague in 1757. On that fatal day Marshal Browne's two sisters were seated at their needlework in an upper chamber. Below in the hall were gathered the servants. Suddenly the great door to the hall was flung open and a tall general officer, fully accoutred, clasping his hands tightly across his breast, hastily entered and made for the curving staircase. From his breast blood flowed terribly staining his white uniform. The Irish servants, spellbound with fear for a moment, watched him pass, and then, plucking up their courage, followed him upstairs and into the room where the two Browne sisters were busy at their needlework. When they reached that chamber there was no vestige of the mysterious intruder and the mistresses of the castle vowed that they had seen no one. Yet the frightened asseverations of the servants so impressed them that they became convinced the apparition was their brother who had just met his death on some battlefield. So certain were they of this that they immediately ordered mourning, had masses celebrated and held a great wake to which all the neighbourhood was invited. It was not till a fortnight later that authenticated information reached the castle of the death of Marshal Browne at Prague on the very day and hour the servants had seen the spectre. Here, without invidious comment, we may return to the more matter-of-fact career of Thomas Wogan Browne.

That perspicacious gentleman married a rich English Protestant lady and it was possibly with her money that he began the enlargement and adornment of Castle Browne in 1788. For a time he was recognized as a man of some importance in Kildare, even achieving the distinction of being dismissed from the Commission of the Peace for Kildare, Dublin and Meath Counties by a suspicious government; but as the months passed and the difficulties of his position increased before his politic eyes his importance, at least in the opinion of the more militant Catholic gentry, took on a sad and wasted autumn hue. Driven, perhaps, by the Zeitgeist of weariness or the apparent impossibility of successful struggle against such over-

whelming odds as the Penal Code, he forsook his heritage as a
Catholic. Yet he was the friend of Hamilton Rowan and the host
of Theobald Wolfe Tone, whose body lies some four miles south of
Clongowes Wood in the ivy-covered edifice of Bodenstown Church.
While little is known of Thomas Wogan Browne's relations with
Wolfe Tone there is a circumstantial tradition that emphasizes his
friendship with Hamilton Rowan. Rowan, then living at Rathcoffey
in a new house built on the site of the old Wogan castle, once
escaped a party of British troopers by fleeing across the fields, racing
up the front stairs of Castle Browne, flinging his hat out the library
window on to the ha-ha as a blind and dashing into a room with
a camouflaged door in the northeast tower. The soldiers, hot on his
heels, fired futile volleys after him. Generations of Clongowes boys
have inspected the tiny holes in the mahogany front door to the
Round Room of the castle and been told that they were caused by
the slugs fired at Hamilton Rowan by infuriated British troopers.
The fact that the holes are on the wrong side of the door does not
lessen the interest and thrill of the tradition.

Thomas Wogan Browne, who in spite of forsaking his heritage
as a Catholic remained one in mind and spirit, died during the great
days when the Emperor Napoleon was marching towards Moscow
in the disastrous campaign that was to break the backbone of his
empire. Commanding the Saxon division of the Emperor's forces
was Lieutenant General Michael Wogan Browne, younger brother
and heir to Thomas and a worthy successor in martial exploits to
that Marshal Browne who died at Prague. When this far-flung adventurer, a very king of wild geese, learned of his elder brother's
death he secured leave of absence and hastily returned to Ireland.
He did not stay there long. Finding the estates of Castle Browne
heavily encumbered and discouraged by the oppressive laws being
enforced against Roman Catholics, he sold his inheritance to Father
Peter Kenny, S.J., who, though an individual purchaser because of
the edict against Catholic establishments purchasing property, was
in reality the representative of a group of Irish Jesuits determined to
inaugurate a school. The sale, in spite of the antagonism of the English governors, was completed in the early spring of 1814. Castle
Browne was immediately renamed Clongowes Wood and on April
5, 1814, Father Kenny took up residence there and dedicated the

castle to Blessed Luigi Gonzaga, S.J. On May eighteenth the first student's name, John MacLornan (or MacLorinan) of Dublin, was entered in the Clongowes Academic Register and actual teaching began on July third just five weeks before the solemn Restoration of the Society of Jesus by Pope Pius VII. Thus the long history of the Norman castle, a history tense with forays against the Pale and the hollow bellow of Cromwell's cannon and melodramatic escapes and murders and bleeding spectres, came to a peaceful end in the Aristotelian and Aquinian bosom of the Society of Jesus of the Roman Catholic Church.

VI

It was to this castle, now in a continuous development under the Jesuit fathers for seventy-four years, that James Joyce was delivered by his father and mother at the opening of the September term in 1888. The boy was approximately six years and seven months old but when he was asked his age he replied, "Half past six." For some time thereafter he was known among his classmates as Half-Past-Six. An old boy remembers him principally because of his diminutive size. We have here, then, a small lad, the youngest in the school, with weak eyes covered by spectacles, thin bony arms and legs, almost effeminate hands and feet, highly nervous and fearful but animated by a definite consciousness of what was justice and what was not, malleable to influences but blessed with the beginnings of an indestructible personality, embarking upon an educational voyage through time under Jesuit direction that was to last until he was twenty years of age. As these thirteen or fourteen years under the guidance of the black-soutaned fathers of the Society of Jesus were the years of his intellectual and emotional development and formation, the creation of the mould, as it were, into which his personality was poured, they are of enormous significance to his career as a man of letters. The four years at Clongowes may be described as a noviatiate, the preparatory training for all that was to follow.

This college was a particularly apposite selection for an imaginative boy. Within the broad limits of its green-grassed demesne lingered vestiges of all the varying layers of civilization, perceptible hints and reminders of the historical progression that had evolved

the modern Ireland, this Parnell-dominated land, of young James
Joyce. Speedily enough the boy's curiosity was aroused concerning
the historical and legendary aspects of the castle. There was hardly
a spot to which he might wander that did not speak to him of the
violent and ambiguous past. Even the half-doubtful heroes and
heroines of the dark and distant Ireland that was a portion of the
dimly-sensed mythos rose through the soil to greet him. On Clongowes ground was the grassy mound in which Queen Buan was
supposed to rest. This queen, the royal consort of Mesgegra, King
of Leinster, had fallen dead on the highway when her husband's
conqueror, the Ulster Champion Connall Cernach, most redoubt-
able of the Red Branch Knights, had boasted to her that he carried
Mesgegra's decapitated head in his painted chariot. And not far
away was the Ford of Clane where the two champions had fought
their tremendous combat. Clane itself and the adjacent village of
Prosperous had witnessed the beginnings of the Rebellion of '98.
From the castle steps the boy could see the ruined barbican of Rathcoffey Castle, memorial to Cromwell's ravages, and but a short stroll
in another direction was the Browne Mortuary Chapel built by
Stephen Fitzwilliam Browne. Then, too, there was the Jesuit bury-
ing plot where slept the fathers who had taught at Clongowes. Here,
almost side by side, in death lay three distinct epochs in the long
history of Ireland: the epoch of the mythos exemplified by Buan and
her tragic story; the epoch of romance with its white-cloaked spectre
and its tortured chatelaine and the clattering feet of Hamilton
Rowan represented by the Brownes; and the epoch of the boy's reality, the black soutanes with their false sleeves, the suave diplomacy
and the raised voice of admonition in the chapel represented by the
Jesuit fathers. Ancient savagery, the hot romance of political struggle
and the steel hand in the velvet glove that was the Church, all were
there.

There is ample reason for this insistence on the historical sig-
nificances, the ghostly nuances, so to speak, of Clongowes Wood, for
they formed a shadowy background for the first school days of
James Joyce. Against this background was the noisy matter-of-fact
reality of study classes, and of play in the three broad playgrounds.
The studies for a small lad, the youngest tadpole in the Third Line,
were simple and elemental, consisting of spelling, of sums, of writ-

ing lessons, a little Latin, and plenty of religious inculcation; in fact, the old Jesuit system for small boys. This method of Jesuit teaching derived from the Ratio Studiorum, a correlated system organized as early as 1599. But many changes, both compulsory and politic, had taken place in this scheme of teaching by the time James Joyce was delivered into Jesuitical hands. For instance, the Conservative Government's policy of state aid to secondary schools in Ireland through Intermediate Examinations with their prize moneys for both students and schools, a policy put into effect in 1878, did its part in remoulding the teaching methods at Clongowes. But though the *matter* was changed so as to make it possible for boys to compete in the Intermediate Examinations of each June on a level with boys from non-Jesuit schools, the administrative principles, regulations, and general *form* of study remained essentially an outgrowth of the time-tried Ratio Studiorum. The man who was the innovator in this particular field at Clongowes was the Jesuit now embalmed for posterity as Father Dolan in *A Portrait of the Artist as a Young Man.* He was Father James Daly, Prefect of Studies at Clongowes Wood College for thirty years.

Father Daly had been educated at the Jesuit College of Notre-Dame de la Paix at Namur, Belgium. In the early eighties he had been prefect of studies at Belvedere College, Dublin, and at Crescent College, Limerick. When he came to Clongowes in 1887 he knew his mind and made no bones about expressing it. He was a born martinet and organizer, a type who should never have been with the Society of Jesus but rather with the Christian Brothers or the Fathers of the Holy Ghost. First of all, he revolutionized the existent plan of studies at Clongowes. He placed all classes before the dinner hour, allotted increased hours to mathematical and scientific studies, regularized examinations, and otherwise established a timetable precision for the routine of the school. Under Father Daly disappeared those dominating interests outside the study hall and classroom that had existed during the gentler days of previous prefects. Ambitious for the ascendancy of the college in the educational hierarchy of Ireland, he saw to it that his new uncompromising system of studies conformed with the existing public programmes throughout the country. The immediate results justified his efforts. Actual study and classroom ploughing reached such a peak that by 1888, the very year

James Joyce entered the school, Clongowes Wood College was at the top of the list of efficient Irish educational establishments.

The sixteenth century Jesuit system of school organization and administration, however, was left untouched by the iconoclastic Father Daly. Not even he, if he had so desired, could break with that time-honoured tradition. Over all, students and masters, at Clongowes ruled the benevolent figure of the Rector, Father John S. Conmee. He was an old Clongownian, having studied at the school from 1863 to 1867, in which latter year he had been debate medallist. Leaving a mastership at St. Stanislaus' College, Tullabeg, the year before that school was merged with Clongowes he came to the castle as rector in 1885. He was a man of skill and tact and endowed, as not many Jesuit fathers are, with a distinct literary gift. Under his supervision the school, apart from the many religious services in the chapel, was divided into two sections. One, which included all studies and teaching and matters pertaining to them, was under the Prefect of Studies and masters. The other, including recreations, rest and meals, was under the supervision of the Minister, responsible only to the Rector, and four prefects of discipline. Three of these prefects were in charge of the three lines into which the student body was divided: the Third Line of small boys, the Lower Line of older boys, and the Higher Line of oldest boys. The discipline was simple and patriarchal. No boy, no matter how old or brilliant or responsible he was, had any disciplinary authority over any other boy. Fagging, that dubious tradition in English public schools, did not exist. Even the masters could not demand any personal services from boys in their classes. It was the elder Pitt, Earl of Chatham, who once declared that he "scarce observed a boy who was not cowed at Eton." This was a remark that he could never have made about a Jesuit school. Father Timothy Corcoran, the historian of Clongowes Wood College, who, interestingly enough, was a fellow student (although in an older line) with James Joyce at the school, has succinctly enunciated the ideal of Jesuit educational organization. "The aim of the Jesuit system, in a word," he has written, "is to forestall the development of the bully, with all the sinister associations of that term; it sought to secure and to develop that independent personality that has no use for, no toleration of, the subjection of boyhood to the perils of fagging and irresponsible punishment."

That "independent personality" was also the objective of the recreations at Clongowes. The broad playing fields, green-grassed and beautifully kept, that flank one side of the castle and the new buildings were and are continually alive with the darting figures of boys during the periods of play. Running with them, urging them on, may be seen the black-gowned figures of the prefects. The sharp crack of the bat on the ball or the thud of the shoe against the bounding football mingles with the shrill cries. Cricket, for many years the most important game at Clongowes, may be described as reaching its apogee about the time that James Joyce entered the college. Already the names of Meldon, Hosty, Harrington, and Maunsell were legendary as famous batsmen or bowlers and in Joyce's own years there were Ross, Comyn, Magee, and Rath to admire, above all, Rath who during the season of 1890-91 bowled out Phoenix, practically a Gentlemen of Ireland eleven, by disposing of four wickets for two runs. So important was cricket to the school that every season a professional was imported from England to coach the boys. It was in Joyce's entrance year, too, that the English game of Rugby was introduced. The year before, 1887, the association game had made its appearance on the Clongowes playing fields. These two types of football pushed out of favour and general playing the older game of gravel football, a rougher sport that had delighted generations of Clongowes boys and been responsible for more than one broken knee and torn hand. Of lesser significance, and more adapted to the younger students, were such pastimes as stilts and rounders.

Third-line boys, naturally enough, were not so affected by Father Daly's new scheme of studies or the rapid modernization and development of sports as were the students of the two upper lines. After all, spelling and sums and a little Latin do not afford much opportunity for new and drastic methods of teaching. And professional cricket coaches are not going to spend much time on the Half-Past-Sixes of the school. Yet the new progressive spirit that animated Clongowes must have seemed frightening enough to young Joyce fresh from Bray and the tenderness of his mother. After all, the instruction of the Jesuit masters, kindly as they may

have been, was a different matter from Mrs. Conway's explanations
of where the Mozambique Channel was and which was the longest
river in America. The lot of a child less than seven years old who is
removed from his home and placed in a boarding school amongst
strangers is not a happy one, generally speaking, until a period of
adjustment has been completed. There are fearsome elders to meet
and face without flinching, and, most trying of all, there is a horde
of schoolmates to encounter, estimate, select, and avoid. Some of
these classmates become fixtures in the memory but many of them
fade out like mist breathed on a glass, their very names dissolving
into thin air. They become less real than Queen Buan under her
grassy mound. The oblique observation of the small boy decides
which are "stinks" and which are "decent fellows." It was naturally
so with Joyce. Of the one hundred and five boys who are registered
as first entering Clongowes in 1888 with Joyce there is not one who
reappears in later life as a close friend of the artist. One must attend
the Belvedere years for that. Yet the Clongowes class of 1888 included a fairly representative group from the greater part of Ireland.
The boys came from Dublin and Belfast and Tipperary and Kil-
kenny and Wexford and Cork and Killarney and Tyrone and
Donegal and Galway and Athlone and Limerick and Athy and
Tara and a dozen other places and districts. There were even boys
from London and Liverpool and Scotland and Jamaica and India
and Spain and Portugal. Surely amongst them were all shades of
temperament and decency and maliciousness. How close did any
one of them ever come to Half-Past-Six? Certain names, to be sure,
are embalmed like small midges in amber in *A Portrait of the
Artist as a Young Man*. Notably, there are Rody Kickham of
Dublin (whose first name was Rodolph and not Roderick) and
John Cantwell of Dublin and Cecil Thunder of Dublin (who
entered Clongowes in 1889) and Anthony MacSwiney of London (also 1889) and Jack Lawton of Middleton (who didn't enter until 1890). There are boys from the upper lines too: Domi-
nick Kelly of Waterford and Michael Saurin of Hill of Down,
West Meath, and Paddy Rath, that great cricketer, of Ennis-
corthy and Argentine. These, however, are little more than the
shadows of boys bearing real names, integral and infinitesimal bits
of the greater background that was Clongowes and against which

the sharply-defined and distinctly lonely figure of Stephen Dedalus stands out all the clearlier. They are merely representative hints of all the boys whose names do not appear, the boys who made up that fluctuating sea of small hates and enthusiasms through which James Joyce swam from 1888 to 1891. None of them were important as individualities. All of them were important as an environment. Two of them, unnamed by Joyce but listed in the old roster of the class of 1888, still arouse a faint curiosity. Who was Peter Joyce of Castleblakeney, Galway, and who was the boy from Dublin who rejoiced in the resplendent cognomen of Patrice B. du Chateau?

### VII

Little remains to be said of the years that James Joyce passed at Clongowes Wood College. Here he was in perhaps the most fashionable Jesuit school in Ireland, certainly the fairest to view, a school that had already taught more than one boy destined to inherit or achieve a famous name, the sons of Daniel O'Connell, for instance, or John E. Redmond or that O'Gorman Mahon, duellist and politician, who proposed Daniel O'Connell for Parliament at the Clare election of 1828 and Parnell for the chairmanship of the Irish party in 1880, or Frank Mahony, Father Mahony, "Father Prout," who wrote "The Bells of Shandon" and is described by G. U. Ellis as "a bright-eyed, scholarly little rascal, with a store of ribald stories and an unslakable thirst." He had his share of illnesses and confinements in the infirmary; he ventured timidly into sports because of his glasses and pint-size; he played his part in the scholarly contests of the two teams into which his class of Elements was divided—one wearing the white rose of York for insignia and the other flaunting the red rose of Lancaster; he attended religious services and said his prayers every night; he returned home for the holidays and listened to the loud political argumentations around his father's dinner table; in short, he did what all the other boys at Clongowes Wood College did.

The one instance in which he rose to a brief eminence in the eyes of his fellow students had nothing to do with sports or studies. It had to do with justice. He had been exempted from work because his glasses were accidentally broken, and Father James Daly, who flogged first and asked questions afterward, soundly pandied him when he discovered him not writing out his lesson. The injustice and humiliation of the undeserved punishment aroused a fierce resolution in him. He would go directly to the Rector, Father John S. Conmee, enter that sacred room at the other end of the castle where no little lad not directly sent for dared to venture, and lay a complaint against the fire-snorting prefect of studies. He suspected that the Rector would side with Father Daly. He feared that if this happened his life at the college would be unbearable thereafter. But there was justice to be considered and justice was all. So to the Rector he went, slipping by the higher-line boys and hurrying through the long dark corridors, and told the story and the Rector, listening gravely to the protest, promised that justice should be done. It was done—immediately—and the boys had the astonishing fact before them that the Rector, the first in the school, had interfered vigorously and without hesitation on behalf of the smallest lad in the lowest class against an all-powerful second. It was an affair to be remembered and discussed by succeeding classes of Clongowes boys in the fifty years that followed.

Events of great consequence to Ireland paralleled the boy's years at Clongowes Wood College. One must have some idea of them, for they had a direct effect on James Joyce; indeed, it was because of the tragic culmination of this series of momentous events that he was stung into putting words on paper to express his adolescent indignation. It was the shocking period of the snarling jackals and the hunted lion, in other words, the tragic fifth act of Parnell's career. The Ironic Power had arranged a practically-unceasing series of violently-dramatic events to run equidistant with James Joyce's childish progress at Clongowes Wood College. He may have heard little or nothing about them from the black-soutaned fathers in his Jesuit milieu but we may be sure that he heard much, and heard it in unabashed language too, during the holidays and vacation periods that he passed in the less-politic bosom of his family. John Stanislaus was never a man to repress his opinions and the fever of the times permeated him as it did every other adult in the city of Dublin.

Parnell's tragic fifth act may be said to have commenced on April 18, 1887, when the first article on "Parnellism and Crime," accusing the Irish leader of being an accomplice of the Phoenix

Park murderers and advocating assassination as a political means,
appeared in *The* [London] *Times*. This was before James Joyce
entered Clongowes Wood College but the really great scenes happened after he had been committed to the care of the Jesuit fathers.
The Commission appointed to inquire into Parnell's possible guilt
existed from September 17, 1888, to November 22, 1889, holding one
hundred and twenty-eight sittings and examining over four hundred
and fifty witnesses. All Ireland and England followed the developments in wild fevers of antagonistic partisanship as the Conservative
jackals endeavoured to drag down the Irish lion. It was on February
20, 1889, that the white-bearded rascal, Richard Pigott, who had
forged the letters implicating Parnell, entered the witness box and
was remorselessly destroyed by his cross-examiner, Sir Charles
Russell. James Joyce had just passed his seventh birthday. When
Pigott betrayed himself through the spelling of the word 'hesitancy' (he had written it 'hesitency' in one of the forged letters
and so spelled it on the witness stand in a list of words dictated
to him) [1] and fled from England a day or so later, and, on March
first, killed himself in the Hotel Embajadores, Madrid, just as
the police were about to lay hands on him, James Joyce was
eagerly looking forward to the Easter vacation and the companionship of his mother. It is not difficult to imagine the excitement in the Joyce household during those thrilling weeks when
Parnell's triumphant vindication raised him to a plane of popularity that even he had never known before. John Stanislaus,
while not of Parnell's party, was nationally-conscious enough
to rejoice as full-heartedly as the rest of his countrymen at the
clean-cut victory of the Irish Leader. And his young son, no
longer Half-Past-Six but Half-Past-Seven, was beginning to understand what it was all about. At least, he was aware that there was
a Hero and that there was Justice.

Parnell's triumph, great as it was, did not endure long, however.
The victorious summer turned into a winter of discontent when
Captain William O'Shea (on December 24, 1889) filed a petition for
divorce from his wife and cited Parnell as co-respondent. The decree
was granted to the petitioner by Mr. Justice Butt on November 17,
1890. There was a brief and ominous lull and then the jackals real-

[1] This word 'hesitancy' is played upon in *Finnegans Wake*, page 421 *et seq.*

ized that they had their prey at last. The lion was down. Gladstone's letter with its famous line stating that Parnell's retention of the leadership of the Irish party would render his [Gladstone's] leadership of the Liberal party "almost a nullity" proved to be the death-blow. The closing scenes of the tragedy followed in rapid succession. There was the shambles of invective in Committee Room 15, the split in the Irish party on December sixth, the dethronement of Parnell, his last heartbreaking campaign in Ireland to regain his power while the priests of the Roman Catholic Church and the cohorts of that squat Judas, Timothy Healy, afterward chosen as first Governor General of the New Ireland, blocked him at every turning, his marriage to Mrs. O'Shea on June 25, 1891, and his sudden death on October sixth of this same year.

All this turmoil of political savagery and personal tragedy reacted vividly on the blossoming imagination of young James Joyce. He had passed his ninth year when the final scene was played. He listened to his father and his father's friends, heard their raised voices and saw their flushed faces over the dinner plates, and, with a mental perception already developed beyond his years, comprehended far more than his elders divined. His own indignation, the indignation of a nine-year-old boy who has seen injustice done and sensed the dark ruthlessness behind the smiling Irish nature, mounted as the mercury in the thermometer mounts on a midsummer day. It demanded an outlet. This outlet took the form of a violently-written attack on Timothy Healy. John Stanislaus, who had become exceedingly pro-Parnell during the last scenes of that Leader's débâcle, was so pleased with his son's prose production that he took it to the firm of Alleyn and O'Reilly and had it printed in the form of a small pamphlet. No copy of this juvenile outburst against the injustice and treachery of man is known to exist but it is still possible that some fortunate explorer fumbling through yellowed papers in a neglected Dublin garret may chance upon this Joycian opus number one of the year 1891.

It was to these last scenes of the Parnell tragedy that James Joyce's years at Clongowes Wood College drew to a close. After the termination of the spring season of 1891 he did not return to the pleasant castle of studies, religious instruction, historical memories and legends. The grave-mound of Queen Buan was left behind with the shot-riddled door of the Round Room. Before he left, however, he was received definitively into the bosom of the church by the rite of Confirmation and took Aloysius for his saint's name: James Augustine Aloysius Joyce. It had a fine long sweep. There being no scholastic reason for his departure (he had not reached the higher lines) it would seem to be due to financial necessity. Certainly it was about this time that John Stanislaus's carefree progress downhill from modest affluence to poverty became accelerated. But though the boy returned no more to Clongowes Wood College it continued to exist in his mind, a vivid reality of sights and scenes and impressions, of legends and dreams and broodings, a sacred place of the coming to consciousness that would be reflected again and again, like sunlight in a shifting mirror, in all the work he would do thereafter.

# Two

YOUNG Joyce had plenty of time to reflect on his first school and to compare the simple but organized life conducted there with the rather hit-or-miss existence of his home, for it was nearly two years before he was entered at another educational establishment. During this interim his powers of perception grew mightily. He commenced to see the world as a series of bright shifting scenes where he was not always at home and where there was much that teased his rapidly-forming mind. From the very first he seems to have been a careful observer of all that went on around him. He was slight in physique, highly nervous, sensitive as a girl, and blessed or cursed (as one may look at it) with an introspective nature. This made him the hub, so to speak, of his own little universe and even of that greater universe outside his cognition where the phenomena of Time moved in cloudy mystery. Even as a lad he was instinctively reaching for a comprehension of that greater universe and many mistily-conceived queries about it were already moving like invisible fish in deep waters and stirring faint currents. In times to be, they would all come to the surface and bring to the mature mind nostalgic rumours of boyhood sharp with the sounds and smells of vanished days.

It was about 1892 or maybe a little later—the exact chronology does not matter, for it is a cross-cut of Time that is considered here —that John Stanislaus Joyce took his eldest son on a visit to Cork. The reason for the trip was to attend the sale of some Joyce properties there. Cork was a new experience for the boy and he was never to forget this early introduction to the pleasant city. There were charming streets and houses to see and a lilt of language to hear that differed from Dublinese. There was Queen's College to visit and the son inspected the desk where the father had carved his initials more than twenty years before. There were old friends of John Stanislaus to meet and old stories to be heard. It was an agreeable diversion in a period of attendance on Time that had been

38

practically all vacation, the playtime, so to speak, between two institutions, between Clongowes Wood College and the new house of learning to which the boy was to be sent.

Once returned from Cork to Dublin (for the family were now living in the city itself at 13 Fitzgibbon Street), John Stanislaus began to concern himself with the necessary resumption of his son's education. He would not send the boy to the Christian Brothers. "Is it with Paddy Stink and Micky Mud?" The father possessed a formidable pride of caste and never forgot that he was a Joyce of *the* Joyces and not a descendant of some scraper of the soil who had appropriated that name from the master of the big house. No, he declared with his usual vigour, let the boy stay with the Jesuits. He had begun with them and, after all, they might be of some aid to him in later years. Meantime the son was discovering Dublin, wandering for the first time, timidly at the beginning but with a growing confidence as he mastered the topography, about the streets and along the busy quays, pausing by old monuments and shop windows, regardant of the flowing streams of life: the multitude of cabs, the swaggering British soldiers, the sable-clad priests, the loitering jackeens with the breath of porter on them, the sharp-tongued servant girls, the scurrying men of business, all that motley and restless mass of humanity that quickened the pulse of the small metropolis. In the face of all this movement his reactions were complex. He was becoming aware of the bigness and disorderliness of life and, perhaps, of his own incapacity to dominate it. He did not realize that here lay all the loose materials of his future art, that Dublin would devour him and that he, in turn, would devour Dublin. Yet the perceptive urge within him caused him to move about the city like the seeing eye of a camera registering beyond forgetfulness the multitudinous facets of the shifting scene.

John Stanislaus, having inquired of his many friends, settled upon Belvedere College in Belvedere House on Great Denmark Street as the proper school for his sons. It was not too far away and, most important of all, through some wangling with influential personalities, James, and his younger brother, John Stanislaus Jr., as well, would be admitted without payment of the customary fees. This was important for a father whose fortune was melting like the snows of this very month. On April 6, 1893, then, James Augustine

Joyce was entered as a New Boy in III of Grammar at Belvedere College and his brother, John Stanislaus Jr., then aged eight, was entered in Elements.

II

Ghosts of great days haunt the spacious rooms of Belvedere House. It had been raised during the time of Grattan's Parliament (1775) when Dublin was noted for its wit, genius, and luxury; and a wealth of ingenuity and art went into its making. George Rochfort, second Earl of Belvedere, for whom it was built, expended twenty-four thousand pounds on the Georgian mansion. It is, according to all authorities, the best-preserved house of its period in Dublin today. The principal rooms are a delight to the antiquary of architecture. The splendid staircases, the elaborately-decorated mantelpieces of genuine Borsi work, the exquisite stucco designs of Venetian artists that adorn the ceilings and walls, the organ with paintings on it by Angelika Kauffmann, the Venus drawing room, the Diana and Apollo rooms (now the college library), all these fastidious achievements of a gracious, sophisticated, and vanished era are carefully preserved by the Jesuit fathers. They, after all, have no more fear of Venus, Diana, and Apollo than they have of Angelika Kauffmann. It was in 1841 that the Society of Jesus purchased the mansion for the astoundingly low sum of eighteen hundred pounds and translated it into a college. Forty-three years later (1884) Killeen House, the adjoining town residence of Lord Fingall, was purchased for the school by the then President, the Very Reverend Father Thomas Finlay, S.J. During this year, also, a gymnasium was added and the north side of the quadrangle was built up to contain a boys' chapel, classrooms and laboratories. The result was one of the most comfortable and best-equipped Jesuit town schools in Ireland. Like Clongowes Wood College, Belvedere House possesses its romantic phantom (never known to walk, however), that of Mary Molesworth, wife to the old debauchee of the Second George's court, Colonel Rochfort.

To this house James Joyce came at the age of eleven years and two months, a rather grave observant boy, still wearing glasses, whose mind, filled with the placid memories of Clongowes and the new phenomena of Dublin, was adjusting itself with avidity towards the necessary goal of *comprehension*. He found nothing particularly foreign or unexpected in the college for it was conducted on practically the same lines as Clongowes. The Jesuit system of secular studies and religious inculcation was maintained and the classes, as in all the schools of this type controlled by the Society of Jesus, were divided from beginning to matriculation into Elements, Rudiments, III of Grammar, II of Grammar, I of Grammar, Poetry and Rhetoric. There was a higher, lower and third line too. But if Joyce found the curriculum in all essentials similar to Clongowes he speedily discovered the Rector to be quite the reverse of that urbane student of the humanities, the Very Reverend Father John S. Conmee, S.J., who had been his court of last appeal at his first school. The head of Belvedere College was Father James Henry, S.J., a fanatical Roman Catholic convert who wore whiskers. His character was harsh and warped but despite these serious flaws he was a man of breeding. From all accounts, he cannot be compared with Father James Daly of Clongowes, the man with the pandybat and a personality temperamentally unfitted to the Society of Jesus.

If Joyce found a grim character in Father Henry, who, by the way, taught the Latin classes and taught them with vigour, he was compensated in the discovery of George Stanislaus [1] Dempsey, a lay teacher who conducted the English courses. Dempsey was a man respected and loved by his students. His own affection and enthusiasm for English communicated itself to those who studied under him and his decency of character made his classes popular and pleasant hours in the long school day. Joyce became very fond of Dempsey as the Belvedere years passed by and the teacher reciprocated this feeling. It will not be going too far to suggest that in George Stanislaus Dempsey we find the first positive influence in Joyce's early artistic and literary awakening. The instinctive passion that the boy had for the English language was fostered and encouraged by the teacher.

Now, it is extremely difficult to estimate the influence of a

[1] If, as probable, Father Conmee's middle name was Stanislaus, this was the fourth Stanislaus to impinge on Joyce's young life, the others being his father and his brother. The name of St. Stanislaus Kostka, one of the three patrons of holy youth (with St. Aloysius Gonzaga and St. John Berchmans) was given, as that also of the patron of Poland, in their view, at least, by many Irish mothers to their sons born about the middle of the last century out of religious and political sympathy with the Poles. The tenor air in *The Bohemian Girl,* "When the fair land of Poland," always brought down the house.

teacher on a student in the junior grades, far more difficult than to recognize the influences of professors in the senior colleges where the undergraduate has already achieved a definite personality and a purpose and is attracted or repelled by what his professor has to give. In the junior grades the student's mind is still in process of formation and being shaped, so to speak, by a more simple and elementary manipulation. The universal essentials of education are being mapped on the more or less submissive mind much as the artist drafts his preliminary sketch in charcoal on the white canvas, putting there the necessary lines that will be subtilized later. In the higher school, the senior college, the sketch will be filled in under the guidance of the sensitive professor who perceives the purpose of the sketch or else the student, already aware of where he wants to go, will revolt from the influence of the teacher and proceed on his own undisciplined way. Therefore, when we consider Joyce's years at Belvedere College, years that stretched from his eleventh to his sixteenth year, we must be careful not to read too much into any positive influences. It is obvious that his urge towards literature was congenital and that an early and consistent passion for an independence of utterance and logical ratiocination (soon to be Aristotelian in essence) agitated his constantly-swelling intelligence. Such a mind might have been spoilt in the formation. That it wasn't is perhaps due to the pertinacity of that mind as much as to the direction of teachers. As we shall see, Joyce's independence grew out of himself alone and matured despite (and because of) antagonistic influences. Of these influences, influences of repulsion, we may say, more will be noted later. We must believe, in the light of the years that follow, that Joyce would undoubtedly have been the Joyce he became if there had been no George Stanislaus Dempsey. Yet, at the same time, we must believe, also, in the light of the years that follow, that George Stanislaus Dempsey was a fortunate event in the growth of the budding artist. Indeed, until his demise some ten years ago Dempsey continued to be a warm partisan of his former pupil, attempting to persuade the college authorities to print Joyce's verse in the college magazine. And some of the innumerable books of reference which Joyce used in the composition of *Finnegans Wake* came to him from his old teacher.

Among the other instructors under whom Joyce sat during his

five years at Belvedere College may be briefly noted: Father Ryan, S.J., who taught French (according to all accounts another misplaced cleric who should have been a Christian Brother), Mr. Foy, brother-in-law to Dempsey, who taught Physics, and a Mr. Loup from whom Joyce first began to learn the Italian language at the age of twelve. Italian, by the way, was at this time the Cinderella of languages. Joyce, having to take a fourth language, had chosen it himself, although his father desired him to take Greek and his mother German. Only one other boy at Belvedere was learning Italian. He was Albrecht Connolly. The school doctor's name was Redmond and it was he who ordered the boy to stop wearing glasses in 1894. Joyce did not put them on again for ten years. Neither must one forget the physical culture coach, Sergeant Major Wright, a forthright individual who put the students through their paces in military style. Joyce, who often amazed the worthy Sergeant Major by tirelessly repeating a half-lever although he was far from muscular, eventually became secretary to the gymnasium, a most peculiar post for a youth whose interest in feats of physical prowess was practically nil. And here a further word may be said about his physique. He was not strong at all. But he was animated and sustained by a sort of electrical nervous energy that sometimes made it possible for him to do things that his lack of muscles would seem to render impossible. There were occasions during his boyhood, and they have continued all his life, when in moments of joyous excitement a sort of dancing vitality possessed him and caught his lean body up and sustained him long after stronger men sank exhausted in their chairs.

Belvedere College was a comparatively small place and because of this the communal life was rather closely knit. All the boys knew one another although they were in varying degrees of intimacy and separated, as all boys do, into cliques. Elements, naturally, did not walk and talk with Senior Grade. Yet there was a solidarity in the school that could not be found in English institutions of the same rank. As at Clongowes, there was no fagging and perhaps this happy release from the customary torture of the younger boys had something to do with the pleasant equality of the students. Joyce adjusted himself without delay to this environment. With an awareness of values that had come to him since his Clongowes days he made no bosom friends but he admitted friendlier contacts with his fellow students than he had before. He was consistent in his relationships with classmates and because of this he was well-enough liked. If his gravity of demeanour sometimes raised an invisible wall between him and his companions, these same companions, all tacit conformists in the Roman Catholic atmosphere of the time, were too heedless or indifferent to notice it. Their minds were almost wholly concerned with the surface aspect of things. Indeed, there does not appear to have been one boy of Joyce's years at Belvedere introspective or analytical enough to penetrate beyond the Jesuit conception of life and culture. Joyce, with his independent and restless will, his scorn of stupidity and placid acceptances and his secret anger at the minor shifts and indelicacies of cowardly boys, walked, then, for the most part alone even when he was in intercourse with those about him. It was, perhaps, this unpretentious and instinctive aloofness, as well as his class distinctions, that made him Captain of the School when he reached the Senior Grade.

His relations with his instructors were courteous and uneventful. Curiously enough, he got along very well with the rather harsh Rector, Father Henry, each personality, perhaps, discovering and respecting the forthright individuality of the other. It is possible that his excellence and assiduity in classwork had something to do with this pleasant state of affairs. Joyce was a natural student, no prodigy, to be sure, but one who loved culture and saw and found in it an outlet for himself and the phantasmal hopes and despairs that were now agitating his nature. Languages appealed to him; the glories of English letters seduced him and the dialectics of the humanities enticed his pondering nature. He was all-embracing in his pursuit of what had been thought and written concerning life and art and outside the college walls he supplemented what he had imbibed within them by an inquisitive investigation of the so-called subversive writers. Their violence and gibes eventually became an acidulous antidote to the dogmatic precisions of Jesuit philosophy. The dark bile of Byron, for instance, curdled the innocuous milk of 'Lawn' Tennyson.

It was in the English course at Belvedere that Joyce became most noticeable and by the time he had reached II of Grammar, his third year in Great Denmark Street, he was famed for his essay writing. It was the task of the week for him, an appealing labour towards which his will was spontaneously drawn. These essays, on set subjects, bore such simple titles as "Make Hay While the Sun Shines," "A Walk in the Country" and "Perseverance." There 'was small chance for any possible heresy in them. One, called "My Favourite Hero," was about Ulysses and the youth's praise of the Greek wanderer rather irritated the instructor who considered such enthusiasm for the wily husband of Penelope as not quite orthodox, at least from the point of view of the Society of Jesus.[1] Money prizes were awarded for the best of these class essays and Joyce won many of them. This money he generally expended on his family, taking them to theatres (already a passion with the boy) or to fine dinners in popular restaurants. The family, perhaps because of this largess, thought (and continued to think through all the years that followed) that the school compositions were the best things Joyce ever wrote or ever would write. "A Walk in the Country" possessed greater charm for them than *A Portrait of the Artist as a Young Man,* and the noble sentiments expressed in "Perseverance" touched John Stanislaus more closely than *Ulysses.* Perhaps these essays, which exist only in rumour now, *were* good; but schoolboy merit is seldom an indication of future major literary ability and it is to be expected that the Belvedere essays, if they existed today, would hardly convince the reader that their youthful author would develop into a world-famous figure in letters. The literary bent was there, without a doubt, but what it would amount to was a secret known only to the mysterious spirit of the future.

Joyce was translating, too, at this period—a necessary part of his Latin studies—and there remains extant his English version of Ode III, 13 from Horace. As it is the earliest of his writings that exists today, a rather charming curiosity from the pen of a fourteen-year-old boy, it may be quoted.

> Brighter than glass Bandusian spring
>   For mellow wine and flowers meet,
> The morrow thee a kid shall bring
>   Boding of rivalry and sweet

[1] See page 306 of *Finnegans Wake* for a comic list of essay titles. "We've had our **day** at triv and quad and writ our bit as intermidgets."

Love in his swelling forms. In vain
He, wanton offspring, deep shall stain
Thy clear cold streams with crimson rain.

The raging dog star's season thou,
  Still safe from in the heat of day,
When oxen weary of the plough
  Yieldst thankful cool for herds that stray.
Be of the noble founts! I sing
The oak tree o'er thine echoing
Crags, thy waters murmuring.

At this moment (to pause midway in the Belvedere years) we have the picture of a lean, grave-mannered boy, manifestly older in temperament than his years, an excellent scholar with an aptitude for languages and compositions, obedient to those in authority because of a natural orderliness of mind, independent in judgement, impatient of stupidities, popular enough with his companions but never giving too much of himself to them, intellectually inquisitive and leavened by a half-mocking sense of humour. All this, be it remarked, was sufficiently obvious to the attentive observer. Invisible to view and the guarded secret of the youth was the troubled growing soul reacting sometimes rebelliously and sometimes inchoately to the admonitory voices that sought to influence it, the voice of John Stanislaus telling him to be a gentleman above all things, the voices of Jesuits urging him to be a good Roman Catholic, the voices of professional patriots demanding that he labour for the uplift of his country and the voices of school comrades desiring him to be a decent chap. Often enough these voices sounded hollow and meaningless, feeble whips of exhortation powerless to drive the mysterious phantoms from his mind. It was to these voices and the subtle influence of elders that he reached adolescence and the more serious problems of his final years at Belvedere.

There was the Church and there was puberty and there was Dublin.

No one can observe the growth of a boy in a Jesuit school without considering the religious element. It was a Jesuit (and he was thinking of Ireland as he wrote) who declared: "The faith of a Catholic nation is of the essence of its nationality, which, therefore, perishes with its faith." For the Irish bishops and the Society of

Jesus, then, Church and State were indivisible and the inculcation and preservation of the Faith were sacred and unceasing duties. At Belvedere College, naturally enough, there was plenty of religious instruction and as Joyce grew older his sensitive nature reacted to it more vigorously and passionately, perhaps, than would duller- or grosser-witted minds. At first he had accepted Roman Catholicism as the fish accepts the ocean, a world into which he had been born and which was his natural element; but as time passed on and increasing capabilities of ratiocination toughened his mind he began to view the Church in a different light. It remained his element but it was suffused with mysteries that teased his mind. The sense of sin, of guilt, of worldly defilement and the cleansing power of absolution became painfully vivid to his adolescent nature. Especially was this true when he reached the age of puberty. Sitting in his place in the chapel during the annual Retreat held before the feast day of St. Francis Xavier—the patron saint of Belvedere College—he listened spellbound to the vigorous admonitions and earnest pleadings of the Jesuit fathers and the ancient controlling power of the religion held absolute sway over his perturbed mind. His mother, too, an unreasoningly pious woman whose piety increased as she aged, would have been pleased to see her eldest son reveal a vocation for the Church. With the influence of his Jesuit teachers subtly directed upon him and the emotional instigation of his mother pushing him toward the Holy of Holies there was a period during the Belvedere years when Joyce actually entertained the idea of entering the Jesuit order. Father James Joyce, S.J. At least, it was alliterative. That the idea soon passed was due to a complexity of reasons, not the least of them, perhaps, being an instinctive understanding that he could never take the vow of celibacy.

Pubescence played a great part in the mental struggles of this period. With the awakening of the body the entire aspect of living changed and the youth found himself in the midst of a dreadful struggle of reorientation in a life where all the values had suddenly shifted. The warnings of preceptors took on a deeper significance while body and mind engaged in an unsuspected warfare. On the one hand was nearly ten years of Jesuit teaching and on the other the blind intuitive urgencies of the body with all the stews of secret Dublin for shameful refuge. An ordinary youth would pass through this period rather lightly and with no regrets; but the extraordinary youth (and this was Joyce's case) would take it more seriously, feeling himself lost at times, achieving difficult victories over himself, and eventually arriving at a profounder comprehension of the dark mysteries of life. It was so with Joyce. He experienced in turn the guilty joy of a blasphemous *non serviam* to the Victorian and Roman Catholic conceptions of deportment and thought that ruled nineteenth-century Dublin, the overwhelming despair of the sinner fallen from God's grace and the ætherial joy of the brand snatched from the burning through penance, absolution and the redeeming arms of the Church.

That all this storm and stress of the soul was complicated and increased by the budding artist, the enwombed artificer, in the youth is without doubt (for after the event one may read backward); but that he was conscious of this fact at the time is extremely dubious. He had yet to realize the reason for his existence, yet to comprehend that it was the unconsciously self-dramatizing imagination of the lonely artist who enlarges himself at the expense of the apparent world that carried him from the nadir of despair to the zenith of a paradisal overlordship of the disastrous flaws of time. That knowledge was to come later, not so very much later, when passing from Belvedere to University College (in other words, passing from boyhood to an early maturity that was the threshold of manhood) he had readjusted himself to the two worlds visible and invisible from which he drew his spiritual sustenance. At that moment, we may say, he saw his vocation in its mythic guise, "a hawkfaced man flying sunward above the sea."

The last year or two at Belvedere was silver-streaked with the steady progression towards this revelation. Joyce continued to be the excellent scholar, the omnivorous reader, the composer of youthful poetry. His interests in music widened and the discovery that he possessed an excellent voice was a great delight to him. He sang often at private parties and those who remember him at the age of thirteen or fourteen declare that he possessed a child's tenor voice and could sing B natural. (Curiously enough, his voice seems never to have changed. There was a day or two's hoarseness and the child's tenor became a man's treble.) The independence of his opinions toughened. There was little he would take for granted; he was insistent in putting all controversial matters to the test of reason. He maintained an easy ascendancy among his classmates, becoming, as has been pointed out, Captain of the School in his last year. He budded forth as an amateur actor, playing the rôle of the pedagogue in Anstey's *Vice-Versa* and basing his conception of the part on the personal peculiarities of Father Henry, much to the delight of the audience and of the Rector himself. He endeavoured, not without anguish, to adjust himself to the increasing squalor of his home; for it was about this time that John Stanislaus's journey down the hill of fortune became precipitate. At the college he avoided all mention of his father and when one of the boys insolently asked him why he moved from house to house so often he could do no more than silently turn away.

And there was Dublin.

By this time all its ways and monuments were familiar to him. The tentative explorations of the uncertain boy had been succeeded by the assured examination of the observant youth, a youth, be it noted, with a memory like a written register wherein the possessor might turn back the pages whenever he chose and review again the place and movement that had vanished in time. From Drumcondra where he lived to Harold's Cross with its memories of Lord Edward Fitzgerald and Robert Emmet he had tramped the streets and by-lanes, wandering from the narrow and nauseous thoroughfares of Nighttown (relics of Lady Morgan's "dear dirty Dublin") to the tree-shaded expanse of St. Stephen's Green, loitering before the shop windows in Grafton Street where was set the slab commemorating Wolfe Tone and watching the trams clanging beneath the Nelson Pillar on Sackville Street, reclining on the sands by Clontarf where Brian Boru smashed the Danes in 1014 and listening to the hiss and slap of the Irish Sea: and all this, wide streets, grey buildings, pebbly expanses, reeking lanes, Phoenix Park, Castle, Mansion House, museum and kip peopled with the heterogeneous types of a metropolis achieved a curious unity in his mind. Dublin was a unique personality and yet again it was all life. Beneath its strident surface hum and roar lay buried the same dark mythos that was concealed in Queen Buan's grave-mound at Clongowes. One might plunge into it and discover all the material that one needed in a lifetime.

And there was the Time-Spirit, the crosscurrents of contemporary evolution, as well, the urge and feel of this Ireland in which the boy was growing up. Parallel with the transformation of Joyce from a boy to a youth proceeded the curious and sometimes barbarous fluctuations of the Zeitgeist. Ireland was undergoing a change although at first it was barely perceptible to the hasty observer.

So far as the political scene was concerned the spectacle was not edifying. The years from 1893 to 1898 were those of the muddy backwash from the Parnell débâcle. Ireland, as a whole, was in a stupor agitated by a series of nightmares. A split and incoherent party engaged in internecine warfare and nowhere was there visible a leader who could fit into the place left vacant by the Uncrowned King. The ineffective Justin McCarthy, titular head of the Irish party, could do nothing but pose as a respectable figurehead. T. M. Healy, the Man in the Gap, was generalissimo of the more vitriolic wing of the anti-Parnell group while John Dillon, advised and sustained by William O'Brien, directed the kindlier. The pro-Parnell minority, shaken and weakened by violent emotion, was impotent. It was the representatives of this battered, broken and bitterly-divided Irish party that were returned to Westminster at the General Election of 1895, a group of unreasonable prejudiced Parliamentarians who betrayed the best interests of their country by their private civil war. Alas, for those simple and trusting peasants (and there were many of them) who fondly believed that the Uncrowned King lay not in his grave but awaited in hiding the propitious hour when he could step into public life again and seize the reins of power. Parnell would never return; he slept too soundly beneath his Glasnevin coverlet. It was not until 1898, Joyce's last year at Belvedere, that the political scene brightened and that was due to the passing of the Local Government Act, a drastic piece of legislation that destroyed landlord power in Irish administration. One might say that it marked the exit of "the garrison" and the entrance of the people. It also marked, be it remembered, the exit of John Stanislaus Joyce from the office of the Collector General of Rates.

But deplorable as the political scene was it had its recompenses. Perhaps it was because of this angry futility of national struggle, this excuse-me-while-I-cut-your-throat-Kathleen-ni-Houlihan attitude of the elected representatives, that a minority of intelligent and cultured people turned their faces and minds away from the dispiriting picture and concerned themselves with a profounder expression of the country. It was during these years that the so-called 'Irish Literary Renaissance had its gestation and birth. Perhaps the immediate seed of this movement had been planted as far back as 1889 when W. B. Yeats's *The Wanderings of Oisin* was published. But, to be arbitrary, one can as well take the years 1893 and 1894 as marking the real birth of the Renaissance. It was in the former year that Douglas Hyde founded the Gaelic League with its insistence on the study of the Irish language and W. B. Yeats published *The Celtic Twilight,* the very title of which finally served to describe an aspect of Irish letters. And in the latter year appeared Hyde's *Love Songs of Connacht,* A.E.'s *Homeward: Songs by the Way* and Yeats's *The Land of Heart's Desire.* During this year, too, while Joyce was composing his first respectable essays at Belvedere, Edward Martyn [1] and George Moore were living in The Temple, London, Martyn in Pump Court and Moore in King's Bench Walk. They engaged in frequent conversations concerning a possible literature for Ireland. Martyn was expressing a desire to return to his native land and write in Irish and Moore was ironically thinking, "Far more true would it be to say that an Irishman must fly from Ireland if he would be himself," a thought, by the way, that would almost seem to be a vague prophecy of James Joyce. Martyn, it is interesting to note, was already under the influence of Henrik Ibsen, an influence that in a very few years would be knocking at the mind of the Belvedere schoolboy.

As time passed on, the new literature—mainly under the impetus of W. B. Yeats (George Moore later admitted that the Irish Renaissance "rose out of Yeats and returns to Yeats")—became increasingly evident even to casual readers. In 1895 (year of the lamentable General Election) appeared Yeats's *Poems,* and in the next year (1896) a slim volume entitled *Two Essays on the Remnant* introduced a new critic who signed himself John Eglinton (W. K. Magee). The year 1897 was notable for three publications, Sigerson's *Bards of the Gael and Gall,* T. W. Rolleston's *Deirdre* (the first of several dramas on that unhappy Celtic heroine), and

---

[1] Martyn, who made an attempt to introduce modern prose drama into Ireland with *The Heather Field,* seems to have been completely shelved by the Abbey Theatre authorities. The play was not revived even during the Abbey Jubilee Celebration a few years ago. Martyn's book, *Morgante the Lesser,* is practically unknown and he has received little or no recognition for his munificence in endowing the Pro-Cathedral Palestrina Choir.

Yeats's *The Secret Rose*. During the autumn of 1898 (year of the Local Government Act and the downfall of John Stanislaus Joyce) W. B. Yeats, Edward Martyn and George Moore sat about a London tea table with Lady Augusta Gregory and conceived the idea of the Irish Literary Theatre. And with that inception the Irish Literary Renaissance may be said to have been, if not full-blown, well on the way to complete flowering.

Joyce could have been only vaguely aware of all this national literary gestation, for the greater part of his time at Belvedere was occupied with imbibing the past and his constant reading in the National Library was mainly confined to the great European figures, that new discovery, Ibsen, for instance, who was so soon to become the god of his idolatry. In his home (or his various homes) he was not likely to hear much abstract comment concerning nascent literary movements. Politics, yes. There is no doubt but that John Stanislaus, rolling a ferocious eye behind his glass, roundly damned the state of national affairs and the Local Government Act that had put him out of office and rewarded him with a meagre pension. His few heroes, Parnell, for example, received an equally vehement approbation. But poets, by God, were another matter. The only poets John Stanislaus recognized were those poets of sound called tenors. And, of course, Thomas Moore, because tenors sang his mellifluous verses. At the moment the son was more concerned with Ulysses than he was with Cuchulain; the odes of Horace were his immediate problem and not Douglas Hyde's recovery of old Gaelic songs; and for his private pleasure there was all of Europe. Yet he was close to an important door, his hand almost upon it, during his last year at Belvedere. What his convictions would be about Irish nationalism (as expressed in both literary form and political agitation) lay just behind that door. That he would arrive at them cold-bloodedly was a foregone conclusion; for the youth of sixteen, unlike most youths of sixteen, distrusted enthusiasms.

It was during the summer of 1898 that Joyce passed out of Belvedere College, leaving behind him the last remnants of his boyhood.

There must have been serious debate in the household of John Stanislaus as to what should be done with the eldest son. The director of studies at Belvedere College, when he was informed that Joyce had definitely decided not to join the Jesuit order, suggested a position in Guinness's Brewery, and John Stanislaus desired his son to read for the Bar. But neither of these prospects appealed to the eldest son. They were equal prisons of the mind to him, two dungeons where the wings of Dedalus could never beat the air. The mysterious urges that had been clamouring within him for some time warned him against these cul-de-sacs of life. His path lay elsewhere and now a word or a gesture would reveal it to him. Admirably enough, it was the easygoing John Stanislaus who finally made the decisive gesture. It was in his decision to permit his son to go on to University College, to register with the Faculty of Arts, to have four more years of freedom wherein to prepare himself for the serious business of life that Joyce almost immediately found himself and his vocation. He had escaped. Years later, turning back into his past, he was to recapture this necessary moment of his liberation in a sentence: "So he had passed beyond the challenge of the sentries who had stood as guardians of his boyhood and had sought to keep him among them that he might be subject to them and serve their ends."

In the College Register of University College, now preserved among the archives at Earlsfort Terrace, Dublin, James Joyce is listed under the year 1898.

### III

University College (Jesuit, of course) was contained in what had been formerly the Georgian town mansion of one 'Buck' Whaley, a swashbuckling roisterer of the eighteenth century whose vehement and oft-repeated oath was that no Roman Catholic priest should ever pass over his threshold. It faced on St. Stephen's Green. The college, inaugurated in November 1883, was a reorganization of the Arts and Science faculties of the collapsed Catholic University founded by John Cardinal Newman some thirty years before. As an institution of learning it had its distinct limitations. For instance, it operated under the old Royal University and was therefore controlled and influenced by the character and regulations of that body. This made for a rigidity in the curriculum. As examples

of this may be cited the facts that there was no differentiation between Major and Minor subjects—all marks being of the same
value, that candidates were asked identical questions in Orals and
that graduates preparing for Studentships had to take *three* languages—all on the same level—in the Modern Language groups.
If we except the Arts courses, there was far from a variety of subjects taught. Science and Economics were imperfectly represented;
Engineering and Law were mere shadows; Technology, Theology,
and Education did not exist at all; and Medicine, located in a building of its own on Cecilia Street, was in all essentials a separate
college.

The Faculty during Joyce's time (the famous Father Gerard
Manley Hopkins [1] was a member long before) was adequate but not
exceptional. The Very Reverend Father William Delany, S.J., a
former rector of Tullabeg College in King's County, was the President. As an administrator he appears to have been efficient and fair-
minded. When Joyce matriculated the Chair of English was held
by Professor Thomas Arnold, son of Dr. Arnold of Rugby and
brother to Matthew Arnold. The Fellowship in English was in the
hands of Father Joseph Darlington, a convert to the Roman Catholic Church, who is pictured, by the way, in *A Portrait of the Artist
as a Young Man* as the dean of studies who lights the fire and
engages in an æsthetic conversation with Stephen Dedalus. Professor Arnold died in 1900 and his successor was Father George
O'Neill, S.J. In 1901, a year before Joyce received his degree, Father
Darlington was transferred to the Chair of Metaphysics, held previ-
ously by Father T. A. Finlay, S.J., and John Bacon, M.A., succeeded
to the Fellowship in English. It was under these teachers, then,
Arnold, Darlington, O'Neill, and Bacon, that Joyce sat during his
English courses.

All of them appear to have been efficient, capable, well-grounded
men with no great imagination and subtly biased, of course, by
their Roman Catholic faith and affiliations. They were diggers in
accustomed ditches. What they had to give had been given a thousand times before to numberless students who sought no more than
they could find in the limited horizons of their instructors. There

---

[1] A year or so ago the contributor of University College Notes to a Dublin daily paper
describing the ceremony of the extension or renovation of the Aula Maxima of the College
wrote of it as "hallowed by the memories of Cardinal Newman, Father Manly Hopkins
and James Joyce"(!). The names, however, are not, from one point of view, incongruous.

were no wings in the precise and pre-orchestrated (so to speak) progression of these teachers through the myriad mysteries of language and its innumerable nuances. Nothing more, in fact, than the rather tame journey towards a foreseen and dogmatic end. What they had taught yesterday they taught today and would teach again tomorrow. The magic was not there. They were bound by the severe obligations of the Faith they professed. Yet within their limits (and the limits of Jesuit thought are not small) they furnished a foundation that was solid and upon which a man could place his two feet and feel that he was not in sinking sands. It might, of course, be alien terrain but it was firm enough for the leap to other continents of thought.

When the English courses are considered one thinks automatically of the library, that abounding well from which the students of English draw their pails of knowledge in the form of books. University College was decidedly inadequate in this necessary reservoir. There was no comprehensive library in 'Buck' Whaley's mansion. But not far away, on Kildare Street (that short thoroughfare flanked with Leinster House, the National Museum of Science and Art and the Kildare Street Club where the landowners of Ireland once gathered to drink their whiskies), was the National Library of Dublin and this became a sort of appropriated annex to University College. It had long been familiar ground to Joyce. Time after time he had passed through the spacious horseshoe vestibule and mounted the richly-carved staircase to the lofty reading room, also horseshoe in shape, to seek the books whose titles were quick in his mind. Often enough he had loitered under the colonnade (and would stand there again and again) watching the birds fly high over the jutting end of Molesworth Street, auguries, perhaps, of his own approaching flight into time. The Librarian of this impressive edifice, Charles Lyster, warmly welcomed the students from St. Stephen's Green and preserved a smiling tolerance when he heard his great building referred to as "the library of University College."

Next to the English classes, those of most interest to Joyce were the Latin and Modern Language courses, for, from the very first, a passion for words possessed him. When he entered the college Father Thomas O'Nowlan, S.J., was professor of Latin but in 1901 Professor Semple succeeded to the Chair. French was taught

by Edouard Cadic, a Breton and so of Celtic extraction. The other
modern languages, German, Italian, and Spanish, were not popular
and therefore no ample provision for them was made. Then there
were the Irish studies. Father Edmund Hogan, S.J., a man great
in his way as a scholar and editor of ancient texts, had the Chair
of Irish Language, History, and Archæology. Others who gave
series of lectures on the resuscitated tongue were John McNeill,
Patrick Pearse and Douglas Hyde, all of whom, by the way, now
occupy important niches in the long panorama of Ireland's struggle
for freedom. Curiously enough, Irish was not noticeably popular at
University College, Father Hogan's class sessions one year (1901-2)
containing but three students.

Of less interest to Joyce but particularly strong in staff was the
Mathematics Department. Here were Joseph Gibney, a singularly
good teacher; Henry McWeeney, held in great regard by his many
students; and Matthew Conran, M.A., besides several assistants of
excellent calibre. Professor Preston, a Trinity College man and
author of several important textbooks on Heat and on Light, taught
Science, but his equipment was so miserable that he laboured under
great difficulties. Biology was in the hands of George Sigerson
whose personal interests made the course more Zoology than Botany.
And Political Economy was taught, first, by W. P. Coyne and,
later (1901), by Father T. A. Finlay, S.J. There was no Chair in
History, the Lecturer on this subject being W. J. Carbery, M.A.
Metaphysics has already been mentioned, but the name of Professor
Magennis may be added to those of Father Finlay and Father Darlington.

To this college and to these teachers, then, Joyce came, aged
about seventeen, fairly tall, steely-blue-eyed, and with quite definite
ideas about life and letters. The growing arrogance that had been
a simple awareness of superiority at Belvedere had hardened into
an attitude that was as self-protective as it was challenging. There
was a *noli me tangere* aura about him that puzzled his companions.
The religious faith he had professed (and, for a period, violently)
as a boy was dying down in his spirit as a ruddy coal dims in a
neglected fire. University College, being Jesuit, had its religious
coloration, of course; there was the Chapel to attend and there were
the clerical obligations of the teachers, all fishers of souls; there
was also the influence of the Jesuit students reading for their De-

gree, young enthusiasts well-equipped to meet argument with argument and achieve artful victories by dialectic; there was the Sodality intended to promote devotion to the Blessed Virgin and all Christian virtues among students: but none of these influences, obvious or subtle, appear to have had any domination over Joyce. The admonitions of the teachers were an old story to him; he discovered that he could argue with the Jesuit students and employ a dialectic as formidable as their own; and, being a non-resident, he found it a simple matter to casually ignore the Sodality.

The sinews of his thought were constantly strengthened by his solitary dialectical exercises with Aristotle and Aquinas, two great instructors whose teachings were to occupy his mind for the next half dozen years, and his reasoning (because of the inward "push" of his will) naturally converged towards an æsthetic end that had little or nothing to do with religion. He saw himself as one apart (and this seems to have come quite suddenly, a mystic revelation, as it were, that had flashed through his spirit with the knowledge that he was to go on to the senior college) and his secret determination was to maintain himself as an independent personality in a milieu of knee-benders. Perhaps this is one of the reasons why from the first he preferred to associate with the medical students from Cecilia Street, or from Trinity College, rather than with the Arts students who sat around him each day. The subserviency of the Arts men repelled him; their conformity disgusted him; and in their parochialism he saw nothing but a blind end. It was different with the medical students. Medical Dick and Medical Davy were hard-tongued, blasphemous, disenchanted men who possessed no illusions about the human body and its weaknesses. Flesh was flesh to them and if spirit was spirit they did not mewl too much about it. Yet the fierce angry idealism that was germinating within Joyce was not stemmed in any way by his companionships. They might add unprintable words to his vocabulary (always a relief for scorn and impatience), but he was not influenced and, apparently, neither did he influence. In a history of University College, compiled twenty-eight years after Joyce's departure, an anonymous contributor states in a footnote: "During his student days James Joyce was not taken seriously. It was understood that he had a weird sort of talent but no one in the college seems to have guessed that he was destined to achieve almost world-wide celebrity." Of course, they didn't. The actual importance of the nonconformist has never been recognized in Ireland.

Yet Joyce was not long in assuming a notable place among his fellow students. His very independence and his emphatic refusal to run with the herd assured him of this. It does not matter now whether he was liked or disliked but the chances are that there was more bewilderment than dislike. The man was "weird." His fellow students simply could not grasp his attitude. However, a few among them gravitated towards him and he accepted them as repositories of the nonconformist and æsthetic problems that were perplexing him and constantly teasing his mind towards further conjectures. There was J. Francis Byrne, for instance (the Cranly of *A Portrait of the Artist as a Young Man*), a youth very ecclesiastical and ascetic in temperament, with whom he walked and talked often, emptying his mind of the thousand and one emotional and intellectual puzzles that aggravated his reason. There was a young man named Cosgrave (the Lynch of *A Portrait of the Artist as a Young Man* and *Ulysses*) who was, perhaps, Joyce's most constant companion, a youth much more salty and earthy in nature than Byrne. And there was George Clancy (the Davin of *A Portrait of the Artist as a Young Man*). Clancy, an intense Nationalist, made it his mission in life at University College to propagandize for the Gaelic League. He had known Michael Cusack (the Citizen of *Ulysses*) and had sat often with the fanatical old patriot and founder of the Gaelic Athletic Association in An Stad, the tobacco shop kept by the Irish humorist, Cathal McGarvey, on North Frederick Street. Yet, friendly as he was with Joyce, Clancy could never impregnate his companion's mind with fervid Nationalist ideals. Years later (in 1921) Clancy was sacrificed to those ideals when, as Lord Mayor of Limerick and "the heart" of the Sinn Fein movement in that district, he was shot down in his home by Black and Tans.

There were other students with whom Joyce came into more or less intimate contact, Francis Skeffington, for instance, who, upon his marriage, added his wife's name to his own and became Sheehy-Skeffington, and who, during the bloody Easter Week of 1916, was "executed" by a half-deranged British officer although he was a noncombatant (Skeffington is present in *A Portrait of the Artist as a Young Man* under the name of MacCann), but none of them appear to have touched Joyce so closely, to have seen him without armour, so to speak, as Byrne, Cosgrave, and Clancy. As a matter of fact, Joyce did not need friends; he was quite sufficient unto himself; and the minds to whom his own kindled were not plentiful in Dublin.

By 1899 Joyce had made his mark at University College. For one thing, he was noted for his absorption and ability in languages. He studied Italian all through the four years, always being the only student in that particular class. His instructor was Father Ghazzi, and when he took his degree in Romance Languages he was the only male candidate in Ireland who presented Italian. French came easily to him and it became a habit to read out his French themes during the language session. He translated from Maeterlinck, Verlaine, and other Gallic poets and there still exists his version of Verlaine's "Les sanglots longues."

A voice that sings
Like viol strings
  Through the wane
Of the pale year
Lulleth me here
  With its strain.

My soul is faint
At the bell's plaint
  Ringing deep;
I think upon
A day bygone
  And I weep.

Away! Away!
I must obey
  This drear wind,
Like a dead leaf
In aimless grief
  Drifting blind.

German he acquired by laborious translation and he toiled doggedly at Henrik Ibsen's mother tongue so that he might read the great plays in the original. But Gaelic he would not touch. At the earnest solicitation of George Clancy he attended some of the

Irish classes conducted by either Patrick Pearse or another but dropped out in disgust and boredom at the continual ridicule aimed by the overenthusiastic lecturer at English: sound, sense, syntax and all. The resuscitation of what he considered dead tongues did not interest him at all; it was living languages, their evolution and possibilities, their dramatic extension into planes where the living word became the living thing itself that called to him and started him on his endless journey. For the patriotic importance of Irish he did not care a fig. He knew that he would never write in that language any more than he would in Choctaw and he knew also that there would never be anything but an artificial audience (a forced hothouse growth in Ireland itself, at the most) for works written in that tongue. And he feared, too, that a national immersion in Gaelic would cut Ireland still further off than she was from the great central current of European culture, a culture that recognized no fixed country boundaries but was universal to all.

In the spring of this year (1899) Joyce, with another gesture, impressed his independence on his fellow students. The London tea-party of the autumn before, that party attended by W. B. Yeats, Edward Martyn, George Moore, and Lady Augusta Gregory, bore its fruit in Dublin and the taste was bitter in the mouths of ultra-patriotic Irish Roman Catholics. On the eighth of May was given the first performance of W. B. Yeats's *The Countess Cathleen* and Edward Martyn's *The Heather Field* in the Antient Concert Rooms, a first performance that more nearly approached a riot than a pre-mière. A body of students from University College, mostly members of the Central Branch of the Gaelic League and including Skeffington, Clancy, Louis J. Walsh, James Clandillon, Ford and Conroy, raided the hall and howled down the performance, their indignation arising from the central motif of Yeats's play—the selling of her soul to the devil by the Countess Cathleen (Ireland) to save her starving people. It was unpatriotic; it was blasphemy; it was heresy. Kathleen ni Houlihan sell her soul to the devil, indeed! To the devil with W. B. Yeats! The next day a manifesto directed against the play was set forth on a table at University College and all the students were gently coerced into signing it. That is, all except one. Joyce contemptuously refused to add his signature to the rest.

This gesture, slight as it may have seemed at the time, is important in its revelation of Joyce's character. The adamantine nature he was developing (callous arrogance to some and intellectual crankery to others) was based upon a sound rock of self-integrity. He refused to compromise for the sake of other people's feelings; he would neither join movements nor be stampeded into giving lip service to them when, with his distrust of crowd enthusiasms, he saw them all as fatal cages where the imprisoned will would die; and he would permit neither religious nor patriotic chains to bind the free flight of the falcon, now unhooded, that was his soul. Such an attitude required moral courage in the Dublin of the end of the century. The city, then, was an exuberant stage for movements, nationalistic, literary, dramatic, religious, and he who dared to walk alone, admitting a fealty to none of these movements, was suspect. Where was he going and what was his purpose? The most gossipy city in the world wanted to know. If he was alone, it boded no good for the New Ireland. And Joyce in the face of all this suspicion was (intellectually) decidedly alone. It was not that he desired to be a solitary. He was no hermit seeking a mystical Thebäid wherein to meditate all by himself. On the contrary, he was a full-blooded young man welcoming companionship and even eager to mingle in the student life surrounding him; but he would not succumb to blandishments, coercions, or the subtle influence of those who (for missionary reasons, patriotic heat or exalted ego) sought to direct his progress.

It is proof of his willingness to make part of the scene about him that in this year (1899) he was a candidate for the auditorship of the Literary and Historical Society of University College against Hugh Kennedy. Kennedy, the late Chief Justice of the Irish Free State, won. Joyce, probably, was considered a little too "weird" for this particular post, too likely, perhaps, to inject an atmosphere into the Literary and Historical Society that might be termed subversive. No, Joyce was in no sense of the word an anchorite. Padraic Colum, recalling Joyce's University College days, writes: "He was very noticeable among the crowd of students that frequented the National Library or sauntered along the streets between Nelson's Pillar and Stephen's Green. He was tall and slender then, with a Dantesque face and steely blue eyes. His costume as I see him in my mind's eye now included a peaked cap and tennis shoes more or less white. He used to swing along the street carrying an ashplant in his hand for a cane." And Constantine P. Curran, a fellow student, describes him as "tall, slim and elegant; an erect and loose carriage; an up-tilted, long, narrow head, with a chin that jutted out arrogantly; firm, tight-shut mouth; blue eyes that for all their myopic look could glare suddenly or stare with indignant wonder; a high fore-head that bulged under high, stiff-standing hair." Joyce, it will be observed, had travelled a far way from little Half-Past-Six who dared to present his grievances to the Rector of Clongowes Wood College. With the new century came the new man.

IV

The Christmas issue of the *Clongownian,* 1899, announced that James Joyce had obtained Second Class Honors in Latin at Uni-versity College. And that was the first and last mention of the former Clongownian in the school magazine. So far as Clongowes Wood College was concerned, James Joyce passed out with the nineteenth century. What actually happened was that James Joyce passed *in* with the new century. Within four months he was to have his first article printed in one of the oldest and most important English periodicals. But before that is considered it is necessary to glance at this new century.

There are soothsayers who will assert that the passing of a century has a mystic influence (like the moon on tides and cats, perhaps) over the lives of mankind. Maybe this is so. It does not matter. Certainly from a literary and social point of view we look back at 1900 as an epochal point of time. It marks for us the end of that decadent movement in letters called Fin-de-Siècle. It is also a convenient date whereon to hang the finally defunct body of that smug and stuffy way of life labelled Victorianism: this in spite of the fact that Queen Victoria outlived her century by a handful of months. For Dublin it was marked less by death than by birth. Not many months before Arthur Griffith, with William Rooney, had founded the *United Irishman,* a paper which may be said to have been the journalistic cradle of Sinn Fein. Naturally, politics were in the air and a new optimism was sweeping over the country. Excited young cubs were beginning to growl. W. B. Yeats and his group were continuing their theatrical experiments (the 1900 programme included Alice Milligan's *The Last Feast of the Fianna,* George Moore's adaptation of Edward Martyn's *The Tale of a Town,* produced as *The Bending of the Bough,* and Martyn's *Maeve*) and violent argumentation pro and con electrified the atmosphere. For instance, in the March issue of the *New Ireland Review,* D. P. Moran was declaring: "Practically no one in Ireland understands Mr. Yeats and his school; and one could not, I suggest, say anything harder of literary men. For if a literary man is not appreciated and cannot be understood, of what use is he? He has not served his purpose. The Irish mind, however, was wound down to such a low state that it was fit to be humbugged by such a school." Mr. Yeats, although so rapped on the knuckles, went determinedly on with his plans. He would give the Irish a New Literature if he had to cram it down their gullets.

As for the social scene in Dublin, it was as vibrant and *mouvementée* as the politics and the literary alarums and excursions. A gaiety and brilliance that they have possibly never known since pervaded the old houses and streets. The wealthier folk from the country came up to town and took houses for the Season. There were great dinners, crowded dances, opera, the races, the theatre, and elaborate vice-regal functions where diamonds and decorations glittered under the crystal chandeliers. Bicycling was still popular; automobiles, those queer 'horseless carriages,' were just being introduced; the paved ways echoed to the 'steelyringing' clop-clop of hoofs as the unending processions of conveyances flashed by. And the streets echoed, too, with exuberant students, who, impregnated, perhaps, by the heady spirit of the twentieth century, expressed themselves with an unruly Irish temperament. For example, on St. Patrick's Day, 1900, Trinity College men attacked the Lord Mayor's procession as it passed through College Green and greeted Timothy Harrington, the Lord Mayor, with a superripe orange on his dignified nose. Dublin, to sum up, possessed everything that London possessed—except Parliament.

There exist brief flashes of Joyce, pictures from the memories of those who knew him at the time, during this period: Joyce, with a few companions, killing time and talking in the Winter Gardens, a public house on the corner of St. Stephen's Green and Cuffe Street; Joyce playing handball with Fitzgerald-Kenney, later to be Minister for Justice of the Irish Free State, and beating him; Joyce singing at private parties and functions ("singing Nationalist songs, too, begod!" remarked one diver into the past); Joyce selling old books to George Webb on the quays; Joyce swimming strongly in the salt water off Clontarf while Skeffington, his little straw-coloured beard thrust forward, posed coyly as Venus Transiens; Joyce swaggering through the special door for distinguished visitors at Eccles Street Convent on the night of a concert and announcing to the astonished Mother Superior, "I'm Joyce!"; Joyce conversing glibly with Byrne in a sort of dog Latin while the listeners laughed; Joyce, evasive, slightly withdrawn and coldly polite with Thomas E. Kettle who had been magnified by university students into a second Parnell; Joyce, clothed in his hostess's best bonnet and cashmere shawl, parodying the Queen Mother in *Hamlet,* rocking with grief in a chair and moaning, "Ah, the poo-er girrll!" while Ophelia, another student, strewed the carpet with cauliflowers; and Joyce acting in an amateur production of *Cupid's Confidant,* an original play by Miss Margaret Sheehy (now Mrs. Sheehy-Casey), the daughter of David Sheehy, M.P. He played the part of the villain, Geoffrey Fortesque, and one Dublin paper printed an extraordinarily long criticism of Joyce's acting (it was written by J. B. Hall, Dublin's leading dramatic critic) in which the young Thespian was favourably compared to the earlier Charles Wyndham, or even Charles Matthews, for his poise and finish. This was a very human Joyce with a sense of the ridiculous that was often extravagant and a vitality that was inexhaustible.

He could be serious too. His adoration of Ibsen had reached a peak and he expressed it in the composition of an essay on the Norwegian dramatist's latest play, *When We Dead Awaken,* which had been published in Copenhagen during December 1899. This essay he sent to the *Fortnightly Review* where it appeared, under the title of "Ibsen's New Drama," in the April issue of 1900. It was signed James A. Joyce. One must pause for an instant to recognize what a remarkable achievement this was: an eighteen-year-old Irish youth barely half through his college terms writes an article on a Norwegian dramatist whom he has read in the original and that article appears in one of the most prominent periodicals in England. His companions were thunderstruck. Padraic Colum declares: "We, the fry swimming about in the National Library, looked with some reverence on the youth who already had an article published in The Fortnightly Review." Joyce received a considerable sum for the sixteen-page essay and the windfall was expended on a trip to London to hear Duse who was then giving a season at the Lyceum Theatre. On this occasion the budding author called on the then editor of the *Fortnightly Review,* the late William Courtney, and that gentleman was considerably astonished to see a beardless stripling of seventeen enter his office.

The article itself was, and remains, an intelligent contribution to Ibsen commentary. It amply fulfils its objective of presenting the gist of a single play with clarity and indicating its special properties and unique importance in the cultural world at the turn of the century.

Twenty years have passed since Henrik Ibsen wrote 'A Doll's House' [begins the young critic], thereby almost marking an epoch in the history of drama. During those years his name has gone abroad through the length and breadth of two continents, and has provoked more discussion and criticism than that of any other living man. He has been upheld as a religious reformer, a social reformer, a Semitic lover of righteousness, and as a great dramatist. He has been rigorously denounced as a meddlesome intruder, a defective artist, an incomprehensible mystic, and, in the eloquent words of a certain English critic, 'a muck-ferreting dog.' Through the perplexities of such diverse criticism, the great genius of the man is day by day coming out as a hero comes out amid the earthly trials. The dissonant cries are fainter and more distant, the random praises are rising in steadier and more choral chaunt. Even to the uninterested bystander it must seem significant that the interest attached to this Norwegian has never flagged for over a quarter of a century. It may be questioned whether any man has held so firm an empire over the thinking world in modern times. Not Rousseau; not Emerson; not Carlyle; not any of those giants of whom almost all have passed out of human ken. Ibsen's power over two generations has been enhanced by his own reticence. Seldom, if at all, has he condescended to join battle with his enemies. It would appear as if the storm of fierce debate rarely broke in upon his wonderful calm. The conflicting voices have not influenced his work in the very smallest degree. His output of dramas has been regulated by the utmost order, by a clock-work routine, seldom found in the case of genius. Only once he answered his assailants after their violent attack on 'Ghosts.' But from the 'Wild Duck' to 'John Gabriel Borkman,' his dramas have appeared almost mechanically at intervals of two years. One is apt to overlook the sustained energy which such a plan of campaign demands; but even surprise at this must give way to admiration at the gradual, irresistible advance of this extraordinary man.

After an enumeration of Ibsen's plays dealing with modern life, Joyce goes on to give a very full synopsis of *When We Dead Awaken,* larding it with patches of dialogue and emphasizing the development of the theme by expository comment. He wants his readers to understand what this play is all about and to grasp the implications, the nuances of the dramatist's finely-disciplined thought, and he succeeds in making this possible by his own clear-cut presentation. That done, and it fills the greater part of the essay, he writes:

Such is the plot, in a crude and incoherent way, of this new drama. Ibsen's plays do not depend for their interest on the action, or on the incidents. Even the characters, faultlessly drawn though they be, are not the first thing in his plays. But the naked drama—either the perception of a great truth, or the opening up of a great question, or a great conflict which is almost independent of the conflicting actors, and has been and is of far-reaching importance—this is what primarily rivets our attention. Ibsen has chosen the average lives in their uncompromising truth for the groundwork of all his later plays. He has abandoned the verse form, and has never sought to embellish his work after the conventional fashion. Even when his dramatic theme reached its zenith he has not sought to trick it out in gawds or tawdriness. How easy it would have been to have written 'An Enemy of the People' on a speciously loftier level—to have replaced the *bourgeois* by the legitimate hero! Critics might then have extolled as grand what they have so often condemned as banal. But the surroundings are nothing to Ibsen. The play is the thing. By the force of his genius, and the indisputable skill which he brings to all his efforts, Ibsen has, for many years, engrossed the attention of the civilized world. Many years more, however, must pass before he will enter his kingdom in jubilation, although, as he stands today, all has been done on his part to ensure his own worthiness to enter therein. I do not propose here to examine into every detail of dramaturgy connected with this play, but merely to outline the characterization.

This Joyce proceeds to do and there is more than one good touch in the outline. As for instance: "Beside his portraits [Ibsen's portraits of women] the psychological studies of Hardy and Turgenieff, or the exhaustive elaborations of Meredith, seem no more than sciolism." Finished with his comments on the characters, the young critic passes on to a consideration of "the frequent and extensive side-issues of the line of thought." He writes:

Again, there has not been lacking in the last few social dramas a fine pity for men—a note nowhere audible in the uncompromising rigor of the early eighties. Thus in the conversation of Rubek's views as to the girl-figure in his masterpiece, 'The Resurrection Day,' there is involved an all-embracing philosophy, a deep sympathy with the cross-purposes and contradictions of life, as they may be reconcilable with a hopeful awakening—when the manifold travail of our poor humanity may have a glorious issue. As to the drama itself, it is doubtful if any good purpose can be served by attempting to criticize it. Many things would tend to prove this. Henrik Ibsen is one of the world's great men before whom criticism can make but feeble show.

Appreciation, hearkening, is the only true criticism. Further, that species of criticism which calls itself dramatic criticism is a needless adjunct to his plays. When the art of a dramatist is perfect the critic is superfluous. Life is not to be criticized, but to be faced and lived. Again, if any plays demand a stage they are the plays of Ibsen. Not merely is this so because his plays have so much in common with the plays of other men that they were not written to cumber the shelves of a library, but because they are so packed with thought. At some chance expression, the mind is tortured with some question, and in a flash long reaches of life are opened up in vista, yet the vision is momentary unless we stay to ponder on it. It is just to prevent excessive pondering that Ibsen requires to be acted. Finally, it is foolish to expect that a problem, which has occupied Ibsen for nearly three years, will unroll smoothly before our eyes on a first or second reading. So it is better to leave the drama to plead for itself. But this at least is clear, that in this play Ibsen has given us nearly the best of himself. The action is neither hindered by many complexities, as in 'The Pillars of Society,' nor harrowing in its implicity, as in 'Ghosts.' We have whimsicality, bordering on extravagance, in the wild Ulfheim, and subtle humor in the sly contempt which Rubek and Maja entertain for each other. But Ibsen has striven to let the drama have perfectly free action. So he has not bestowed his wonted pains on the minor characters. In many of his plays these minor characters are matchless creations. Witness Jacob Engstrand, Tonnesen, and the demonic Molvik! But in this play the minor characters are not allowed to divert our attention.

And a short summarizing paragraph concludes the essay.

It is easy to see, in the light of what followed, the reasons for Joyce's worship of Ibsen. There was, first of all, the independence of the Norwegian from all submissions. There was his freedom from the strangling halters of nationalistic and religious conformity. There was his abnegation of sentimentalism in any shape whatsoever. There was his logical precision, his cold realism, his concern with spiritual conflict, and his contemptuous refusal to tolerate the "legitimate hero." These were the ends towards which Joyce was moving although in his own way and, perhaps, somewhat darkly. He possessed more of the poetical temperament than Ibsen (and was to be partially coloured by it always) but he subjected it to as severe a discipline as Ibsen subjected the plots of his plays.

Indeed, at this period Joyce was composing a respectable amount of poetry. The greater part of it was written in fixed French verse forms, villanelles, triolets, rondels and the like (the villanelle in *A Portrait of the Artist as a Young Man* is an example of this early work), and all of it appears to have been experiments in craftsmanship rather than expressions of emotion. The young man was teaching himself how to gain his effects. Most of this delicate labour was collected into two copybooks under the titles, *Moods* and *Shine and Dark*. In 1902 or 1903 Joyce turned these books over to George Clancy and they seem to have been lost in the years that followed. At this period, too, Joyce (naturally enough with the great example of Ibsen before him) was essaying the drama form. This resulted in a five-act play called *A Brilliant Career.*[1] That, also, has been de-

---

[1] Joyce sent this play to William Archer, the translator of Ibsen, who wrote a long letter in reply. Among other things Archer declared: "You seem to me to have talent, possibly more than talent, yet I cannot say that I think your play is a success." And again: "I have been trying to read some elaborate symbolism into the third and fourth acts to account for their gigantic breadth of treatment." These acts dealt with a plague. The play was dedicated by the author to his own soul. When John Stanislaus, sitting up in bed, read this dedication, he exclaimed, "Holy Paul!"

stroyed or lost. It is probable that nothing of importance to letters vanished in the disappearance of these poems and this play, but, so far as an indication of the literary development of Joyce is concerned, it is regrettable that they do not exist.

To return to Ibsen: a pleasant surprise greeted Joyce some time after his article appeared in the *Fortnightly Review*. He was swinging in his garden about dawn with the young lady whose attributes are set forth in the character of Gerty MacDowell in *Ulysses* (they had just returned from a dance) when a letter from William Archer, the English critic and champion of Ibsen, was brought to him. In it was a quotation from the Norwegian dramatist expressing his pleasure at Joyce's article. Here was the first authentic personal connection with a great writer, a slight and insignificant little link, perhaps, but yet a link, a touch across time, an acknowledgement that Henrik Ibsen was aware of the existence of James Joyce. For an eighteen-year-old youth and hero-worshipper this was an inexpressible moment. Some time later, to anticipate by a season, Joyce set forth his admiration for Ibsen in a letter which he wrote first in English and then turned into the mother tongue of the great dramatist.

8 Royal Terrace,
Fairfield, Dublin.
March, 1901.

HONOURED SIR,

I write to you to give you greeting on your seventy-third birthday and to join my voice to those of your well-wishers in all lands. You may remember that shortly after the publication of your latest play, 'When We Dead Awaken,' an appreciation of it appeared in one of the English reviews—The Fortnightly Review—over my name. I know that you have seen it because some short time afterwards Mr. William Archer wrote to me and told me that in a letter he had had from you some days before, you had written, 'I have read or rather spelled out a review in The Fortnightly Review by Mr. James Joyce which is very benevolent and for which I should greatly like to thank the author if only I had sufficient knowledge of the language.' (My own knowledge of your language is not, as you see, great but I trust you will be able to decipher my meaning.) I can hardly tell you how moved I was by your message. I am a young, a very young man, and perhaps the telling of such tricks of the nerves will make you smile. But I am sure if you go back along your own life to the time when you were an undergraduate at the University as I am, and if you think what it would have meant to you to have earned a word from one who held as high a place in your esteem as you hold in mine, you will understand my feeling. One thing only I regret, namely, that an immature and hasty article should have met your eye rather than something better and worthier of your praise. There may not have been any wilful stupidity in it, but truly I can say no more. It may annoy you to have your works at the mercy of striplings but I am sure you would prefer hotheadedness to nerveless and 'cultured' paradoxes.

What shall I say more? I have sounded your name defiantly through the college where it was either unknown or known faintly and darkly. I have claimed for you your rightful place in the history of the drama. I have shown what, as it seemed to me, was your highest excellence—your lofty impersonal power. Your minor claims—your satire, your technique and orchestral harmony—these, too, I advanced. Do not think me a hero-worshipper—I am not so. And when I spoke of you in debating societies and so forth, I enforced attention by no futile ranting.

But we always keep the dearest things to ourselves. I did not tell them what bound me closest to you. I did not say how what I could discern dimly of your life was my pride to see, how your battles inspired me—not the obvious material battles but those that were fought and won behind your forehead, how your wilful resolution to wrest the secret from life gave me heart and how in your absolute indifference to public canons of art, friends and shibboleths you walked in the light of your inward heroism. And this is what I write to you of now. Your work on earth draws to a close and you are near the silence. It is growing dark for you. Many write of such things, but they do not know. You have only opened the way—though you have gone as far as you could upon it—to the end of 'John Gabriel Borkman' and its spiritual truth—but your last play stands, I take it, apart. But I am sure that higher and holier enlightenment lies—onward.

As one of the young generation for whom you have spoken I give you greeting—not humbly, because I am obscure and you in the glare, not sadly, because you are an old man and I a young man, not presumptuously nor sentimentally—but joyfully, with hope and with love, I give you greeting.

Faithfully yours,

JAMES A. JOYCE.

Mr. Henrik Ibsen,
Arbens Gade, 2,
Kristiania.

With the essay and this letter the influence of Ibsen over Joyce and the reasons for it should be amply plain.

It is proper to pass on here (noting, by the way, that Joyce took his First University Examination in the autumn of 1900) to the independent young man's attitude towards the proposed National Theatre for Ireland, the project that so kindled the enthusiasm of W. B. Yeats, George Moore, Edward Martyn, and Lady Gregory. Joyce would have none of it. He saw in it a betrayal of the artist, a surrender to the mob and a throttling of that intellectual freedom that knows no nationalistic boundaries. In vehement conversation he protested against it and, finally, in the summer of 1901 he thought he had found a periodical that would carry his written protest. This was *St. Stephen's,* a University College journal which first appeared on June 1, 1901, under the editorship of Hugh Kennedy assisted by Felix Hackett, John O'Sullivan, J. C. McHugh, James Murnaghan and Arthur Clery. But Joyce reckoned without the censor. His protest was refused and he was forced to print it, together with Francis Skeffington's "A Forgotten Aspect of the University Question," an argument for co-education, in the form of a twopenny pamphlet.

As "The Day of the Rabblement" is so important an expression of Joyce's opinions at this time, it is here quoted at length:

No man, said the Nolan,[1] can be a lover of the true or the good unless he abhors the multitude; and the artist, though he may employ the crowd, is very careful to isolate himself. This radical principle of artistic economy applies specially to a time of crisis, and today when the highest form of art has been just preserved by desperate sacrifices, it is strange to see the artist making terms with the rabblement. The Irish Literary Theatre is the latest movement of protest against the sterility and falsehood of the modern stage. Half a century ago the note of protest was uttered in Norway, and since then in several countries long and disheartening battles have been fought against the hosts of prejudice and misinterpretation and ridicule. What triumph there has been here and there is due to stub-

---

[1] University College was much intrigued by this personage whom it supposed to be an ancient Irish chieftain like the MacDermott or the O'Rahilly. As a matter of fact, he is Giordano Bruno of Nola. He appears constantly throughout *Finnegans Wake* in the particularized dress of Browne and Nolan (the name of one of the leading booksellers and stationers in Dublin), and, in fact (a hint to critics), his metaphysical dualism accompanies throughout Giambattista Vico's theory of history.

born conviction, and every movement that has set out heroically has achieved a little. The Irish Literary Theatre gave out that it was the champion of progress, and proclaimed war against commercialism and vulgarity. It had partly made good its word and was expelling the old devil, when after the first encounter it surrendered to the popular will. Now, your popular devil is more dangerous than your vulgar devil. Bulk and lungs count for something, and he can gild his speech artly. He has prevailed once more, and the Irish Literary Theatre must now be considered the property of the rabblement of the most belated race in Europe.

It will be interesting to examine here. The official organ of the movement spoke of producing European masterpieces, but the matter went no further. Such a project was absolutely necessary. The censorship is powerless in Dublin, and the directors could have produced 'Ghosts' or 'The Dominion of Darkness' if they chose. Nothing can be done until the forces that dictate public judgement are calmly confronted. But, of course, the directors are shy of presenting Ibsen, Tolstoy or Hauptmann, where even 'Countess Cathleen' is pronounced vicious and damnable. Even for a technical reason this project was necessary. A nation which never advanced so far as a miracle play affords no literary model to the artist, and he must look abroad. Earnest dramatists of the second rank, Sudermann, Björnson and Giacosa, can write very much better plays than the Irish Literary Theatre has staged. But, of course, the directors would not like to present such improper writers to the uncultivated, much less to the cultivated, rabblement. Accordingly, the rabblement, placid and intensely moral, is enthroned in boxes and galleries amid a hum of approval—la bestia Trionfante—and those who think that Echegaray is 'morbid,' and titter coyly when Melisande lets down her hair, are not sure but they are the trustees of every intellectual and poetic pleasure.

. . . . . . .

Meanwhile, what of the artists? It is equally unsafe to say of Mr. Yeats at present that he has or has not genius. In aim and form 'The Wind Among the Reeds' is poetry of the highest order, and 'The Adoration of the Magi' (a story which one of the great Russians might have written) shows what Mr. Yeats can do when he breaks with the half-gods. But an æsthete has a floating will and Mr. Yeats's treacherous instinct of adaptability must be blamed for his recent association with a platform from which even self-respect should have urged him to refrain. Mr. Martyn and Mr. Moore are not writers of much originality. Mr. Martyn, disabled as he is by an incorrigible style, has none of the fierce, hysterical power of Strindberg, whom he suggests at times, and with him one is conscious of a lack of breadth and distinction which outweighs the nobility of certain passages. Mr. Moore, however, has wonderful mimetic ability, and some years ago his books might have entitled him to the place of honour among English novelists. But though 'Vain Fortune' (perhaps one should add some of 'Esther Waters') is fine, original work, Mr. Moore is really struggling in the backwash of that tide which has advanced from Flaubert through Jakobson to d'Annunzio: for two entire eras lie between 'Madame Bovary' and 'Il Fuoco.' It is plain from 'Celibates' and the later novels that Mr. Moore is beginning to draw upon his literary account and the quest of a new impulse may explain his recent startling conversion. Converts are in the movement now and Mr. Moore and his island have been fitly admired. But however frankly Mr. Moore may misquote Pater and Turgenieff to defend himself, his new impulse has no kind of relation to the future of art.

. . . . . . .

In such circumstances it has become imperative to define a position. If an artist courts the favour of the multitude he cannot escape the contagion of its fetishism and deliberate self-deception, and if he joins in a popular movement he does so at his own risk. Therefore, the Irish Literary Theatre, by its surrender to the trolls, has cut itself adrift from the line of advancement. Until he has freed himself from the mean influences about him—sodden enthusiasm and clever insinuation and every flattering influence of vanity and low ambition—no man is an artist at all. But his true servitude is that he inherits a will broken by doubt and a soul that yields up all its hate to a caress; and the most seeming dependent are those who are the first to reassume their bonds. But Truth deals largely with us. Elsewhere there are men who are worthy to carry on the tradition of the old master who is dying in Christiania. He has already found his successor in the writer of 'Michael Kramer,' and the third minister will not be wanting when his hour comes. Even now that hour may be standing by the door.

October 15, 1901.

Joyce was in his nineteenth year when this protest appeared and it had been a year of great intellectual activity for him. Part of the summer he had occupied in translating with immense difficulty Gerhart Hauptmann's *Vor Sonnenaufgang* and *Michael Cramer* (two versions),[1] Hauptmann being the successor to Ibsen announced

[1] Joyce still possesses a great admiration for *Michael Cramer*. In writing thirty-four years afterward to thank Hauptmann for a copy of the play that the dramatist had autographed for him at the instance of Ezra Pound, Joyce expressed the fervent hope that his manuscript translation might never meet the eye of the great German dramatic poet.

in the last paragraph of "The Day of the Rabblement." He had made it a point to call on A.E. (George Russell) bearing with him his manuscript poems and A.E. had been very kind, smiling through his beard and puzzling his head at the same time over this young man who was so sure of himself and so arrogant in his sureness. Joyce plied him with all sorts of questions about mystical matters and A.E. conceived the quaint misconception that the insistent cross-examiner desired to join the Hermetic Society. The Irish Literary Theatre, impervious to the University College student's blast, was producing *Diarmuid and Grania,* by W. B. Yeats and George Moore, and *Casad-an-Sugan (The Twisting of the Rope*), by Douglas Hyde, and Joyce sat through them inwardly stewing all the time. In the autumn he passed his Second University Examination.

The dissatisfaction he felt with the Dublin scene had mounted to boiling point. Though he was strong enough in his own will to stand aside from movements and mob enthusiasms he already experienced the dangers of those more insidious influences of family, religious milieu and the sapping obligations of his social environment. In a way, so far as the parochial aspects of the Irish literary scene were concerned, he was re-echoing unconsciously the thoughts of Alexandre Dumas *père* who had written in the 1850's: "Oh, gentlemen! you who are engaged in matters of French dramatic art, ponder this seriously. France, with its powers of assimilation, ought not to restrict itself to National Art. She ought to seize upon European Art, cosmopolitan, universal art—bounded in the North by Shakespeare, in the East by Aeschylus, in the South by Calderon and in the West by Corneille. It was thus that Augustus, Charlemagne and Napoleon conceived their Empires." Joyce, without doubt, would have placed other names for his boundaries but the implications of Dumas's apostrophe would have been the same.

He was now well on the way to an æsthetic of his own, a philosophy of art, so to speak, that he was building on foundations furnished by Aristotle and Aquinas and which had nothing peculiarly Irish in it at all. Plato he distrusted. The Greek epics, curiously enough, he dismissed. They were before Europe, he told Padraic Colum, and outside the tradition of European culture. The *Divine Comedy* was Europe's epic. He was constantly reading, constantly writing poetry, constantly brooding over the great end of letters, constantly living in a world that was quite the reverse of his more or less squalid surroundings. It was the comparison of those two worlds that aroused his dissatisfaction. The picture that he drew in *A Portrait of the Artist as a Young Man* of Stephen Dedalus walking from the North Side of Dublin to University College is obviously his own.

The rain laden trees of the avenue evoked in him, as always, memories of the girls and women in the plays of Gerhart Hauptmann; and the memory of their pale sorrows and the fragrance falling from the wet branches mingled in a mood of quiet joy. His morning walk across the city had begun; and he foreknew that as he passed the sloblands of Fairview he would think of the cloistral silverveined prose of Newman; that as he walked along the North Strand Road, glancing idly at the windows of the provision shops, he would recall the dark humour of Guido Cavalcanti and smile; that as he went by Baird's stone cutting works in Talbot Place the spirit of Ibsen would blow through him like a keen wind, a spirit of wayward boyish beauty; and that passing a grimy marine dealer's shop beyond the Liffey, he would repeat the song by Ben Jonson which begins:
I was not wearier where I lay.

His mind when wearied of its search for the essence of beauty amid the spectral words of Aristotle or Aquinas turned often for its pleasure to the dainty songs of the Elizabethans. His mind, in the vesture of a doubting monk, stood often in shadow under the windows of that age, to hear the grave and mocking music of the lutenists or the frank laughter of the waistcoateers until a laugh too low, a phrase tarnished by time, of chambering and false honour, stung his monkish pride and drove him on from his lurking place.

Being so caught and held by the enchantment of art and wildly conscious now of what his objective in life was to be it is little wonder that he endured a wilful alienation from his environment during his last year at University College. The religious faith that had been steadily dying down in his mind became extinct. He felt that he had outgrown his friends, or that they, doubting him and in pious fear of his flight beyond them, were insidiously seeking to sap his morale. He saw his instructors as the sergeant majors of conformity. He regarded the New Literature of the New Ireland as a dish salted to the taste of the rabblement. His own home was a place of dejection for him. John Stanislaus, bereft of a regular livelihood, was precariously existing by accepting temporary employment from time to time with the Dublin Corporation and the Dublin County Council and acting as election agent before the revising barrister for parliamentary returns. To all this a bold *non serviam* was fiercely arising in Joyce's mind, the credo he was to word later in *A Portrait of the Artist as a Young Man:* "I will not serve that in which I no longer believe, whether it call itself my home, my fatherland or my church; and I will try to express myself in some mode of life or art as freely as I can, using for my defence the only arms I allow myself to use, silence, exile and cunning."

### v

1902 was the year of the hegira. It was marked by three events of importance to the young Joyce: the publication of an essay on James Clarence Mangan in *St. Stephen's* for May, the taking of his Bachelor of Arts degree on October thirty-first, and his flight from Dublin in the early winter.

The essay on James Clarence Mangan is interesting in retrospect for two reasons: its definite change of style from the bared prose of the Ibsen article and the reason for the subject chosen. The prose is literary—approaching floweriness, poetical, and, at times, Paterian, as we shall see from some excerpts. It is the craftsmanship of a poet writing about a poet and in love with the fine fall and delicate (almost precious) balance of syllables. Indeed, the essay might have served to decorate the recently-defunct pages of Mr. Arthur Symons's *Savoy* magazine or Mr. Henry Harland's *Yellow Book.* Yet it was soundly reasoned and served to set forth some of Joyce's ideas on classicism, romanticism, poetry and art. To enlarge upon the reason for the subject chosen is a more subtle endeavour. First of all, there appears to have been an identification (slight, perhaps) of elemental urge between the essayist and Mangan. Joyce found that the poet was little known in his own country, "a rare and unsympathetic figure in the streets," that "a fierce energy" moved behind his banter, that the best of his work "was conceived by the imagination," and that he was an artist at his supreme moments who rose above "literature." Then, too, he was drawn to Mangan because his conception of the poet limited by patriotic passion afforded him, the commentator, opportunity to indicate the fatality of such weakness. "In the final view the figure which he [Mangan] worships is seen to be an abject queen upon whom, because of the bloody crimes that she has done and of those as bloody that were done to her, madness is come and death is coming, but who will not believe that she is near to die and remembers only the rumours of voices challenging her sacred gardens and her fair, tall flowers that have become the food of boars."

And to give an example of the essayist's prose:

He could not often revise what he wrote, and he has often striven with Moore and Walsh on their own ground. But the best of what he has written makes its appeal surely, because it was conceived by the imagination which he called, I think, the mother of things, whose dream we are, who imageth us to herself, and to ourselves, and imageth herself in us—the power before whose breath the mind in creation is (to use Shelley's image), as a fading coal. Though even in the best of Mangan the presence of alien emotions is sometimes felt, the presence of an imaginative personality reflecting the light of imaginative beauty is more vividly felt. East and West meet in that personality (we know how): images interweave there like soft luminous scarves and words ring like brilliant mail, and whether the song is of Ireland or of Istambol it has the same refrain, a prayer that peace may come again to her who has lost her peace, the moonwhite pearl of his soul, Ameen. Music and odours and lights are spread about her, and he would search the dews and the sands that he might set another glory near her face. A scenery and a world have grown up about her face, as they will about any face which the eyes have regarded with love. Vittoria Colonna and Laura and Beatrice—even she upon whose face many lives have cast that shadowy delicacy, as of one who broods upon distant terrors and riotous dreams, and that strange stillness before which love is silent, Monna Lisa—embody one chivalrous idea, which is no mortal thing, bearing it bravely above the accidents of lust and faithfulness and weariness: and she whose white and holy hands have the virtue of enchanted hands, his virgin flower, the flower of flowers, is no less than these an embodiment of that idea. How the East is laid under tribute for her and must bring all its treasures to her feet! The sea that foams over saffron sands, the lonely cedar on the Balkans, the hall damascened with moons of gold and a breath of roses from the gulistan—all these shall be where she is in willing service: reverence and peace shall be the service of the heart, as in the verses "To Mihri"

> My starlight, my moonlight, my midnight, my moonlight,
> Unveil not, unveil not.

Here, surely, is the Stephen Dedalus of *A Portrait of the Artist as a Young Man* intoxicated with the enchantment of soft phrases flowing into one another.[1] One hardly cares whether it means anything (or could have been said in three sentences) or not. Present, too, in this essay is the Stephen Dedalus who strode the streets of Dublin and either alone or with a friend or two puzzled out in his mind a workable æsthetic philosophy, endeavouring to establish a logical conception of art by which the creator might be guided.

It is many a day [Joyce begins his essay] since the dispute of the classical and romantic schools began in the quiet city of the arts, so that criticism, which has wrongly decided that the classical temper is the romantic temper grown older, has been driven to recognize these as constant states of mind. Though the dispute has been often ungentle (to say no more) and has seemed to some a dispute about names and with time has become a confused battle, each school advancing to the border of the other and busy with internal strife, the classical school fighting the materialism which attends it, and the romantic school to preserve coherence, yet, as this unrest is the condition of all achievement, it is so far good, and presses slowly towards a deeper insight which will make the schools at one. Meanwhile no criticism is just which avoids labour by setting up a standard of maturity by which to judge the schools. The romantic school is often and grievously misinterpreted, not more by others than by its own, for that impatient temper which, as it could see no fit abode here for its ideals, chose to behold them under insensible figures, comes to disregard certain limitations, and, because these figures are blown high and low by the mind that conceived them, comes at times to regard them as feeble shadows moving aimlessly about the light, obscuring it; and the same temper, which assuredly has not grown more patient, exclaims that the light is changed to worse than shadow, to darkness even, by any method which bends upon these present things and so works upon them and fashions them that the quick intelligence may go beyond them

---

[1] Joyce set some of Mangan's poems to music, among them "Morn and Eve" and "The Swabian Love Song." He has also set to music about eight of Yeats's poems, one by Rochester and one of his own—"Bid Adieu," to which the American musician, Edmund J. Pendleton, has added a charming pianoforte accompaniment.

to their meaning, which is still unuttered. Yet so long as this place in nature is given us, it is right that art should do no violence to that gift, though it may go far beyond the stars and the waters in the service of what it loves. Wherefore the highest praise must be withheld from the romantic school (though the most enlightened of Western poets be thereby passed over), and the cause of the impatient temper must be sought in the artist and in his theme. Nor must the laws of his art be forgotten in the judgement of the artist, for no error is more general than the judgement of a man of letters by the supreme laws of poetry. Verse, indeed, is not the only expression of rhythm, but poetry in any art transcends the mode of its expression; and to name what is less than poetry in the arts, there is need of new terms, though in one art the term 'literature' may be used.

Literature is the wide domain which lies between ephemeral writing and poetry (with which is philosophy), and just as the greater part of verse is not literature, so even original writers and thinkers often be jealously denied the most honourable title; and much of Wordsworth, and almost all of Baudelaire, is merely literature in verse and must be judged by the laws of literature. Finally, it must be asked concerning every artist how he is in relation to the highest knowledge and to those laws which do not take holiday because men and times forget them. This is not to look for a message but to approach the temper which has made the work, an old woman praying, or a young man fastening his shoe, and to see what is there well done and how much it signifies. A song by Shakespeare or Verlaine, which seems so free and living and as remote from any conscious purpose as rain that falls in a garden or the lights of evening, is discovered to be the rhythmic speech of an emotion otherwise incommunicable, at least so fitly. But to approach the temper which has made art is an act of reverence and many conventions must be first put off, for certainly the inmost region will never yield to one who is enmeshed with profanities.

This was the Joyce of 1902. This is the way that he thought and wrote and talked. There is hardly need of excessive reiteration of what he thought or of paraphrasing in simpler language the processes and conclusions of his æsthetic journeys. That may be left to the critical commentators. What he had to say he said plainly enough and the reader sufficiently interested in the development of this astonishing young man (barely past his twentieth year in 1902) may follow his progress in his own words. It was the painstaking twisting of the rope (not Dr. Douglas Hyde's rope), the careful selection and intertwining of selected strands, that furnished him the cable that would carry him from parochial Dublin to the universal Europe of his dreams. One more excerpt, the last paragraph of this essay on Mangan (in reality an affirmation of the essayist's own ideals), and we have finished with it.

Beauty, the splendour of truth, is a gracious presence when the imagination contemplates intensely the truth of its own being or the visible world, and the spirit which proceeds out of truth and beauty is the holy spirit of joy. These are realities and these alone give and sustain life. As often as human fear and cruelty, that wicked monster begotten by luxury, are in league to make life ignoble and sullen and to speak evil of death the time is come wherein a man of timid courage seizes the keys of hell and of death, and flings them far out into the abyss, proclaiming the praise of life, which the abiding splendour of truth may sanctify, and of death, the most beautiful form of life. In those vast courses which enfold us and in that great memory which is greater and more generous than our memory, no life, no moment of exaltation is ever lost; and all those that have written nobly have not written in vain, though the desperate and weary have never heard the silver laughter of wisdom. Nay, shall not such as these have part, because of that high, original purpose which remembering painfully or by way of prophecy they would make clear, in the continual affirmation of the spirit?

Joyce, by the time this essay appeared in print, was widely noted for his arrogance, his mental pugnacity, his emphatic declarations of what he believed to be so (sometimes in language that burned the ears of his listeners) and his ability to polish off a victim in a limerick. He had become, in a sense, a 'character' in a city that was noted for its 'characters.' He had encountered the greater part of the group of budding poets who looked up to A.E. as a seer and his opinion of them was often more scorching than complimentary. He had met Lady Gregory and slated one of her books in a Dublin newspaper. He had gone to visit W. B. Yeats and Yeats is reported to have complained, "Never have I encountered so much pretension with so little to show for it." Yet Yeats was friendly and willing to advise Joyce about the literary life. The two men met seven or eight times. Indeed, there have been false reports about the relations of the two men that might lead one to think that there was an element of contempt on the part of the younger for the older. This was never so. Joyce realized that Yeats had grown up in an earlier æsthetic atmosphere (William Morris, etc.) in which he had no part, but he never undervalued Yeats's great contribution to letters. In April Joyce had attended Clarendon Street Hall and witnessed the first performances of A.E.'s *Deirdre* and W. B. Yeats's *Cathleen-ni-Houlihan*. They did not change his attitude toward a parochial Irish Theatre and he continued to demand productions of Ibsen and Hauptmann. He began to read Henry James and was vastly pleased with *The Portrait of a Lady*. He was decidedly "in the swim," to word it colloquially. At the same time he was a lone wolf.

As the spring merged into a pleasant summer and the hot days came the unrest with his lot mounted within him like a rising fever. He could see no outlet for himself in Dublin, no way in which he could adjust himself and his huge ambition to the environment that hemmed him in on all sides and that offered him neither sympathy nor audience. Dublin was like a cramped house, a house crowded with strangers all intent on their own petty jealousies, momentary enthusiasms and emotional compromises. He was better away from it all. Even John Stanislaus was coming to the conclusion that his son's literary intransigence was facing an insurmountable barrier in reactionary Dublin and, towards the end of this season, he was advising Joyce to seek a freer atmosphere in which to live and work according to his own ideas. And when the son received, on October thirty-first, his degree of Bachelor of Arts in the Faculty of Arts of University College the last link with the intellectual Dublin of his time was broken.

His decision to leave Ireland was immediate. He possessed no money; his family could spare him but little; it was doubtful that he would be able to support himself in a foreign land; yet go he must. The bright star of Paris was calling. Perhaps, because he was very adept with languages now, he could gather about him students of the English tongue and sustain himself from their fees. Perhaps he could write articles for English periodicals and sell poetry to the London weeklies. There would *have* to be something, for his departure was an inexorable necessity. And knowing this he set about it with no compunctions and with no loss of time. A few farewells were said; a few garments of clothing were flung into a bag with a few manuscripts; and by the time the first cold winds came beating across the Irish Sea Joyce was regarding the receding Mourne Mountains as they faded with Ireland into the west of his boyhood and youth.

# *Three*

WHEN Joyce left Dublin in this late autumn of 1902 he had fully determined to break from the parochial civilization in which he had been bred and forge for himself, alone and single-minded, an unfettered reality and an æsthetic integrity that he did not believe existed amongst his race. He was twenty years old and arrogant and intellectually fearless. His faith in himself was boundless. He would employ for his defence against the mass pressure of the scornful and malicious Dublin circle that doubted him the only weapons he commanded—silence, exile and cunning. By his silence to their objurgations and stolid insistence he would discomfit them, by his exile he would escape them and their choking atmosphere and by his mercurial cunning he would outwit them. They could not break through that bristling hedge of defence. Already he had issued his first challenge to what he described as "the most belated race in Europe" in the paragraphs that made up "The Day of the Rabblement." That had been written almost exactly a year before and he had discovered no necessity to modify his opinions in any degree since. His campaign, as he mistily saw it, was simple enough: first, he would preserve himself intact; second, he would orientate himself in the great world of thought; third, he would achieve such things as were controlled only by the universal laws of art, things unaffected by any narrow nationalisms or pietistic slaveries. He was moving doggedly in a straight line toward his cloudy objectives and if his path lay parallel with that of the Wild Geese it was not for any patriotic reasons. He did not mourn the Romantic Ireland that Yeats buried in the grave of O'Leary. It was something far different that he sought, a loveliness, in fact, that had not yet come into the world and a deliverance from the contagious fetishism of the multitude. It was only through exile that he could free himself from mean influences. The shortest way to Tara was via Holyhead.

London, a London of smoky-bellied skies, drizzling rains, and

stuffy inertia, was his first halt on the road to freedom. It was a
lethargic metropolis. The sad young men of the nineties had either
committed suicide or joined the Roman Catholic Church; Alfred
Austin, author of that immortal couplet:

> They went across the veldt
> As hard as they could pelt

was poet-laureate; Edward VII was By the grace of God, of Great
Britain, Ireland, and of the British dominions beyond the seas, King,
Defender of the Faith, Emperor of India; the Boers had been
thrashed; Thomas Hardy had been silenced; Oscar Wilde was successfully dead at last; Henry James was pouring tea for Mrs. Hum-
phry Ward at Rye; H. G. Wells had emerged as the doyen of the
younger writers; in short, a Truly British God was in His Edwardian Heaven and all was well with the world.

Joyce was too wise to consider pausing long in this milieu, his
haven was Paris, but stay some days he did. He was greeted at the
Euston Station early in the morning by William Butler Yeats,
who, kindliness personified, bought him breakfast and proffered
himself as cicerone through the mild Purgatorio of London. Perhaps the elder poet saw in Joyce a promising adjunct to his own
movement although the emphatic dicta of "The Day of the
Rabblement" might have forewarned him that a complete independence, uninfluenced by movements or men, was Joyce's objective. Yeats was wise enough to perceive that he could not help
the younger man to any great degree. He could introduce him to
a few editors and, much more to the point, bring him into contact
with some of the young men who already were making tentative
gestures towards a new contemporaneity. The poetry which Joyce
brought with him Yeats considered frankly the poetry of a
young man who was but practising at his instrument and taking
a pleasure in the mere handling of the stops. "Remember what
Dr. Johnson said about somebody, 'Let us wait until we find out
whether he is a fountain or a cistern.'" Yet, at the same time, he
was convinced that Joyce's technique was superior to that of any
young Dublin man whom he had met in his time. If there was an
element of rather conscious patronage in his attitude towards this
slender youth with the jutting jaw and hard blue eyes it was but

natural and Joyce undoubtedly experienced a warm feeling of friendliness towards the older poet.

Yeats did what he could for Joyce. He carried him off to visit C. Lewis Hind, then editor of the *Academy* and to be famed the very next year as the man whom Joseph Conrad assaulted, and that turgid individual was kind enough to ask Joyce for some "moments of his spiritual life." Joyce, non-committal about his spiritual divagations, demanded some new books for review, cannily divining that it might prove advantageous to eat while in Paris. C. Lewis Hind explained that all he had to do (as editor of the *Academy,* which was then a sort of livelier *Athenaeum*) was to thrust his head out a window and shout and a hundred reviewers would leap up from nowhere, reviewers then as now being very much like the dragon's teeth that Cadmus sowed. Encouraged by this reception but receiving no books, Joyce, still accompanied by Yeats, proceeded to visit a gentleman by the name of Dunlop who was about to launch a periodical with the Browningesque title, *Men and Women.* Would Mr. Joyce send something from Paris for it? Mr. Joyce would. Later he did, but as the periodical died stillborn the "something from Paris" never saw the light of day.

One evening Yeats took the young man to see Arthur Symons. Symons, still throwing forth a pallid yellow glow from the recently-defunct nineties, resided at 134 Lauderdale Mansions, Maida Vale, in a corner flat which he had occupied for nearly two years since leaving Fountain Court, The Temple, where he had entertained Paul Verlaine. There was a piano there, a Broadwood designed by Burne-Jones, and upon this instrument the fin-de-siècle poet and critic played while Joyce, charmed always by music, sat quietly in his chair and listened. He must have seemed very far away from the progression that was his determination as he rested inert and observed the knickknacks of the nineties (there must have been a Beardsley drawing or two on the wall), the Burne-Jones piano and the pallidly yellow-glowing player. Years later when Symons was to know Joyce better he remarked that the Dubliner "seemed to me a curious mixture of sinister genius and uncertain talent." But in 1902 he knew nothing about him, except what Yeats had to say, and he was filled with a kindly solicitude. What he had to offer was not the meat that Joyce desired at all. Symons was bound heart

and soul to an epoch that was *démodé*. It is doubtful that Joyce
saw anything romantic about the nineties. They represented a weak
herd urge to him and, though he could employ the semi-Paterian
phraseology of the time as in his essay on James Clarence Mangan,
the very essence of his nature was to avoid the herd. The tougher
fibre of Ibsen drew him more strongly than the "hard gem-like
flame" of Walter the Epicurean. Therefore, as he sat and listened to
Symons's playing while the lights winked goldenly on the furniture and the ghosts of Beardsley and Dowson peered across the
threshold and the lank lock of hair on the forehead of Yeats fell
forward he must have sighed for a clean whistling wind, biting
with salt, from the Norwegian fiords.

Yet at the same time he was carrying in his pocket a manuscript of precise French and English verse forms. This was not
so inconsistent with his Aristotelian conception of art as it may
seem. Those verses, like most of the lost verses of his early years,
were exercises in the exactitude of words and rhythms. They
were exactly what Yeats described them to be, the poetry of a
young man who was practising at his instrument and taking a
pleasure in the mere handling of the stops. To suggest that
Joyce's passions were involved in them would be absurd. Yet
they cannot be dismissed from any comprehensive view of his development. He felt like that at the time; he felt like practising; he
felt like disciplining his control of the coloured counters we call
words. When the greater passions demanded expression the labour
expended on these deftly-chased cameos would prove of inestimable
value to him.

A short time after his meeting with Arthur Symons the young
Joyce was in Paris, having travelled by way of Newhaven and
Dieppe, and arranging his meagre baggage in a small room in the
Grand Hôtel Corneille in the Rue Corneille, that hostelry of which
Thackeray had written decades before: "If you are a poor student
come to study the humanities, or the pleasant art of amputation,
cross the river forthwith, and proceed to the Hôtel Corneille, near
the Odeon."

II

The Paris of 1902 had little in common with the Paris of today although there are vestiges still of that vanished city. It had begun to turn into Cabotinville after the turn of the century, after the Exposition that celebrated the demise of the nineteenth century, but it had yet to achieve that dubious eminence. It was a Paris un-contaminated by American influences, bars, cocktails, illuminated *boîtes* like monstrous hæmorrhages, Negro dancers and jazz bands. Yet if it seemed slower in movement it was more excitable and effervescent in emotional and intellectual ferment. Parisians, then, fought over ideas other than political dogmas. Life was simpler and more primitive (for instance, there were no autobuses until 1906 and porcelain bathtubs were luxuries) and it provided more time and a fitter setting for spiritual and intellectual conflict. The Bo-hemia of Murger had not quite disappeared. This carefree and disorderly existence was represented at one extreme by that noc-turnal wanderer, Paul-Jean Toulet, and at the other by Jean Moréas, who, in top hat and fiercely-glittering monocle, presided over his young disciples at the Café Vachette. The new world was on the way, to be sure, but it had not arrived. *L'Art Nouveau,* introduced by the Exposition of 1900, was steadily permeating a society that continued to vociferate over the complicated *affaire Dreyfus.* It was the elections of this very year that forced the *chute* of the anti-Dreyfus league directed by Jules Lemaître and Madame de Loynes. A new kind of liberalism was knocking at the door. Frenchmen were reading the books of foreign authors as they had never read them before. From the shop windows winked the names of Dostoev-sky, Tolstoy, Fogazzaro, Ibsen, Sudermann, Hauptmann and Björn-son. And in September Emile Zola, high priest of Naturalism, was found asphyxiated in his home in the Rue de Bruxelles. With his death a whole period of French letters came to a close.

Even more illustrative of what a far step it is from our times of proletarian *bagarres,* sit-in strikes and rampant communism to 1902 is an enumeration of the impressive number of visits by roy-alty that kept President Emile Loubet busily shaking hands and delivering addresses of welcome. There were the Shah of Persia,

Muzaffar-ed-Din, and Carlos I, King of Portugal, and George, King of Greece, and the Prince and Princess Royal of Saxony. Then, too, not royalty but treated like royalty, there were the Boer generals, Botha, De La Rey and De Wet. All these names represent to us vanished thrones and lost causes, a civilization that is as dead as a doornail today and a traditional respect that was blown to fragments long ago. There was, of course, social ferment in 1902 (France has never been without it) but it was not the dominating passion of the day. In the workmen's districts the disciples of Fourier agitated; there were religious excitements and demonstrations against the clergy (in this year the schools controlled by the Church were ordered closed); however, all this was more of a presage, a writing on the wall, albeit in large letters, than an actuality. It did not dislocate the humming tempo of the metropolis.

To this Paris came Joyce, twenty years old, practically penniless, boiling with ideas and determinations, with no plans except the certain one of writing and the rather curious idea of enrolling as a medical student at the Ecole de Médecine. As he gazed about his small room in the Grand Hôtel de Corneille and put his penny notebooks in order he must have wondered a trifle anxiously about the future, for all that he possessed in the way of weapons to burst open the door to Fortune's comfortable salon were two letters of introduction, an English pound or so, some manuscript poems and a vague desire to teach English to ambitious Frenchmen. The letters of introduction were neither important nor calculated to launch Joyce auspiciously into the presence of Fortune. One was a general note from Timothy Harrington, then Lord Mayor of Dublin, announcing to the world at large that he was acquainted with Joyce's father and that he wished the best of success to the son. The second letter was from a Dr. Maclagan of London and it was addressed to Dr. Jacques Rivière, the Parisian specialist in physicotherapy.[1] Joyce presented this letter. It benefited him to the extent of providing him with a few lunches at the doctor's home in the Rue des Mathurins. These, however, turned into rather embarrassing séances. Dr. Rivière constantly inquired about his good friend Dr. Maclagan in London and Joyce, who had never even seen the physician, was nonplussed

[1] Who, by the way, is still alive.

what to answer and sought safety in vague indeterminate replies. He had received the letter of introduction from Lady Gregory.

The young man's poetry was less important than the letters so far as providing food was the objective. There was, of course, Yeats in London to do what little he could but with all the good will in the world behind them a scant dozen or so of lyrics could hardly augment a non-existent income or add perceptibly to a literary reputation. Nothing but a book could do that. The determination to write was savagely strong in Joyce's mind, but it must be remembered that while he possessed a general idea of the direction he was travelling and even the framework of an æsthetic he was still in a formative state. Much of his resolution would express itself in assiduous preparation rather than in actual creation. The critical faculty, the ability to estimate one's self in a fairly objectified manner, developed so early in Joyce, must be allowed to reach out on all sides and intensively explore the intellectual phenomena of the past and present and so orientate itself in the panorama of Time. The æsthetic must be consolidated and applied to the raw material that was to be transmuted into literature.

Joyce proceeded towards this goal by means of a harsh pedantry, a scornful examination of what had been achieved already. He had no mercy for "easy" writing, grammatical slips or loose ends. If one desired to play an instrument one should play it well or not at all. We have, then, the spectacle of the young man assiduously analyzing the works of his contemporaries as well as the literature of the past and pouncing upon their lapses with an unholy glee. Herbert Spencer, Edmund Gosse, William Butler Yeats, it did not matter how eminent the name, were examined with a searching eye and down went their barbarisms and untidinesses with the English language in a battered notebook under the ironic heading: "Memorabilia." Even at twenty years of age Joyce's precision in the use of words was evident. The future great grammarian was implicit in the impatient young man. With what undisguised scorn he carefully copied out the meaningless imbecilities of the day.

> When the autumn night was hot
> (Peach and apple and apricot)
> Under the shade of a twining rose,
> Deep in the high-walled garden close,

> Guenevere, red as a sunset glows,
>     Plighted her love to Lancelot.
>
> Overhead at a window, unseen
> (Apple and filbert and nectarine), . . .

Knowing the vigour of expression that Joyce then used to relieve his exasperated feelings we may imagine what he said when he happened upon this ripe gooseberry of English poesy by the late Sir Edmund Gosse. Very carefully after the versifier's name he inscribed the letters LL.D. Then strolling out into the crude sunlight that flooded the pale-yellow streets of the city now in its early wintry aspect he would meditate upon an exact and inspired literature that would be as sturdy as the squat towers of Notre-Dame.

### III

During these first days in Paris the idea of the study of medicine persisted beside that of discovering a literary form free from influences and founded upon a personal æsthetic. This idea (and it could never have been very strong) was speedily dissipated. When Joyce applied for entrance to the preliminaries of the *Etudes Physiques, Chimiques et Naturelles* at the Collège de Médecine he discovered that the authorities would not recognize his Dublin degree. Piqued by this refusal to permit him to do what he imagined he would like to do he went directly to Dr. Brouardel,[1] *doyen* of the Faculty at the Collège de Médecine, and demanded his aid. Dr. Brouardel eventually wangled a provisional card that admitted Joyce to lectures. He attended class in the Rue Cuvier once and never went there again. The reason for this abrupt termination of the study of medicine was not so much that he immediately lost interest but that he discovered fees must be paid in cash and without delay. Not having the cash he lost no time in putting the idea of medicine behind him. It is fairly obvious that he was not particularly heartbroken.

The pound or so he possessed had almost immediately disappeared. The expected journalistic and literary activities did not materialize. Neither did the Frenchmen anxious to pay for learning

[1] There is an avenue near the Bois de Boulogne in Paris called after Dr. Brouardel— but not on account of what he did for Joyce.

the English language although eventually he did secure two students. In short, it was not long before he was in a practically-starving condition. Indeed, at one desperate moment he attempted to pawn his suit of clothes at the *mont-de-piété* but the clerk there refused to accept it. It was *trop sale.* Occasional small money orders from his mother and infinitesimal loans from two or three acquaintances almost as poverty-stricken as himself just kept his head above water. But he was always hungry. As he tramped the vivacious streets, avoiding the rolling carriages driven by *cochers* in white hats, and smelled the freshly baked loaves of bread and observed the shopgirls munching their *chaussons* of pastry and sniffed the rich odour of steaming coffee and the heady fragrance of spiced beans and saw the great bowls of cooked vegetables in the *crémeries,* he comforted himself with the thought that it would be painful to eat anyway. For during this winter Joyce suffered from ferocious toothaches, toothaches so intense that though he was ravenously hungry he dreaded the effect of the first mouthful. The pain in his teeth that followed rendered him speechless for several minutes. It is important to remember this trouble of the teeth, for certain authorities have assumed that from it were engendered the grave eye ailments of his later years. And if this is so it may be postulated that the toothaches of 1902-3 have indirectly affected the progress and development of English letters, for it is demonstrable that Joyce's eye afflictions have shaped his handling of creative literature to a surprising degree.

We have here, then, a lonely young man in shabby clothes, a Latin Quarter hat and a peculiar long overcoat and with aching teeth and empty stomach striving haphazardly to make an impression on a world that did not even know he existed. Some few in Dublin were smilingly aware of his own estimate of himself but if they subscribed to it, and there is no evidence that any one of them did, they were careful not to admit it so loudly that they would be overheard. That gossiping, backbiting, scandalmongering free-and-easy, whisky-and-porter-drinking community, wise as its years and foolish as its impulses, proceeded blithely on its way and permitted Paris and the four corners of the earth to shelter the man who was not stamped in its pattern. Inconsistent city! City of Leonard MacNally and Robert Emmet!

In the meantime Joyce applied himself to his writing and his reading, expending much less time on the former than he did on the latter. Sparse as his composition was, however, there still exists some of it although in a changed form. The major labour of this green season of his career was the creation of a dozen or more plotless sketches, flashes of life, manifestations of mood and place, which he called *Epiphanies*. Years later several of these fragments, greatly revised and brought to a perfection they lacked in 1902 and 1903, were introduced into *A Portrait of the Artist as a Young Man*. Except for this work and the revision of one or two poems there is nothing that can be laid to his credit during this parlous period. Perhaps he was too hungry. Perhaps the *paresse* of a young artist in a new place was too much for him. Anyway, his life stultified into a simplified poverty-stricken attempt to carry the high arrogance and lonely pride that so set him apart from the young Dubliners of his time like a cloak that would not be too threadbare seen from a distance. If he could not subscribe with a cringing knee to shibboleths he despised or compromise for the sake of ease he could, at least—and it must have been cold comfort at the moment, live in himself and for himself. What he found there was enough to incite his progression.

The routine of his days as the bleak winter settled down on Paris, that cold, snowless, rainy interregnum between the sparkling autumn and the restless spring, was uneventful. He would rise late in his dark little lair in the Grand Hôtel Corneille, glance on the floor by the door for the envelopes from the English journals which never came, and proceed to a small *crémerie* in the narrow Rue Saint-André-des-Arts where he could procure a steaming bowl of chocolate for three sous. If he were particularly penniless (and this state he endured most of the week) he would purchase a bowl from the strident-voiced women in wooden clogs who stood beside their smoking cauldrons in the streets. There even arrived a period when he regarded the most modest prices as beyond his means and then he put a pathetic plan into effect. An impecunious student (without a doubt one of medicine) at the Grand Hôtel Corneille informed him that it was far too expensive to pay one franc ten centimes for a meal and advised him to cook in his hotel room. Joyce thereupon purchased a second-hand pot and a spirit lamp and gravely cooked stews, rice and chocolate in the solitary receptacle, a receptacle, by the way, that he never cleaned out. The mingled *gout* must have been indescribable. Murger would have appreciated this. A letter to his mother, written upon his twenty-first birthday, reveals his condition so succinctly and clearly at this time that it needs no comment.

> Grand Hôtel Corneille.
> Paris, 2. February, 1903.

Dear Mother,

Your order for 3/4 of Tuesday last was very welcome as I had been without food for 42 hours. Today I am twenty hours without food. But these spells of fasting are common with me now and when I get money I am so damnably hungry that I eat a fortune (1/—) before you could say knife. I hope this new system of living won't injure my digestion. I have no news from "Speaker" or "Express." If I had money I could buy a little oil stove (I have a lamp) and cook macaroni for myself with bread when I am hard beat. I hope you are doing what I said about Stannie, but I dare say you are not. I hope the carpet that was sold is not one of the new purchases that you are selling to feed me. If this is so sell no more or I'll send the money back to you by return of post. I think I am doing the best I can for myself but it's pulling the devil by the tail the greater part of the time. I expect to be served with my bill (1/6/o—with oil) any day and then my happiness is complete. My condition is so exciting that I cannot go asleep at night often till four in the morning and when I wake I look at once under the door to see if there is a letter from my editors and I assure you when I see the wooden floor only morning after morning I sigh and turn back to sleep off part of the hunger. I have not gone to see Miss Gonne nor do I intend to go. With the utmost stretching your last order will keep me Monday midday (postage half a franc probably)—then, I suppose, I must do another fast. I regret this as Monday and Tuesday are carnival days and I shall be the only one starving in Paris.

> Jim.

It is, perhaps, necessary to point out here that Miss Maud Gonne, the inspiration of so many of W. B. Yeats's poems and a beautiful woman who came close to being a sort of Irish Joan of Arc, was living in Paris during Joyce's dark winter there. It was just about this period that she met Major John MacBride, who had led the Irish Brigade in Kruger's army against the British troops during the Boer War. Later she married (and still later divorced) him. She had invited Joyce to call upon her but he felt that his suit of clothes was *trop sale* for such a social visit.

The eating places which Joyce patronized at this time (when

he patronized any) were the usual cheap bistro-affairs, for the most part, the sort of haunts which young writers and artists with more ambition and ability than money have frequented since writers first sought Paris as the arena for their development. There was the *crémerie* in the Rue Saint-André-des-Arts (now vanished), the Crémerie-Restaurant Polydor in the Rue Monsieur-le-Prince (at last account still in existence) to which Joyce went only when he possessed a few extra francs and where he enjoyed the rice cooked with cinnamon, and the Café-Restaurant des Deux-Ecus on the Place des Deux-Ecus on the right bank.

Having breakfasted on chocolate or merely a few gulps of fresh air, Joyce would saunter across the Seine, glancing with longing at the huge Norman armoires in the windows of the antiquaries and the display of iron rings in Arnou's shop on the Rue Racine, and so up the drab Rue Richelieu to the Bibliothèque Nationale, that cold mausoleum of dead minds, where he would pass part of the day reading the works of Ben Jonson. During this winter he digested the complete works of that hard-minded intellectual Elizabethan worthy. After his meagre dinner he would saunter across the Boulevard Saint-Michel to the Bibliothèque Sainte-Geneviève and forget his loneliness in a perusal of Victor Cousin's translation of Aristotle. His mental pabulum was not unusual, it will be seen, but it is interesting now to speculate as to the reasons why he was particularly drawn to Ben Jonson. His readings or, rather, rereadings in Aristotle were but a continuance of the road he had naturally found and followed under Jesuitical direction. But Jonson was different. Was it the sinewy qualities and classical exactness of Jonson that charmed him? Was it the Elizabethan's propensity for delineating "humours" and "vapours," the curious and eccentric attitudes towards life of his herd of characters? Or was it the lyrics that were strewed through the plays? It was probably an amalgam of all these characteristics of Ben Jonson. He found in the plays a precision, a marshalling of motives, an attentiveness to character, an Aristotelean exactness, a lyric impulse and a disciplined humour that merged without dissonance into his own budding philosophy of letters. There was, without a doubt, a solidity about Jonson that attracted him, a "toughness," if the word may be used, that was as removed from sentimentality as the mind of Aristotle is removed from the mind of Plato. That he studied the works of Jonson with unusual attentiveness is evident from the quotations to be found in one of the notebooks he kept at this time (and which still exists), such quotations, for instance, as the lovely song beginning:

> I was not wearier where I lay
> By frozen Tithon's side, tonight,
> Than I am willing now to stay
> And be a part of your delight;
> But I am urgéd by the day,
> Against my will, to bid you come away.

The first line of this lyric, it may be pointed out, is quoted in *A Portrait of the Artist as a Young Man*.

Then there are excerpts in the notebook from *Cynthia's Revels, The Poetaster, Volpone, or The Fox, Epicœne, or The Silent Woman, The Devil is an Ass, The Staple of News* and *The New Inn*. Certainly the young writer seeking a metrical discipline could travel far without finding a better model than Jonson.

It is unnecessary to enlarge upon Joyce's continued interest in Aristotle. As his mind matured, and one must remember the influences under which it matured, his exploration of the reasoning of the master of Aquinas achieved a profundity that would have done credit to an experienced specialist in the subject. Aristotle still represented to him Dogma, a Rock set against the turbid tides of inchoate metaphysics. He was System, co-ordination, rationalization. He was the reverse of Plato and Plato's beautiful and ineffectual mysticism. Joyce, with the gigantic fetish of exactitude ever before him and an intense concern for the unities, with his worship of Ibsen and his scorn for the empty twilight of the Irish theatre, naturally found in Aristotle a firmer base from which to spring than the quicksand of Romanticism left by the backwash of the nineties. The sentences that he copied down in his notebook from the various works of the Stagirite show us what arrested his mind and in what direction it was travelling. For instance:

"The soul is the first entelechy of a naturally organic body."

"That which acts is superior to that which suffers."

"Only when it is separate from all things is the intellect really itself and this intellect separate from all things is immortal and divine."

"The principle which hates is not different from the principle which loves."

"The intellectual soul is the form of forms."

"Speculation is above practice."

"Necessity is that in virtue of which it is impossible that a thing should be otherwise."

"God is the eternal perfect animal."

"Nature, it seems, is not a collection of unconnected episodes, like a bad dream (or drama?)."

These utterances, perhaps not in the exact words of Aristotle, from the *Psychology* and the *Metaphysic* give some idea of the attempt that Joyce was then making to establish for himself a reasonable metaphysic for life and æsthetic for art. He was finding his way, not too slowly, by a tough reasoning process and the steps of his progression are indicated by the short original notes he set down at this time and was to continue a year or so later in Pola and Trieste. Indeed, these notes were the loose bricks from which he was to build up the æsthetic definitions so beautifully exposited to Lynch in *A Portrait of the Artist as a Young Man*. Lynch was quite correct in remarking that they possessed the true scholastic stink but nevertheless they played a vast part in liberating Joyce from the musty æsthetic urges of his youthful environment. It is both instructive and fascinating to observe the young Dubliner clarifying his mind and sharpening his intellect during this immersion in Aristotle (and Aquinas too, of course), setting down, for instance, such detached paragraphs as:

Desire is the feeling which urges us to go to something and loathing is the feeling which urges us to go from something: and that art is improper which aims at exciting these feelings in us whether by comedy or by tragedy. Of comedy later. But tragedy aims at exciting in us feelings of pity and terror. Now terror is the feeling which arrests us before whatever is grave in human fortunes and unites us with its secret cause and pity is the feeling which arrests us before whatever is grave in human fortunes and unites us with the human sufferer. Now loathing, which in an improper art aims at exciting in the way of tragedy, differs, it will be seen, from the feelings which are proper to tragic art, namely terror and pity. For loathing urges us from rest because it urges us to go from something, but terror and pity hold us in rest, as it were, by fascination.

When tragic art makes my body to shrink terror is not my feeling because I am urged from rest, and moreover this art does not show me what is grave, I mean what is constant and irremediable in human fortunes nor does it unite me with any secret cause for it shows me only what is unusual and remediable and it unites me with a cause only too manifest. Nor is an art properly tragic which would move me to prevent human suffering any more than an art is properly tragic which would move me in anger against some manifest cause of human suffering. Terror and pity, finally, are aspects of sorrow comprehended in sorrow —the feeling which the privation of some good excites in us.

And now of comedy. An improper art aims at exciting in the way of comedy the feeling of desire but the feeling which is proper to comic art is the feeling of joy. Desire, as I have said, is the feeling which urges us to go to something but joy is the feeling which the possession of some good excites in us. Desire, the feeling which an improper art seeks to excite in the way of comedy, differs, it will be seen, from joy. For desire urges us from rest that we may possess something but joy holds us in rest so long as we possess something. Desire, therefore, can only be excited in us by a comedy (a work of comic art) which is not sufficient in itself inasmuch as it urges us to seek something beyond itself; but a comedy (a work of comic art) which does not urge us to seek anything beyond itself excites in us the feeling of joy. All art which excites in us the feeling of joy is so far comic and according as this feeling of joy is excited by whatever is substantial or accidental in human fortunes the art is to be judged more or less excellent: and even tragic art may be said to participate in the nature of comic art so far as the possession of a work of tragic art (a tragedy) excites in us the feeling of joy. From this it may be seen that tragedy is the imperfect manner and comedy the perfect manner in art. All art, again, is static for the feelings of terror and pity on the one hand and of joy on the other hand are feelings which arrest us. It will be seen afterwards how this rest is necessary for the apprehension of the beautiful—the end of all art, tragic or comic,—for this rest is the only condition under which the images, which are to excite in us terror or pity or joy, can be properly presented to us and properly seen by us. For beauty is a quality of something seen but terror and pity and joy are states of mind.

James A. Joyce, 13 Feb., 1903.

. . . There are three conditions of art: the lyrical, the epical and the dramatic. That art is lyrical whereby the artist sets forth the image in immediate relation to himself; that art is epical whereby the artist sets forth the image in mediate relation to himself and to others; that art is dramatic whereby the artist sets forth the image in immediate relation to others. . . .

> James A. Joyce, 6 March, 1903, Paris.

Rhythm seems to be the first or formal relation of part to part in any whole or of a whole to its part or parts, or of any part to the whole of which it is a part. . . . Parts constitute a whole as far as they have a common end.

> James A. Joyce, 25 March, 1903, Paris.

*e tekhne mimeitai ten physin*—This phrase is falsely rendered as "Art is an imitation of Nature." Aristotle does not here define art; he says only, "Art imitates Nature" and means that the artistic process is like the natural process . . . It is false to say that sculpture, for instance, is an art of repose if by that be meant that sculpture is unassociated with movement. Sculpture is associated with movement in as much as it is rhythmic; for a work of sculptural art must be surveyed according to its rhythm and this surveying is an imaginary movement in space. It is not false to say that sculpture is an art of repose in that a work of sculptural art cannot be presented as itself moving in space and remain a work of sculptural art.

> James A. Joyce, 27 March, 1903, Paris.

Art is the human disposition of sensible or intelligible matter for an æsthetic end.

> James A. Joyce, 28 March, 1903, Paris.

Joyce even posited to himself certain questions the answers to which might further clarify his convictions and strengthen the æsthetic that he was beginning to preach and practise. He was, it will be observed, his own master and student, setting himself problems which he was to resolve by the dialectic of his own æsthetic. Some of these questions were incorporated into the dialogue between Stephen Dedalus and Lynch in *A Portrait of the Artist as a Young Man* but the answers were not set down. It is, therefore, pertinent to this brief exposition of Joyce's intellectual activity in Paris to reveal a few of them here:

Question: *Why are not excrements, children and lice works of art?*
Answer:   Excrements, children and lice are human products—human dispositions of sensible matter. The process by which they are produced is natural and non-artistic; their end is not an æsthetic end: therefore they are not works of art.

Question: *Can a photograph be a work of art?*

Answer: A photograph is a disposition of sensible matter and may be so disposed for an æsthetic end but it is not a human disposition of sensible matter. Therefore it is not a work of art.

Question: *If a man hacking in fury at a block of wood make there an image of a cow (say) has he made a work of art?*

Answer: The image of a cow made by a man hacking in fury at a block of wood is a human disposition of sensible matter but it is not a human disposition of sensible matter for an æsthetic end. Therefore it is not a work of art.

Question: *Are houses, clothes, furniture, etc., works of art?*

Answer: Houses, clothes, furniture, etc., are not necessarily works of art. They are human dispositions of sensible matter. When they are so disposed for an æsthetic end they are works of art.

It is to be regretted that the answer to one immortal question in *A Portrait of the Artist as a Young Man* is unobtainable; namely, the response to: *"Is the bust of Sir Philip Crampton lyrical, epical or dramatic? If not, why not?"* The memorial to Sir Philip Crampton, placed at the junction of D'Olier Street, Townsend Street and Great Brunswick Street in Dublin, is one of those atrocities that once seen are never forgotten. Dubliners affectionately refer to it as the Pineapple or the Artichoke.

Joyce had just passed his twenty-first year when he reached this dialectical peak of his development and while he may appear ultra-solemn and rather pompously pedantic there is equal evidence of a tenaciously-exploring mind that was mining through the hard rock of ratiocination towards a satisfying intellectual haven. *Navigare necesse est.*

More than one commentator has pointed out that the young university men of Joyce's youth were all brought up in a rigorously-classical atmosphere, that they were forced into assiduous application to classical studies, and that their knowledge, far from being unusual, was quite the general rule. They lisped Latin in their cradles and devoured Aristotle as later generations of young men devoured Mr. Edgar Wallace. All this may be so but it does not lessen the impressiveness of Joyce's scholarship. Even his schoolfellows, as we have seen, were aware of his greater command and seriousness. And, after all, it is the influence of scholarship on the man that matters and not the unimportant fact that a vast number of inconsequential youths ingested it much as a poll-parrot might retain the phrases of some patient teacher, gabbled dog Latin to one another and then emerged into manhood uninfluenced by the culture that had been crammed down their throats. Joyce digested his classical education as well as ingesting it.

IV

This systematized method of constant reading and speculation together with his penniless state did not afford Joyce much time for wandering or dalliance with the fleshpots of Paris or convivial friendships; but, all the same, there were several cafés which he visited at odd hours (although at this time he drank no alcohol at all) and a number of fleeting contacts with fellow wanderers. There was, of course, no Byrne with whom to walk and talk the night away. That companionship had ended when Joyce left Dublin. The café most frequented by Joyce was in the Carrefour de l'Odéon, not a stone's throw from Sylvia Beach's bookshop, Shakespeare and Company (which, of course, did not exist then), where *Ulysses* was to be published twenty years later. In this café Joyce met and conversed with a rather motley group of individuals. There was one Riciotto Canudo, an Italian; a German poet named Theodor Däubler; an individual named Eugene Routh and another called Villona. To find a common ground between their varying languages they often conversed in Latin. They were all enormous men physically and the slender Joyce in the midst of them must have seemed like an antelope who had wandered by mistake into a herd of elephants. The conversations were literary and the intellectual pugnacity of Joyce amidst this gathering is evident through the fact that once his vehemence offended the German poet, Däubler, so deeply that the young Dubliner narrowly escaped a challenge to a duel.

This man Däubler deserves a brief paragraph to himself. He was born in Trieste in 1862 and was therefore forty when Joyce encountered him. Today he merits a small niche in the pantheon of German letters. He was essentially esoteric and in his three solid volumes entitled *Nordlicht* he appears as a sun worshipper and hails the Aryan race as the sun's favourite child.

> Es sind die Sonnen und Planeten alle,
> Die hehren Lebensspender in der Welt,
> Die Liebeslichter in der Tempelhalle
> Der Gottheit, die sie aus dem Herzen schwellt.

Whether or not he rhapsodized in his customary exalted philosophic vein to Joyce about the sanctity and prodigious future of the Aryan blood strain is a mystery but if he did it is easy to see why the young Irishman nearly entangled himself in a duel. Any ideal so foggy that it had to be taken on faith and personal prejudice alone was apt to draw harsh and ironical comment from Joyce.

There are two other men whom he met at this period, John Millington Synge, the Irish dramatist, and one Joe Casey, who deserve some enlargement. Synge was in financial straits too, and he had decided to sell out the few belongings remaining to him in a garret in the Rue d'Assas and return to Ireland. Like Joyce he was lonely, arrogant and rather harsh in his reactions to life. The younger writer saw in him a dark tramper of a man and Synge saw in Joyce an ego with a mind that resembled Spinoza's. They met seven or eight times, lunching in the humble bistro-restaurant in the Rue Saint-André-des-Arts where a four- or five-course meal could be procured for one franc ten centimes. Synge would thrust his dark, crude face across the table and talk volubly, his subject always being literature. He was dogmatic in his convictions, argumentative to the point of rudeness and inclined to lose his temper. Once Joyce led him up to his chamber in the Grand Hôtel Corneille and showed him the notebook wherein he copied down the ungrammatical "Memorabilia" which he culled from the books he read. Synge examined the excerpts and his teeth flashed. He studied Yeats's

> And more I may not write for them that cleave
> The waters of sleep can make a chattering tongue
> Heavy as stone, their wisdom being half silence

and Herbert Spencer's

> Hereafter her rank will be considerably higher than now

and Walter Sichel's

Honest manly Jack Fielding . . . Everybody is thinking about themselves

and Theodore Watts's

But after its (Tyranny) dethronement when human nature has become infinitely perfectible how can . . .

and flung down the notebook with a violent oath. "What of it?" he exclaimed. "It is not important at all."

Although he disliked what he considered Joyce's pedantry he yet was curious enough about the young man's opinions to submit to him a manuscript copy of his play, *Riders to the Sea*. Joyce, running true to form, complained that the manner in which the catastrophe was brought about was faulty.

Joe Casey, who appears in *Ulysses* under the name of Kevin Egan, was of a decidedly different type from Synge. He was not intellectual at all. He was a typesetter for the Paris edition of the New York *Herald* but before that he had been a dynamitard during the Irish Fenian troubles, one of the innumerable band of reckless men who ventured their lives and careers that Ireland might be freed from English domination. Now he hid in Paris safe from the authorities who sought him and gained his meagre livelihood by labouring for an American newspaper. Joyce had no political interest in Casey but he enjoyed being with the simple and straightforward old man. They lunched many times together in the small bistro-restaurant des Deux-Ecus which was diagonally across the road from the old Herald building on the Rue du Louvre. It was an unpretentious place with a zinc bar in one room and half a dozen discoloured marble-topped tables in the other. There, with his shabby hat tilted over his eyes and rolling his cigarettes with ink-stained fingers while the garçon poured his absinthe, Joe Casey would sit and talk to Joyce, describing Ireland's militant past, explaining how he had been with Colonel Richard Burke at the Clerkenwell explosion and speculating on the future. There was a son, too, Patrice, who was serving his time in the French army and who lived, when in Paris, with his mother in the rue Git-le-Cœur, Madame Casey having separated long before from her flea-bitten old lion of a husband. This son would appear occasionally at the

Café-Restaurant des Deux-Ecus and gobble his spiced beans and listen benevolently to the oft-repeated stories of his father. Both Casey *père* and Casey *fils* loaned small amounts of cash to Joyce from time to time.

There remain to be mentioned the two language students whom Joyce finally secured and whose small fees made it possible for him to escape starvation on certain days. The first was one Joseph Douce, a manufacturer of champagne, who, curiously enough, was intensely socialistic in his attitude toward life. He was somewhat impressed by his young teacher and invited him to dinner several times. The other student, whom Douce found, by the way, was a man named Auvergniot.

This completes the list of Joyce's acquaintances in Paris if we except the few students whom he encountered from time to time as he made his peregrinations about the Latin Quarter. They, however, were no more than passing shadows, momentary streaks of shade across the path such as trees fling as one walks rapidly onward.

If it be asked what Joyce received from his friends and acquaintances at this time the answer must be exactly what it has been for the remainder of his life—exactly nothing. What he took from them is another matter. He might be a trifle stimulated (as, for instance, in the case of Synge, who, apparently, offered him the opportunity of attack and exposition (in a letter to his younger brother, Stanislaus, at this period, he wrote: "But thanks to God, Synge isn't an Aristotelian. I told him part of my æsthetic; he says I have a mind like Spinoza.")) but that was all. Human beings with their reactions, their inconsistent hopes and denials and unintelligent responses to life were curious automata to be sharply observed and then ticketed away in the prodigious portfolio of the brain. They were never props upon which to lean or sources from which one might drink the tepid waters of sympathy. Even at twenty-one Joyce had realized that only from himself could he draw the strength for living. The closest he had come to friendship (and that had never been a dependent friendship) was with Byrne. After Byrne there was no one. One might even add, there was only documentation.

In fact, that is what he took from practically all the people with whom he came in contact. There is, assuredly, no living writer today who has drawn more completely from memory (memory of himself as well as others) to populate his books than Joyce. Whether under their own names and aspects or most slightly disguised, they have all come from a world that once actually existed or still does exist. Yet they have been translated from reality to what might be called a superreality. They cast greater shadows and assume Titanlike aspects. Translating Joe Casey into Kevin Egan and the twenty-one-year-old James Joyce into Stephen Dedalus is a form of major sorcery. The importance of these friends and acquaintances, then, to Joyce in 1902-3 seems to be that they were part of his documentation (unconscious, as yet) of the fantastic exertion called living. They neither influenced nor remoulded his mind or his attitude toward sentient existence and art. He developed himself alone and he achieved his æsthetic by himself in the shabby chamber at the Grand Hôtel Corneille and the draughty reading rooms of Parisian libraries.

There is little more to be described about Joyce's bleak winter and early spring in Paris. He attended a few plays and operas, among them one of the first performances of Claude-Achille Debussy's *Pelleas et Mélisande* at the Opéra-Comique and Heijermans's *La Bonne Espérance* at the Théâtre-Antoine with Signoret in the cast. He heard Jean de Reszke sing in *Pagliacci* and thought the Polish tenor's voice very like his father's voice. This performance was a special gala, and Joyce, much to his anguish, had to pay seven francs fifty centimes for a seat in the gallery. He saw Réjane. He interviewed Henri Farman about the Gordon Bennett Cup Races and sold the interview to the *Irish Times*. Desiring to continue the training of his voice he called upon a voice teacher in the Rue du Four but was disappointed to discover that the teacher desired his fee in advance for giving him lessons. He made a few trips out of Paris, one as far as Clamart and several to the confluence of the Seine and the Marne where he sat contentedly watching the mingled waters flow by. If he could not have Anna Liffey he would have Anna Sequana. He ventured on one major trip to Dublin for the Christmas and New Year holidays where he remained quietly at home and mixed not at all in the life of his native city. It was, taken *in toto,* a lonely life, an arduous existence filled with disappointments and drabnesses and that he managed to maintain it with an air and a gesture of confidence is ample testimony to his doggedness of determination and supreme faith in himself.

v

The winter marched towards the spring. Various occurrences, exerting no obvious influence on Joyce's life or thought, revealed the tempo and taste of the time, illustrating the sort of world in which the young man existed. Early in January the bearded Socialist, Jean Jaurès, was elected Vice-President of the Chamber of Deputies much to the disgust of the conservative Right. On the seventh day of this month Pierre Wolff's *Le Secret de Polichinelle* was produced at the Théâtre-Gymnase and brought a new descriptive phrase into the French language. On the twenty-ninth Augusta Holmés, the composer, died in her home in the Rue Juliette-Lamber, having (like so many freethinkers before her) made her peace with the Church at the very last moment. This same day, too, witnessed the death of another composer, Robert Planquette, whose *Les Cloches de Corneville* (better known in English as *The Chimes of Normandy*) must have been familiar to Joyce. During February Emile Zola's posthumous novel, *Vérité,* appeared in the bookshop windows and proved to the world that the vogue of Naturalism was rapidly sinking into oblivion. Maria Christina, dowager queen of Spain, and her daughter, the Infanta Maria-Theresa, added their illustrious names to those of the many royalties visiting the agreeable Paris of plump Monsieur Loubet. On March seventh Gaston Paris, the great authority on mediæval French literature, died, and eight days later (the fifteenth) Ernest Legouvé, author of that ancient war horse of the theatre, *Adrienne Lecouvreur,* breathed his last. On the twenty-second day of the month the silk-hatted seconds of Jean Jaurès and Godefroy Cavaignac met to complete the arrangements for a duel between their principals. On the twenty-ninth Anatole France's *Crainquebille* had its première at the Renaissance. To sum up, it was a typical Paris season, with deaths, theatrical productions, publications and duels to excite the mind and reassure the forgetful that time marched on.

How much Joyce knew or cared about it all is a mystery. He was, possibly, too engrossed in himself to expend much time in examining the peculiar phenomena of Parisian life; but the sum total of things coloured his environment and so impinged upon his apprehension. Towards the end of this month of March he was gloomily setting down a page of bookkeeping in one of his note-books to convince himself (possibly) that he possessed absolutely nothing. This page deserves to be copied out for it reveals more clearly than any extensive description can the cramped circumstances and hand-to-mouth existence that the young man endured at this time.

If one remembers that there were twenty-five francs to the pound in 1903 it is obvious from the above statement that Joyce was existing on little more than a pound a week, part of that being borrowed money hastily sought at climactic moments of extreme hunger. Today that would be tantamount to living for a week in Paris on one hundred and seventy-eight francs (providing the French money is not again devaluated before this page is published) or approximately twenty-five francs a day. It is possible, of course, but it is damned disagreeable, especially when one's rent comes out of it. And in Joyce's case the situation was further complicated by the fact that his money was uncertain and at least half of it was borrowed. It will be noted that while he paid seven francs in debts (without a doubt to Casey) he still owed the staggering sum of forty-four francs and fifty centimes (almost two pounds!). The prospects for the month of April, then, were far from rosy.

VI

It drew near Easter and the shop windows burst into spring colours. The newspapers announced that the *carême* of 1903 at Notre-Dame de Paris would be preached by Père Janvier. Joyce, always attracted by the singing voice and the liturgical chants, determined that he would hear what he could of the church music during the solemn season of the Resurrection. *That,* at least, was free. On Good Friday morning he went to Notre-Dame de Paris and attended the services. After that, being at a loose end and quite penniless, he started to roam about the streets of the city and continued his peregrinations until long after the night lamps were

2nd. month:

from 20 February to 20 March 1903 (exclusive of hotel-bill)

Received   6.40  
        21.40  
        9.50  
        25.20  
        17.00  
        79.50 and

             40.20  
             38.70 (Hotel-bill)            £3/4/9½  
    1.50    1.50                  £   4/8  
    81.00 francs                    £3/0/1½

Debts paid 1.50                      £1/6/0  
       5.50                        £4/6/1½  
       7.00 francs  
    74.00 francs

Hotel-bill 30.00 (probably)  
          1.80                 **Present Debts**  
          .80                Chown ...... 10.00  
     32.60 francs      fr. c.    Casey fils .... 2.00  
  106.60 francs Hotel-bill   33.00    Casey ........ 5.50  
                                 Casey ........ 2.00  
                                   19.50  
          (And Gogarty £1/0/0 = 25.00)  
                                   44.50

TOTAL EXPENSES  
     106.60       =       £4/6/1½  
       .40          =          3  
     107.00                 4/6/4½  
         Remainder   0

JAMES A. JOYCE.

illuminated and shining across the shadowy streets. He liked so to walk, repeating his own poems to himself as he passed unnoticed and unnoticing through the ancient thoroughfares where the chattering theatregoers hurried towards their lighted portals. When he finally and reluctantly returned to the Grand Hôtel de Corneille it was after eleven o'clock at night and the little Place de l'Odéon lay deserted under the spring stars. Entering the hotel Joyce discovered that a telegram awaited him. That was curious for he could imagine no one, not even Mr. C. Lewis Hind or Mr. Dunlop of *Men and Women,* sending him a telegram. With some fear and suspicion, then, he tore open the blue oblong of paper and read, "Mother dying come home father." For an instant he was dumbfounded and at a loss as to what to do. He did not possess a franc in his pockets and yet he knew that before the morning he must raise the fare to Dublin. Where could he go at midnight in Paris to borrow money? He might knock up Casey in his Montmartre lair in the Rue de la Goutte-d'Or but Casey would never have enough cash to pay for a passage from Paris to Dublin. Then he thought of his language student, the socialist-minded champagne manufacturer, Joseph Douce. At least, it was a chance. He hurried from the Grand Hôtel de Corneille and tramped through the practically-deserted streets to Douce's place of residence. The building was dark and locked. After great trouble and long waiting (for Paris concierges were as deaf in 1903 as they are today) he succeeded in being admitted. The champagne manufacturer, somewhat tousled and in his nightshirt, his full blond beard ruffled in the night breeze, read the telegram which Joyce handed to him, listened to the young man's plea and then proved himself worthy of his name. He produced three pounds in French money and presented it to Joyce.[1]

The next morning Joyce was on his way back to Dublin, travelling by way of Dieppe, Newhaven, London and Holyhead, his Bohemian days in Paris being over for all time.

---

[1] Joyce's father returned this sum promptly to Monsieur Douce and wrote him a florid letter of thanks which was an expression of his Irish Francophile sentiments. John Stanislaus had what would be considered today (and he kept it until he was an old man) an exquisite calligraphy of which he was very vain. It was finer and more ornate even than that of Joyce's Uncle Willy who wrote a legal scrivener's hand. When John Stanislaus wrote a letter every noise in the house had to cease—and, if possible, in the neighbouring streets as well. An untimely knock at the hall-door would be greeted by a melodious outburst of curses.

# Four

I T was the same Dublin (how could it have changed in so short a time?), but Joyce observed it from a new point of vantage that curiously shifted all its values. He was detached. The months in the city by the Seine afforded him a means of comparison for the city by the Liffey. He could view Dublin now with an objectivity of which he had been incapable before, seeing it from the outside as well as the inside, understanding that it was only a small portion of a greater world and that the unique Irish Roman Catholic civilization modified by English infiltration of which it boasted was not an end-all in itself but a local phenomenon that dwindled mightily when considered beside the cosmopolitan flavour of Paris. The peculiar stuffiness and smugness of the post-Boer War era in Ireland must have seemed as quaint as it was irritating when he compared it with the broader and meatier conception of life in France. It was not alone that practically everything meeting the eye was different, the deportment of the people, for instance, the ugly public houses in place of the brighter cafés, the indulgence in whisky and porter instead of wines and apéritifs, the theatres and what was presented in them, the vistas of streets and squares and monuments, the magazines and newspapers displayed for sale, indeed, the thousand and one inconsequentia that compose an atmosphere, but the very mind and being of the two peoples, the Dubliners and the Parisians, were inexorable poles apart. It was curious, too, to note the surprising variances of French and Irish Roman Catholicism. If Paris was a lamp for lovers lit in the wood of the world, what was Dublin? A place of the dying, perhaps, where the leaping thought was speedily caged. We may guess, then, that a gloomy irritability possessed Joyce as he recognized anew and with wiser eyes his native city and suffered from the realization that the tragic necessity which had drawn him back had replunged him in a small, bickering, treacherous world which did not desire him (the arrogant nonconformist) any more than he desired it.

For the moment, however, he could not regard it too bitterly. Once settled in his father's house at 7 St. Peter's Terrace, Cabra, he had the tragedy of his mother to live with and to face. She was dying and dying in extreme pain. The incurable cirrhosis of the liver that was eating her life away manifested itself frighteningly in the constant vomiting of green bile. When she died on the thirteenth of August, after four months and five days of this persistent bilious retching, Joyce had dwelt for practically the same period of time in the sombre household, hearing the hushed footsteps of his brothers and sisters, comforted perhaps a little by his uncle William Murray and his aunt Josephine, observing the grief and bewilderment of John Stanislaus and realizing with a dull and helpless pain that no effort could vanquish the gulf that existed between him and the dying mother.

It was not within his power to bridge that gulf. Mary Jane Joyce was dying in the sanctity of the bosom of her Church, that vast spring whose holy waters had refreshed and sustained her throughout the forty-four years of her life, and her eldest son, whose inner dæmon had snatched him from submission to that great master, could only stand apart and grieve that the two wills could not meet and mix. He was incapable of bending his knee to the powerful phantom that, once acknowledged, would devour him as it had devoured so many about him and half a civilization as well. His independence was his reason for existing, the solid foundation upon which he must build the metaphysic of his art, and all his blood cried out that subservience, even an instant's surrender, would be a veritable death in life. Even a false lip service, a pseudo-genuflection for pity's sake, so easy to perform and yet so momentous to himself, would be an unforgivable self-betrayal and place him in the ranks of those whom he despised. Compromise would lead to compromise until the will was sapped and the outwardly-conforming shell contained nothing but dull regrets and still-born gestures. There was only one road, brambly and stony as it was, to travel. There was only one device to obey. *Non serviam.*

Emphasis, delicately as it must be put, is necessary here if we are to understand (however fragmentarily) the painful and lonely development of Joyce. His mother's death appears to have been a powerful challenge to his will as well as a great sorrow to his heart.

It was Time's remorseless way of testing the integrity of the young man (now just past his twenty-first birthday) and its reverberations were to sound through many years of his life. One can but guess at certain aspects of it (for these are matters never worn upon the sleeve), but the important deduction seems to be that it flung Joyce into a violent inner conflict from which he emerged hardened, rather bitter, and sometimes reckless of the consequences. It was, in a way, a test of his inviolability to the usual compromises of the flesh and will.

After Mary Jane Joyce had been laid away in her last resting place in Glasnevin Cemetery, Joyce appears to have been thrown very much upon himself. Released from the tension of his home (and there was nothing to be found there but a heart-breaking effort to make ends meet) he sought to renew himself again in the lively city. Literary projects, reading, the composition of poetry, ideas whereby he might make money, and an immersion in whatever Bohemian life Dublin had to offer caught him up and fairly filled his days. It is by his brief participation in the Bohemian life (if one may name it so) that he is best remembered in his native city today. He ran with the jackeens, so to speak. Accompanied generally by medical students (always his favourite companions in Dublin) he explored the stews and byways of Nighttown and became a noticeable figure in the more popular public houses that dotted the city. Davy Byrne's on Duke Street, Conway's near the Westland Row Railway Station, The Ship in Lower Abbey Street, Barney Kiernan's near the Four Courts, the Scotch House, the Ormonde Bar on the quays, all of them knew the young man, and if he was sometimes the worse for liquor (for he was beginning to drink now) it was not because he imbibed excessively but because he could carry so little. He who was born to be a wine drinker became a man of straw when attempting brief bouts with Irish whisky and heady black porter.

There were reasons for this immersion in the more reckless side of Dublin life and they would seem to be concentred in a violent desire to forget himself, to shake free of the gloom (Baudelaire's "spleen") that oppressed him, to deny for the moment that he was apparently caught in a coil that was none of his choosing. He was disorientated as only the artist in an antagonistic environment can be disorientated and his long hours in the National Library (for he was as noticeable there as he was in the public houses) failed to furnish him with that intellectual anchor that moors the sedentary bookman placidly in any haven that he may be. Joyce was too active, too disturbed, too nervously adjusted, too dissatisfied for that. A.E. and John Eglinton might be able to sit still in Dublin but the young man was incapable of such composure. He possessed more chaos in him than the editor of the *Irish Homestead* imagined and there was a world in the making there. Even the poetry that he was creating (precise lyrics suggestive of Elizabethan and Jacobean singers) afforded him but momentary calm. He might arrogantly declare, "I have written the most perfect lyric since Shakespeare," but we may guess that the boast was as much a self-protective gesture against the doubting Thomases surrounding him as it was an affirmation of his satisfaction with himself. He was like a man seeking for something that was not to be found in Dublin and growing bitter with the futility of his laborious chase. John Eglinton has pictured him at this crucial period as a young man with "a pair of burning dark-blue eyes, serious and questioning, fixed on me from under the peak of a yachting cap; the face is long, with a slight flush suggestive of dissipation, and an incipient beard is permitted to straggle over a very pronounced chin, under which the open shirt collar leaves bare a full womanish throat. The figure is fairly tall and very erect, and gives a general impression of a kind of seedy hauteur." One needs but add the ashplant and one has Stephen Dedalus.

Such was Joyce between the time of his mother's death and his second (and final) flight from Dublin somewhat more than a year later. His chronic pennilessness stemmed in no way his arrogant flowering. Neither did it divert his mind from its constant fidelity to an æsthetic that was assuredly shaped with no idea of monetary return. He desired the wherewithal to live in comfort as every reasonable man does but he could not adjust himself to the popular taste of Dublin, not even to the more precious taste of the Yeats-A.E.-Gregory inner circle. The Nationalist movement in letters and politics continued to antagonize him and he made no secret of his scorn for it. That scorn expressed itself in a barbed malicious wit that left no hide unpricked. Truth within the balanced scheme of his conception of art was his solitary concern, truth about himself as well as truth about Dublin. The devil take all sentimental softenings and lip services to the false gods whose bellies were stuffed with straw. The truth about himself he began to see as a sort of autobiographical novel, a story of his school and college days through which would walk thinly disguised or disguised not at all the variegated personalities, family, instructors and companions, who had influenced (however briefly) his own development. It would be a portrait of the artist as a young man. The truth about Dublin he envisaged in a possible series of short stories, or sketches, depicting various facets of the city's social and political life.

By the beginning of the new year (1904)—a year that was to have a lasting influence on his life and art—he had commenced work upon these projects. At the same time he was casting about for a means to live. He had left his father's house and was existing precariously in cheap rooms. He exchanged quarters often, possibly at the behest of worried landladies who desired their rent. One flash of him exists as wandering through the streets of Dublin and carrying the iron poles of his bed with him. Passing an open window he saw a young woman sitting within and paused to declaim some poetry to her. As she appeared to listen with pleasure, he attempted to climb over the railings before the house and tore the seat of his trousers on an iron spike. A shriek of laughter from the watching mother of the young woman sent him on his way. Some time l er while he was parading along O'Connell Street still bearing the iron poles of his bed the loud voice of a mercurial medical student, a boosing companion, halted him. "You drunken ——!" cried the acquaintance. "The whole arse of your breeches is gone!" It was this same Medical Davy who once, encountering Joyce in a yachting cap, demanded, "Where's she moored, commander?"

Joyce, at this time, was borrowing small sums of money and wearing hand-me-down garments that were given him by more affluent companions. Yet his arrogance appeared to increase with his poverty. Extravagant schemes to make money blossomed in his unbusinesslike mind and one of the most impossible of them was the establishment of a daily halfpenny paper. He conceived this brilliant plan with Francis Skeffington. The paper was to be called the *Goblin* and it would suppress all politics and confine itself to the arts. A daily cartoon would adorn its pages. One Gillies, once Scotch manager of the *Freeman's Journal* and later editor of the *Irish Bee Keeper,* was to be the business manager. What a huge success the publication of a daily paper without politics would have been in Dublin! The quixotic idea got no further than the registration of the title. Joyce, by the way, was later appointed sub-editor of the *Irish Bee Keeper* and held the post for about twenty-four hours.

But a job of sorts (paying just enough to keep body and soul together) did turn up in the early spring of 1904. Joyce secured a position teaching at Clifton School, Summerfield Lodge, Dalkey Avenue, Dalkey, under a headmaster named Francis Irwin, T.C.D. He taught there for about four months. Both the place and the job are of interest in a consideration of Joyce's life and work. If we except his brief language-lesson experience in Paris, it was his first attempt to exist by teaching others, a form of livelihood that was to be his sole means of precarious support for many future years. No one seems to know whether or not Joyce was a good teacher at this time. The deduction would seem to be that he was bored by the experience and continued it to the end of the school year primarily for the few pounds it brought him. Yet it was an episode that never slipped from his mind and he drew copiously from Clifton School and Francis Irwin, T.C.D., for an entire section in *Ulysses.*

Dalkey itself, town and island, was not without interests both historical and legendary. It was originally a Danish foundation (Dalkey means Thorn Island) and the bay so resembles the Bay of Naples that many of the houses and streets were given Neapolitan names—Sorrento, for instance, and the Vico Road. The island was for many years a mock-kingdom and the election of the king (a travesty recently resumed) was an annual opportunity for humorous and exaggerated parody. John Dowland, the Elizabethan composer, is supposed to have been born in Dalkey. It will be observed how places and times meet in a curious mixture here. The beaked galleys of the Danes, a wild Irish island, Sorrento and its evocation of the sirens. Giambattista Vico and his *Scienza Nuova,* the phantom of a kingdom that exists only in the Comic Mind, the clear un-Irish strains of Elizabethan airs, and all the manifold emanations that meet and mix from these disparate things must have penetrated the subconscious mind of Joyce and there awaited their hour. They belonged to an unborn myth where a bluff Dublin alderman was also a king and where four old men and a donkey trudged around the Vico Road.

While Joyce was still teaching at Clifton School he removed temporarily from Dublin and went to live in the Martello Tower at Sandycove adjoining Glasthule with one of his medical companions, Oliver St. John Gogarty. These squat solid battlements crowned with parapet and gunrest (there were originally fifteen of them between Dublin and Bray) were built during the period of the National Defence Act of 1804 when Pitt feared that the Emperor Napoleon might invade the British Isles. What were left of them (for six or seven had been either demolished by workmen or destroyed by the erosion of their sites by the sea) could be rented from the government as summer headquarters for those who desired close proximity to Dublin Bay. Life in the Martello Tower during the spring of 1904, from most accounts, was raffish and exuberant. There was a great flow of persiflage and wit, a comparative freedom from the "reformed conscience" that fettered so much of Dublin existence, and (no strange thing in the city by the Liffey) a subtle interplay of pronounced personalities congenitally antagonistic to one another. Joyce's residence there was not of long duration. He was too much of an individualist to permit himself to be submerged by lesser individualities, no matter how strident or mocking they might be, and his peculiar tenancy in Time was not to be usurped by any scoffing jester.

During this last year of his impatient existence in Ireland Joyce laboured fitfully at his literary conceptions. He had practically perfected in his own mind the long-pondered æsthetic based on the teachings of Aristotle and Aquinas and with it as master he was determined to create an art in letters that had never existed in his native country. All that he was doing now would last and take a definite place in the canon of his achievement. These first labours fell into three classifications and they may be considered briefly in turn. First of all, there was his poetry, not the French forms of *Moods* and *Shine and Dark*—for they were either lost or still in the possession of George Clancy—but a handful of lyrics that were, for the most part, the product of this very year. They were the poems that he recited in a beautiful voice to his companions while strolling along the streets of Dublin in the spring and summer evenings, each poem the formal and rather precious liberation of a rhythm. The appropriate inclusive title for them occurred to Joyce by a Rabelaisian chance. One of his bouncing companions, a sharp-witted intelligent zany, often sought solace (to put it delicately) in the generous charms of a hot-blooded widow and to this widow's home one evening went Joyce, companion, poems, and several bottles of beer. Joyce read his poems aloud while the widow listened and emptied the bottles of beer. After a time necessity (that knows no master) urged the widow to rise and retire precipitately behind a screen that was in the room. An instant later there sounded a brave and unabashed tinkle from the hidden corner. Joyce's companion shouted with joy. "By God!" he cried, "she's a critic! You hear how she appreciates your poems?" "Critic or no," replied Joyce gravely, "she has given me a title for my book. I shall call it *Chamber Music.*"

Much more important to Joyce than the poems, however, were his prose ventures for to them he could apply the full measure of discipline demanded by his æsthetic. He had commenced work on the series of short stories that were to capture various facets of the Dublin scene and his ambition at the moment was to sell them to the *Irish Homestead,* A.E.'s periodical, profanely called the "pig's paper" by the younger Dublin literati. Eventually Joyce did sell two of them but after that the *Irish Homestead* would accept no more, evidently considering them too lacking in patriotic sensibility and idealistic sentiment for the taste of the Irish public. At the same time the young writer was making a tentative approach to the autobiographical novel that was swelling in his mind. Its structure was still somewhat cloudy but he did write out a trial introductory chapter for the purpose of submitting it to an editor. Early in this year John Eglinton had founded a small periodical called *Dana: A Magazine of Independent Thought,* edited from 26 Dawson Chambers, Dawson Street, and to him Joyce went with his introductory chapter. Eglinton himself has described his reception of this proffered manuscript. "He observed me silently as I read," he wrote, "and when I handed it back to him with the timid observation that

I did not care to publish what was to myself incomprehensible, he replaced it silently in his pocket." Eglinton, however, did take one of the poems and Joyce managed to exact a small payment for it.

With the arrival of early summer (on June tenth, to be precise) an event of great and lasting importance happened to the young man, an event that put for the moment even his writing out of mind. He became acquainted with Nora Joseph Barnacle, a charming auburn-haired young woman from Galway who had recently ventured into the buzzing hive of Dublin to earn her way in life. She was neither literary-minded nor, it would seem, prepared to cope with the vagaries and temperament of an artist; yet her freshness, her humour, her joyous disposition, and her transparent honesty captivated Joyce and it was not long before he was completely in love with her. She, on her part, observed the erect blue-eyed writer with the arrogant self-assurance and, perhaps, not realizing what she had found or to what far journeyings the meeting would eventually lead her, reciprocated this love. With this encounter Joyce's life changed. The stews of Nighttown knew him no longer and the reckless cast of his days was subtly diverted to another end. He had passed his twenty-second birthday and the serious business of life, the difficult task of living in a world that would offer no help to the artist, loomed like some monstrous jinni out of the *Arabian Nights* before him.

It was a problem that would occupy his mind incessantly during the immediate months that followed. But, for the moment, he appears to have relished life in Dublin, to have explored it as a man who is half-conscious that he will never revisit old haunts again makes his final pilgrimages to the familiar places, recognizing them anew as enduring landmarks in a spiritual journey through time and subtly acknowledging their permanence in the intricate labyrinth of his art. What acute consciousness Joyce had of all this is problematical. One can but guess from the fragmentary testimonies of those who knew (or thought they knew) him at this crucial period of his life. The important fact remains that the Dublin of 1904 with all its monuments and peoples and unique contemporary atmosphere rested indelibly fixed in his mind and formed the background for nearly all the work that he was to do thereafter.

II

There is no evidence that anything unusual happened to Joyce six days after his first meeting with Nora Barnacle and yet he has so implanted the date of June 16, 1904 ("Bloomsday"), in the mind of the reading public that one may well pause and consider it for a moment. If Joyce dipped into the newspapers that day he discovered, first of all, breathless reports of the tragic sinking of the excursion steamer, *General Slocum,* in the East River with a great loss of life. The headlines fairly screamed:

### APPALLING AMERICAN DISASTER

EXCURSION STEAMER GENERAL SLOCUM ON FIRE
NEAR HELL GATE, EAST RIVER, N. Y. HARBOUR
500 LIVES LOST
WILD SCENES OF PANIC
CHILDREN THROWN OVERBOARD
WOMEN TRAMPLED TO DEATH

He learned, too, that the Russian Army under Lieutenant General Baron Stackelberg was retreating before the Japanese forces and that there were rumours the Nipponese had almost reached Port Arthur. In Paris the Roman Catholic sisters acting as nurses at the Invalides had been expulsed and replaced by lay nurses. And from Ascot came the results of the Coronation Stakes for three-year-old fillies:

Pretty Polly (W. Lane) ............... 1
Montem (H. Jones) ................... 2
Pieria (K. Cannon) ................. 3

Betting had been five to one on the winner.

As for Dublin itself, the news was slight. There were no explosions, sinkings, murders, or wars. The great summer sale of Todd Burns and Company ("Bargains in Every Department") was open. At the Dublin Stock Exchange a lady had applied for membership. The Committee would consider the application at an early date. In the Northern Police Court before Mr. Mahony, Mr. Gerald Byrne, Solicitor, applied for the transfer of the license of 5 and 6 North Strand Road from the name of Ellen Delany to that of Ellen

Walsh. The application became necessary owing to the marriage of the proprietress of the establishment. Mr. Mahony proved to be a humourist. *Vide:* Mr. Mahony: Did Mr. Walsh marry the public house? (Laughter.) Mr. Byrne: No, sir. He married the widow. Mr. Mahony: The solicitors and the clergy are getting all the publican's money. (Laughter.) At the Gaiety Theatre Mrs. Bannerman Palmer was announced in *Leah, the Forsaken;* at the Theatre Royal, Eugene Stratton, the World-Renowned Comedian; at the Queen's Theatre, the Elster-Grime Grand Opera Company in *The Lily of Killarney;* at the Empire-Palace, the Great Marie Kendall and Company; and at the Tivoli, the Mysterious Lilith, Greatest Sensation of Modern Times, with W. J. Churchill, comedian. The Norddeutscher Lloyd announced passages on its magnificent steamers to New York third class for two pounds and to Boston same class for two pounds thirteen and six.

Many things not recorded by the newspapers and of no apparent interest at all must have taken place under the young summer sun of the city. John Eglinton, sub-librarian of the National Library, undoubtedly traversed the short distance to the offices of *Dana.* A.E., bearded and in homespun tweeds and possibly pushing his bicycle, made his way either to that mausoleum of books guarded by Mr. Lyster or to the headquarters of the *Irish Homestead* to consult with Mr. Norman. A "touched" eccentric of many names ending in Farrell strode along Nassau Street bearing a sabre under his arm. Another eccentric, hurrying to nowhere, took meticulous care to pass outside all the lampposts as he traversed the city. Davy Byrne leaned over his bar in Duke Street and conversed with friends. The sporting fraternity placed bets on the outcome of the Ascot Gold Cup. John Stanislaus Joyce, breathing the ambient air with pleasure, strolled along O'Connell Street with, perhaps, his friend, little Alfred Bergan. British sentinels marched up and down at the gates to the Castle and before the Viceregal Lodge in Phœnix Park. Tugs from Messrs. A. Guinness, Sons and Company passed down the Liffey to the port. Cricket bats sounded from the Park of Trinity College. Through the portals of establishments on Grafton Street and Wisdom Hely's on Dame Street passed expectant shoppers and through the doors of Kiernan's and Conroy's and Burke's passed expectant drinkers. Two Irish-American visitors sought for the spot where

Robert Emmet was executed opposite St. Catherine's Church on Thomas Street. Afterward they would go on to Werburgh Street in The Liberties where Lord Edward Fitzgerald and his captor, Major Sirr, lay buried. A funeral cortège passed, carriage wheels squeaking and horses' hoofs ringing on the pavement stones, on its way to Glasnevin while male pedestrians paused and lifted their hats. In the National Maternity Hospital on Holles Street a doctor and nurses attended a difficult birth. A wedding party dismounted before St. Teresa's Church, Clarendon Street. An overrouged drab leaned out of a Purdon Street window and yawned. Before the Nelson Pillar the clanging tramcars shunted and started on their respective runs to Blackrock, Rathgar and Terenure, Ringsend, Harold's Cross and a dozen other places.

And through all this welter of life wandered Joyce, erect, in yachting cap, threadbare suit and tennis shoes, swinging his ashplant and registering the sights and sounds and smells and feel of the day like some delicately-adjusted machine. It was a day like all others and yet it was all days in one. The coigns of houses lined against the sky, the signs above the shops, the churches and banks and government buildings, the faces and voices and names of those who passed, the creaking gulls on the Liffey, the rumble of porter barrels, the gush of warm sour odour from drinking places, the coloured displays in the windows, the traffic of the roadways, all these multitudinous facets that made up Dublin and *was* the city had been captured and interned in the young man's capacious memory. He detested it, perhaps, but he was filled with it. It was as much a part of him as he was a part of Dublin. He would never forget it as he would never forget his own childhood and youth and, because this was so, memory—the thing seen and apprehended for what it was—would always play a great part in his art.

And so the day that was to be immortal in literature passed unvisited as yet by the dark padding ruminating figure of Leopold Bloom, canvasser of newspaper advertisements and most sympathetic of cuckolds.

As the summer drew toward its close Joyce was preparing himself for a new venture that had to do with art and yet nothing at all with writing. He had decided to compete in the Feis Ceoil, the Irish festival of music that was held in Dublin at annual intervals and always aroused a higher degree of interest and speculation than any other musical event in the lively capital. Worthy singers had emerged from the Féis Ceoil and Joyce, whose high clear tenor voice (typically Irish) had reached a technical excellence, mainly through a natural discipline and intuitional artistry, had, at the time, the sudden ambition to be one of them. He loved singing (after all, it was an hereditary accomplishment in his family) and there were moments when he even meditated making it his major career. The power of the voice, for him, ran close second to the power of the word. Each was an exalted revelation. After all, both powers were powers of expression, the communication of emotion, and through both powers he could liberate the eternal rhythms that swelled within him. Even so, one may speculate as to whether Joyce the concert tenor would ever have reached that significant completeness of *giving* that is so vast a part of Joyce the writer. That he never did become a professional singer is perhaps the answer. The world that he had within him could never have been communicated fully by the music of the voice.

Joyce was the last competitor to enter the Feis Ceoil of 1904, his registration being twenty-two in a group of contestants numbering twenty-two. He had received a few singing lessons from Benedetto Palmieri, professor for the voice in the Dublin Academy of Music, but the fees had been high and his almost chronic penniless state had forced him to relinquish this important coaching. Later he had gone to Vincent O'Brien, John McCormack's teacher, and gathered a few further hints on handling his voice. That was all. It was an inadequate preparation for an event that would theoretically bring together the best burgeoning voices in Ireland but Joyce possessed confidence in himself and his own natural artistic ability. Where the arts were concerned he was far from timid. He might have other timidities, might in fact be a curious amalgam of sensitive superstitions and nervous fears, but he was entirely unselfconscious when it came to those profound expressions that were liberated by musical notes and written words. Dogs he feared like the devil but critics he scorned; a clap of thunder would send him cowering into a windowless closet but the hisses or laughter of a multitude moved him not at all; the heave and toss of the ocean twisted his stomach with fright but a blind venture into an unknown foreign land hardly stirred his pulses. And so an appearance on the platform at the Feis Ceoil to sing with a voice that was largely self-trained aroused no nervousness in him. It was the expression of an art and as so a natural expression of himself.

The great day came. Luigi Denza, professor of singing at the London Academy of Music and composer, among other songs, of "Funiculi-Funicula," was the adjudicator. When it came Joyce's turn to sing he stepped forward and sang "Come, ye children," an air from Sir Arthur Sullivan's *The Prodigal Son*. It went well and was flatteringly received. Signor Denza opened his eyes with pleasure. Then followed a long farewell Irish melody and the rendition of this aroused a tumult of approbation. Signor Denza began to think of the Gold Medal. Joyce appeared to be on the verge of a triumph that might have vitally affected his career in years to come. But at that moment the ever-watchful Fate of the young man (who seems sometimes to have stepped backward in order to move forward) intervened. For his third effort Joyce was handed a sheet of music unknown to him and ordered to sing it at sight.[1] This seemed to the budding tenor a monstrously inartistic thing to do (much like asking a blindfolded sculptor to carve a statue) and, flatly refusing, he marched from the platform. He did not regard it as a test of the beauty of the voice or the musicianship of proper delivery to sing at sight. Preparation and awareness were essential qualities of all art. Denza, the adjudicator, somewhat bewilderedly (for he had been greatly impressed by Joyce's voice) delivered a speech praising number twenty-two's talent and announced regretfully that he would not be able to award the Gold Medal to the young man as he had failed to complete the required programme.

At the moment Joyce considered this a definite unjust setback and there followed a day or two of fuming while the disappointed contestant criticized the regulations of the Feis Ceoil in a rich blistering language that was a joy to his companions. However, an immediate sequel revealed to him that nothing had been lost at all, except, of course, the Gold Medal. He received a letter from Benedetto Palmieri, his former teacher, requesting a rendezvous.

---

[1] As a matter of fact, Joyce cannot read music well. He never could learn to play the piano from sheet music though he began to take lessons from a Mr. Haughton at Clongowes Wood College when he was a small lad. Many years later, in Trieste, he resumed study with Giulio Veneziani but he asked so many questions that the piano teacher gave up his difficult job in despair.

Joyce went. Palmieri, with astute Italian business logic, proceeded straight to the point. Denza, it seemed, had written to the professor of the Dublin Academy of Music and extolled in glowing terms the virtues and potentialities of Joyce's voice. Palmieri, therefore, had an offer to make. As long as Joyce possessed no money and small prospects of gaining any he (Palmieri) would teach the young man gratis for three years provided the young man would sign an agreement to turn over to the professor a certain per cent of his earnings as a singer during the first ten years of his professional career.

Palmieri was too late, for Joyce had already decided to leave Ireland.

The desire, like a hot iron, had been prodding him for a long time. His disaffection with Dubliners and Dublin, an aggravation of the spirit troubling him since the autumn of 1902 when his brief wild-goose flight to Paris had given him—despite his poverty—a tantalizing taste of a broader civilization, was now an incurable malady of the mind intensified by nearly all that he saw and heard. There was no stable place for him in Dublin. He did not fit into the untidy enthusiastic all-for-Kathleen-ni-Houlihan scheme of things and he was incapable of remoulding himself so that he might become an acquiescent part of it. He still distrusted enthusiasms. The renascent dramatic and literary movement that had already found a haven in the newly-organized Irish National Theatre (a coming to maturity, as it were, of the Yeats-Martyn-Moore Irish Literary Theatre) quite failed to carry him along on its ambient tide. Mr. Joseph Holloway might be planning already the reconstruction of the old theatre in Abbey Street with Miss A. E. F. Horniman's subsidy and W. B. Yeats might be busily assembling the casts for his own *The Countess Cathleen* and *On Baile's Strand,* Lady Augusta Gregory's *Spreading the News* and the dark tramper Synge's *In the Shadow of the Glen,* but Joyce's interest in it all was a scornful negative interest, an interest shot with disappointment and disdain. The Irish National Theatre was turning out exactly as he had feared and prophesied. Of course it would be successful and rouse the plaudits of the rabblement but that in itself would be its own damnation in the unflickering eyes of art. The young poetasters, A.E.'s brood of fledglings, who were so busily revising their manuscripts for Maunsel and Company, aroused not even a tepid interest in Joyce.

The novelists and essayists shrank to zero when measured by his precise definitions of what creative letters should be. As for the editors, he had already sampled them in his dealings with *Dana* and the *Irish Homestead* and found them to be as limited in the larger vision as was the entire literary movement.

There are spurious thinkers who might say that Joyce could have easily isolated himself from these particularities of a nationalistically-excited moment and attended to his own work in a seclusion that was impregnable. But there are no Thebäids in Ireland and even if there were Joyce was no anchorite. Neither are there any seclusions of the spirit that are impregnable. The parish priest sees to that. As a matter of fact, it was not the particularities that mattered, they were but the obvious results; it was the spirit, the general atmosphere, the civilization of Ireland itself that rose like a stone wall between Joyce and the æsthetic freedom that he demanded. From every side it pressed on the young man, seeking to stifle his independent will, striving to force him into a conformity that was an abnegation of himself, and endeavouring to net his soaring impulses with the traditions of years and the authorities of the masses. This invisible and practically omnipotent power was both forthright and insidious in its insistencies and persuasions. It spoke through the mouths of families and friends; the common gestures of living were animated by it; it flavoured and coloured the civilization it had captured and vanquished. It was from all this that Joyce desired to extricate himself and he knew that he would find his freedom only in flight. One cannot destroy a slave civilization any more than one can destroy the masters who have subdued it but one can evade it by stepping outside of it and so freeing one's self from its powerful impulsions. Joyce knew this. He did not want to live for Ireland (as Ireland was); he wanted Ireland to live for him (as its mythic substance was pictured in his mind). For that to happen he would have to go away and take his own Ireland (the real Ireland, perhaps) with him.

Feeling so about his native land could not but enlarge his desires and expectations of the great world that lay beyond the frontiers of Ireland. It was not England that he thought of (*that* was as stuffy and limited as the Emerald Isle) but Continental Europe, the Europe of Ibsen and Maeterlinck and d'Annunzio and Giacosa and Hauptmann where a man could write without being smothered by religious and social obligations and oppressions. Perhaps that great world was not quite so free as Joyce imagined but in comparison to his own land it appeared to be the very acme of liberation. It was an old saying that art was respected abroad whereas it was only tolerated in the British Isles and tolerated only if it conformed. That being so, exile for Joyce would really be a sort of coming home, at least an entrance into the spiritual domain whose air he had to breathe if he was to live. He was animated, then, during this autumn of 1904 by practically the same urges (though more maturely objectified by himself) that had driven him from Dublin in 1902. His aspirations were the same and his intended means of achieving them had not changed. This final period in Ireland had been but an unhappy interim, an arrestation by callous chance of a journey through time commenced two years before.

Besides his disgust with Ireland and his expectations of the larger world that lay beyond the waves of the English Channel there was a third element that was violently pushing him toward flight. It was Nora Barnacle, his present wife.

The first days of autumn discovered Joyce busily preparing for his second hegira from the land of his birth. The thin sheaf of poems that made up *Chamber Music* was placed in order and dispatched to Arthur Symons in London with a plea that he seek an English publisher for them. Symons, although his vogue was dimming in the plush complacencies of the Edwardian era, continued to remain a modest power in the London literary scene, and, as he had expressed some interest in Joyce's work, the young man experienced no hesitancy in calling upon him for aid. Symons immediately submitted the manuscript to a young publisher named Grant Richards. So much done, there remained the vital decision of where to go and how to live. Joyce, though impractical in many ways, was not foolish enough to imagine that Nora Barnacle and himself could exist on his problematical literary earnings. What were they, anyway? A few pounds, perhaps, from *Chamber Music,* provided it was immediately published, and a few pounds more from periodicals for the short stories—provided they were accepted. All the rest was in the realm of unachieved conceptions. There remained, then, the possibilities of some sort of hackwork, an uneventful drudgery that would keep body and soul together until the great days of recognition and royalties arrived. Journalism? Well, that was too uncertain. He had thought of that two years before in Paris and discovered that he was temperamentally unsuited for it, that, indeed, it was a way of slow inglorious death. He was absolutely incapable of writing anything that he did not believe or feel and what he believed and felt was not what the eminently safe and commercially-bulldozed journals of the post-Boer War era desired. Teaching, then? That sounded more practical. His excellent knowledge of modern languages stood him in good stead here and he had already acquired some brief experience. Such a grind might prove obnoxious to him but, at least, it did not conflict with his æsthetic ideals. But to teach one must secure a billet.

Where and how? At first Joyce conceived the idea of going to Sweden, to Stockholm, and settling there as a teacher of the English language. There was something fresh and invigorating in his conception of the Scandinavian air that called to him. The 'how' of his question settled that. The 'how,' of course, was an employment agency and the one to which he applied in England had no vacancies in Sweden. But it averred that it did have a post in the Berlitz School in Zurich. Joyce, really having no choice in the matter, decided that Switzerland would do and accelerated the preparations for his departure. There was clothing to be assembled (some of it secondhand) and money (a part of it borrowed) to be collected. The trial chapter and notes for *Stephen Hero* and the jottings for the short stories that would make up *Dubliners* were packed away in the young man's scanty luggage. There were a few farewells to be made. These were easy for Joyce sensed the lack of faith in his acquaintances and comrades and this, as always, heightened his arrogance and steeled his determination. John Eglinton was sure that he would come back begging to Dublin; J. Francis Byrne was certain that he would become a drunkard; Cosgrave, the "lecherous lynx," prophesied that he would develop into a nymphomaniac; Skeffington, the bearded, knickerbockered, stout reformer of society, averred that he had made the mistake of his life in the comrade he had chosen. All of them appeared to think that he was an obstinate creature with no sense of values (Dublin values, to be sure) leaping into the limitless void; none of them remembered the indomitable wings of Dedalus. Joyce's pugnacious jaw thrust forward. By God, he would show them all! In ten years' time he would give them a novel to talk about!

Joyce and Nora Barnacle left from the North Wall on the eighth day of October to seek a new world of their own.

# *Five*

THE young couple arrived in Paris on the tenth of October and drove in an open carriage from the imposing barracks of the Gare Saint-Lazare to the Gare de l'Est. As the horse trotted up the long crowded stretch of the Rue Lafayette, Joyce, seated beside his charming young companion and gazing out at the familiar colour of the French capital, people hurrying in all directions and cabs rattling to and fro, must have contrasted in his mind his present status with the bleak half-year that had ended eighteen months before when his father's succinct telegram had abruptly withdrawn him from the fringe of the Bohemian life of Paris. Then he had been unanchored, as it were, able to sail on whatever seas he chose, to venture any tempest, and to change his course at will. His only duty was towards his art, an onerous duty but one that disciplined all his senses. Now everything was different. He had assumed a responsibility that would inevitably change the entire course of his life. He was no longer the complete master of his destiny in so far as he would have to correlate another's with his own. He would be compelled to work now and work hard and not alone at that search for literary perfection that was the abiding passion of his days and nights. He would have to labour for bread, to accept the unwelcome drudgery of dull routine in a language school that two might not be hungry. He would have to create a world that would please a second person. What time would be left for creative writing? Not as much as he desired, perhaps, but yet sufficient to make the adventure worth while. He had announced to his companions in Dublin, companions, of course, who scoffed in the natural Irish fashion, that he would produce a great book, at least, a book that pleased *him,* in ten years' time. That would be in 1914. There was time to spare, then, time to venture upon the complications of a *ménage* and assume the responsibilities of living as well as the responsibilities of art. In spite of the scepticism of his friends he was sure that his instinct was a proper one. He would see to it that what had been ventured in passion would be vindicated by reason. He would prove himself a human being as well as an arrogant brain.

During this solitary day in Paris he found time to call upon his earlier benefactor, Dr. Jacques Rivière, and secure a small loan from him to augment the scanty sum that was carrying him and the choice of his heart into the dubious future. On the eleventh of the month the venturesome couple were in Zurich and settling themselves and their luggage in a modest third-rate hotel, the Gasthaus Hoffnung.[1] An immediate disappointment shocked Joyce into a grave recognition of the responsibilties he had so unthinkingly assumed. There was no position waiting for him in the Berlitz School. The employment agency that had dispatched him on this wild-goose chase was a swindle. What could he do? Return ignominiously to Dublin and admit defeat? Try to write for newspapers and endeavour to live the life of the impecunious free lance? He remembered Paris, those freezing months when he had starved for forty hours at a stretch, and shook his head. However, the director of the Berlitz School in Zurich, one Malacrida, had a better idea. He would query the various schools on the Continent for a possible vacancy while Joyce attended in Zurich and stretched his scanty means to cover as many days as possible. Joyce attended for three weeks.

In the meantime there was Zurich to be explored.

The wide lake rippled gently under fleecy-clouded skies and fresh autumn winds and sometimes there was a hint of winter, of icy rains and invisible snows in the fleeting gusts. Far away were the shining snow-capped peaks of mysterious mountains. Villages glimmered in the near distance as one gazed across the waters, Zollikon, Kilchberg, Erlenbach. One turned from the lake by the regal Hôtel Baur au Lac and sauntered back along the wide lime-tree-shaded Bahnhofstrasse where the shop windows winked luxury at the pedestrian and immediately before the pleased eyes lifted the congested congeries of the city dominated by the double towers of the Grossmünster and climbing to the high fringe of pine trees so soon to be covered with their white mantles of snow. The blue

---

[1] It is now called the Gasthaus Speer. Curiously enough, when the Joyce family returned there in 1915 this hotel bore the name Gasthaus Doeblin.

and white tramcars clattered by, their gongs sounding warning. The two rivers that split the town—the Limmat and the Sihl—coursed through the coloured quarters, snakelike and silent under the miniature bridges. From the bank of the Limmat rose the Shipfe, the old section, with its seventeenth-century houses parading toward the sky. Everywhere there was something to engage the eye, the Fraumünster, the Peterskirche, the white vision of the University, the Polytechnic, the Stadttheater. The streets were animated. On all sides passed the robust, self-confident Zurichers, arguing, laughing, marvellously certain of themselves. And for the imaginative mind of the scholar there were the memories of the mighty who had strode the streets of Zurich and found it a place to remember and love, Klopstock, Wieland, Goethe, Kleist, Pestalozzi, Keller and Richard Wagner.

Joyce experienced an almost immediate sympathy for Zurich. Perhaps even its remoteness from Roman Catholic Dublin enlarged its virtues. It pleased him. Its sweep and height seemed to give him room to breathe. Its delicate white wines warmed his palate and the Swiss-German language assuaged his ear. He regretted that there was no place for him in this active and desirable city for he felt that he could work here, that he could carry on with serenity the literary projects that were in his mind, the series of short stories to be called *Dubliners* and the novel, *Stephen Hero,* whose introductory chapter he had shown to John Eglinton so short a time before. But he was no longer the complete master of his own fate. There was another to consider and a livelihood to be won.

He was desperately low in funds when the director of the Berlitz School informed him that the long-sought vacancy had been located at last. It was in Trieste, an immediate city of the Austro-Hungarian Empire although its population was predominantly of Italian blood. There Joyce was to report to the Berlitz School and, presumably, begin his labours as a teacher of the English language. It was during the first week in November that the young couple started for the mysterious city. As the train chugged out of Zurich station Joyce must have sighed a little. Zurich had pleased him so much. But perhaps the day would come when he would live in Zurich again and live there for a long time, long enough, indeed, until the city became almost as familiar to him as his own Dublin.

The train rushed southward and after an interminable period halted in the station of what appeared to be a great city, surely the end of the strange new journey. The young couple dismounted from their compartment and made their way out of the station and into the streets. A puzzled inquiry brought them the disturbing information that they were in Laibach (now called Ljubljana) some seven hours from Trieste. The train they had deserted was already hooting its way through the darkness, for it was night, and there would be no more traffic for the south and Trieste until the dawn came. The two travellers crept into a near-by garden and remained there until the morning. There was an Observatory here and they watched and counted the stars, that great wheel of light that glowed above the mysterious city, and agreed that they were bright and glorious. The rich odour of autumnal earth suspired about them and they were not unhappy at all.

In the morning they continued their journey and this time they left the train in Trieste without making an error of place. But once in the strange streets they were in a quandary. Where would they find lodgings? Joyce had failed to provide himself with this information before he left Zurich. It was necessary that he do something immediately about it. Therefore, he deposited his worried partner in a garden opposite the station and started off to make inquiries. Reaching a small noisy café crowded with sailors he entered but no sooner had he asked his question than a squad of Austrian police drove up to the door and arrested everybody in the place, including Joyce himself. The sailors were British sailors being rounded up, as usual, by local police at the request of the commander of the visiting squadron, which was about to move on, and the police, hearing Joyce speak English, thought he was a naval deserter attempting a flight in civilian garb. The indignant sailors, on the other hand, were convinced that Joyce was a police spy sent after them when he responded to the officials in Italian. For a moment the situation seemed ugly. But after great argument, many explanations and the display of such identity papers as he carried the young man was reluctantly released and information as to possible habitations given him. Somewhat shaken by this unexpected experience he hurried back to the garden opposite the station. It was a perilous and disconcerting beginning and the young wanderers ventured rather timorously into the streets of what they thought would be their new home for a long period to come.

II

The lot of a Berlitz School teacher is an arduous one and in the case of a man like Joyce, whose interest in his teaching was only perfunctory, it proved to be a deadly boring grind. For a salary amounting to approximately eighty pounds a year he taught a heterogeneous group of people, ranging from counts and baronnesses to hard-headed Jewish commercials and stokers and cooks, a colloquial English calculated to carry them through English-speaking countries without serious linguistic mishaps. The objective always was immediate vocabulary and a minimum of grammatical drudgery. If Joyce, who regarded his teaching as no more than a disappointing but necessary interruption of his proper life, was sometimes dry and ironical with his bewildered students they do not appear to have liked him the less for that. As a matter of fact, despite his scorn for his routine he was extremely conscientious. His career as a teacher may be said to have really begun in Pola to which town he was sent very soon after he reported to the director of the Berlitz School in Trieste. There, settled in a chamber at Via Medolina, 7, he commenced the laborious task that was to continue until the thunders of the Great War deafened all ears to the niceties of language. This drudgery of teaching ran parallel with the composition of *Dubliners, A Portrait of the Artist as a Young Man, Exiles* and a good portion of *Ulysses*.

Pola, he decided, was a queer old place, but it possessed its virtue in that it brought him his first Italian friends. They were Alessandro Francini-Bruni, a young Florentine, and his recently-acquired wife. Francini-Bruni taught the official Tuscan to those students in the Berlitz School anxious to get rid of their harsh Triestine dialect. As he was a qualified critic of the Italian language it is interesting to note what he once said about Joyce's command of the tongue. "At that time [the first months in Pola] he spoke a rather odd Italian," Francini-Bruni declared, "an Italian covered with wounds and scabs. It was, in fact, a dead language, come to join the babel of living tongues."

Once settled in Pola the young man resumed his labours in what spare time he could grasp for himself on the literary ventures that his romantic flight from the North Wall had interrupted. The notebooks were unpacked and the ink bottle uncorked. The novel tentatively called *Stephen Hero* absorbed the larger part of his energies. It was to be (as has been pointed out before) an autobiographical book, a personal history, as it were, of the growth of a mind, his own mind, and his own intensive absorption in himself and what he had been and how he had grown out of the Jesuitical garden of his youth. He endeavoured to see himself objectively, to assume a godlike poise of watchfulness and observance over the small boy and youth he called Stephen and who was really himself. He recalled, not without nostalgia perhaps, the progressive steps of that youth's march towards maturity and piled up page after page of memories, of observant comment, of fastidious characterizations, always aiming towards his objective—the portrait of the artist as a young man. The notebook he had started in Paris was continued and in it he set down the unhesitating march towards that æsthetic upon which his art was based and which his hero was to enunciate. As, for instance:

Bonum est in quod tendit appetitus.

S. Thomas Aquinas.

The good is that towards the possession of which an appetite tends: the good is the desirable. The true and the beautiful are the most persistent orders of the desirable. Truth is desired by the intellectual appetite which is appeased by the most satisfying relations of the intelligible; beauty is desired by the æsthetic appetite which is appeased by the most satisfying relations of the sensible. The true and the beautiful are spiritually possessed; the true by intellection, the beautiful by apprehension, and the appetites which desire to possess them, the intellectual and æsthetic appetites, are therefore spiritual appetites. . . .

J.A.J. Pola, 7 XI 04.

Pulcera sunt quae visa placent.

S. Thomas Aquinas.

Those things are beautiful the apprehension of which pleases. Therefore beauty is that quality of a sensible object in virtue of which its apprehension pleases or satisfies the æsthetic appetite which desires to apprehend the most satisfying relations of the sensible. Now the act of apprehension involves at least two activities, the activity of cognition or simple perception and the activity of ~~consequent satisfaction~~ recognition. (If?) the activity of simple perception is like every other activity, itself pleasant (,?) every sensible object that has been apprehended can be said in the first place to have been and to be ~~beautiful~~ in a measure beautiful; and even the most hideous object can be said to have been and to be beautiful in so far as it has been apprehended. In regard then to that part of the act of apprehension which is called the activity of simple perception there is no sensible object which cannot be said to be in a measure beautiful.

With regard to the second part of the act of apprehension which is called the activity of recognition it may further be said that there is no activity of simple perception to which there does not succeed in whatsoever measure the activity of recognition. For by the activity of recognition is meant an activity of decision; and in accordance with this activity in all conceivable cases a sensible object is said to be satisfying or dissatisfying. But the activity of recognition is, like every other activity, itself pleasant and therefore every object that has been apprehended is secondly in whatsoever measure beautiful. Consequently even the most hideous object may be said to be beautiful for this reason as it is *a priori* said to be beautiful in so far as it encounters the activity of simple perception.

Sensible objects, however, are said conventionally to be beautiful or not for neither of the foregoing reasons but rather by reason of the nature, degree and duration of the satisfaction resulting from the apprehension of them and it is in accordance with these latter merely that the words 'beautiful' and 'ugly' are used in practical æsthetic philosophy. It remains then to be said that these words indicate only a greater or less measure of resultant satisfaction and that any sensible object, to which the word 'ugly' is practically applied, an object, that is, the apprehension of which results in a small measure of æsthetic satisfaction, is, in so far as its apprehension results in any measure of satisfaction whatsoever, said to be for the third time beautiful. . . .

J.A.J. Pola, 15 XI 04.

## The Act of Apprehension.

It has been said that the act of apprehension involves at least two activities—the activity of cognition or simple perception and the activity of recognition. The act of apprehension, however, in its most complete form involves three activities—the third being the activity of satisfaction.

By reason of the fact that these three activities are all pleasant themselves every sensible object that has been apprehended must be doubly and may be trebly beautiful. In practical æsthetic philosophy the epithets 'beautiful' and 'ugly' are applied with regard chiefly to the third activity, with regard, that is, to the nature, degree and duration of the satisfaction resultant from the apprehension of any sensible object and therefore any sensible object to which in practical æsthetic philosophy the epithet 'beautiful' is applied must be trebly beautiful, must have encountered, that is, the three activities which are involved in the act of apprehension in its most complete form. Practically then the quality of beauty in itself must involve three constituents to encounter each of these three activities. . . .

J.A.J. Pola. 16 XI 04.

It is to be hoped that some ambitious young student of æsthetics in one of the greater universities will, sooner or later, base a painstaking thesis on the æsthetic reasoning and development of the youthful James Joyce. In the notes set forth above and in *A Portrait of the Artist as a Young Man* there is plenty of material from which to work.

In this same early *cahier,* too, Joyce set down odd scraps, phrases and hints for the novel and they reveal so clearly the widely-searching antennæ of the creator exploring for precisions and motives that a selection from them should be set down here, affording the reader a behind-the-scenes peep, as it were, into the artist's intimate workshop.

Greek culture (Iliad) Barbarian (Bible)

Spiritual and temporal power
Priests and police in Ireland

Catacombs and vermin
La Suggestione Letteraria

Ireland—an afterthought of Europe

Beauty is so difficult

I once saw a bleeding Christ—(W. Yeats) quoting Beardsley

Old Murray and Dante
'Miss Esposito, I never see a rose but I think of you.'
'I got the highest marks in mathematics of any man that ever went
   in.'

'Ah, Paris? What's Paris? The theatres, the cafés, *les petites femmes des boulevards.*'
Ladies' bonnets. High mass at the Pro-Cathedral.
Signs of Zodiac. Earth a living being.
'The English have their music-hall songs but we have the melodies.'
Moments of spiritual life.
'That queer thing—genius.'
'Synge's play is Greek,' said Yeats, etc.
'With all his eccentricities he remains a dear fellow.'
Dr. Doherty and the Holy City

---

Strangers are contemporary posterity—Chamfort.

The artillery of heaven
Mrs. Riordan and the breadcrumbs
Spittin' and spattin' on the floor
Consumatum est
Dog an' divil
Make death a capital offence in England; end of modern English plays; Fr. Delaney.
'Yisterday' F. Butt Moloney (Clery)
Kinahan and Boccaccio
Kinahan Enc. Britt. 'Socialism'
The ice-cream Italian—Rossetti
The marsupials
Art has the gift of tongues
'Special reporter' novels

'on our side every time'
centripetal writing
every bond is a bond to sorrow
With men women do not think independantly
What is the ambition of the hero's valet?
Love—an intimate, desirous dependance.
Church calls it a low vice to serve the body, to make a God of the belly, and a high virtue to make a temple of it.
The egoist revenges himself on his loves for the restrictions his higher morality lays upon him.
Unlike Saul, the son of Kish, Tolstoy seems to have come out to find a kingdom and to have found his father's asses.

Coyne: Beauty is a white light.
Joyce: Made up of seven colours.

Coyne and religious landscape
"The blanket with the hole in the middle was not the dress of the
    ancient Irish but was introduced by the indecent Saxon."
Shakespeare, Sophocles and Ibsen
Walshe didn't know how anyone could know more about Ibsen
    than F. Butt did.
Starkey thinks Ibsen's mind a chaos. "Hedda should get a kick in
    the arse."
I am unhappy all day—the cause is I have been walking on my heels
    not from the ball of my foot.
The music-hall, not Poetry, a criticism of life.
The vulgarian priest

————————

### Byrne

Features of the Middle Age: a pale, square, large-boned face, an
    aquiline nose with wide nostrils rather low in his face, a tight-
    shut lifeless mouth, full of prejudice, brown eyes set wide apart
    under short thick eyebrows and a long narrow forehead with
    short coarse black hair brushed up off it resting on his temples
    like an iron crown.
The Grand Byrne.
Wicklow.
Brutal 'bloody' 'flamin''
Thomas Squaretoes
Talking like a pint
Deprecate eke so
Did that bloody boat the Seaqueen ever start?
Immoral plebeian
His Intensity The Sea-green Incorruptible
to make me drink
Stannie takes off his hat

There was a page, too, devoted to notes for the series of short
stories he was writing.

### For 'Dubliners'

High instep
Foretelling rain by pain of corns

'the world will not willingly let die'
'which, if anything that the hand of man has wrought of noble and
    inspiring and beautiful deserves to live deserves to live'
'that way madness lies'
The United States of Europe
Sick and indigent roomkeepers
Logue: a handsome face in repose
Lightning: a livid woundlike flash
God plays skittles: thunder
Tips: palm-oil
To scoff—to devour
Medieval artist—lice in a friar's beard
The cold flesh of priests
A woman is a fruit
Paris—a lamp for lovers hung in the wood of the world
To take the part of England and her tradition against Irish-America
Mac—Be Jaze, that put the kybosh on me

---

### S. D.

Six medical students under my direction will write Paradise Lost
    except 100 lines.
The editor of the Evening Telegraph will write the Sensitive Plant
    Hellenism—European appendicitis.

And during this short period in Pola he wrote the fourth story
in that series. He called it "Hallow Eve" but when it was finally
published it appeared under the title of "Clay."

At the same time he gave himself some bitter amusement in
concocting a satiric attack on his Dublin contemporaries that was
compact with all the arrogance of his scornful youth. He had it
printed as a broadside and dispatched to all the victims mentioned
in it. It was called "The Holy Office."

> Myself unto myself will give
> This name, Katharsis-Purgative.
> I, who dishevelled ways forsook
> To hold the poets' grammar-book,
> Bringing to tavern and to brothel
> The mind of witty Aristotle,
> Lest bards in the attempt should err

Must here be my interpreter:
Wherefore receive now from my lip
Peripatetic scholarship.
To enter heaven, travel hell,
Be piteous or terrible,
One positively needs the ease
Of plenary indulgences.
For every true-born mysticist
A Dante is, unprejudiced,
Who safe at ingle-nook, by proxy,
Hazards extremes of heterodoxy,
Like him who finds a joy at table,
Pondering the uncomfortable.
Ruling one's life by commonsense
How can one fail to be intense?
But I must not accounted be
One of that mumming company—
With him who hies him to appease
His giddy dames' frivolities
While they console him when he whinges
With gold-embroidered Celtic fringes—
Or him who sober all the day
Mixes a naggin in his play—
Or him whose conduct "seems to own"
His preference for a man of "tone"—
Or him who plays the ragged patch
To millionaires in Hazelpatch
But weeping after holy fast
Confesses all his pagan past—
Or him who will his hat unfix
Neither to malt nor crucifix
But show to all that poor-dressed be
His high Castilian courtesy—
Or him who loves his Master dear—
Or him who drinks his pint in fear—
Or him who once when snug abed
Saw Jesus Christ without his head
And tried so hard to win for us
The long-lost works of Eschylus.
But all these men of whom I speak
Make me the sewer of their clique.

That they may dream their dreamy dreams
I carry off their filthy streams
For I can do those things for them
Through which I lost my diadem;
Those things for which Grandmother Church
Left me severely in the lurch.
Thus I relieve their timid arses,
Perform my office of Katharsis.
My scarlet leaves them white as wool.
Through me they purge a bellyful.
To sister mummers one and all
I act as vicar-general,
And for each maiden, shy and nervous,
I do a similar kind service.
For I detect without surprise
That shadowy beauty in her eyes,
The "dare not" of sweet maidenhood
That answers my corruptive "would."
Whenever publicly we meet
She never seems to think of it;
At night when close in bed she lies
And feels my hand between her thighs
My little love in light attire
Knows the soft flame which is desire.
But Mammon places under ban
The uses of Leviathan
And that high spirit ever wars
On Mammon's countless servitors,
Nor can they ever be exempt
From his taxation of contempt.
So distantly I turn to view
The shamblings of that motley crew,
Those souls that hate the strength that mine has
Steeled in the school of old Aquinas.
Where they have crouched and crawled and prayed
I stand, the self-doomed, unafraid,
Unfellowed, friendless and alone,
Indifferent as the herring-bone,
Firm as the mountain-ridges where
I flash my antlers on the air.
Let them continue as is meet

To adequate the balance-sheet.
Though they may labour to the grave
My spirit shall they never have
Nor make my soul with theirs as one
Till the Mahamanvantara be done:
And though they spurn me from their door
My soul shall spurn them evermore.

With such labours as these Joyce filled the larger part of his spare time; yet he found opportunity, too, to enjoy the lighter and more frivolous side of life. Though non-committal and averse to giving himself to strangers he was always willing to unloosen his 'talktapes' with friends and intimate acquaintances. There were joyous dinners with the Francini-Brunis, much drinking of light wines and even the extravagance of a trip on the little steamer to the Island of Brioni. He was in a light-hearted country where every tiny feast was enlarged into a holiday and he relished that way of living. For the time being he was comparatively light-hearted, too, taking his colour from his surroundings. His work seemed to march and his material necessities were sufficiently satisfied. Though he was not living like a king neither was he living like a poor student of the humanities in Paris. True enough, his book of verse did not seem to travel rapidly towards the printing press. Impatient at the delay and hearing from Arthur Symons that Grant Richards was in bankruptcy he dispatched a note to that publisher.

7 via Medolina,
Pola, Austria.

The Manager,
Grant Richards,
London.

DEAR SIR,

I wrote to you at the beginning of October last from Dublin asking you to let me know what you had decided to do with the book of my verses ("Chamber Music") which Mr. Arthur Symons gave you to consider and in reply I received a card from you saying that you would let me know definitely in a day or two. May I ask you to tell me by return whether you intend to print them or not and, in case you do not intend to print them, to send them to me without delay as I want to try and publish them somewhere as soon as possible and I have already refused to accept the offer of another publishing firm because I thought there was a prospect of your bringing the book out.

Faithfully yours,

JAS A JOYCE.

16 January 1905

Grant Richards eventually replied:

I must apologize for not having sooner answered your letter with reference to the MS. of your verses. I regret to say that it is not at present possible for me to make any arrangements for the publication of the book, but I may say that I admire the work exceedingly and if you would leave the matter open for a few weeks it is possible that I might then be able to make you some offer. The MS. I regret to say has been packed up by some mistake with some furniture of mine that has been warehoused and it is not easy for me at the moment to get at it so that in any case I shall be glad if you can leave the whole question over for a short time.

Even this did not dispirit the young man too much. He had yet to be weakened by the slow torture of the procrastination of publishers.

III

Early in March 1905, Joyce was recalled to Trieste where a position similar to the one he held in Pola awaited him in the Berlitz School at Via S. Nicolò, 32. He secured living quarters at Piazza Ponterosso, 3 III. and settled down to his sedentary labours. He would have to work harder than ever now for he had known for some time that he would be a father by midsummer. With the promptitude of most expectant fathers he had already selected two names for the newcomer. If it were a boy he would call him George after his brother who had died at an early age; if it were a girl he would call her Lucy.

Time now marched fast. The pile of manuscript called *Stephen Hero* grew mightily. New stories for *Dubliners* were sketched out and then written. And he dove into the variegated life of Trieste with the pleasure of a dolphin diving in familiar waters. Every aspect of the city seemed to please him, the picturesque life along the quays, the diverse ways of the Città Vecchia with their wine-shops and cheap restaurants, the oxcarts rumbling through the streets, the constant processions when red blankets hung out of windows and candles glimmered behind them, the Albanians in native costumes and the brilliantly shawled women—for none of them wore hats—leaving the theatres, the countless barrels of coffee outside the shops and their rich odour impregnating the air, the giant watermelons piled in the squares and the lights flaring on their crimson succulence until two or three o'clock in the morning, the Sunday loiterers playing bowls or *mora,* the carnival masks crowding the streets on Shrove Tuesday, the nutria caps and fur coats and coloured collars and silk shawls passing on all sides, the side-whiskered image of the Emperor Franz Joseph in white tunic adorning every tobacco shop, the huge powdered beadle at the Opera who bawled for carriages and the three opera seasons themselves— the Christmas and Carnival season at the Teatro Communale and the summer season in the open-air theatre and the autumn season at the Politeama, the excited jabber of buyers and sellers in the markets for there were no set prices, the smell of fish and the sight of sea spiders cooked in their shells, the innumerable taverns bearing Christian names and, above all, the Triestines, charitable, witty, irreligious, sceptical, fond of cakes and the black wine of Istria and the fortified *vin rosé*—the Opollo from Lissa. Even the 'bora,' that dreadful wind that blew so fiercely through the town that ropes had to be stretched across the streets to aid pedestrians, fascinated him as one of the irresistible phenomena of nature. Many years later he remarked to a friend: "I cannot begin to give you the flavour of the old Austrian Empire. It was a ramshackle affair but it was charming, gay, and I experienced more kindnesses in Trieste than ever before or since in my life . . . Times past cannot return but I wish they were back."

If, however, the town with its multiple attractions pleased him, so much could not be said for his personal life. Despite the ground he had covered (and in July he was enumerating what he had achieved in a letter to his brother Stanislaus—". . . in these nine months I have begotten a child, written 500 pages of my novel, written three of my stories, learned German and Danish fairly well, besides discharging the intolerable (to me) duties of my position and swindling two tailors") he was increasingly dissatisfied with

his place in time. He was impatient with what he regarded as the
sluggishness of the tide that was carrying him on. And he became
suspicious and sensitive at what he was convinced was the scornful rudeness of people observing the condition of his partner in
life. Indeed, it became necessary for him to change lodgings once
or twice and finally he moved into the household of a Jew, Moisè
Canarutto, next door to the Berlitz School. It was from this place,
Via S. Nicolò, 30, that he walked one day early in July across
Trieste and into the adjoining wood.

The damned monotonous summer was over [he wrote to his brother]
and the rain and soft air made me think of the beautiful (and I am serious) climate of Ireland! I hate a damn silly sun that makes men into
butter. I sat down miles away from everybody on a bench surrounded
by tall trees. The Bora (the Trieste wind) was roaring through the tops
of the trees. I sniffed up all the fragrance of the earth and offered up
this following prayer (not identical with that which Renan offered upon
the Acropolis):
'O. Vague Something behind everything.
For the love of the Lord Christ change my curse-o'-God state of affairs.
   Give me for Christ's sake a pen and an ink-bottle and some peace
   of mind, and then, by the crucified Jaysus, if I don't sharpen that
   little pen and dip it into fermented ink and write tiny little sentences about the people who betrayed me, send me to hell. After all,
   there are many ways of betraying people. It wasn't only the Galilean
   suffered that. Whoever the hell you are, I inform you that this is a
   poor comedy you expect me to play and I'm damned to hell if I'll
   play it for you. What do you mean by urging me to be forbearing?
   For your sake I refrained from taking a little black fellow from
   Bristol by the nape of the neck and hurling him into the street when
   he spat some of his hatched venom at me. But my heroic nature
   urged me to do this because he was smaller than I. For your sake
   I allowed a cyclist to use towards me his ignoble and cowardly manners, pretending to see nothing, pretending that he was my equal.
   I sorrowfully confess to you, old chap, that I was a damn fool. But
   if you will only grant that thing I ask you for I will go to Paris
   where I believe there is a person by the name of Anatole France
   much admired by a Celtic philologist by the name of Goodbetterbest
   and I'll say to him, "Respected master, is this pen pointed enough?"
   Amen.'

On Thursday the twenty-seventh of July at nine o'clock in the evening Joyce's first child was born and the excited father received his first felicitations from the aged Jewish aunt of Canarutto who approached him smiling and nodding and saying, *"Xe un bel maschio, signore."*

During this period Joyce's state of mind was not improved by the misfortunes of *Chamber Music*. Grant Richards could not publish the verses (in the near future, anyway) unless the author furnished part of the money. Both Heinemann and T. Fisher Unwin flatly refused the book. A short story, "Hallow Eve" ("Clay"), was rejected by the *Literary World*. All this exasperated the young man and increased his restlessness. Pictures of Ireland, of Dublin, constantly flashed through his mind and he desired someone who knew his native city as intimately as he did as a companion for walks and conversations. He thought instinctively of his brother Stanislaus with whom he possessed so much in common and to whom he had written so many letters concerning his ambitions, hardships and disappointments. It would be a splendid thing to have Stanislaus with him in Trieste for Stanislaus was intelligent and sensitive and endowed with a goodly measure of artistic perception. So as the summer passed Joyce broached this matter to his brother and, receiving a favorable response, set about to make it possible. The way for the advent of Stanislaus was cleared when one of the Berlitz School teachers, who had quarrelled with the director, was discharged. The vacant place was offered through Joyce to his brother and on October 24, 1905, Stanislaus left Dublin and arrived in Trieste a few days later. He was not yet twenty-one years of age but he was quite equipped to act as an adequate foil to Joyce's restlessly-darting mind. With him he brought the aroma and paradoxical temperament of the city by the Liffey, its gossip and irony, its sudden flares of temper and bursts of laughter and mischievous ridicule and exaggeration. At last, Joyce had someone with whom to converse in the way that he desired to converse.

IV

By November Joyce had completed the twelve stories that made up his scheme of *Dubliners* and on December 3, 1905, he sent the manuscript to Grant Richards who appears to have partially extricated himself from the toils of bankruptcy. But before this, on October fifteenth, he had written to that unpredictable publisher:

Via S. Nicolò, 30.

DEAR MR. GRANT RICHARDS,

Mr. Symons wrote to me saying that Messrs Constable and Company, to whom he had spoken of me, had invited me to send them the MS. of my two books. Accordingly I made a copy of 'Chamber Music' and sent it to them today. I am not sure whether you will think this act of mine discourteous but I hardly know what to do. I think you had better keep my verses as it is most probable that Messrs Constable and Company will refuse the book.

The second book which I have ready is called 'Dubliners.' It is a collection of twelve short stories. It is possible that you would consider it to be of a commercial nature. I would gladly submit it to you before sending it to Messrs Constable, and, if you could promise to publish it soon, I would gladly agree. Unfortunately I am in such circumstances that it is necessary for me to have either of the books published as soon as possible.

I do not think that any writer has yet presented Dublin to the world. It has been a capital of Europe for thousands of years, it is supposed to be the second city of the British Empire and it is nearly three times as big as Venice. Moreover, on account of many circumstances which I cannot detail here, the expression Dubliner seems to me to bear some meaning and I doubt whether the same can be said for such words as 'Londoner' and 'Parisian,' both of which have been used by writers as titles. From time to time I see in publishers' lists announcements of books on Irish subjects, so that I think people might be willing to pay for the special odour of corruption which, I hope, floats over my stories.

Faithfully yours

JAS A JOYCE.

The young man's history, so far as it concerns the world, becomes from now on the history of *Dubliners*. He had his brother with him, he had his young son to observe, he had his routine at the Berlitz School, he had the *vie mouvementée* of Trieste, and, eventually, he had a house of his own (shared with the Francini-Brunis) at Via Giovanni Boccaccio, 1, on the outskirts of the Italo-Austrian city and all of this was good in so far as it fortified his ambitions as a creative artist. To follow his progress now one must follow the series of letters he wrote to Grant Richards and find reflected in them the struggle of the artist against prejudice, against compromise, against the shoddinesses and hesitations of the British bourgeoisie. Let us start with a letter written on February 28, 1906. Joyce had just received a letter of acceptance for *Dubliners* from the British publisher.

> Via Giovanni Boccaccio, 1.
> Trieste, Austria.

DEAR MR. GRANT RICHARDS,

I hardly know what you wish me to write as a description of the book. I sketched it for you in former letters but perhaps you want a complete description. The only thing I could think of was to ask my brother to write a short account of the book and this I now enclose you. It expresses my aim very well and you are free to use it as well as any notice of your own which seems to you suitable. Naturally you know better than I what is needed.

As for the appearance of the book I am content to leave it to your judgement. I have no books here to select from my library being composed mainly of bundles of old letters. I would not like the book to be too slim in form. If you send me in your reply to this details of, say, two styles of binding I will choose one of them. On one point I would wish you to be careful. I would like the printer to follow the manuscript accurately in punctuation and arrangement. Inverted commas, for instance, to enclose dialogue always seemed to me a great eyesore.

I doubt if June would be a good time to publish the book. I would prefer some date early in May, or, if that is not possible, September.

You have asked me to tell you what I am doing and what my prospects are. I am an English teacher here in a Berlitz School. I have been here for sixteen months during which time I have achieved the delicate task of living and of supporting two other trusting souls on a salary of £80 a year. I am employed to teach young men of this city the English language as quickly as possible with no delays for elegance and receive in return tenpence for every sixty minutes so spent. I must not omit to mention that I teach also a baroness.

My prospects are the chance of getting money enough from my book or books to enable me to resume my interrupted life. I hope these details will not bore you as much as they bore me. In any case, I give them to you only because you have asked for them.

I return you the contract signed by me. I hope you will write to me as soon as possible so that the date of the appearance and form of the book may be soon agreed on. I have sent you a story *Two Gallants* and propose adding one more story to the book. I have written part of it and can promise that it will be ready during March.

Faithfully yours

JAS A JOYCE.

In another letter, written on the thirteenth of March, Joyce acknowledges receipt of the signed contract from Grant Richards and also describes the size of *Stephen Hero*.

Via Giovanni Boccaccio, 1.
Trieste, Austria.

DEAR MR. GRANT RICHARDS,

I am obliged to you for your letter and copy of the contract. If *Dubliners* cannot be published in May I should prefer September. I shall send you in a week or so the last story which is to be inserted between *The Boarding House* and *Counterparts* so that you may proceed with the printing of the book. Being a first offender I cannot judge of the financial prospects of my book of stories. It seems to me, however, that if it had any sale in England you might perhaps be able to arrange an edition for America where there are some fifteen millions of my countrymen.

You suggest I should write a novel in some sense autobiographical. I have already written a thousand pages of such a novel, as I think I told you, 914 pages to be accurate. I calculate that these twenty-five chapters, about half of the book, run into 150,000 words. But it is quite impossible for me in present circumstances to think the rest of the book much less to write it. . . .

I shall be glad to hear from you when you have decided in what form you will bring out *Dubliners*.

Faithfully yours

JAS A JOYCE

One would think that with the contracts signed, the obvious approval of the publisher for the book and the unmistakable quality of the work itself that the way was clear for the publication of *Dubliners*. It is possible that Joyce thought so for a few weeks. But there was an antagonist with whom he had not thought to cope, the British Philistine, that last bulwark of mediocrity in a world that was rushing into the future. The British Printer raised his Moral Thumb, blew his Moral Nose and lifted his Moral Eyebrows. Joyce's letter of May fifth explains all.

Via Giovanni Boccaccio, 1.
Trieste, Austria.

Dear Mr. Grant Richards,

I am sorry you do not tell me why the printer, who seems to be the barometer of English opinion, refuses to print *Two Gallants* and makes marks in the margin of *Counterparts*. Is it the small gold coin in the former story or the code of honour which the two gallants live by which shocks him? I see nothing which should shock him in either of these things. His idea of gallantry has grown up in him (probably) during the reading of the novels of the elder Dumas and during the performance of romantic plays which presented to him cavaliers and ladies in full dress. But I am sure he is willing to modify his fantastic views. I would strongly recommend to him the chapters wherein Ferrero examines the moral code of the soldier and (incidentally) of the gallant. But it would be useless for I am sure that in his heart of hearts he is a militarist.

He has marked three passages in *Counterparts:*

'a man with two establishments to keep up, of course he couldn't . . .'

'Farrington said he wouldn't mind having the far one and began to smile at her . . .'

'She continued to cast bold glances at him and changed the position of her legs often; and when she was going out she brushed against his chair and said "Pardon," in a Cockney accent . . .'

His marking of the first passage makes me think that there is priestly blood in him: the scent for immoral allusions is certainly very keen here. To me this passage seems as childlike as the reports of divorce cases in *The Standard*. Or, is it possible that this same printer (or maybe some near relative of his) will read (nay more, actually collaborate in) that solemn journal which tells its readers not merely that Mrs. So and So misconducted herself with Captain So and So but even how often she misconducted herself with him. The word 'establishment' is surely as inoffensive as the word 'misconducted.'

It is easier to understand why he has marked the second passage, and evident why he has marked the third. But I would refer him again to that respectable organ the reporters of which are allowed to speak of such intimate things as even I, a poor artist, have but dared to suggest. O one-eyed printer! Why has he descended with his blue pencil, full of the Holy Ghost, upon these passages and allowed his companions to set up in type reports of divorce cases and ragging scenes and cases of criminal assault—reports, moreover, which are to be read by an 'inconveniently large section of the general public'?

There remains his final objection to the word 'bloody.' I cannot know, of course, from what he derives the word or whether, in his plain blunt way, he accepts it as it stands. In the latter case his objection is absurd and in the former case (if he follows the only derivation I have heard for it) it is strange that he should object more strongly to a profane use of the name of the Virgin than to a profane use of the name of God. Where is his English Protestantism? I myself can bear witness that I have seen in modern English print such expressions as 'by God' and 'damn.' Some cunning Jesuit must have tempted our stout Protestant from the path of righteousness that he defends the honour of the Virgin with such virgin ardour.

As for my part and share in the book I have already told you all I have to tell. My intention was to write a chapter of the moral history of my country and I chose Dublin for the scene because that city seemed to me the centre of paralysis. I have tried to present it to the indifferent public under four of its aspects: childhood, adolescence, maturity and public life. The stories are arranged in this order. I have written it for the most part in a style of scrupulous meanness and with the conviction that he is a very bold man who dares to alter in the presentment, still more to deform, whatever he has seen and heard. I cannot do any more than this. I cannot alter what I have written. All these objections of which the printer is now the mouthpiece arose in my mind when I was writing the book, both as to the themes of the stories and their manner of treatment. Had I listened to them I would not have written the book. I have come to the conclusion that I cannot write without offending people. The printer denounces *Two Gallants* and *Counterparts*. A Dubliner would denounce *Ivy Day in the Committee Room*. The more subtle inquisitor will denounce *An Encounter,* the enormity of which the printer cannot see because he is, as I said, a plain blunt man. The Irish priest will denounce *The Sisters*. The Irish boarding-house keeper will denounce *The Boarding-House*. Do not let the printer imagine, for goodness sake, that he is going to have all the barking to himself.

I can see plainly that there are two sides to the matter but unfortunately I can occupy only one of them. I will not fall into the error of suggesting to you which side you should occupy but it seems to me that you credit the printer with too infallible a knowledge of the future. I know very little of the state of English literature at present nor do I know whether it deserves or not the eminence which it occupies as the laughing-stock of Europe. But I suspect that it will follow the other countries of Europe as it did in Chaucer's time. You have opportunities

to observe the phenomenon at close range. Do you think that *The Second Mrs. Tanqueray* would not have been denounced by a manager of
the middle Victorian period, or that a publisher of that period would
not have rejected a book by George Moore or Thomas Hardy? And if a
change is to take place I do not see why it should not begin now.

You tell me in conclusion that I am endangering my future and your
reputation. I have shown you earlier in the letter the frivolity of the
printer's objections and I do not see how the publication of *Dubliners*
as it now stands in manuscript could possibly be considered an outrage
on public morality. I am willing to believe that when you advise me not
to persist in the publication of stories such as those you have returned
to me you do so with a kind intention towards me; and I am sure you
will think me wrong-headed in persisting. But if the art were any other,
if I were a painter and my book were a picture you would be less ready
to condemn me for my wrong-headedness if I refused to alter certain
details. These details may now seem to you unimportant but if I took
them away *Dubliners* would seem to me like an egg without salt. In
fact, I am somewhat curious to know what, if these and similar points
have been condemned, has been admired in the book at all?

I see now that my letter is becoming nearly as long as my book. I
have touched on every point you raise in order to give you reason for
the faith that is in me. I have not, however, said what a disappointment
it would be to me if you were unable to share my views. I do not speak
so much of a material as of a moral disappointment. But I think I could
more easily reconcile myself to such a disappointment than to the thousand little regrets and self-reproaches which would certainly make me
their prey afterwards.

Believe me, dear Mr. Grant Richards,

Faithfully yours,

Jas A Joyce.

On May thirteenth, having received an unsatisfactory reply
from Grant Richards, Joyce continued his self-defence.

Via Giovanni Boccaccio, 1.
Trieste, Austria.

Dear Mr. Grant Richards,

I am sorry that in reply to my letter you have written one of so
generalizing a character. I do not see how you can expect me to agree
with you about the impossibility of publishing the book as it is. Your
statement that no publisher could issue such a book seems to me some-

what categorical. You must not imagine that the attitude I have taken up is in the least heroic. The fact is I cannot see much reason in your complaints.

You complain of *Two Gallants,* of a passage in *Counterparts* and of the word 'bloody' in *Grace*. Are these the only things that prevent you from publishing the book? To begin at the end: the word 'bloody' occurs in that story twice in the following passage:

'At dinner, you know. Then he has a bloody big bowl of cabbage before him on the table and a bloody big spoon like a shovel, etc.'

This I could alter, if you insist. I see no reason for doing so but if this point alone prevented the book from being published I could put another word instead of 'bloody.' But this word occurs elsewhere in the book in *Ivy Day in the Committee-Room,* in *The Boarding-House,* in *Two Gallants:*

'And one night, man, she brought me two bloody fine cigars, etc.'
                                                          *Two Gallants.*

'Here's this fellow come to the throne after his bloody owld mother keeping him out of it till the man was grey, etc.'
                                    *Ivy Day in the Committee-Room.*

'. . . if any fellow tried that sort of a game on with his sister he'd bloody well put his teeth down his throat, so he would . . .'
                                              *The Boarding-House.*

The first passage I could alter. The second passage (with infinite regret) I could alter by omitting the word simply. But the third passage I absolutely could not alter. Read *The Boarding-House* yourself and tell me frankly what you think. The word, the exact expression I have used, is in my opinion the one expression in the English language which can create on the reader the effect which I wish to create. Surely you can see this for yourself? And if the word appears once in the book it may as well appear three times. Is it not ridiculous that my book cannot be published because it contains this one word which is neither indecent nor blasphemous?

The objections raised against *Counterparts* seem to me equally trivial. Is it possible that at this age of the world in the country which the ingenuous Latins are fond of calling 'the home of liberty' an allusion to 'two establishments' cannot appear in print or that I cannot write the phrase 'she changed the position of her legs often'? To invoke the name of *Areopagitica* in this connection would be to render the artist as absurd as the printer.

You say it is a small thing I am asked to do, to efface a word here and there. But do you not see clearly that in a short story above all such effacement may be fatal? You cannot say that the phrases objected to are gratuitous and impossible to print and at the same time approve of the tenor of the book. Granted this latter as legitimate I cannot see how anyone can consider these minute and necessary details illegitimate. I must say that these objections seem to me illogical. Why do you not object to the theme of *An Encounter,* to the passage 'he stood up slowly saying that he had to leave us for a few minutes, etc. . . . '? Why do you not object to the theme of *The Boarding-House?* Why do you omit to censure the allusions to the Royal Family, to the Holy Ghost, to the Dublin Police, to the Lord Mayor of Dublin, to the cities of the plain, to the Irish Parliamentary Party, etc.? As I told you in my last letter I cannot understand what has been admired in the book at all if these passages have been condemned. What would remain of the book if I had to efface everything which might give offence? The title, perhaps.

You must allow me to say that I think you are unduly timid. There is nothing 'impossible' in the book, in my opinion. You will not be prosecuted for publishing it. The worst that will happen, I suppose, is that some critic will allude to me as the 'Irish Zola.' But even such a display of the critical intellect should not be sufficiently terrible to deter you from bringing out the book. I am not, as you may suppose, an extremely business-like person but I confess I am puzzled to know why all these objections were not raised at first. When the contract was signed I thought everything was over: but now I find I must plunge into a correspondence which, I am afraid, tends only to agitate my nerves.

The appeal to my pocket has not much weight with me. Of course I would gladly see the book in print and of course I would like to make money by it. But, on the other hand, I have very little intention of prostituting whatever talent I may have to the public. (This letter is not for publication.) I am not an emissary from a War office testing a new explosive or an eminent doctor praising a new medicine or a sporting cyclist riding a new make of bicycle or a renowned tenor singing a song by a new composer: and therefore the appeal to my pocket does not touch me as deeply as it otherwise might. You say you will be sorry if the book must pass from your list. I will be extremely sorry. But what can I do? I have thought the matter over and looked over the book again and I think you are making much ado about nothing. Kindly do not misread this as a rebuke to you but put the emphasis on the last word. For, I assure you, not the least unfortunate effect of this tardy correspondence is that it has brought my own writing into disfavour with myself. Act, however, as you think best. I have done my part.

Believe me, dear Mr. Grant Richards,

Faithfully yours,

JAS A JOYCE.

Three further letters may be quoted as revealing to what point Joyce permitted himself to be driven by the Moral British Printer. The first is dated the tenth of June.

Via Giovanni Boccaccio, 1.

Trieste, Austria.

DEAR MR. GRANT RICHARDS,

I see by reference to letters that you were sending the book to the printers two months ago. Its transit, however, has been delayed by a copious and futile correspondence which my original reply to your objections certainly did not provoke. This correspondence has been a cause of great and constant worry to me and I now recognize how useless it has been.

I pointed out to you clearly in my last letter that it was I who had made efforts to narrow down the difficulties between us, difficulties which, I think, it would have been much wiser to raise at an earlier stage. I am unable to gather from your letter of this morning whether you hold to your first claims of six weeks ago or whether you agree to the concessions I made in my letter of a fortnight ago. I will ask you to let me know this definitely.

I have nothing further to add to what I have written in defence of my book but I may repeat that, in my opinion, you have allowed yourself to be intimidated by imaginary persons. You may have difficulties of which I know nothing for I imagine it is not public opinion which deters you. My bag of suggestions is nearly empty but I present you with this last one. Buy two critics. If you could do this with tact you could easily withstand a campaign. Two just and strong men, each armed with seven newspapers—*quis sustinebit?* I speak in parables.

As regards me, I leave this delightful city at the end of next month and go to Rome where I have obtained a position as correspondent in a bank. As the salary (£150 a year) is nearly double my present princely emolument and as the hours of honest labour will be fewer I hope to find time to finish my novel in Rome within a year or, at most, a year and a half. I mention this because in a former letter of yours you were kind enough to inquire about my financial position.

Believe me, dear Mr. Grant Richards,

Faithfully yours,

Jas A Joyce.

On the sixteenth of June Joyce wrote again, this time at length and with another attack on the Moral British Printer.

Via Giovanni Boccaccio, 1.
Trieste, Austria.

Dear Mr. Grant Richards,

I have turned to your letter of May 16th last and particularly to the first paragraph where I read that in consideration of three omissions conceded by me you allowed me to retain a word originally written in one of the stories. These three concessions I am still disposed to make on certain conditions.

The second paragraph of the same letter contains a withdrawal of one of your objections and a statement that one other phrase in the story under discussion should come out. In that story there are two other phrases marked by somebody's blue pencil; and in reply to your letter I stated that I was disposed to modify the passage but that I could not omit it. You now say that one of the two phrases must come out and I presume you choose this solution in preference to the one proposed by me, namely, a modification of the passage which contains the two phrases objected to. I am still disposed to make either concession, that is, either to modify (without omitting) the passage or to allow you to cancel whichever of the phrases you prefer to cancel on certain conditions.

The third paragraph of your letter of 16 May stated that you wished to omit another story of the original book but that you would not insist on this if I gave way on the other points. I replied by making the concessions mentioned above.

In the fourth and fifth paragraphs of the same letter you said that the story *Two Gallants* should certainly be omitted adding that you supposed I could omit it with an easier mind since it did not form part of the original book. I replied to this by pointing out that I had already agreed to make an omission in that story, that it was one of the most important stories in the book in my opinion, that I saw no way in which it could be rewritten and that its omission would mean in my opinion a mutilation of the book. I am still disposed to make the omission I agreed

to make of the word 'bloody' in that story if you are disposed to include
it in the book.

I suppose you are now quite clear as to my present position. The
concessions which I made in reference to the original book I made solely
with a view to the inclusion of *Two Gallants,* which, if it did not actually form part of the original book, you knew to be in preparation and
finally wrote for when the book was going to press. If you cannot possibly include *Two Gallants* with the omission I volunteered to make, the
motive which would induce me to make the other concessions disappears and I am disposed to allow you to print the book without it as I
originally wrote it, though, as I have told you, I regard such an omission
as an almost mortal mutilation of my work.

The spectre of the printer which I thought I had laid rises again in
your letter of the 14th instant. This apparition is most distasteful to me
and I hope he will not trouble the correspondence again. I do not seek
to penetrate the mysteries of his being and existence, for example, how
he came by his conscience and culture, how he is permitted in your
country to combine the duties of author with his own honourable calling,
how he came to be the representative of the public mind, how he happened to alight magically on what he was designed to overlook, and
(incidentally) why he began the process of printing my book at the third
page of the sixth story, numbered in the manuscript 5A. These for me
are mysteries and may remain so. But I cannot permit a printer to write
my book for me. In no other civilized country in Europe, I think, is a
printer allowed to open his mouth. If there are any objections to be
made the publisher can make them when the book is submitted to him:
if he withdraws them he pays a printer to print the book and if he
cannot withdraw them he decides not to trouble the printer by asking
him to print the book. A printer is simply a workman hired by the day
or by the job for a certain sum.

I am delighted and surprised to learn that nowadays it is impossible
to buy a critic of importance. Evidently since I left the British Isles some
extraordinary religious revolution has taken place. I expect to hear
shortly that the practices of self-stultification and prostitution have gone
out of fashion among authors.

In the last paragraph of your letter you seem to suggest the possibility
of our meeting in Rome. I should be glad of such a meeting as correspondence on debated points appears to me most unsatisfactory. However, by dint of exchanging six or seven letters, I hope we have now
arrived at a clear understanding of our respective attitudes.

In conclusion I thank you for replying to me so quickly and will be glad if you will answer this with equal promptness.

Believe me, dear Mr. Grant Richards,

Faithfully yours,

JAS A JOYCE.

A final letter, dated July ninth, sums up the concessions and changes that Joyce was reluctantly willing to make in his manuscript.

Via Giovanni Boccaccio, 1.

Trieste, Austria.

DEAR MR. GRANT RICHARDS,

I return you today the MS of *Dubliners* which you suggested in your letter of 19 June that I should alter at certain points. I have read it carefully from beginning to end and have made the following alterations:

I have rewritten the first story in the book *The Sisters* and included the last story *A Little Cloud* which you asked me to send on with the others.

I have corrected a few small errors and rearranged and renumbered the stories in the middle of the book, so that the book should now consist of fourteen stories in the order in which I have placed them.

I have deleted the word 'bloody' in six places, namely, on page 4 of *Two Gallants*, on page 7 and twice on page 16 of *Ivy Day in the Committee-Room*, and twice on page 16 of *Grace*.

I have deleted the passage you objected to in *Counterparts* and have rewritten the incident in the way I engaged to do.

I will not conceal from you that I think I have injured these stories by these deletions but I sincerely trust you will recognize that I have tried to meet your wishes and scruples fairly. And I will ask you to write to me, as soon as possible after receipt of the MS, in order that I may know definitely what you intend to do. This address will find me until the 28th July.

Faithfully yours,

JAS A JOYCE.

It would be superfluous to comment at any length on this correspondence. Everything that should be said is said and said well by the young author. Today it sounds strange (and almost unbelievable) that a long correspondence between an author and his prospective publisher should be mainly concerned over the word 'bloody' and a phrase describing a woman who changes the position of her legs frequently. But one must remember that the year was 1906 and the period that stuffy post-Boer-War time when smugness and gentle sentiment hovered like an anæsthetical miasma over the British Isles. Strange, too, is the idea that a printer could wield such influence over a publisher's mind and decisions but that is a phenomenon peculiar to England and even today it has not been wholly eradicated. It is as curious as the stringent libel laws of England. Taken altogether Joyce's epistolary duel with Grant Richards is revelatory of two grievous matters: the impossible world he lived in so far as the freedom of the artist was concerned and the brutal and disheartening struggle to vindicate his own theories that loomed before the young writer. Such a prospect (and one calculated to sap the courage from most men) Joyce faced without one weakening gesture. He would be reasonable (as his letters show) but there was a point beyond which he would not be driven. He believed too thoroughly in his own art (arrived at by such arduous steps) to quail before the mumbling magisters of British public taste. Exile had strengthened him by making him independent. He would march along his lonely road with his own pride for a buckler.

v

During this aggravated period of correspondence with Grant Richards Joyce was occupying himself with many other matters as well. There was his novel, *Stephen Hero,* upon which he laboured spasmodically and which he conceived as a huge book running to sixty-three chapters and totalling more than three hundred thousand words. As we have seen (in a letter to the English publisher) by March 1906, he had completed about half of this ambitious work. He continued to hesitate about the title, shifting from *Stephen Hero* to the original title, *A Portrait of the Artist,* and then to *Chapters in the Life of a Young Man.* None of them sounded quite right. For want of a definitive title, one that would express clearly the object of his book, he returned, for the time being, to *Stephen Hero.* There is no doubt whatsoever but what the long-drawn-out argumentations over *Dubliners* partially dammed the progress of the novel.

At this time, too, he was seriously considering studying for the operatic stage. Sinico, a Triestine maestro to whom he went, informed him that his voice had an extremely beautiful timbre and that two years' hard work should make him ready for the stage. But this was a dream. He was never to be a professional singer, an interpreter, because the dæmon of creation struggled too fiercely within him. Singing would continue to be, as it had been in the past, his avocation and the delight of his friends. The only permanent mark that Maestro Sinico left on Joyce's career was the use of his name for the unfortunate woman in the short story called "A Painful Case."

It must not be supposed that there were not lighter moments in the young writer's life during this spring and early summer of 1906. Despite the laborious travail of the Berlitz School and the thwarted fortunes of literary ventures Joyce was continuously susceptible to joyous explosions of *camaraderie*. There were evenings in the house on the Via Giovanni Boccaccio when Francini-Bruni would get into the infant Giorgio's carriage, suck at a milk bottle and cry, squeal and regurgitate like a baby while Joyce trundled him about the place. This would be at midnight. And after the clowning was over Joyce would sing Gregorian chants and the excitable Francini-Bruni, who had a high shrill laugh like a goat, would kiss the singer in an ecstasy of joy. Many a bottle of Triestine wine was emptied over the midnight table while the dark-blue-eyed Giorgio, now grown into a plump serious-countenanced baby, slept placidly in his crib and his mother sat by and commented with her rich native Irish humour on the frivolities of the two men.

But with all this an increasing restlessness pervaded Joyce's life. Even the presence of Stanislaus, with his introduction, as it were, of a doubled Dublin atmosphere into the house, could not stem it. The rut of the Berlitz School, the forced economy of life in Trieste, the feeling of being shut away from the world, the futile correspondence with Grant Richards, all these things, perhaps, merged into a general dissatisfaction that troubled Joyce's mind and finally aroused in him a desire to get away from Trieste, to change his scene and see if that would change his fortune. The visions of other cities beckoned to him, Rome, Genoa, Marseilles. He began to cast about him for a means of escape, any sort of line that would pull him out of his familiar waters. The feeling that he must go was intensified by the conviction that his billet at the Berlitz School was unstable, certain occurrences there suggesting to him that he was to be let out. Where, then, should he go? He perused the daily papers and searched the advertising columns for possible vacancies to which he might be suited. Eventually he happened upon one in the *Tribuna:* the bank of Nast, Kolb and Schumacher in Rome desired a correspondence clerk, one who would be as proficient in English as in Italian. The salary was considerably more than he was getting at the Berlitz School although, even so, it could hardly be called a fortune. But it would seem to be enough upon which to struggle along. And the new scene would be Rome. Joyce sat down and answered the advertisement, the first one he had ever answered, and a few days later he received a response provisionally accepting him if, after his arrival in Rome, the ensuing interview with the manager of the bank was satisfactory. On one of the last days of July 1906, Joyce and his young family turned their backs on Trieste and started for Rome.

# Six

THE Austrian city faded behind them. But even as the three young people (the father but twenty-four years old, the mother twenty-two and the son barely beyond his first year) travelled the uninteresting distance between Trieste and Fiume, where they were to take ship for Ancona, the enervating summer air was spinning with hazards, desires, expectancies and uncertainties. There is no doubt but what Joyce desired to go to Rome. He could just as well have remained in Trieste, his city of the many kindnesses, and devoted himself to private teaching of languages if his billet at the Berlitz School (and this is not certain) had ceased to exist. But, as has been pointed out before, the truth seems to be that he had become restless, that the unvarying routine had wearied him and that he was convinced (a blind urge telling him so) that the time for a change had come. If the mind moved on then the body must move on too. He had been unsettled and indefinite about that change, pondering the possibilities of Rome, Genoa and Marseilles. And here one may speculate for a moment on his decision. Each city appealed to him for a different reason but the appeal of Rome had been the greatest of all. There was, it may be suggested, a deep-rooted reason for that and it lay neither in the advertisement of a vacant position in an unknown bank that had appeared in the *Tribuna* nor the favourable response rewarding the applicant's answer to that advertisement. This was but the outward semblance of the reason, the practical gesture of the deeper urge. Now what was the urge that pushed Joyce into answering an advertisement that ended with the word 'Roma'? What propulsion started him towards the Eternal City? The answer to this lay in himself, in his childhood (shadow and spell of black soutanes moving across the cropped grass of unforgotten football fields), in the droning Latin of plump-paunched priests and their frightening admonitions at hushed Retreats (had he not but recently completed the chapters in *Stephen Hero* describing those days when he walked

161

in the shadow of Rome?), in his conscious struggle to shake off the
incubus that had striven to crush him to conformity at Belvedere
and University College. He yearned to see the Eternal City, where
a legendary Peter became a legendary Rock, as anxiously and as
curiously as a much-driven man desires to gaze upon the face of
his invulnerable persecutor. What was in the centre of this great
web called Roman Catholicism that so entangled the green island
where he was born? What mysterious power had its home in the
House of Peter? The impulse driving him towards this search may
have been wholly clouded to himself at the time but it was there
nevertheless, a primitive reaching, as it were, towards a monstrous
influence born in the blood and strengthened in the breeding but
entirely nullified by the reason. He did not know it but the
Roman days were to influence his comprehension of himself and
what he desired to do, to sharpen his focus on Time, so to speak,
and to clear away the ground upon which he desired to build.

The long-scattered voyagers of that journey, if any still exist,
will hardly remember the slim, piercingly-blue-eyed young man
with the tightly-clamped mouth and the thin threadbare trousers
(to become such a problem in Rome), the charmingly-rousse young
woman and the child not yet out of its swaddling clothes, foreigners all, strangers in a strange land, travelling from one point of
time to another, following a seemingly-reasonless but spontane-
ously-determined path that started in poverty and ended in mystery.
They saw (if they saw anything) a trio coming from nowhere and
going to nowhere, that was all. And it is very possible that Joyce
saw himself in this light as he arrived in Fiume and boarded the
vessel that was to take him across the turbulent waters to Ancona.

From Fiume to Ancona the three travellers slept on deck
(cheapest place of all), the infant Giorgio suffering not the least
harm from the rough knocking about of the voyage. Joyce, from
his brief observation, decided that he admired Fiume, finding in it
a "clean, asphalted town with a very modern go-ahead air . . . far
finer than Trieste," but Ancona aroused a repugnance in him. He
found something Irish "in its bleak gaunt beggarly ugliness." This
repugnance was possibly intensified by the misfortunes of being
swindled out of two lire by the money-changer, half a lira by the
cabman who drove him and his family the three miles from the

pier to the train, and three lire by the insolent railway ticket clerk.

His first activities in Rome were to find decent living quarters, report at the bank of Nast, Kolb and Schumacher on the corner of the Piazza Colonna and the Via San Claudio (this he did on August first) and discover a favourite café. The living quarters (only a single room for three) were secured at Via Frattina, 52. The first visit to the bank was successful. Schumacher, one of the partners and Austro-Hungarian Consul for Rome as well, interviewed him in the typically-gruff Germanic fashion, inquiring his age and desiring information about his father. The responses being satisfactory, Joyce was definitely engaged and assigned to the Italian correspondence department, receiving immediately sixty-five lire for his travelling expenses and a hundred lire advance on his monthly stipend of two hundred and fifty lire. The work was easy and mechanical (albeit dull and arduous) but the hours were long, officially extending from half-past eight o'clock to twelve in the morning and from two to seven-thirty in the afternoon, but often continuing far later into the evening. It was a sedentary occupation; Joyce sat down all day; and it was not long before the rapidly thinning seat of his solitary pair of trousers became one of his major problems in the Holy City. Towards the end of his first month (and it was an extremely hot August) he was gloomily announcing to his brother in Trieste: "There are two great patches on the seat of my trousers so that I cannot leave off my coat in the office and sit stewing for hours." Still later he was forced to wear his tail coat all day. Because of this tail coat he was advanced to the position of reception clerk. This portrait of the artist as a young man attending to stacks of dull Italian financial correspondence in a foreign bank or receiving prospective clients with money to burn while all his desire was to write down the literary images that flashed through his mind and glumly regarding piles of lire and bundles of paper notes that meant leisure for others but not for himself approaches the acme of irony. It was a ridiculous jest of Time that Joyce, himself so prodigal of the few pence that came his way and absolutely impracticable in money matters of any sort, should land, of all places, in a bank. Here was the bewildered eagle sitting in a sparrow's (or, should we say, buzzard's) nest. Yet he accepted his lot with that sort of exasperated fatality that kept him precariously existing in a world where most things seemed to seek to drag him down and strip his unearthly plumage from him. Surrounded by fifty or sixty shiny-panted employees who hissed "signore" at one another all day (every wretched scribbler in account books was a signore) Joyce conformed outwardly but inwardly he was choked with a desperate detestation of "the stupid, dishonest, tyrannical and cowardly burgher class." He hated their smug satisfaction and abhorred the petty cruelties they wreaked on their juniors.

The search for a favourite café was an exasperating adventure also. He could discover nothing comparable to his comfortable haunts in Trieste. There were innumerable little café-bars, humble restaurants, *trattorias,* but they did not fulfil that desire for a *homely* rendezvous where one might be *en salon, en salle-à-manger* and *en café* at the same time. This problem of an agreeable café, a place one entered with the same spirit that one put on an old favourite smoking jacket, is always important when one's home is circumscribed in an overcrowded bedchamber with its unlovely furniture. There is an atmosphere about the proper café that turns it into a second home. It is a place to greet friends, to argue about the matters that concern one closely, indeed, to grow into tune with Time and one's self. There is ample justification for the assertion (as true as most broad statements are) that the majority of the great literary and artistic movements in France were conceived and delivered in cafés and restaurants. Joyce, after some blundering search, fixed upon a little Greek eating place, a forgotten corner formerly frequented by Amiel, Thackeray, Byron and Ibsen, where the bill of fare was in English, a pot containing six cups of tea cost only sixpence and the New York *Herald* (European edition) and *Daily Mail* were provided for sedentary clients. It was not the perfect headquarters that Joyce envisaged, for its clatter and lack of size were drawbacks, but it had to serve. Its cheapness was its great advantage. For Joyce, all the time that he was in Rome just as all the time he had been in Trieste or in Paris, or anywhere, for that matter, suffered from a pinching and humiliating lack of funds. Even in those days of comparative cheapness two hundred and fifty lire a month was hardly sufficient to provide for three people. The natural result of this poverty was a feverish anxiety about the morrow. He could, and he did, apply for and receive advances on his meagre monthly stipend but this only forced him into further arrears when his depleted envelope reached him on the regular payday. There was, too, his brother Stanislaus in Trieste to whom he could (and did) dispatch frantic letters demanding small sums, but Stanislaus, although without family responsibilities, was as badly off as Joyce himself. Therefore the small sums (those tiny sops to the ravenous wolf who had taken up a permanent residence on Joyce's doorstep), though they did arrive occasionally, were few and far between. To augment his insufficient income Joyce sought prospective students of the English language. He watched the advertising columns of the *Tribuna* each day for any intimations of Italians ambitious to conquer Shakespeare's tongue and finally landed one Terzini, a nephew of the Abruzzese painter Michetti. Terzini must have been a likable sort for he did not demur at paying for half a dozen lessons in advance whenever Joyce was blindly floundering in one of his critical financial crises. A second pupil was eventually provided by one of the clerks in the bank. And in November of this year an answer to another advertisement in the *Tribuna* secured for Joyce the dubious honour of teaching by night in a small Ecole des Langues, one of those tuppenny imitations of Herr Berlitz's vaster undertaking to make foreign languages as easy as soothing syrup.

Despite the long hours of labour, the lack of a tranquil and satisfying milieu and the practical invisibility of money Joyce succeeded in maintaining an equanimity that was only infrequently shattered by unfortunate crises. He possessed the severe integrity of his mind, his dogged purpose in life, his inextinguishable sense of humour and his ability to compose himself in the ugly face of adversity. He may have been irritable as the young and highly nervous are irritable but he does not appear to have been ever despondent or hopeless. When a man can jest about his adversity he is superior to it and this was peculiarly Joyce's reaction. He might burst out with the glum reflection that his mouth was full of decayed teeth and his soul was full of decayed ambitions but the next minute he was meditating a new literary venture or heaping rich ridicule on the pseudo artists he had left behind in Dublin. The invulnerable element of which his spirit was fashioned could be shaken but it never could be broken. There are periods during this epoch of his life when Joyce's will to live and the swift onslaught of misfortune have the aspect of an irresistible force in contact with an immovable object.

What did he find in this Rome that he had so desired to see? Its exterior aspects do not seem to have moved him at all. Faithfully, when time permitted and that was only on his free Sundays, he tramped about the streets and gazed upon the monuments of the past. St. Peter's, the Pincio, the Forum, the Coliseum, he directed an inquisitive eye upon them and reacted not at all as the visitor first arriving in Rome is supposed to react. Papal Rome was like the Coombe in Dublin or old Trieste and the new Ludovici Quarter was not so fine as Pembroke township. St. Peter's did not seem to him much larger than St. Paul's in London. The music of the mass "was nothing much" and "some of the rev. gents" had voices like crows. Cardinal Rampolla, whom he had long ago travestied in charades in Dublin and whom he now saw in procession, was "a tall strong man with a truculent face" wearing "a red beretta stuck anyhow on his head." The neighbourhood of the Coliseum was like an old cemetery. The cobbled streets were fearfully noisy. Inside the famous circus when once the gladiators had clashed in fatal combats his ears were assaulted by a tourist's voice proclaiming:

> "Whowail stands the Coliseum, Rawhm sh'll stand;
> When falls the Coliseum, Rawhm sh'll fall,
> And when Rawhm falls—the world sh'll fall,"

and adding cheerfully, "Kemlong, 'ere's the way aht." Guides and postcard vendors drove him to distraction. However, he derived some pleasure in the Coliseum and St. Peter's from the disrespectful spectacle of his small son (who, with infant acumen, had discovered the "echoey" possibilities of the two great piles) shouting at the top of his voice. Indeed, it was Giorgio who adjusted himself to Rome (or, rather, adjusted Rome to himself) with the blander composure. Joyce informed his brother: "Georgie is a great favourite with everyone here. All the people we frequent know his name. He has added to his vocabulary, 'O, Gesù Mio,' 'brutto, brutto, brutto,' and cleans out his ear when told to do so. Also, when we go to the bank in the Piazza Colonna he beats time to the music, amusing the 'smiling Romans' thereby very much. He wears a long mayoral chain with little medals round his neck." Still later Giorgio would march up and down in restaurants flourishing a wooden sword and singing arias from the operas. When less than two years old he hit the high notes. But if Rome was pleasing enough to Giorgio it had fallen far short of Joyce's somewhat abstract expectations. In the midst of all these vestiges of the past he announced plaintively, "I wish someone was here to talk to me about Dublin," and he summed the whole scene up in the declaration that the Holy City reminded him of "a man who lives by exhibiting to travellers his grandmother's corpse."

If the exterior scene struck no sparks from the flint of his mind, what is to be said for the effect of the spiritual entity that is timeless and boundless and is the Rome of the imagination, that mysterious quintessence of a thousand historical, philosophical and religious gestures and divagations? That is more difficult to judge. Joyce was avid enough to discover, to encompass and to extend the bounds of his comprehension; but Rome, it would seem, did not provide that quickening of the senses or instigate that awareness of immeasurable impulses that might have been expected. In *The Marble Faun,* Nathaniel Hawthorne, attempting to circumscribe the effect of Rome on a sensitive nature, wrote: "It is a vague sense of ponderous remembrances; a perception of such weight and density in a bygone life, of which this spot was the centre, that the present moment is pressed down or crowded out and our individual affairs and interests are but half as real here as elsewhere." This sort of romantic escape (for it is no more than that) Rome did not give to Joyce. Yet the city did provide something and that something was an increasingly intensive recognition of himself and a consequent knowledge of where he should begin to build. The very strangeness of Rome sharpened his own outline to his own perception. He was lonelier in Rome, perhaps, than he had been in any city wherein he had dwelt. It was the first metropolis where he could find no one with whom to converse, except an old priest who had him out to dinner once or twice, and the natural result of this drastic isolation was to fling him violently inward upon himself. The savour of Paris and its chatter in little *bistros* and the homeliness of Trieste with Stanislaus always at hand were lacking; yet this loneliness, the positive fact that he was a solitary in the midst of "ponderous remembrances," focused more clearly than ever his sensibilities upon himself and, a logical corollary, the city of his childhood and youth. Rome planted him more firmly in the heart of Dublin and, at the same time, made possible for him an objective perspective of the compact humming metropolis by the Liffey, a Pisgah sight he had lacked before. As a matter of fact, he had never left Dublin; he carried it about with him wherever he went, in his heart, in his brain, in nostalgic returns of the mind; now, existing vicariously in it, he could, miraculously enough, stand aside from it and observe it with a calm clinical eye. It was Rome that sharpened this double vision of immersion and doctoral perception.

There are writers who will submerge themselves in the colours and personalities of the various places in which they rest for a month or a year, who, if in Rome, will, as Hawthorne did, give you a Roman novel or, if in Paris, seize upon the sparkling phenomena of *La Ville Lumière,* but Joyce was never of this category. The farther he travelled and the more alien the aspects of his environment then the more vivid and intense became his absorption in Dublin. "The shortest way to Tara was via Holyhead" still. Although he might stand in the Ludovici Quarter of the Holy City he was spiritually in Pembroke township. When he walked across the Piazza Colonna amongst the "smiling Romans" he walked, at the same time, across St. Stephen's Green, *his* Green. It was not that he did not see what was before his eyes but his entire intellectual and creative being was concentred in a distant milieu (always near to him) that provided him with all the sustenance he required. Curiously enough, this absorption did not parochialize his artistic impulse. By some subtle chemistry of the will he universalized Dublin until it became a microcosm of all life, a city of the mythos, an epitome of human existence and endeavour and mysterious evolution. All of this was not clear to him; the gnostic vision with its mythic significance was yet to come; but as he sat in his noisy *trattoria* before his *polpetta* the vague and enormous shapes were moving cloudily in the depths of his mind. What he was to do was concealed behind veils, but what he was doing already troubled those veils.

## II

During the seven disappointing and laborious months that he existed in Rome there would not seem to have been much time left from Joyce's diurnal routine for literature; and yet certain objectives, momentous in their implications for him and his future, were achieved; and others, inexplicably buried like fecund seeds in the rich soil of his mind, were swelling towards the sun and attending that slow deliverance of Time that would break the earth and let them push into the light of day with all their great blossoms full-blown upon them. The problem that occupied his mind the most and salted his days with a stinging exasperation was the dubious (and, later, impossible) publication of *Dubliners*. He still continued his unavailing duel of letters with Grant Richards, a duel disastrous to him in that there was no cutting edge to his vigorously-flourished sword. It was as ineffectual as Giorgio's wooden weapon. It is only money or influence that puts a sharp blade on such rapiers. The armour of the Philistine is otherwise impregnable. At the same time he unceasingly tested in his mind the value of the stories that made up his manuscript volume. "I have written three paragraphs to add to 'A Painful Case,' but I don't know if I can rewrite it. I would like also to rewrite 'After the Race,' but if G.R. [Grant Richards] sent me proofs I would pass the book as it is. The chase of perfection is very unprofitable." [From a letter to his brother Stanislaus dated August 14, 1906.] The firm of Grant Richards still dithered and procrastinated and Joyce began to prophesy gloomily that the book would only see the light when too late to give its author any pleasure. He had set great store by this collection of fictional sketches for it had occupied a vast part of his mind from 1904 onward. There were times when he had a faintly-guilty feeling of being too harsh to his compatriots and the city that had shaped him; but this feeling (almost a sentimental weakening) was soon enough dissipated by a conviction of the integrity of his impartial objectivity. What he saw and what his logical reasoning powers told him was so he must put down in cold prose. He himself expressed this mixed feeling in a letter he wrote to his brother during this period.

"Sometimes thinking of Ireland," he admitted, "it seems to me that I have been unnecessarily harsh. I have reproduced (in 'Dubliners,' at least) none of the attraction of the city, for I have never felt at my ease in any city since I left it, except Paris. I have not reproduced its ingenuous insularity and its hospitality; the latter 'virtue,' so far as I can see, does not exist elsewhere in Europe. I have not been just to its beauty: for it is more beautiful naturally, in my opinion, than what I have seen of England, Switzerland, France, Austria and Italy. And yet I know how useless these reflections are. For was I to rewrite the book as G.R. suggests 'in another sense' (where the hell does he get the meaningless phrases he uses!) I am sure I should find again what you call the Holy Ghost sitting in the ink-bottle and the perverse devil of my literary conscience sitting on the hump of my pen. And, after all, 'Two Gallants'— with the Sunday crowds and the harp in Kildare Street and Lenehan—*is* an Irish landscape."

By the autumn of this year Joyce realized, to his dismay and chagrin, that still another publishing season would pass without the appearance of *Dubliners*. A full year had wasted itself in epistolary argumentation over literary franknesses that Joyce, with his congenital honesty of purpose and inability to compromise with the social timidities and hypocrisies of the Edwardian scene, would not and could not accept as valid flaws in composition. On September twenty-third he dispatched a further protest to the English publisher:

Via Frattina, 52. II.

DEAR MR. GRANT RICHARDS,

I have been waiting all the week for a letter from you with regard to my book. The month of September is now nearly over and I am still uncertain of its fate. I write to you now because I wish that this suspense of mind in which I live at present may come to an end one way or the other. I need scarcely assure you how disheartening it is for me to see (as I see) that yet another season is going by without my book being published. And yet I think you will not accuse me of being importunate if I ask you to write me definitely on receipt of this letter.

Faithfully yours,

JAS. A. JOYCE.

The response of Mr. Grant Richards was far from definite and by the thirtieth of the month Joyce (now worked into a feverish state of exasperation) had composed a long letter setting forth the meaningless impasse which he sent to Arthur Symons. Although he had not seen Symons for several years he remembered him as sympathetic and willing even to go out of his way (something surprising in most English authors) for a fellow writer at odds and bewildered by the chameleon aspects of London publishers. At the same time he determined to consult an international jurist in Rome and discover if there was any method by which he could force the English publisher to respect his agreement. The British Consul gave Joyce the name of St. Lo Malet and to this presumable Solon the young writer went, carrying with him all the correspondence and the agreement with the firm of Grant Richards. To Stanislaus Joyce forwarded an account of this consultation. "He [St. Lo Malet] discovered some discrepancies. First, G.R. says, 'I read the book myself on behalf of this house'; later, 'the man who read the book for us was Filson Young.' He says an agreement like mine is considered only a personal contract. He advised me to try to come to terms on letter 11 and not to go to law (letter 11 is the letter with which G.R. returned the MS.), as law-suits are long and costly and as other publishers would then be reluctant to publish me. I said I had tried to come to terms on letter 11 unsuccessfully. I told him I had written to Symons and he advised me to wait for Symons' answer before doing anything. . . . In one way, he says, my case is strong since G.R. has broken a contract. But he says the assessment of damages would be very difficult. G.R. has constantly disparaged the book commercially. The contract gave me nothing on the first 500 and G.R. would maintain that it was unlikely my book would reach even that limit. I might be awarded five pounds damages or enough money to enable me to bring out the book myself."

All of this was cold pottage to the impatient young writer. He regarded an immediate publication as a species of self-vindication, an earnest of the pledge he had made himself by the very gesture of his voluntary exile; and he knew, too, that his mind was growing and what was representative of it today would not be so tomorrow. It was a clearing of the decks, so to speak, that he desired, a stripping for action (only to be attained by the appearance of what had been written) so that he might advance into new struggles with that perdurable wrestler called Art. At this vexatious moment

of time the letter he shortly received from Arthur Symons brought
him a substantial crumb of comfort. He could chew upon it while
he waited for the greater feast. Symons wrote:

> I am glad to hear from you again. When I named you to Grant
> Richards, it was before his failure; I should hardly have done it since.
> Still, as he has apparently begun to print your book, I would be inclined
> to give it to him as far as you can without vitally damaging your work.
> If he signed an agreement to publish the twelve stories, why not hold
> him to that: and you could hold over the other two stories for another
> book later. The great thing is to get published, so that people may have
> a chance of reading you. I will write a line to G.R. advising him not to
> lose your book. I hope you will arrange it between you.
>
> Now as to your poems, I feel almost sure that I can get Elkin
> Mathews to print them in his shilling Garland series.
>
> You would get little money from him, but I think it would be worth
> your while to take what he offered—probably a small royalty after ex-
> penses are covered. He did for me a little set of translations from Baude-
> laire's 'Petites Poèmes en Prose.' The cost was £14/14/0, and it is now
> nearly covered when my royalty will begin. Tell me if I may write and
> advise him to take the book. If it comes out I will give it the best review
> I can in the 'Saturday' or 'Athaeneum,' and I will get one or two other
> people to give it proper notices. I hope you are getting on well in Rome.
> Let me have a line promptly about the poems.

This was unexpectedly friendly and it succeeded, to some degree, in diverting Joyce's mind from the unhappy Odyssey of the
*Dubliners* manuscript. He wrote immediately accepting this well-
intentioned offer from the English poet and critic to stand godfather to *Chamber Music*. While he professed no more than a perfunctory interest in the verses, regarding them much in the light
of an idle tuning-up of the rare instrument of his creative instinct
preliminary to the more serious performance of *Dubliners* and that
multitudinously-rewritten and still-truncated autobiographical novel
upon which he had stopped work for some time, he was pleased
enough at the prospect of seeing them published before any of his
prose volumes. If they were printed at all both chronology and
development called for their immediate appearance. It would, at
least, be a logical beginning to the necessary clearing of the decks.
So, for the time being, he had something to occupy his mind, a

not-unwelcome dive back into his immediate past, the arrangement of the verses and a consequent past-springtime diversion from the hovering spectacle of the slow death, or lethal coma, of his unfortunate dealings with Mr. Grant Richards. That lethal coma was near when he wrote on October twenty-second to the English publisher.

Via Frattina, 52. 11.
Rome.

DEAR MR. GRANT RICHARDS,

I have received your letter of the 16th., and my verse MS for which thanks. As I told you in my last letter I can make no further changes in the MS you have at present, the changes made so far having been made solely in order that stories 13 and 14 might be included. If, however, you wish to stand by our agreement with regard to the original twelve stories I will concede what you ask for in your letter of 23 April:

1) suppression of 'Two Gallants' (and of 'A Little Cloud')
2) deletion of passage in 'Counterparts' (already deleted)
3) deletion of word 'bloody' in 'Grace' (already deleted)

If, however, you decide that you cannot publish the original book, as agreed between us, even with these concessions kindly send me back the complete MS by return of post.

Faithfully yours,

JAS. A. JOYCE.

One hears here the veritable death rattle of *Dubliners,* so far as the publishing house of Grant Richards at this period of polite and unadventurous civilization was concerned. Within the next month all dealings with the English firm ceased for Joyce found himself unable to cope with the situation. He was helpless, impractical, penniless and the humiliated sport of stuffy timidities. What could he do? Entirely friendless in Rome, innumerable miles away from London, an Irishman, the creator of a new honesty in English letters, unknown and, therefore, unconsidered, without a book to his name, he was absolutely discomfited and worsted in a world that his reason would permit him to have no part in. The Society of Authors demanded a guinea subscription before it would take up the matter and Joyce, who couldn't even buy himself a new pair of trousers, did not have the guinea. Mr. St. Lo Malet, international jurist *par excellence,* advised against any legal proceedings and requested a pound for his opinion. Joyce gave him ten lire on account and the manuscript of "Two Gallants" to read.

A humorous epilogue to the misfortunes of *Dubliners* grotesquely ended this joyless season. Joyce wrote to John Long, the English publisher, offering him the book and received the amazing reply that if he (Joyce) would send him (Long) the sum of one and a half guineas he (Long) would forward an exhaustive report on the book, written by a novelist of good standing which would be of use to him (Joyce). Still later Long wrote that his reader had advised against the publication of *Dubliners* and so the manuscript returned to roost on Joyce's shelf again. The disastrous campaign was over and *Dubliners* passed into oblivion for a time.

Matters proceeded more merrily with *Chamber Music.* Arthur Symons, true to his promise and with a promptitude exceptional in poets, approached Elkin Mathews and received from him a letter which he forwarded to Joyce.

My dear Symons,

I am very much obliged to you for drawing my attention to Mr. Joyce's work and feel sure from what you tell me of its quality that it will be a great acquisition to my Vigo series. So will you please put me into communication with Mr. Joyce or arrange with him for me to see his MSS.

Faithfully yours,

Elkin Mathews.

This letter was written early in October.

(Arthur Symons, by the way, appears to have visited Rome in January of the following year—for some verses in his *Collected Poems,* "At Sant' Onofrio," are dated "Rome, January 9, 1907"—but there is no evidence that he encountered Joyce.)

During the late autumn evenings after he had given his language lessons and the free Sundays when the bank was mercifully closed Joyce occupied the hours with arranging and slightly revising the thirty-seven short lyrics (one, the poem now called "Tilly" in *Pomes Penyeach,* being suppressed as not in the mood of the others) that were the residuum of his last years in Dublin. What memories they evoked in him were his own secret. He had, how-

ever, long stepped out of the delicate circle of their archaic precision and sought a bleaker, stonier, wind-swept space of reality. Yet
from this harder place of Time it is most certain that he glanced
back at that younger Joyce who tramped the rainy autumn streets
of Dublin and brooded over the dark narrow dimpling waters of
the Liffey, who drifted lonelily across the iron ways of that Paris
lighted by the pale-blue disks of the night lamps and sought to
find himself and found only the beginnings of the long and thank-
less task of living; for to glance backward (but with an eye on the
present as well) had already become an important aspect of his art.

*Chamber Music* was dispatched to Elkin Mathews early in November with a note from the author explaining that the poems had
been in bond for two years and requesting an early decision as to
their acceptability. But publishers are never to be hurried. While
they will press and harry authors most unreasonably they regard
the author's natural impatience as an insolent form of *lèse-majesté*.
Elkin Mathews, like the solid slow-stepping Britisher he was, replied that *Chamber Music* could not be published this side of Christmas but that as soon as he got some pressing work off his hands he
would turn to and examine the manuscript. The manuscript contained exactly 434 short lines, not much labour, one would think,
for a reader, perhaps a half hour's perusal at most. However, towards
the end of January 1907, the agreement arrived and early in February came the proof sheets, those thin long slips that are first the
delight and then the despair of the conscientious writer. Shortly
after receiving them Joyce announced to his brother: "It is a slim
book and on the frontispiece is an open pianner!" Even now, with
the flimsy proof sheets in his hands, a feeling of doubt beset him
for he went on to declare to Stanislaus: "I don't like the book but
wish it were published and be damned to it. However, it is a young
man's book. I felt like that. It is not a book of love-verses at all, I
perceive. But some of them are pretty enough to be put to music.
I hope someone will do so, someone that knows old English music
such as I like. Besides, they are not pretentious and have a certain
grace."

The remainder of the history of *Chamber Music* belongs to the
period succeeding Joyce's forlorn seven months in the Holy City of
"ponderous remembrances."

We have in these various negotiations, then, the collapse of a long struggle for the publication of *Dubliners,* a book that Joyce felt fairly represented him, and the prospect of the imminent appearance of *Chamber Music,* a book that interested him slightly if at all. Such a lost battle and a won skirmish can hardly have been stimulative to his creative urge and yet that irrepressible gift was constantly restless and reaching out towards a vaster expression. Towards the end of his sojourn in Rome the idea for a long short story (the longest he had ever written) to be called "The Dead," and to form the fifteenth and last section of *Dubliners,* possessed him but his precarious situation was so impossible, his days so crowded with drudgery and his mind so agitated that he was quite put off the theme and compelled to postpone it to a future time. Titles of other stories, each one conveying to him its peculiar situation, floated through his mind, "The Last Supper," "The Street," "Vengeance," "At Bay," but circumstances were never favourable to their composition and they remain, even now, in that mysterious limbo of authors' prospective but never accomplished works which so tease the mind of the imaginative reader. It is as though one saw a second volume of *Dubliners* (what a titillating title, "Dubliners: Second Series"!) floating just beyond recognition by eye and mind in the cloudy insubstantiality of the potential past.

More important to Joyce's own future was an idea adumbrated in three brief passages from his letters to Stanislaus during this period. One is at liberty to speculate upon these remarks as one pleases although whatever assumptions one arrives at will be practically baseless so far as definitive facts are concerned. On September 30, 1906, Joyce wrote: "I have a new story for 'Dubliners' in my head. It deals with Mr. Hunter." [1] Again, on November thirteenth: "I thought of beginning my story, 'Ulysses,' but I have too many cares at present." And once more, on February 6, 1907: " 'Ulysses' never got any forrarder than the title." Here, then, for the first time we find the name that was (sixteen years later) to make Joyce world-renowned. The wanderer had found the Wanderer; at least, he had sensed the great presence. It is plain as a pikestaff that Joyce's

[1] To anticipate what was to come later it may be mentioned here that this Mr. Hunter of Dublin was only one of the living models who served for the character of Leopold Bloom in *Ulysses.* There were two others, one in Trieste and the other in Zurich, the former a Greek and the latter a Hungarian.

first conception of the theme carrying that name was a short sketch or story in which some person he had known named Hunter was to play a rôle and this narrative was intended to form an integral part of *Dubliners*. He probably envisaged nothing profounder than the honest recital of a day's peregrinations through the streets of Dublin, the observations and reflections, maybe, of *l'homme moyen sensual*. It is equally obvious that he did nothing about it at the time. For what reason did he put the subject aside in favour of another, "The Dead," which was to finish off his first prose work? One might suggest several reasons: that the idea did not bite at him strongly enough, that it slipped out of his mind in the days that followed, that it was but part and parcel of those other titles, "At Bay," "Vengeance," etc., that constantly streamed through his mind and floated off into the dissipating smoke of the never-to-be-accomplished; but it is equally valid to assume that the subtly-governing dæmon who directs the expression of all great artists put a peremptory halt to it because the artist was not yet ready for this particular adventure. The dæmon saw more than a day's peregrinations from Drumcondra to Rathgar. There was a long road to travel, much water was to flow from near Sally Gap down and under the bridges of the Liffey and several way stations to the theme were to be achieved before Joyce stood face to face with *Ulysses* and saw it for what it must be. The artist was yet to be engulfed consciously in the mythos. For what was the title *Ulysses*, with all its implications of far journeys and perilous meetings with sirens, Cyclops and storm-tossed straits, but the signpost, the sudden signature of direction thrusting momentarily upward from the deep subconscious, pointing along a fog-enveloped road towards a great myth, a legend of man's wandering endeavour and unceasing search for the tranquillity that is implicit in a complete self-recognition and final orientation in the great-waved seas of outrageous Time? And here was Joyce, an exile not many leagues from the wine-dark Mediterranean, a sailor and searcher too, but over abstract waters dangerous with uncharted shoals and rocks, a hero-worshipper of the wily Greek who discomfited his enemies by stratagems of common sense, a father with an infant son just beginning to respond to the stimuli of living, here was Joyce, be it repeated, hearing the great name in his mind but unaware as yet of its thousand and one meanings.

He was not prepared for the event but the seed had been dropped and fecundated during this period of intellectual self-adjustment in Rome. "There is a painful pregnancy in genius," George Santayana once wrote, "a long incubation and waiting for the spirit, a thousand rejections and futile birthpangs, before the wonderful child appears, a gift of the gods, utterly undeserved and inexplicably perfect." The "painful pregnancy" that was to result in *Ulysses* began, then, in the autumn of 1906 and lasted until 1914, the year that convulsed Europe, when the first words were put on paper in the loyal Austrian city of the Emperor Franz Josef, Trieste.

### III

Here it is illuminating to consider those complementary aspects of Joyce's mind not directly associated with his creative endeavours but yet feeding them and playing a part in his æsthetic development, aspects that crowded the narrow interstices of his labour-crammed days and afforded him some pleasures of speculation and observation. They may be assorted under: his reading, those phases of the contemporary activities in Rome that caught at his mind, and his continual absorption in the Irish (or, to be precise, Dublin) scene and what he found in it; in other words, what fed his mind from literature, from the shifting spectacle of his Italian environment, and from his constant return, if only through memory and reports, to the Irish city where he grew to manhood. From the letters he wrote to Stanislaus during this period it will be of revelatory interest to cull a few extracts concerned with his reading.

The first book that appears to have fallen into Joyce's hands in Rome was Oscar Wilde's *The Picture of Dorian Gray*. Curiously enough, he read it in an Italian translation. "I have just finished 'Dorian Gray,'" he wrote on August 19, 1906. "Some chapters are like Huysmans' catalogued atrocities: lists of perfumes and instruments. The central idea is fantastic. Dorian is exquisitely beautiful and becomes awfully wicked—but never ages. His portrait ages. I can imagine the capital which Wilde's prosecuting counsel made out of certain parts of it. It is not very difficult to read between the lines. Wilde seems to have had some good intentions in writing it—some wish to put himself before the world—but the book's rather

crowded with lies and epigrams. If he had had the courage to develop the allusions in the book, it might have been better. I suspect
he has done this in some privately-printed books. Like his Irish
imitator:

> 'Just the reverse is
> The style of his verses.' "

Later in this same month Joyce dislocated his finances by purchasing a copy of George Moore's *The Lake*. It will be remembered
that he had definitive ideas about Mr. Moore, that while he recognized him as an author of wonderful mimetic ability he also saw
him as a struggler in the backwash of that tide which had advanced from Flaubert through Jacobsen to d'Annunzio. In "The
Day of the Rabblement" Joyce had written: "But however frankly
Mr. Moore may misquote Pater and Turgenieff to defend himself,
his new impulse has no kind of relation to the future of art." A
perusal of *The Lake* aroused a jocose contempt in him. On August
thirty-first he wrote to his brother: *"The Times* calls it a prose
poem. You know the plot. She [the heroine of *The Lake*] writes
long letters to Father Oliver Gogarty about Wagner and the Ring
and Bayreuth (memories of my youth!) and about Italy where
everybody is so happy (!!!!!!!!!!!!!!) and where they drink nice
wine and not that horrid black porter (O, poor Lady Ardilaun,
over whose lily-white hand he lingered some years back!) with a
literary man named Ellis—one of Moore's literary men (you can
imagine what . . . a silent second cousin of that terribly knowing
fellow, Harding)—and Father Oliver Gogarty goes out to the lake
to plunge in by moonlight, before which the moon shines oppor-
tunely 'on a firm erect frame and grey buttocks'; and on the steamer
he reflects that every man has a lake in his heart and must ungird
his loins for the crossing. Preface written in French to a French
friend who cannot read or write English (intelligent artist, however, no doubt) and George Moore, out of George Henry Moore
and a Ballyglass lady, explains that he only does it 'because, *cher
ami* (dear friend), you cannot read me in my own language.' Eh?"
Some days later Joyce reverted to *The Lake* again, in response to
some comments by his brother. "Yerra, what's good in the end of
'The Lake'? I see nothing. And what is to be said about the 'lithery'
man, Ellis, and all the talk about pictures and music? Now, tell the
God's truth, isn't it bloody tiresome? To me it is. As for 'Rev.

Oliver Gogarty' I think that may either have been laughingly suggested by O. St. Jesus [Joyce alluded to Oliver St. John Gogarty, his former companion in the Martello Tower at Sandycove] for his greater glory or hawk-eyedly intended by Moore to put O. St. Jesus in an *embarras*. If the latter O. St. Jesus has risen nobly to the situation, I have violated the sanctity of this office by laughing. I remembered Moore's legend about Mrs. Craigie. Thanks be to Christ, they amuse us anyhow." The description of Father Oliver Gogarty plunging into the lake by moonlight reminded Joyce of his rapidly disintegrating trousers for he further remarked to his brother: "Already the moon is threatening to shine on my grey buttocks and I wish someone would send me a pair of Father Oliver's small clothes that he hid among the bulrushes." It is amusing to note that in *Ulysses* (published sixteen years later) Stephen Dedalus refuses a pair of grey trousers offered him by Buck Mulligan (Oliver St. John Gogarty).

The next work to arouse comment from Joyce was Gerhart Hauptmann's play, *Rosa Bernd*. We are already cognizant of his familiarity with the dramas of this German writer. Early in October he wrote: "I finished Hauptmann's *Rosa Bernd* on Sunday. I wonder if he acts well. His plays, when read, leave an unsatisfying impression on the reader. Yet he must have the sense of the stage well-developed in him by now. He never (in his later plays, at least) tried for a curtain so that the ends of his acts seem ruptures of a scene. His characters seem to be more highly vivified by their creator than Ibsen's do but they are also less under control. He has a difficulty in subordinating them to the action of his drama. He deals with life quite differently, more frankly in certain points (this play opens with Rosa and her lover emerging one after the other from opposite sides of a bush, looking at each other first and then laughing) but also so broadly that my personal conscience is seldom touched. His way of treating such types as Arnold Kramer and Rosa Bernd is, however, altogether to my taste. His temperament has a little of Rimbaud in it. Like him, too, I suppose somebody else will be his future. But, after all, he has written two or three masterpieces—a little immortal thing like 'The Weavers,' for example. I have found nothing of the charlatan in him yet."

By November Joyce had plunged into the somewhat muddy waters of George Gissing, reading one after the other *Demos: A Story of English Socialism* and *The Crown of Life*. Both books disgusted him, offending all his canons of art and prose. "Why are English novels so terribly boring?" he demanded. "I think Gissing has little merit. The Socialist in this [*Demos*] is first a worker and then inherits a fortune, jilts his first girl, marries a lady, becomes a big employer and takes to drink. You know the kind of story. There is a clergyman in it with searching eyes and a deep voice who makes all the Socialists wince under his firm gaze. I am going to read another book of his. Then I will try Arthur Morrison and Hardy and finally Thackeray." With a flash of his old Dublin arrogance he concluded: "Without boasting, I think I have little or nothing to learn from English novelists." *The Crown of Life* he found equally bad and decided that Gissing's work reminded him of *pastefazoi,* a sort of Triestine soup. What he thought himself of socialism at this time, the political and economic theory so dear to Gissing, will be discussed later.

Another book that aroused a puzzled scornful comment from him was Seumas O'Kelly's *By the Stream of Killmeen,* a volume of stories sent to him at his own request by his aunt Josephine. He announced to Stanislaus: "The stories I read were about faithful and pure Connacht girls and lithe broad-shouldered open-faced young Connacht men, and I read them without blinking, patiently trying to see whether the writer was trying to express something he had understood. I always concluded by saying to myself without anger something like this, 'Well, there's no doubt they're very romantic young people; at first they come as a relief, then they tire. Maybe, begod, people like that are to be found by the Stream of Kilmeen only none of them has ever come under my observation, as the deceased gent in Norway remarked.' " [1]

Other books mentioned casually by him in his letters at this time were Ferraro's *Young Europe,* several volumes of Guy de Maupassant's short stories, two or three Anatole France narratives and some of the old Italian taletellers such as Sermini and Doni.

---

[1] Joyce, however, has a great admiration for this writer's remarkable short tale, "The Weaver's Grave."

For the most part he did not find the particular magic for which he sought.

His own ideas on writing as a fine art peer out obliquely from the comments on his reading. Fuzziness of conception, disregard for exactitude of expression, sentimentalism, compromise of any sort with one's literary integrity, the failure to intelligently circumscribe an idea, these were flaws that he abhorred and they were flaws that he discovered all too often in the Irish and English books he read. The stuffiness of Edward VII's smug era offended his sensibilities. He was constantly endeavouring "to see if the writer was trying to express something he had understood" and by understanding he meant to see the *thing,* the situation, the emotional resolution exactly and wholly for what it was, to catch it in its static perfection, to apprehend it at the instant of its completeness and so convey it to the reader. Compromise or sentimentality always reduced such an endeavour to bathos. And it was so that he scornfully saw the tentative expression of the Irish writers he had left behind him in Dublin. A.E.'s nest of singing birds were not cygnets to him but a self-satisfied brood of chickens peeping shrilly in a high-fenced barnyard. They apprehended neither terror nor pity; they knew not "the human disposition of sensible or intelligible matter for an æsthetic end" which was art; the old Aquinian *"Ad pulchritudinem tria requiruntur integritas, consonantia, claritas,"* over which Joyce had so pondered during his Dublin, Paris and Pola days, meant nothing to them. Small wonder, then, that he could break out bitterly (and it is by the infrequent weaknesses of a man that we may gauge his strength): "They are all in the public eye and favour. . . . And here am I (whom their writings and lives nauseate to the point of vomiting) writing away letters for ten hours a day like a blue devil on the offchance of pleasing three bad-tempered bankers and inducing them to let me retain my position while (as a luxury) I am allowed to haggle for two years with the same publisher, trying to induce him to publish a book for which he has an intense admiration. *Orco Dio!"* This was the resounding exasperation of a young man but a young man much tried to whom Time had been less than kind.

As for those phases of contemporary activities in Rome that caught at his mind they may (so far as any perceptible stimulation went, and that was but lukewarm) be confined to one: the Socialist Congress then meeting and whose clamorous sessions he followed with a detached but actual interest. The spectacle of the delegates representing various types of socialism plunging into endless internecine warfare concerning conflicting theories of dogma and action, arguing, orating, denouncing and expounding, caused to flicker up anew, but fitfully, that speculative curiosity that had moved him since the days he had first read the anarchist and socialist writers. His own socialism was thin and unsteady and ill-informed and he knew it to be so. Indeed, it was more of a sympathy than a conviction, a feeling that the perfect freedom in life with the absolute minimum of restraining laws was an ideal devoutly to be desired, a feeling that was, of course, no more socialism than it was capitalism. But it naturally followed that no favoured class should have privileges denied a more unfortunate class, that freedom—freedom of the soul, freedom of the will, freedom of the intelligence, freedom of the artistic urge—should be the common property of all, beggars as well as Edwardian noblemen and purse-proud landowners. From this anarchistic conception of the unfettered mind it was but a step to the theory of an economic equality, to a world where hardships engendered by class distinctions and the unfair distribution of the riches of the earth no longer existed. Joyce, lacking or ignoring an exact knowledge of socialism, made that step. But it would be absurd to insist that he was a Marxian or that he acquiesced in any degree to the principle that individual freedom should be subordinated to the interests of the community. He despised the bourgeois class as a class and there is no doubt he knew that his true ideal was an intellectual plane of living unattainable by the mass of mankind. It was pleasant to dream about but all the realities were against it. His intellectual anarchy, then, had little or nothing to do with Karl Marx.

Politics as politics were wearisome to him although infrequent speculative conjectures betrayed his flickering concern with them. The only country that he would like to see changed (and that so

---

[1] Among the many whose works he had read may be mentioned Most, Malatesta, Stirner, Bakunin, Kropotkin, Elisée Reclus, Spencer and Benjamin Tucker, whose *Instead of a Book* proclaimed the liberty of the non-invasive individual. He never read anything by Karl Marx except the first sentence of *Das Kapital* and he found it so absurd that he immediately returned the book to the lender.

changed that the artist might live in it without a feeling of frustration) was Ireland, but as he couldn't change the country he preferred to change the conversation. And so as he followed the windy drift of the Socialist Congress, vaguely admired Ferraro, noted that Labriola reminded him of Arthur Griffith and listened to the wordy clashes between the intellectual and parliamentary Socialists and the starker-minded Syndicalists, his tepid interest in the spectacle grew colder and colder until it congealed and was put out of mind for more important matters. Not even the explosion of a bomb near the bank (a favourite argument among the antagonistic Italian political groups) could arouse more than a momentary horror and disgust in him. He was only reminded anew of the savagery that existed in his so-called civilized world.

The far-away Irish scene made a greater impact on his mind than the bomb explosion in the Café Aragno. From his modest perch in the foreign correspondence department of the Roman bank he followed with an undeviating absorption all the phenomena, great and small, that made up the sum total of Dublin life. His great vexation was that he did not receive enough information. Dubliners, then as now, were exceedingly poor correspondents. But sufficient information (through newspapers and letters) reached him to impress upon his mind the exhilarating effect of the strong yeast that was fermenting in his native city. Dublin, according to all accounts, was one of the liveliest and most pleasant places in which to live during this transitional period of time when the rest of the world's great cities appeared content to drowse in a sort of midsummer lethargy. There was sparkling excitement over art and politics in the air above the Liffey. Hugh Lane was perfecting his plans to inaugurate the Modern Art Gallery and a shoal of young painters (few, alas, of first rank) were slapping pigment on canvas. The Arts Club had been organized and to its sessions came the James Duncans, William Butler Yeats, the Markievicz'—Cassie and Constance, the Orpens, A.E., Maurice Joy, Padraic Colum, Cruise O'Brien, Percy French and a dozen others. "The hairy fairies of Plunkett House," A.E., Sir Horace Plunkett, Edward Stopford, Henry Norman and their cohorts laboured for the Irish Agricultural Organization Society. At the Abbey Theatre, cursed by most Dubliners because it had no bar and one was forced, between the

James Joyce. From the portrait bust by Jo Davidson

41 Brighton Square, Rathgar, Dublin, the house in which James Joyce was born

Mary Jane Joyce, James Joyce's mother. From a drawing by Patrick Tuohy

James Joyce as a baby

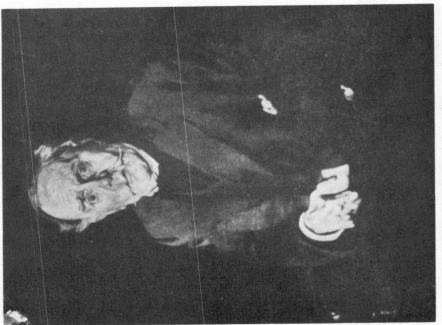

**John Stanislaus Joyce**, father of James Joyce.
From a painting by Patrick Tuohy

James Joyce as a lad at Clongowes Wood College

Courtesy Duane Library, Fordham University, New York

No. 5 Killeen House    No. 6 Belvedere House

Belvedere College, Dublin

*Courtesy "The Belviderian"*

Nos. 7 and 8 Preparatory School

University College, St. Stephen's Green

Joyce and a group of students at University College. Joyce is in the third row back, second from left

George Clancy, J. F. Byrne and James Joyce during University College days

Joyce in his graduation robes

Joyce during the first Paris years

from 23 January 1903 to 20 February 1903 (exclusive of Hotel Bill

Received    25·
            15·50
            27
            24·50
            15·65
            15·10
            ———
            122·75

                              £ 41 5½                    Total Debts

                                                          £ 1 14

Debts       5 0  (Casey)
            10 0  (Chаван)      14 8 ½       + £ 1 0 0 (Gogar
            3·40  (Casey fils)
            ————
            18·40

Hotel Bill (appr)
            30 0                £ 17 2½
            1·20
            2·80
            ————
            34·0      Hotel Bill — 38 f. 70 c

_____

TOTAL EXPENSES

        156·75              £ 5 8 8    £ 6 4 9 ½
          4·70                    3 9         3 9
        ———                 —————      —————
        161·45             £ 5 12 5    £ 6 8 6 ½
        _____

                Remainder — 0


                                    Jas Joyce

Nora Joyce

Joyce during the earlier years of the Zurich period

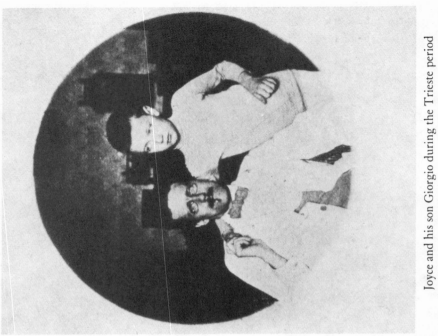

Joyce and his son Giorgio during the Trieste period

Giorgio Joyce at three years of age

Lucia Joyce during the Zurich period

73, Seefeldstrasse, Zurich. One of Joyce's residences

James Joyce in Zurich

Valery Larbaud

Portrait of the Joyce family soon after their arrival in Paris from Trieste.
Left to right: Lucia, Mrs. James Joyce; James Joyce, Giorgio Joyce

Bernard Kiernan's Public House, Dublin

Sylvia Beach and James Joyce

From left to right: James Stephens, James Joyce, John Sullivan

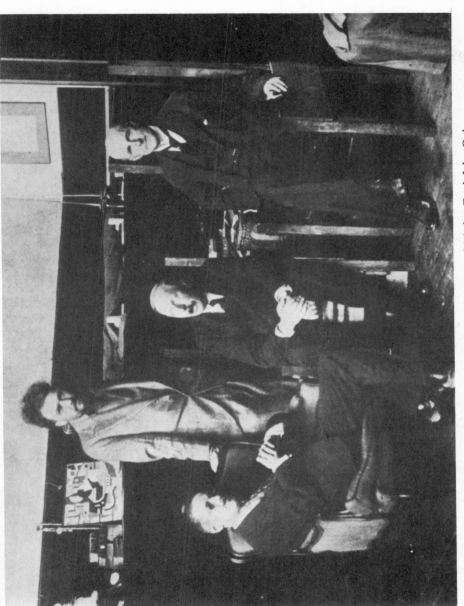

From left to right: James Joyce, Ezra Pound, Ford Madox Ford, John Quinn

Snapshots taken on the lake of Constance in 1932.
Above: James Joyce and his daughter Lucia.
Below: Lucia Joyce (second from left), James Joyce and Nora Joyce (right)

Summer of 1935. Above: Avon (Seine et Marne).
From left to right: Herbert Gorman, Nora Joyce and James Joyce.
Below: Valvins (Seine et Marne). From left to right: Claire Gorman,
Herbert Gorman and James Joyce

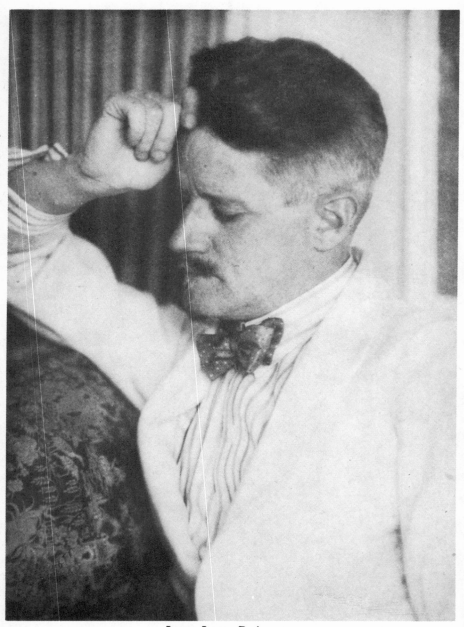

James Joyce: Paris years

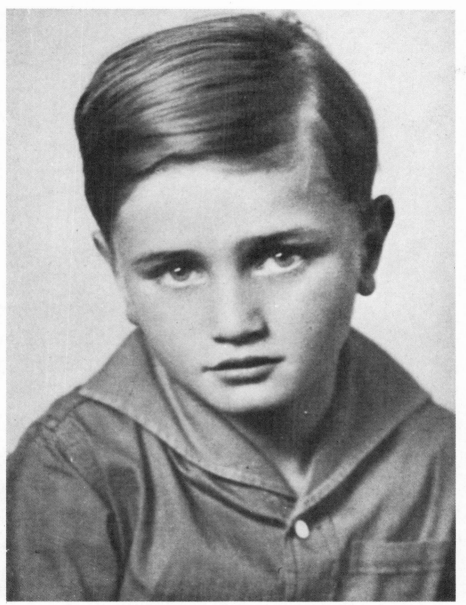

Stephen Joyce, grandson of James Joyce

Corrections sent with final proof, "Work in Progress" (*Finnegans Wake*),
Transition No. 18

Lord of ladders,
what for lungitube!

I am lather of the missed. Areed.

falling hair and for would be joybells to ring sadly ringless hands.
The dame dowager to stay kneeled how she is as first mutherer
with cord in coil. The two princes of the tower royal, daulphin and
devlin, to lie how they are without to see. The date dowager's duffgerent to present wappon and about wheel without to be seen of
them. The infants Isabella from her coign to do obeisence toward
the duffgerent as first futherer with drawn brand. Then the court
to come in to full morning. Herein see ye fail not.
— Viduif forkeg Ili vi rigardas Returnu, forkego Maldefi-
kato O Sire!

Hummels! That crag! Those hullocks! What have you therefore? I fear lest we have lost ours respecting these wildy parts.
How shagsome all and beastful! What do you show on? I show
because I must see before my misfortune so a stark pointing
pole. Can you read the verst legend hereon? To the dunleary
obelisk via the rock what myles knox furlongs; to the general's
post/office howsands of patience/ to the Wellington memorial half
a league wrongwards/ to sara's bridge good hunter and nine to
meet her/ to the point, one yeoman's yard. He, he, he! At that do
you leer? I leer because I must see a buntingcap of so a pinky on
the point. It is for a true glover's greetings and many burgesses by
us uses to pink it in this way. Do you not have heard that the queen
lying abroad/her kingshall come tomorrow, michaelmas? He shall
come by jubilarian with — who can doubt it? — His golden bea-
gles and his white elkox terriers for a hunting on our littlego ill-
come faxes/meynhir mayour, our boorgomaister, in best bib and
sucker, surrounded by his full cooperation and all our pueblos,
shall receive from king at broadstone barrow with a keys of good-
morrow onto his pompey cushion. It will give piketurns on the
tummlippiads and crosshurdles and dollmanovers and vicuvious
pyrolyphics at darkfall for our fancy ladies. You do not have
heard? I have heard anyone tell it yesterday how one should
come on morrow here but it is never here today. Well but remind
that it is always tomorrow in another place. Amen.
True! True! Is rich Mr. Porrter always in his such strong health?
I thank you for the best, he is exceedingly herculeneous. One
sees how he is lot stoutlier than of formerly. One would say him
to hold whole a litteringture of kidlings under his aproham. Has
handsome Mr. Pourater always been so long married? O yes Mr.
Pournter/familys has been marryingman ever since so long time

of lateenth dignisties
it says in book
of that which is.
meet

all
Bracc's Mamnesly

Photo by Mrs. Eugene Jolas
Final proof of "Work in Progress" (*Finnegans Wake*), Transition No. 18

acts, to run across the street and round the corner to Wynn's for a sixpenny 'Baby' Powers, the company was rehearsing a new play that would lay all Dublin by the ears and even have repercussions on Joyce, as we shall see. A quaint individual (Dublin has always abounded in them) called Alabaster was inventing a piano that played colours instead of notes. The Players Club, guided by Arnold Graves, continued to produce dramas with amateur casts. The Gaelic League, directed by its prophet with the waterfall moustache, Douglas Hyde, today President of Eire, industriously propagated the Irish language. Arthur Griffith, that square-jawed fighter, was struggling to establish the Sinn Fein party and build up an organization strong enough to contest a parliamentary election. And in the submerged ranks of Labour the two Jameses, Connolly and Larkin, were proselytizing against that day when they might present a united front to callous capitalism. At another extreme Dr. Esposito was conducting concerts calculated to raise the level of music in Dublin. It was all exciting from the lunatic fringe exemplified by that Endymion who strode the streets with a bare sabre under his arms to the large-bodied lumbering Edward Martyn who forsook his heavy dinners at the Kildare Street Club to dabble in politics, in the language revival, in music, in plays, in a stained-glass renascence, in anything at all calculated to advance the civilization of Ireland.

And Joyce was copying dull letters in a distant Italian bank.

From that lamentable situation he desired to know everything, what books were written, what gossip was retailed in the streets and public houses, what political agitation was in process or impending, in short, the very shape and substance and diurnal being of Dublin. At the same time he was constantly diving back into the past. He demanded old editions of Kickham, Griffin, Carleton, Banim, P. J. Smyth. He wondered if his aunt would send him a great bundle of tram tickets, advertisements, handbills, posters, newspapers, programmes, city maps, all the small flotsam that daily covered the fluctuating waters of the dancing sea that was Dublin.

"Remembering thee, O Sion."

Politics as politics, it has been pointed out, were wearisome to him and yet the Dublin manifestations as he read of them in the *United Irishman* and, later, *Sinn Fein* aroused a rational commentary that would have done credit to any observer before the event. "You ask me," he wrote to Stanislaus, "what I would substitute for parliamentary agitation in Ireland. I think the Sinn Fein policy would be more effective. Of course, I see that its success would be to substitute Irish for English capital, but no one, I suppose, denies that capitalism is a stage of progress. The Irish proletariat has yet to be created. A feudal peasantry exists, scraping the soil, but this would with a national revival or with a definite preponderance of England surely disappear. I quite agree with you that Griffith is afraid of the priests—and he has every reason so to be. But, possibly, they are also a little afraid of him, too. After all, he is holding out some secular liberty to the people and the Church doesn't approve of that. I quite see that the Church is still, as it was in the time of Adrian IV, the enemy of Ireland, but I think her time is almost up. For either Sinn Fein or Imperialism will conquer the present Ireland."

At the time of this letter, the winter of 1906, Sinn Fein as a political organization had existed for but little more than a year. The bloody Easter Week of 1916 was ten years in the future. Yet here was Joyce prophesying either that the infant movement of Arthur Griffith would conquer or British imperialism would devour the country. And here it may be pointed out that Joyce, if anything, was an Irish Nationalist at heart, especially if a lifelong and so far successful battle against English ideas merits that title. "If the Irish programme did not insist on the Irish language," he declared to his brother, "I suppose I could call myself a nationalist." He was as precise and consistent as ever in intimating that he could not offer even lip service to any shift in Irish culture that would cut that country off from the great stream of European civilization. He had declared himself upon that point in "The Day of the Rabblement" and he would continue to declare himself in spite of the professional patriots in Dublin. But he was never a pro-Englander and the accusations brought against him in later years were, as we shall see, nothing less than malicious libels.

IV

It was this continuous absorption in the Dublin scene and the consequent dissatisfaction in being so far from it that gave birth to his restlessness in Rome. To understand him one has to emphasize this many times. As the days passed prosaically one after the other the sensation that he was stifling in a vacuum obsessed him. He was crushed under the "ponderous remembrances" that recalled nothing to him. He brooded more and more about other cities only partially realizing that he would be just as dissatisfied in them as he was in Rome. It might be tempting to exclaim "Lost young man!" here but he was not a lost young man. He knew where he was and where he desired to be. He was a strayed young man, an exile through reason following a road that would lead back to Dublin only when Dublin suffered a sea change into something nearer to his vision of place. Still, the justification for his plight did not lessen its pangs.

This restlessness reached its apogee when one winter day in February 1907 (and by this time he was living in new quarters at Via Monte Brianzo, 51, two rooms on the roof from which he had an excellent bird's-eye view of the Holy City), he chanced upon an English journal and read in it an account of an amazing fracas in Dublin. This was a report of the stormy first night of John Millington Synge's *The Playboy of the Western World* at the Abbey Theatre.

The story of that première, which occurred on January 26, 1907, is familiar to most students of international drama and there is no necessity to expatiate upon it here. Synge's play, with its boastful pseudo parricide, was too strong a meat for the strict Catholic-National-intellectual element that patronized the Abbey Theatre and expected gentle fairy tales about noble peasant boys and pure-souled religious girls in red shawls. It was an unpleasant purgative for queasy stomachs weakened by a fare of innocuous delicacies. Mr. W. J. Lawrence expressed the self-righteous horror of Dublin's professional patriots and Mutual Admiration Society when he wrote (and we can feel the pen shaking in his holy fustigating hand): "The wonder was, could it be possible that there existed anywhere in our Island of Saints, a community so vile as this, where one and all, men and women alike, were lost to all sense of moral decency? The occasional expression of coarse thoughts in coarse language might have been tolerated, but not the implication of abysmal paganism." Even from this distance of time we can hear the outraged yells from the audience at such lines as Christy Mahon's declaration to Pegeen Mike: "I squeezing kisses on your puckered lips till I'd feel a kind of pity for the Lord God in all ages sitting lonesome in His golden chair!" and that other terrific image picturing all the girls of Mayo standing before Christy Mahon in their shifts. What blasphemy! What indecency!

As Joyce read about this hurly-burly in his English journal and the Irish papers that reached him a day or two later a wild exasperation at his own loneliness possessed him and rapidly tautened to the breaking point. "This whole affair has upset me," he burst out to his brother. "I feel like a man in a house who hears a row in the street and voices he knows shouting but can't get up to see what the hell is going on. It has put me off the story I was going to write—to wit, 'The Dead.' " Almost immediately he decided definitely to leave Rome. Let the cursed "ponderous remembrances" remind somebody else of something. Where he should go, however, proved to be a painful problem. Without settling upon that destination he recklessly handed in his notice at the bank. At least the coil was cut and he would *have* to go somewhere. He wrote to various agencies and answered newspaper advertisements in different parts of Italy and France. The idea of Marseilles again crossed his mind and he thought it might be pleasant to labour in a shipping office near the harbour where he could go in and out and see the water sparkling in the bay and hear the din of ships loading and unloading. But this was no more than a passing fancy, a daydream of his quickened imagination. His painful problem was quickly reaching its solution without any particular mental volition on his part. Hard-fisted circumstance and a not-unwilling surrender were seeing to that. Trieste, the city he had left in disgust, began to draw him like an irresistible magnet. He was known there. He remembered that there he would meet people who shared his temperament to some degree. He would be able to talk all he pleased about Dublin with Stanislaus. He recalled with some nostalgia calm evenings when he had strolled along the Triestine streets and thought over the phrases in his stories. Very well, then, though it were no more than the best of a bad bargain he would accept it and return. "There is some element of sanity in this last mad performance of mine, I am sure," he remarked to his dubious-minded brother and he was right. Even the discouraging news, forwarded by Stanislaus, that the Berlitz School would provide no place for him did not change his determination. He would give private lessons, then. In some way he would make ends meet. And he would be able to write in Trieste, something he had found almost impossible in Rome. The last story in *Dubliners* was ready to his pen and behind it there was *Stephen Hero,* which, after all, he thought he would call *A Portrait of the Artist as a Young Man.*

Early in March the three wanderers were back in Trieste.

# *Seven*

THE familiar streets with their picturesque figures hurrying to and fro reassured Joyce and as he settled his family in modest quarters at Via Santa Catarina, 1, he experienced the sensation of the wanderer who had returned to a well-known home. It was not the real home, perhaps, that was Dublin, but it was as close as he, an exile because of a rigorous moral and artistic necessity, could come to a home. There was Stanislaus with whom to converse again and there were the winding ways of the Città Vecchia wherein to wander. The bora roared a welcome to him and the Triestine dialect fell pleasantly upon his ears. The smiling Romans and the multitudinous ruins of the Eternal City faded into the perspective of things that had served their purpose.

Joyce's first task was to procure private students of the English language so that he might support himself and his family and as he had already achieved some reputation as teacher during the Berlitz School days they were not too difficult to find. An acquaintance of this period (Silvio Benco) describes the Joyce of 1907 in these terms: "Tall, thin, smooth-shaven (a member of the giraffe family, he used to say) he might have seemed (and without so much contradicting the facts) an overgrown schoolboy who had developed too rapidly. Except that no one would have taken James Joyce for an overgrown boy, so vivid was the impression of a mature, already decided life in his stiff, automaton-like bearing . . . He was always hastening from house to house to give their hour of English to all the Triestines. Energetic and punctual in his work, devoted to his wife, his children and his house, he was remarkable for his sobriety. But within there was the poetic torment, the keen critical mind, the paradoxical *diablerie* of Joyce."

The young man apparently kept from his students as a whole the knowledge that the teaching of language was distasteful to him and that his entire nature was permeated with a devouring creative urge. But there was one exception and that was a businessman named Ettore Schmitz who in his youth had written a couple of books under the nom de plume of Italo Svevo. To him Joyce revealed himself and his ambitions and the contact between the two men was such that it affected both of them. Schmitz returned to writing, undoubtedly at the instigation of Joyce, and Joyce found in the matter-of-fact unsentimental Schmitz more than one hint for the cloudy figure moving in the back of his mind and who would one day be called Leopold Bloom.

Joyce's salary as a language teacher at the beginning was equivalent to tenpence an hour and there were days when he gave as many as eleven lessons. Later his fees rose to 2/— and 2/6 and in the cases of some classes to 4/— and even 5/—. There was not much leisure, then, for his creative work; that had to go by the board for the time being or be hastily snatched at late at night. As an example of the laboriousness of his days the teaching of a certain Captain Dehan may be cited. Captain Dehan commanded a boat that used to come every fortnight to Trieste from Bari. On these days Joyce would leave his house, walk across the Piazza Giambattista Vico, walk through the tunnel of Montuzza, take an electric tram to the gate of the Free Port, enter and take a horse tram to the Punto Franco, make signals to the ship until a small boat was sent out for him, board the boat and be taken to the ship, climb aboard and have a sailor search for the Captain, look for a quiet spot to give the lesson, give it (the Captain was intensely stupid), then look for a sailor to take him back to the Punto Franco, enter the horse tram and ride to the gate of the Free Port, board the electric tram which would take him to the mouth of the Montuzza tunnel, walk back through it, cross the Piazza Giambattista Vico and so reach his house. For this extraordinary exertion he received payment amounting to thirty pence.

Interrupting the grey routine of 1907 were four events that had their influence on Joyce and his future. The first was the publication of his first book.

On April sixth Elkin Mathews issued an edition of five hundred and nine copies of *Chamber Music,* priced at 1/6. The tome was a small one bound in light-green boards with the title in gold on the side and back and the title page carrying a design with a harpsichord. True to his word Arthur Symons immediately reviewed the little volume in an English periodical and as what he wrote is probably the first piece of any length ever to be written about Joyce it deserves to be set down here:

'Chamber Music,' by James Joyce, an Irishman, who was in no Irish movement, literary or national, has not anything obviously Celtic in its manner. The book is tiny, there are thirty-seven pages, with a poem on each page. [This is not true. There are thirty-six poems on thirty-six unnumbered pages.] And they are all so singularly good, so firm and delicate, and yet so full of music and suggestion, that I can hardly choose between them; they are almost all of an equal merit. Here is one of the finest:

> Gentle lady, do not sing
>     Sad songs about the end of love;
> Lay aside sadness and sing
>     How love that passes is enough.
>
> Sing about the long deep sleep
>     Of lovers that are dead and how
> In the grave all love shall sleep.
>     Love is aweary now.

No one who has not tried can realize how difficult it is to do such tiny evanescent things as that; for it is to evoke, not only roses in midwinter, but the very dew of the roses. Sometimes I am reminded of Elizabethan, but more often of Jacobean, lyrics; there is more than sweetness, there is now and then the sharp prose touch, as in Rochester, which gives a kind of malice to sentiment:

> For elegant and antique phrase,
>     Dearest, my lips wax all too wise;
> Nor have I known a love whose praise
>     Our piping poets solemnize,
> Neither a love where may not be
> Ever so little falsity.

There is a rare kind of poetry to be made out of the kind or unkind insinuations of lovers, who are not always in a state of rapture, even when the mood comes for singing, and it may, like this love-poet, be turned to a new harmony.

> And all for some strange name he read
> In Purchas or in Holinshed.

There is no substance at all in these songs, which hardly hint at a story; but they are like a whispering clavichord that someone plays in the evening, when it is getting dark. They are full of ghostly old tunes, that were never young, and will never be old, played on an old instrument. If poetry is to be a thing overheard, these songs, certainly, will justify the definition. They are so slight, as a drawing of Whistler is slight, that their entire beauty will not be discovered by those who go to poetry for anything but its perfume. But to those who care only for what is essentially poetry in a poem, they will seem to have so much the more value by all they omit. There is only just enough, but these instants are, in Browning's phrase, 'made eternity.'

Perhaps the rare quality of these songs might captivate certain readers. Such a song as *Bright Cap and Streamers* or *Silently She's Combing* ought to catch every fancy, and the graver poems ought to awaken every imagination. But if anything in art is small, and merely good, without anything but that fact to recommend it, it has usually to wait a long time for recognition. People are so afraid of following even an impulse, fearing that they may be mistaken. How unlikely it seems, does it not, that any new thing should come suddenly into the world and be beautiful.

In the old *Freeman's Journal* of Dublin there appeared a sympathetic notice over the initials T. M. K., which every student of modern Irish politics will be able to translate. It was, of course, Thomas M. Kettle. This was to be for more than twenty years the first and last mention of Joyce's name in any Dublin paper, though it seems in the last few years the silence has been broken.

There were other favourable reviews as well and Joyce optimistically ventured to hope that he might gain a few pounds from the sales of the book. In this hope he was disappointed, but the mere fact of the publication of *Chamber Music* was of a greater value at this period than, perhaps, he suspected. It was a book. It was published by a professional publisher at the publisher's risk. In other words, Joyce had joined the great company of professional authors and joined it at a moment when he most needed the strengthening reassurance of that fact. It was not a fortification of his faith in himself as a creator that he needed (for that faith had never faltered) but it was rather an indication that the public (represented by publishers, at least) would accept him and, consequently, that in the near or far future he would be released from routine drudgeries having nothing in common with his art. *Chamber Music* did that for him.

The second event of 1907 was the discovery of Joyce as a writer by Triestine journalists. This was due to Joyce's contribution of three articles to *Il Piccolo della Sera,* then edited by Roberto Prezioso. The budding journalist wrote, of course, in Italian ("The Italian was a bit hard and cautious," comments Silvio Benco) and the subjects had to do with Irish politics. They were, so to speak, the final flickers of Joyce's interest in such matters. The first, called "The Last of the Sinn Fein," was concerned with the apparently dwindling strength of that young militant party. In Rome, as we have seen, Joyce believed that either Sinn Fein or imperialism would triumph in Ireland; he now believed that imperialism was winning and that this was due to the inconsistent Irish nature, always blowing hot and cold by turns. "In Ireland at the psychological moment the traitor always appears," he wrote bluntly and the statement was one that was later paraphrased in *Ulysses.* The second article was called "Home Rule Come of Age" and pointed out that twenty-one years had passed since Gladstone, in 1886, made his statement that the English Liberal party would refuse to legislate for England until England had granted some measure of self-rule to Ireland. But, in the intervening time, Gladstone, "having, with the aid of the Irish bishops, brought about the assassination of Parnell," Home Rule had met with nothing but disaster. The third article was entitled "Ireland in the Dock." All the pessimism of Joyce concerning his country and its future was packed into this indictment. Ireland "does not succeed in making herself understood; she has no means of communicating with the public opinion of England and other countries. The Irish are alleged cut-throats. The true sovereign of Ireland, the Pope, looks upon them as the English do."

Joyce, of course, was observing Ireland from a distance and over a space of three years' exile. If the political pulse was accelerating he could only know it by hearsay, by the letters he received from his family, by the constant stream of Irish newspapers that sped from Dublin to Trieste. He knew it, too, from his deep comprehension of the Irish character, from his instinctive awareness of the mental reactions of the race he considered to be the most beated in Europe. It would be easy to assume that Joyce's own misfortunes with his people had so prejudiced him that he was incapable of taking a neutral attitude and seeing the situation for what it was without personal coloration. But this is not true. He had arrived at his conclusions by a dispassionate reasoning and not without anguish. He loved Dublin and it tortured him to think what inconsiderate and cowardly men had made of the city. His journalism, then, may be regarded as a sort of vent through which he dissipated the bitterness that was swelling his mind. He was all the better for it. Through it he was unconsciously fumbling towards a realization of that atmospheric pressure that colours parts of *Ulysses.* And through it, too, he found a sympathetic personality, Roberto Prezioso, to whom he could read the stories that made up *Dubliners,* and discuss them as he could with no others except his brother Stanislaus and Ettore Schmitz. The small circle was widening.

A third event of importance to him occurred on July twenty-sixth, St. Anne's day, when his daughter, Lucia Anna, was born in the City Hospital of Trieste. This added considerably to his responsibilities and emphasized in his mind anew the necessity for constant labour. With three to provide for out of a precarious livelihood he was to be seen more often than ever dashing from house to house in Trieste to give his English lessons and the day was to come when he mockingly remarked that he had taught everybody in town the English language and would have to move on to another city. With such an unequal contest with fortune it was exceedingly difficult for him to devote much time to his creative labours and they consequently suffered, the huge manuscript of *Stephen Hero* being laid aside for the time being.

But in the early autumn a fourth event in the form of an unexpected letter renewed his interest in his writing. One Joseph Hone, a director of Maunsel and Company, Dublin publishers, wrote to him from Marseilles suggesting that he submit the manuscript of *Dubliners* to the Irish firm. Joyce did so and then waited impatiently for the decision of acceptance or rejection and the possible contract. He was to have a long wait, Irish publishers being, if anything, still more impossible than English publishers.

An unfortunate episode marked this year, also. Shortly before he left Rome Joyce had celebrated a special occasion by dancing through the streets late one night with two postmen during a terrific rainstorm. Some time after he returned to Trieste he developed a rheumatic fever which temporarily atrophied his biceps. This resulted in his first attack of iritis, an ailment that was to torture him annually for the next eighteen years. Grave as this may sound it was but the beginning of the many eye troubles that were eventually to reduce him close to blindness. His doctor in Trieste was Oblath, a student of the famous Brettauer.

If 1907 was a year of few events for Joyce and his future, 1908 may be said to be a year without any events. He continued the dreary round of language lessons, he translated John M. Synge's *Riders to the Sea* into Italian, with the assistance of Dr. Nicolò Vidacovitch he did the same thing with W. B. Yeats's *Countess Cathleen,* he burned a portion of *Stephen Hero* in a fit of momentary despair and then started the novel anew in a more compressed form, he waited in vain for the contract for *Dubliners* from Maunsel and Company, he suffered his second attack of iritis and he received not a penny in royalties from *Chamber Music.* As for the lighter side of life, he went often to the theatre, he became interested in several Triestine musicians including Antonio Smaraglia the little-known blind Polesan composer of the charming opera *Nozze Istriane* and the beautiful opera *La Falena,* and followed their careers attentively, he studied singing for a time under Romeo Bartoli and he read the dramatic criticisms of Giovanni Pozza in the *Corriere.* Late in the year, in December, he conceived an idea which he broached in a letter to his sister Poppie.[1] He wrote:

> Via S. Catarina, 1.
> Trieste, Austria.

DEAR POPPIE,
    Thanks for sending on the music. I have seen your letter to Stannie and his reply, which is enclosed with this. I have an idea which you will tell me if you like. I will send Georgie among you for six weeks or so next summer in charge of Stannie if you think such a proposal would have the effect desired. Neither he nor Stannie would be any expense as (if we can manage the thing at all) we shall pay all expenses of travelling and board with you. Perhaps he might be a good influence in your household and I fancy all of you would be glad to make his acquaintance. He could go about the end of July and come back to Trieste about the

[1] Now Sister Mary Gertrude, Convent of the Order of Mercy, Greymouth, New Zealand.

end of August or first of September. If you like the idea and think it likely to do good I shall write to Pappy myself.

I suppose you will think this a hare-brained idea like all the others I have had hitherto but if you will walk around it for about a quarter of an hour and look at it from all sides it will begin to look right enough.

I will send him gladly if that will make yiz all happy and loving. I told him I was going to, and he has been canvassing all the people in the house for a valise to put his clothes in and go to 'Dubirino.'

Thank you, I feel a little better of the rheumatism and am now more like a capital S than a capital Z. Hoping this will find you as it leaves me at present, thank God, I am, dear sister,

Your most affectionate brother,

Jim.

But when the time came for the projected trip it was not Stanislaus who accompanied the three-year-old Giorgio but Joyce himself. At the last moment the lure of Dublin had been too strong and, furthermore, there was the question of the dilatory tactics of Maunsel and Company concerning the acceptance or rejection of *Dubliners.* That slothful little firm had even outdone Grant Richards in the stupid sin of procrastination. So, about the first of August 1909, Joyce and his young son left Via Vincenzo Scussa, 8, the new address to which they had recently moved, for the city that the father had not seen for five years.

II

The voyagers were met at Westland Row Railroad Station by the entire Joyce family group. During the next few days the returned exile had an opportunity of discovering what Dublin thought of his appearance and he humorously set the verdicts down in a letter he wrote to his brother.

> Aunt J.: lost all boyishness
> Cosgrave: in splendid health
> Eglinton: looking very ecclesiastical
> Gogarty: Jaysus, man, you're in phthisis
> O'Leary Curtis: much more mature
> Sheehan: very thin
> Eileen: very foreign-looking
> Keohler: you look 35

Mrs. Skeff.: not a bit changed
Skeff.: somewhat blasé
Everybody: melancholy
Russell: like a man of business

While the family at 44 Fontenoy Street regaled themselves with the infant Giorgio, Joyce set about his business immediately with the firm of Maunsel and Company. He discovered that one George Roberts was the man with whom to treat. For the time being all went well and by the twentieth of the month the contract for the publication of *Dubliners* was signed by both parties and stamped at the Stamp Office. With this off his mind, as he thought, he proceeded to renew his acquaintance with the familiar city, wandering about the streets and visiting old companions. It was, he discovered, the same Dublin, the very replica of the image he had carried about Europe in his mind for five arduous years. The well-known thoroughfares and squares and buildings, the Liffey running gently between her narrow quays, the green expanse of St. Stephen's Green, the grey-brown bulk of Trinity College, the General Post Office and the Mansion House and Leinster House and the National Library and the Nelson Pillar and the statue of O'Connell and the bookstalls on Bachelor's Walk and the Rotunda and Davy Byrne's and The Ship and the stews[1] and Eglinton and A.E. walking sedately along the street, all were there as he had remembered them and would remember them again for a definite purpose when the special dæmon of creation that had briefly visited him in Rome reached upward in his mind once more.

His activities beyond this replunge into the variegated life of his native city were few. He attended the première of George Bernard Shaw's *The Shewing Up of Blanco Posnet* and wrote a critique on it which he sent to the *Piccolo della Sera*. He wrote to Synge's brother about the rights of production of the Italian translation of *Riders to the Sea* and received such an unsatisfactory re-

---

[1] There is nothing in Paris resembling this old Nighttown (now vanished) and to see something like it one has to go to the Vieux-Port at Marseilles. Curiously enough, the whole quarter was dominated by the Roman Catholic Church of the city, the Pro-Cathedral on Marlborough Street, so called because the other two cathedrals, St. Patrick's and Christ Church, are now Protestant. Dubliners facetiously referred to the Pro-Cathedral as the Cathedral of the "Pros." The three churches appear from time to time throughout *Finnegans Wake*, *Marlborough the Less*, *Greatchrist*, *Holy Protector* and so on.

sponse that he decided to let the brother "follow J.M.S. to the Wicklow quarter of hell." He applied in turn to the *Irish Times,* the *Express* and the *Mail* for authorization to interview. Enrico Caruso, who was singing in Dublin at the time, and was politely refused. He went to the new recently-reorganized National University to discover if the Board planned a professorship in Italian (with the idea of applying for it) and found that there would be only a lectureship in commercial Italian at £100 a year. It did not appeal to him. And he decided to bring his sister Eva back to Trieste with him and so make life easier for the mother of his children.

By the second week in September, with his signed contract for *Dubliners* in his pocket, he was shepherding his sister Eva and his son George by way of London, Boulogne, Basle, Zurich, Innsbruck and Laibach to Trieste.

One would think that this dip back into the past would have been sufficient for one year but Fate in the form of a motley quartet of impresarios decreed otherwise. No sooner was Joyce back in Trieste than he met four businessmen who together controlled two cinemas in the Austrian city and one in Bucharest. They were Antonio Machnich, an upholsterer who had invented a new type of sofa-bed; Giovanni Rebez, a leather merchant; Giuseppe Caris, a draper; and Francesco Novak of Pirano, proprietor of a bicycle shop. Through Dr. Nicolò Vidacovitch Joyce interested this quartet in the idea of introducing cinema theatres into Ireland, and especially in Dublin. There were hurried negotiations between the little group and on the twenty-first of October Joyce was back in Dublin again with a contract to open cinemas in Dublin, Belfast and Cork and a limited amount of money with which to finance them. Stanislaus, who had dreamt vainly of returning to Ireland, remained in Trieste and took over Joyce's language students whose names were like a melody: Popper, Bolaffio, Veneziani, Castelbolonese, Sordina, Höberth, Bertoli and Latzer.

For a brief period Joyce the businessman superseded Joyce the artist. He trotted about Dublin examining premises suitable to be translated into cinema theatres, interviewed the theatre inspector about licenses and familiarized himself with the laws governing such ventures. Eventually he decided upon a site at 45 Mary Street as being the most feasible. So much done, he wired for Antonio Machnich (at the same time remarking in a letter to his brother: "If M. makes as many mistakes travelling as he does in writing Italian he will end in Archangel!") and occupied himself with other affairs. Among these other affairs was the curious one of securing for himself an agency in Trieste for Irish tweeds.[1] It was not long before the young Dubliner discovered that Joyce the businessman could not exist simultaneously with Joyce the artist. One or the other must go. The businessman went.

Machnich and Rebez and Novak arrived in Dublin early in November and at a moment when Joyce, his expense money exhausted, was fearful that the lease of 45 Mary Street would be voided for non-payment of rent. With the arrival of the trio, none of whom could speak English, the construction of the Volta Theatre (so named in honour of Alessandro Volta) was hurried forward. The trio and Joyce made a hurried trip to Belfast (which the Verdi-loving foreigners persisted in calling Falstaff) to look over the ground there. They found no site but Joyce discovered W. B. Reynolds, music critic of the Belfast *Evening Telegraph,* who had set to music several of the songs from *Chamber Music.* This, undoubtedly, interested him far more than possible sites for cinema theatres. Back in Dublin (December second) Joyce the artist was further elated by the promise of George Roberts of Maunsel and Company that first proofs of *Dubliners* would be ready the following week. The young writer (with an astounding optimism) had already figured out that if the book sold twelve thousand copies the royalties would total £500.

However, for the moment Joyce the businessman was predominant. In a letter written to his brother at this period he gives a clear picture of his activities:

It is 1 a.m. I have just come home from Mary Street where I have been for the last hour or so in a cellar under the house in the middle of electric wires. The show is not open yet. Every day there are disappointments. If I were to write you all the confusion here you would not find it amusing in the least. On Saturday night, for example, I was up till 4.30 a.m. sending express letters and telegrams for the Società to Trieste,

[1] He got the agency and did, in fact, succeed in clothing several of his Triestine male pupils in Irish homespuns ordered by them.

London and Bucharest. I got home and a cannon woke me up at 7 a.m. I rose in the pelting rain and got to Kingsbridge. We left for Cork at 8 a.m. and arrived at 1 p.m. For five rainy dreary hours we were mooning about Cork. At 6 p.m. we left for Dublin, and arrived at 11.30 p.m. I was home at midnight, dined and sat down to write with the result that I got to my ricketty, naked bed at 3 a.m. Since this work began I have never been in bed before 3 or 3.30.

I have no end of trouble and anxiety concerning landlords and builders, etc. Now the electrical engineer has left us in the lurch and the Società blames me for choosing him. How was I to know? (I forgot to say that the trip to Cork was put down to my expenses and cost me my share of outlay. . . .) I sent two advance posters to you today (designed by me) and that is all the news I have. I have not even got the Licence yet, as the Recorder is not sitting at present, though I have had plenty of Irish promises. I am busy night, noon and morning. To my advt. in the papers for staff hands, etc., I got nearly 200 replies and had to interview about fifty of them. I did not wish to write either to you, Schmitz, Francini or Vidacovitch until the ball is open, as I know the *scalogna* that follows me. I will wire the moment we open.

In spite of obstacles, however, the Volta Theatre opened on the Monday of Christmas Week with a program of Italian films and so large was the crowd that milled about the strange new venture that the police had to be called to keep them in order. Half an hour before the opening a Sinn Fein electrician, probably convinced that the cinema had nothing to do with the freedom of Ireland, abruptly quit and Joyce was forced to scour Dublin for a substitute. On Christmas Day Machnich and Rebez returned to Bucharest leaving Joyce and Novak to carry on the Volta, which, though the weather was extremely bad, managed to draw a fairly good business.

Joyce almost immediately decided to return to Trieste. There were two strong reasons for this contemplated departure. He was suffering from iritis again and he desired to be treated by his Triestine doctor. Also, he had received the disturbing news from Stanislaus that his landlord had served a writ for non-payment of rent and there was danger of the entire family being flung out into the street. This was a problem that required immediate attention. Furthermore, he was anxious to take his sister Eileen back to Trieste with him. All these considerations pushed him into speedy action and by the first week in January 1910 he was on his way back to the only city that he could really call home.

The further history of the Volta Theatre proved disappointing enough. Novak discovered that it was easier to run a bicycle shop in Pirano than to direct a cinema in Dublin. The language, the climate, the people were too alien and incomprehensible. After five months the bewildered foreigner gave up the unequal struggle, and the Società, much against the will of Joyce who argued three weeks against it, sold out the theatre to an English company. It was Joyce's first and last active venture into the hard-headed world of business. If it proved anything it proved that such a world was the very last one into which he should venture. He could (and, as we have seen, did) work hard but his impracticality in matters concerning money was such that he was certain to be fleeced or bested. He simply did not have the knack. In the case of the Volta Theatre some months later (in June) he received the sum of one thousand crowns as a liquidation of his partnership.

### III

When he returned to Trieste with Eileen he was penniless. A desperate note dispatched by hand to his brother during February reveals his condition.

Dear Stannie,

There is a summons here and people are calling for bills. I have no money whatever. I have four new pupils next week but till then cannot get anything. Kindly come here unless we are to starve.

Jim.

There appears at this period to have been a series of differences between Joyce and his brother Stanislaus. Perhaps Stanislaus felt that he could no longer meet the emotional demands of his highly-nervous brother. Both had lives to lead, both had ambitions and both were high-strung and impatient. Joyce was desperately grasping to right and left for the means (and he meant to have them at all cost) to preserve himself against illimitable disaster. A dæmon prodded him on and that dæmon was ruthless in its intensity. It became for the writer (who was but twenty-eight years old) an almost hysterical struggle to keep his head above the cold waters of complete material failure. Another sombre note, sent by hand to Stanislaus on March twelfth, reveals the perilous situation.

DEAR STANNIE,

I know nothing of any forty crowns. Zannoni's man was here six times in three days. He had orders to take the piano yesterday, but I prevailed on him to wait another day. As I have already paid 300 crowns, I think it would be silly to lose it. Kindly send me today at least one month for him and I will pay the other. And in addition some money for the house, which you arranged to give if I paid the bills. If not, I must sell part of my furniture. I do not understand your obscure threats, but I paid the money. I got away relying on your promise to keep the house going.

JIM.

The forty crowns mentioned in this letter was for the part support of their sister which both brothers had agreed to share. Stanislaus's prolonged absences from the house were the result of frequent quarrels with his sister and occasionally with his sister-in-law. Joyce invariably acted as a jocular peacemaker.

Casting about on all sides for the means of preserving himself and his family Joyce remembered that he had never received a penny from *Chamber Music*. On the fourth of April he wrote to his English publisher:

Via Vincenzo Scussa 8,
Trieste, Austria.

Elkin Mathews, Esq.,
London.

DEAR SIR,

It is now three years since you published *Chamber Music* and I would like to hear if the sales have brought in anything to my profit. Therefore I would ask you to send me an account to date by return.

When I was in Belfast last autumn Mr. W. Reynolds, musical critic of the *Belfast Evening Telegraph,* gave me some settings he had made of certain of the songs and complained to me that you had refused to give him permission to set them. Illness and various business prevented me from writing you earlier on this matter. I cannot understand why you did not give him leave. I had a letter today from Mr. O'Brien Butler, the Irish composer . . . who writes that he admires the verses very much and will perhaps set some of them. Should he write you thereon I do not see why such permission should be withheld. I was told in Dublin that a Mr. Hughes had also done some of the songs and one has even been set by a young Italian musician here. Seeing that no fewer than five composers seem to have been at work on the book and in the light of the press notices which were all very favourable I am quite at a loss to understand how the book has brought me in nothing so far.

I will ask you for a line in reply and trust it may be of an encouraging nature.

Perhaps it will interest you to know that my long delayed book of stories *Dubliners* will come out in Dublin early in June published by Messrs Maunsel.

Very truly yours,

JAMES JOYCE.

As was to be expected there were no royalties.

Joyce, too, was mistaken about the publication date of *Dubliners*. Late in the previous year the Irish publisher, apparently frightened by a frank reference to King Edward VII in the story called "Ivy Day in the Committee Room," had asked Joyce to change the passage. Reluctantly he had done so. But this had not satisfied the publishers. An unexpected, new and malevolent spirit seemed to enter into their correspondence and they deliberately procrastinated on the publication of the book and eventually demanded that the author either completely kill or drastically change the passage in question. Joyce, remembering his futile epistolary duel with Grant Richards (and was it not curious that Grant Richards and George Roberts had the same initials?), refused with some fury to compromise any further. On July 10, 1910, he wrote an ultimatum to the Irish firm, having, as will be noted, changed his address again.

Via della Barriera Vecchia 32, III.
Trieste
(Austria)

MESSRS MAUNSEL AND COMPANY,
Dublin,

In a letter I wrote you some time ago I proposed either deletion of the passage in dispute with a prefatory note of explanation by me or arbitration as a solution of the matter. No reply has been sent me.

If no reply is sent me to this letter I shall consider that you have no intention of publishing the book and shall communicate the whole.matter of the dispute in a circular letter to the Irish press and at the same time take legal action against you through my solicitor in Dublin for breach of contract.

Yours sincerely,

JAMES JOYCE.

Joyce received no satisfaction from this letter. The Dublin publisher seemed to be animated by an unreasonable animosity that had not existed during the earlier part of 1909. It was as though a new and evil influence antagonistic to Joyce had crept malevolently into the attitude of the little firm and was determined to completely suppress the publication of *Dubliners*. Joyce was at a loss as to what he could or might do to assert his own rights. He wrote letters; by mail he consulted a Dublin solicitor; no satisfactory solution appeared. What, in the name of God, did the idiots mean by their suddenly-changed front? Who was behind it all? Joyce could not answer that question and it is difficult to answer it today. One can but suspect and suspicions cannot be put down on paper. There is some reason to believe that the influence was exerted by a person who is no longer alive.

In the meantime Joyce continued the drudgery of his language lessons, often living from hand to mouth while he frantically watched time flow by and knew that all he had dreamt of accomplishing was either choked or in a forced abeyance. The summer of 1910 merged into the autumn and then into a rainy winter. A new year arrived inauspiciously enough and he passed his twenty-ninth birthday with nothing but the slim green volume of *Chamber Music* to show for all his efforts. ·Giorgio was nearly six years old and Lucia was not far from four. The slim young Dubliner aged and a light-brown beard concealed the pugnacious jaw that had once thrust forward so aggressively in the National Library. Winter softened into spring and spring into summer. There appeared to be no means of bridging the widening impasse between the harassed author and Maunsel and Company. So Joyce put his threat into action. He wrote a circular letter and dispatched it to the Irish press.

Via della Barriera Vecchia 32, III.
Trieste, Austria.

SIR,

May I ask you to publish this letter which throws some light on the present conditions of authorship in England and Ireland?

Nearly six years ago Mr. Grant Richards, publisher, of London, signed a contract with me for the publication of a book of stories written by me entitled *Dubliners*. Some ten months later he wrote asking me to omit one of the stories and passages in others which, as he said, his printer refused to set up. I declined to do either and a correspondence began between Mr. Grant Richards and myself which lasted more than three months. I went to an international jurist in Rome (where I lived then) and was advised to omit. I declined to do so and the MS. was returned to me, the publisher refusing to publish notwithstanding his pledged printed word, the contract remaining in my possession.

Six months afterwards a Mr. Hone wrote to me from Marseilles to ask me to submit the MS. to Messrs Maunsel, publishers, of Dublin. I did so: and after about a year, in July 1909, Messrs Maunsel signed a contract with me for the publication of the book on or before 1 September 1910. In December 1909 Messrs Maunsel's manager begged me to alter a passage in one of the stories, *Ivy Day in the Committee Room,* wherein some reference was made to Edward VII. I agreed to do so, much against my will, and altered one or two phrases. Messrs Maunsel continually postponed the date of publication and in the end wrote, asking me to omit the passage or to change it radically. I declined to do either, pointing out that Mr. Grant Richards of London had raised no objection to the passage when Edward VII was alive and that I could not see why an Irish publisher should raise an objection to it when Edward VII had passed into history. I suggested arbitration or a deletion of the passage with a prefatory note of explanation by me but Messrs Maunsel would agree to neither. As Mr. Hone (who had written to me in the first instance) disclaimed all responsibility in the matter and any connection with the firm I took the opinion of a solicitor in Dublin who advised me to omit the passage, informing me that as I had no domicile in the United Kingdom I could not sue Messrs Maunsel for breach of contract unless I paid £100 into court and that, even if I paid £100 into court and sued them, I should have no chance of getting a verdict in my favour from a Dublin jury if the passage in dispute could be taken as offensive in any way to the late King. I wrote then to the present King, George V, enclosing a printed proof of the story with the passage therein marked and begging him to inform me whether in his view the passage (certain allusions made by a person of the story in the idiom of his social class) should be withheld from publication as offensive to the memory of his father. His Majesty's private secretary sent me this reply:

'Buckingham Palace.

The private secretary is commanded to acknowledge the receipt of Mr. James Joyce's letter of the 1 instant and to inform him that it is inconsistent with rule for His Majesty to express his opinion in such cases. The enclosures are returned herewith.

11 August, 1911.'

Here is the passage in dispute:

'—But look here, John,—said Mr. O'Connor.—Why should we welcome the king of England? Didn't Parnell himself . . . ?—Parnell,—said Mr. Henchy,—is dead. Now, here's the way I look at it. Here's this chap come to the throne after his old mother keeping him out of it till the man was grey. He's a man of the world and he means well by us. He's a jolly fine decent fellow, if you ask me, and no damn nonsense about him. He just says to himself:—*The old one never went to see these wild Irish, By Christ, I'll go myself and see what they're like.*—And are we going to insult the man when he comes over here on a friendly visit? Eh? Isn't that right, Crofton?—

Mr. Crofton nodded his head.

—But after all now—said Mr. Lyons, argumentatively,—King Edward's life, you know, is not very . . .—Let bygones be bygones,—said Mr. Henchy.—I admire the man personally. He's just an ordinary knockabout like you and me. He's fond of his glass of grog and he's a bit of a rake, perhaps, and he's a good sportsman. Damn it, can't we Irish play fair?—'

I wrote this book seven years ago and hold two contracts for its publication. I am not even allowed to explain my case in a prefatory note: wherefore, as I cannot see in any quarter a chance that my rights will be protected, I hereby give Messrs Maunsel publicly permission to publish this story with what changes or deletions they may please to make and shall hope that what they may publish may resemble that to the writing of which I gave thought and time. Their attitude as an Irish publishing firm may be judged by Irish public opinion. I, as a writer, protest against the systems (legal, social and ceremonious) which have brought me to this pass.

> Thanking you for your courtesy
>> I am, Sir,
>>> Your obedient servant.

18 August 1911.                                                JAMES JOYCE.

So far as is known but two Irish newspapers took the trouble to print this circular letter. They were *Sinn Fein,* Dublin, and the *Northern Whig,* Belfast. If Joyce thought that Maunsel and Company would now go ahead and print his book as it stood except for this one mangled passage, his angry *carte blanche* putting all the responsibility on the publisher, he was grievously mistaken. Maunsel and Company did nothing of the sort and a year slid by with nothing at all accomplished in the way of breaking the deadlock between the two principals. In the meantime Joyce fumed and racked his mind for a possible means of procedure. A disgust for Trieste possessed him and he even made two trips to the University of Padua where he underwent examinations first written and then oral with other candidates for teaching English in Italian public schools. The result was that he was awarded 90 per cent for proficiency in the Italian language and literature but subsequently was disqualified by the Board of Education in Rome on the ground of the inadequacy of his Dublin degree. Not even the intervention of influential friends in Trieste including Senator Mazzoni and a language pupil Carlo Galli, then Italian consul-general in Trieste and at present one of the Italian leading diplomatists, was potent enough to remedy this official decision which deserves a very high place indeed in the Annals of Comic Opera Culture. Joyce was working again, when he had the time, on the third version of the novel (now definitely called *A Portrait of the Artist as a Young Man*) and he planned to make it much shorter than that behemoth of two thousand written pages he had envisaged under the title of *Stephen Hero.* But the spectre of a mangled *Dubliners* danced constantly before his eyes. His disciplined æsthetic, so based on the precision of words, the harmony of parts and the completeness of apprehension, was outraged by the increasing demands for deletions from the Dublin publisher. He felt far away and helpless, too far from the field of battle to accomplish anything on his own behalf, and he realized that he would have to go to Dublin if matters were to be settled. He was not anxious to go. He had been back twice and each time his pleasure in the city had been dissipated by the parochialism of the natives. Ireland had become for him an "ignorant and famine-stricken and treacherous country." Nearly a year before, when he had received a few lines from Maunsel and Company apprising him of the third inexplicable postponement of the publication of *Dubliners,* he had written furiously to Stanislaus: "I know the name and tradition of my country too well to be surprised at receiving three scrawled lines in return for five years of constant service to my art and constant waiting and indifference and disloyalty in return for the 150,000 francs of continental money [evidently from the Volta Theatre project] which I have deflected into the pockets of hungry Irishmen and women since they drove me out of their hospitable bog six years ago." Since then, his opinion of Ireland, and especially Dublin, had not changed. It was, in fact, the fury of the lover at the hideous flaws in his sweetheart, a wounded pride and a just resentment at malevolent and superstitious injustice.

But, strong as his reluctance at the moment was, to Dublin he must go. This time he planned to take his entire family with him and the added expense was a problem that caused much worry and desperate planning on his part. The money was eventually raised (part of it by neglecting to pay the overdue rent for his flat) and late in July the four travellers were in Dublin.

### IV

The mother and two children went on immediately to Galway, to the home of the mother's uncle, Michael Healy, His Majesty's Inspector of Customs and Receiver of Wreck for Galway, and a day or two later, Joyce, having called at the office of Maunsel and Company without any satisfaction, followed them. Michael Healy was an excellent man of the old type, broad-minded, sympathetic in nature and generous (he aided Joyce, for whom he had the greatest affection and admiration, monetarily several times later on during the war and Joyce, with an ironic observation of his precarious state, had signed his acknowledging letters "Flotsam, Jetsam, Lagging and Derelict"). Joyce enjoyed life very much in Galway. He rowed and cycled and drove about the countryside, observing with pleasure the freshness of the fields and the simplicity of the natives. At Oughterard he visited the little graveyard he had pictured in his long short story, "The Dead," and discovered there a headstone with the name "J. Joyce" engraved upon it. It was in Galway, too, that he became interested in a cure for the foot and mouth disease that was devastating Irish cattle (the seed of one of the motifs in *Ulysses*) and wrote a letter to William Field, M.P., President of the Irish Cattle Traders' Society. He received no response to it. The only writing he did was two articles on the Aran Islands for the *Piccolo della Sera*. An idea that he conceived of interviewing Marconi for the Triestine journal came to nothing, it being impossible to get into direct touch with the great Italian inventor of wireless telegraphy. This was his one and only visit to the so-called Joyce country in Connemara.

During these relatively calm days in Galway Joyce was worried and badgered by the attitude of his latest landlord in Trieste. That individual, desiring his overdue rent and seeing no way of getting it, had decided to evict the Joyce family from the premises and rent them to a more opulent tenant. Joyce, learning of this, explained the matter in a letter to Stanislaus: "The story about the flat is this. I received on the 24th Feb. notice. That was unpleasant but valid. I then with Nora went about looking for a flat and visited thirty. The house-agent *himself* stopped me in the Via Bellini and asked me had I found a flat. I said no. He said the matter would be smoothed over, to leave it to him, that he did not want me to leave as he did not know what kind of people might come into the flat, that Picciola the landlord was very fond of me and intended to take English lessons from me during the winter, and that if any repairs were necessary he even believed that Picciola would pay for them. . . . Similar conversations took place *four* times. I told the porter and everyone who visited the flat that I was remaining. When I paid the last quarter I asked had he spoken to Picciola. He said he would see in a few days and repeated the story about the English lessons. I consider (and will contest by force and law) that this is a verbal revocation of notice. On the strength of it I left Trieste. I have written the whole story to Picciola himself and said if he will not have me in the house, I shall vacate the flat for the 24th Feb. or 24th Nov. For the 24th Aug. *no*. The house-agent did a wise thing to rescind the contract with the incoming tenant. Tell him to sign a contract with nobody. He has played a double game (as I told Picciola, who is a pig in any case) and has only himself to blame. But for his intervention I should have found a flat. I have written to Eileen to explain the matter to Serravallo. If in spite of that Picciola insists on putting me and my family on the street I promise you you will see some fun in the house. If he does so he is an inhuman person and I will treat him as such. I am however sure that he would agree to my proposal. In the meantime, if you have nothing better to do, call again on the house-agent and let him know that I intend to remain in that house after the twenty-fourth of August, and if anything happens the result will lie at his door. Take possession of the house till I return. Don't let any debts trouble you. Tell them I am away "*,.*' will return in the month of September. They would get the same answer at Economo's [1] door and would salute and go away. Fano, perhaps, would be nasty, not the others." The vexed situation was finally solved by Joyce giving up the flat while Stanislaus found another at Via Donato Bramante, 4.

Towards the end of the writer's holiday in Galway the negotiations over *Dubliners* started a swift march toward a climax. Joyce had written to Hone, the original applicant on the part of Maunsel and Company for the book, demanding fair treatment but received an answer from George Roberts suggesting that the deadlock might be broken if Joyce were to sell the sheets to Grant Richards. "You stated that his printer would not print the book. This would be obviated by him taking over the sheets printed by us." Joyce had no intention of retiring so from the Irish battlefield. He possessed a signed and stamped contract and he meant to make Maunsel and Company live up to it. That was why he was in Ireland. A day or so after he received this surprising suggestion from George Roberts he engaged a Dublin solicitor named George Lidwell to represent him.

Returning to Dublin Joyce called immediately at the offices of

[1] Baron Leon Economo was the wealthiest Greek merchant in Trieste and a pupil of Joyce.

the publishing firm and had a two hours' conference with George Roberts. It ended in a willingness to compromise on the part of the writer. He would omit "An Encounter," delete and change the passage in "Ivy Day in the Committee Room," change the names of the public houses in "Counterparts" (Davy Byrne's to Andy Kehoe's, Mulligan's to Quinlan's, the Scotch House to the Manx House), change the name of the pawnbroker Terry Kelly to Micky Grim, change the name of Sydney Parade in "A Painful Case" to White Church and all this on condition that the book be published before October. Padraic Colum, who was present, looked over the proofs and demanded if the book was all about public houses. George Roberts, who had twice left the room in a temper, refused to commit himself to anything and suggested that Joyce return again in a few days. At that time the writer would be apprised as to the publisher's legal adviser's decision concerning the changes.

When Joyce went back on the twentieth of August George Roberts still had no decision to offer. He listened carefully while Joyce defended the book from the first story to the last, demanded suspiciously if there was sodomy suggested in "The Sisters," asked what simony was, requested the information if the priest in "The Sisters" was suspended only for the breaking of the chalice and wanted to know if there was more in "The Dead" than appeared on the surface. Joyce attempted to answer all this calmly and then sought his solicitor, George Lidwell, who had read the proofs, and asked for a letter from him giving his opinion that the book was not liable to a libel action. Lidwell reluctantly wrote the following note:

DEAR SIR,
        Re "Dubliners."
    Referring to our correspondence concerning the stories 'Ivy Day in the Committee Room' and 'An Encounter' as the passages you have shown me are not likely to be taken serious note of by the Advisors of the Crown, they would not interfere with the publication, nor do I consider a conviction could be easily obtained.
                                                    Yours faithfully,
                                                    GEORGE LIDWELL.

Joyce took this note to George Roberts on the twenty-first but the manager of the publishing firm said that it was no good to him since it was not written to him. The harried writer then sought out his solicitor and requested him to dispatch a parallel note to Maunsel and Company. This the timid-minded solicitor refused to do, offering as the only reason for his refusal the fact that Maunsel and Company was not his client. Why not, he suggested smoothly, let the vexed portions of the book go and write another story about Ringsend which had many historical associations? It began to dawn on Joyce that his solicitor was far from militant. He shrugged his shoulders and hurried back to George Roberts. Roberts was as adamantine as ever. He demanded a letter from Lidwell on the whole case stating where the author stood and what he proposed to do about it. Joyce, sensing an ugliness in the situation that had not been so apparent before, countered by offering to sign an agreement to indemnify the firm to the extent of £50 (that being his estimate of the cost of the first edition) if the book were confiscated. George Roberts met this offer with a demand for two sureties of five hundred pounds each. With just indignation Joyce retorted that no person in his proper senses would consent to that and that in any case it could never be proved whether or not the author were responsible for the firm's losses. Whereupon George Roberts declared the discussion at an end and added that Maunsel and Company would act on its legal advice and not publish at all.

That evening Joyce wrote the following letter to the publisher's manager:

21st August, 1912.

Dear Roberts,

I enclose Copy of my solicitor's letter to me which confirms what I asserted all through our correspondence, the legal innocence of the passages you took exception to.

Nevertheless, in order to end this interminable discord I have decided to close with your proposal of the other day, very reluctantly and entering my protest at the same time. That proposal was the omission of 'An Encounter' from the book.

I agree to that on the following conditions:

1) That the following note be placed by me before the first story: *This book in this form is incomplete. The scheme of the book as*

*framed by me includes a story entitled An Encounter which stands between the first and second story in this edition. J. J.*

2) That no further changes be asked of me.

3) That I reserve the right to publish the said story elsewhere before or after the publication of the book by your firm.

4) That the book be published by you not later than the 6th of October, 1912.

I believe that you will change your opinion very shortly after the publication of the book, and believe also that its reception will strengthen your hand so far as to lead you to include the omitted story in subsequent editions.

Sincerely yours,

JAMES JOYCE.

George Roberts's surprising answer to this reached Joyce on the twenty-third and it came like an exploding bomb. The manager of Maunsel and Company wrote:

*Without prejudice*

DEAR MR. JOYCE,

I am sorry to find by your letter of the 21st inst. that our recent conversations have led only to misunderstandings.

It is quite erroneous on your part to assume that provided the solicitor advising you expresses the view that certain passages in your book are free from risk of legal action, I should be prepared to take his opinion. On the contrary, at our last interview, I told you plainly that the opinion of our legal advisers should have to be taken, and that in fact, I was about to take it.

Pursuant to that understanding I submitted the whole matter to them, and I regret to say that they find the book to abound in risks of action for libel. They advise me that in practically every case where any going concern (e.g. public house, restaurant, railway company or other existing firm, person or body corporated with vested interests) is mentioned by actual name, then, having regard to the events described as taking place in connection with them, there is no doubt that actions for libel would lie.

As the instances are so numerous they do not detail them, but confine themselves to the general statement that being so the publication of the book by Maunsel and Company is out of the question; and I am advised further that even if the objectionable were struck out there would still remain the risk of some of them having been overlooked; and to provide for this risk should publication be contemplated they advise that the author must under clause eleven of the agreement be bound in two sureties of £500.—.—(five hundred pounds) each to meet possible damages, or in the alternative, lodge the sum of £1000 in our bank.

In that case they advise me under clause two of the agreement, the time and manner of publication is at our sole discretion. Serious as is the foregoing part of their opinion, what follows is so serious from the point of view of Maunsel and Company that I ask your particular attention to it. They advise that the author has committed a breach of guarantee contained in clause eleven by offering for publication a book which as he should know is clearly libellous; and they recommend, if I so desire, that Maunsel and Company proceed against you in order to recover all costs charges and expenses for time, labour and materials expended on the book. I should be extremely sorry to have to take proceedings against you to protect the interest of Maunsel and Company, but as it appears that the chance of selling the sheets is very remote, I must ask you to make a substantial offer towards covering our loss.

Failing your doing that I shall have most reluctantly to put the matter in other hands.

Faithfully yours,

GEORGE ROBERTS.

Joyce took this letter immediately to his solicitor. George Lidwell read it and admitted that his client had been badly treated. At the same time he advised the angry young author that he could do nothing about it and that the publisher was quite right. What he (Lidwell) had seen of the book *was* objectionable. Joyce then sought advice of his father who airily told him to put the letter in his pocket, buck up, take back the manuscript and find another publisher. But Joyce was obstinate. He went to George Roberts again and offered the defence which he wrote down later that day and sent to his brother:

1.) A railway company is mentioned once and then exonerated from all blame by two witnesses, jury and coroner.

2.) Public houses are mentioned in four stories out of fifteen. In three of these stories the names are fictitious. In the fourth the names are real because the persons walked from place to place ('Counterparts').

3.) Nothing happens in the public houses; people drink.

4.) I offered to take a car and go with Roberts, proofs in hand, to the three or four publicans really named and to the Secretary of the railway company. He refused.

5.) I said the publicans would be glad of the advertisement.

6.) I said that I would put fictitious names for the few real ones but added that by so doing the selling value in Dublin of the book would go down.

7.) I said that even if they took action for libel against Maunsel that the jury would be a long time before awarding damages on such a plea.

8.) I said that his legal adviser was a fool to advise him to sue me. If he sued me (even if I lived in Dublin) a jury would say he had the MS. for ten months and I was not liable for his error of judgement. But if he sued me in Trieste I would hold the whip and would laugh him out of court.

9.) I suggested that his lawyer encouraged correspondence and litigation for his own profit.

George Roberts walked about, made notes on a paper and finally agreed to consult his legal adviser again. But this was the end. A week later the Maunsel manager demanded that every proper name in the book be fictionalized, that changes be made in the first paragraph of "Grace," in three paragraphs of "Ivy Day in the Committee Room" and in a portion of "The Boarding House." Joyce flatly refused to make the latter group of changes, whereupon the Manager told him to pay over thirty pounds for the sheets and seek another publisher. A day or so later Joyce, thinking he might publish the book himself with his brother's aid, agreed to this proposition but a new snag held up even this humiliating solution. The printer refused to hand over the sheets, decided to forgo all claim to the money due him, had the type broken up and destroyed the edition. There has never been any valid explanation for this crude sacrifice and wanton destruction on the part of the printer. It may be pointed out here that the printers were Falconer and Company who did a lot of work for various Roman Catholic societies and were in a small way official printers to the Crown.

Joyce, defeated and helpless, left Ireland about the middle of September (he has not set foot in that country since) [1] and

---

[1] He was invited to Ireland twice by the late William Butler Yeats in connection with the Tailteann Games and then in connection with the foundation of the Irish Academy of Letters. These invitations (the first was personal) and this membership were declined by

returned to Trieste. Behind him was a mystery; before him years
of hard work. At Flushing, Holland, where he changed travel
connections he occupied the long halt in the station waiting room
in concocting "Gas from a Burner."

> Ladies and gents, you are here assembled
> To hear why earth and heaven trembled
> Because of the black and sinister arts
> Of an Irish writer in foreign parts.
> He sent me a book ten years ago.
> I read it a hundred times or so,
> Backwards and forwards, down and up,
> Through both ends of a telescope.
> I printed it all to the very last word
> But by the mercy of the Lord
> The darkness of my mind was rent
> And I saw the writer's foul intent.
> But I owe a duty to Ireland:
> I hold her honour in my hand,
> This lovely land that always sent
> Her writers and artists to banishment
> And in a spirit of Irish fun
> Betrayed her own leaders, one by one.
> 'Twas Irish humour, wet and dry,
> Flung quicklime into Parnell's eye;
> 'Tis Irish brains that save from doom
> The leaky barge of the Bishop of Rome
> For everyone knows the Pope can't belch
> Without the consent of Billy Walsh.
> O Ireland my first and only love
> Where Christ and Cæsar are hand and glove!
> O lovely land where the shamrock grows!
> (Allow me, ladies, to blow my nose)
> To show you for strictures I don't care a button
> I printed the poems of Mountainy Mutton
> And a play he wrote (you've read it I'm sure)
> Where they talk of "bastard," "bugger" and "whore"
> And a play on the Word and Holy Paul
> And some woman's legs that I can't recall

him. He has not even sought refuge there during the present calamitous events in Europe.
Having a vivid memory of the incident at Castlecomer when quicklime was flung into the
eyes of their dying leader, Parnell, by a chivalrous Irish mob, he did not wish a similar
unfortunate occurrence to interfere with the composition of the book he was trying to write.

Written by Moore, a genuine gent
That lives on his property's ten per cent:
I printed mystical books in dozens:
I printed the table-book of Cousins
Though (asking your pardon) as for the verse
'Twould give you a heartburn on your arse:
I printed folklore from North and South
By Gregory of the Golden Mouth:
I printed poets, sad, silly and solemn:
I printed Patrick What-do-you-Colm:
I printed the great John Milicent Synge
Who soars above on an angel's wing
In the playboy shift that he pinched as swag
From Maunsel's manager's travelling-bag.
But I draw the line at that bloody fellow,
That was over here dressed in Austrian yellow,
Spouting Italian by the hour
To O'Leary Curtis and John Wyse Power
And writing of Dublin, dirty and dear,
In a manner no blackamoor printer could bear.
Shite and onions! Do you think I'll print
The name of the Wellington Monument,
Sydney Parade and Sandymount tram,
Downes's cakeshop and Williams's jam?
I'm damned if I do—I'm damned to blazes!
Talk about *Irish Names of Places!*
It's a wonder to me, upon my soul,
He forgot to mention Curly's Hole.
No, ladies, my press shall have no share in
So gross a libel on Stepmother Erin.
I pity the poor—that's why I took
A red-headed Scotchman to keep my book.
Poor sister Scotland! Her doom is fell;
She cannot find any more Stuarts to sell.
My conscience is fine as Chinese silk:
My heart is as soft as buttermilk.
Colm can tell you I made a rebate
Of one hundred pounds on the estimate
I gave him for his Irish Review.
I love my country—by herrings I do!
I wish you could see what tears I weep
When I think of the emigrant train and ship.

That's why I publish far and wide
My quite illegible railway guide.
In the porch of my printing institute
The poor and deserving prostitute
Plays every night at catch-as-catch-can
With her tight-breeched British artilleryman
And the foreigner learns the gift of the gab
From the drunken draggletail Dublin drab.
Who was it said: Resist not evil?
I'll burn that book, so help me devil.
I'll sing a psalm as I watch it burn
And the ashes I'll keep in a one-handled urn.
I'll penance do with farts and groans
Kneeling upon my marrowbones.
This very next lent I will unbare
My penitent buttocks to the air
And sobbing beside my printing press
My awful sin I will confess.
My Irish foreman from Bannockburn
Shall dip his right hand in the urn
And sign crisscross with reverent thumb
*Memento homo* upon my bum.

## V

With this second disappointment and defeat over the publication of *Dubliners* Joyce may be said to have reached the nadir of the bad luck that engulfed him. Eight years' work and struggle had gone for apparently nothing. He was thirty years old and all that he could show the public for those years was a slim book of verse for which he had not received one penny. As he settled down again in Trieste and applied himself once more to the dreary routine of teaching the English language to his counts and cooks he must have realized how apparently hopeless was his continual struggle against the Philistines. His failure in Dublin had intensified the bitterness he felt towards that city and its inhabitants. He was convinced that a conspiracy to crush him completely existed amongst his former companions in that lively centre of mingled religiosity and ruthlessness. Their scorn of him was engendered by fear and their mocking voices were heightened by envy. Yet apparently hopeless as his struggle against them was he would not surrender to the compromises that might reinstate him in their Lilliputian circle. Æsthetic paralysis lay that way and he could not succumb to it. He would rely still on the ancient weapons of his early youth, silence to their scorn and objurgations, exile from their choking atmosphere, and a cunning through which he would discomfit them. He would continue to write too, and write in the only way that his integrity would permit him to write.

VI

By 1913 he was teaching in the Commercial Academy as well as carrying on his private lessons in English. He delivered a number of lectures, among them a series on *Hamlet* as well as others on Daniel De Foe, William Blake, and the Island of Saints and Sages. In the series on *Hamlet* he outlined the theory that he was later to incorporate in *Ulysses*. The final draft of *A Portrait of the Artist as a Young Man,* assiduously laboured at whenever he was free from his routine, approached the end and he felt satisfied with it. It was a book in which he had pictured his youth with an uncompromising fidelity to facts and an implicit indictment of the civilization that had attempted to mould him into an image of itself. What would Dublin think of that? And surging upward in his consciousness was a sequel to *A Portrait of the Artist as a Young Man,* the very theme that had bitten at him briefly in Rome and which he had put aside, a work to be called *Ulysses* and which would carry still further into the heretofore unexplored terrain of letters the æsthetic theories upon which his art was based.

It is an old and trite saying that it is darkest just before dawn but it will serve at this period of Joyce's slow advance towards recognition. The year 1913, which began so sombrely with Joyce resettled in Trieste much to his father's disgust and apparently doomed to remain there in indefinite isolation, ended with light breaking before him. The incipient gleam in this case was the American poet, Ezra Pound, then settled in London. Pound, who must have heard of Joyce through W. B. Yeats, was compiling the first *Imagist Anthology* and he wrote to the Dublin exile asking him if he might use the poem from *Chamber Music* beginning "I hear an army charging upon the land," in that selection.

Joyce immediately agreed and in the correspondence that followed Pound learned that *A Portrait of the Artist as a Young Man* was practically completed. At that time Pound was advisory editor to a publication called the *Egoist,* formerly the *New Freewoman,* and he was searching about for new prose writers of a modernistic calibre to contribute to it. The *Egoist* was edited by Miss Dora Marsden and later by Miss Harriet Weaver. Already gathering about that advanced publication were such new writers as Wyndham Lewis, Richard Aldington, H.D., and T. S. Eliot. Joyce had fallen into good hands. He sent on the first portion of *A Portrait of the Artist as a Young Man* and it was immediately accepted for serial publication. This was a decided advance for the Irish writer and it added to his courage to go on in his integral fashion.

Another unexpected development during this year vindicated Joyce's fortitude.

Grant Richards reopened negotiations for the publication of *Dubliners* in London. Perhaps a light from heaven had fallen upon him or, more probable, the name of Joyce was being bruited about so much in the advanced literary circles of the English capital that he succumbed to a sort of autosuggestion. Whatever it was, Joyce lost no time in sending on the manuscript that had been the cause of two disastrous campaigns.

The year 1914 opened, then, to an auspiciously turning tide for Joyce. As he wrote 'finis' to *A Portrait of the Artist as a Young Man* and added the dates "Dublin, 1904. Trieste, 1914" he knew that he had rounded one of the most difficult capes of his difficult life. Times might continue to be hard but never in the same frustrated way they had been in the past. He possessed his well-wishers now and an imminent audience was in the near distance. A new pot of literary urges was boiling in London (assiduously stirred by the indefatigable Ezra Pound) and the Edwardian epoch was rapidly receding into the past. Discreet gentility was on the wane, a fearless realism increased rapidly, and more than one young man (freed from the shackles of slavish tradition) was preparing to 'blast' the public with new and unexpected experiments in technique and words. When, early in the new year, *A Portrait of the Artist as a Young Man* began to appear in the pages of the

*Egoist* Joyce found himself in the vanguard of this revolutionary group.

And there was *Dubliners*. Grant Richards was procrastinating again and on the eight of January 1914, Joyce wrote briefly:

Dear Mr. Richards,

I am sorry to press you but I must ask you to let me hear from you by return of post with regard to my book 'Dubliners' as I am naturally most anxious to have the matter settled one way or another after so many years.

Sincerely yours,

James Joyce.

It was not until the twentieth of the month (and after Joyce had written a second letter to him) that the English publisher replied and to this response the impatient author answered:

Via Donato Bramante 4, II.
Trieste, Austria.

Grant Richards, Esq.,
London.

Dear Mr. Grant Richards,

In reply to yours of 20 inst:

The book is in the form approved of by me, i.e., with one or two slight changes already made.

I am willing to omit the preface from the book and to have it replaced by the introduction you speak of.

There is not the least fear of an action. If you have read between the lines you will see that the constant objection raised in Dublin were excuses and nothing more. Some person paid the Dublin printer for his work. I did not.

As to modification of the present text all things considered had we not better waive this point?

I am willing also to take for sale here 120 copies at trade price.

I think of publishing two of the stories in an American magazine and the Italian version of one (Ivy Day) in the Nuova Antologia, where the book is promised an article of notice. If so would you wish it to be known that the publication by you in book form is to be expected?

I daresay you know your own business better than I, but I fancy the 'curious history' of 'Dubliners' is of notable effect.

Sincerely yours,

James Joyce.

Grant Richards definitely accepted the book (his second acceptance of it in eight years) and the epistolary discussion turned to the terms of the new contract. On the third of February (one day after his thirty-second birthday) Joyce wrote:

DEAR MR. GRANT RICHARDS,

In reply to yours of 29 ult:

I agree to the terms in our old contract but there are a few points on which it is better to be clear.

1) I think you should agree to withhold the Continental (Tauchnitz, etc.) rights for two years. This would allow me to sell the English edition even after the 120 copies which are now sold. It is understood that I take these at the trade price of 2/6 (£15).

2) In view of a possible success I think the royalty of 10 per cent. should apply to, say, the first 8,000 copies. After that I think you could well increase it to 15 per cent.—if only in recognition of my troubles with the book.

Could you bring out the book in May? I undertake to return proofs sent me corrected within two days of receipt.

I hope our troubles are now at an end and wish your house and myself and the ill-fated book good luck.

Sincerely yours,

JAMES JOYCE.

The troubles between author and publisher *were* at an end for on March fourth Joyce returned his copy of the agreement signed and on the twenty-fourth received a signed copy from Grant Richards. The manuscript was given to the English printer (who miraculously appears to have offered no objections at all to the subject matter) and by the last of April Joyce was posting to London the first corrected proofs. June (instead of May which the author regarded as his lucky month) witnessed the publication of *Dubliners* in England. It was a fair-sized volume bound in dark-red cloth with the title stamped on the side and back in gold. The long struggle stretching from 1906 to 1914 had concluded in a victory for the writer. His script was published as he desired it published and even the few compromises he had been willing to submit to for the sake of a quick publication had evaporated on the way. The history of this book and the dogged pertinacity of its author, it will be admitted, are unique in the annals of English publishing.

It was while the negotiations and printing of *Dubliners* were in process that Joyce, hardly pausing to catch breath after the completion of *A Portrait of the Artist as a Young Man,* embarked on the great book that in 1904 he had announced he would write in ten years' time. In this spring of 1914 he began *Ulysses,* setting down, first of all, the preliminary sketches for the final sections. It would be more precise to say that he began "to put" *Ulysses* on paper, for the theme, as a whole, had been swelling in his mind for some years, growing secretly at first from the seed fecundated in Rome, then blossoming into his consciousness, and finally completely absorbing it. No one, not even Professor George Santayana, can adequately circumscribe the thousand and one urges and motifs, conscious and unconscious, that eventually coalesce into a work of art. One can but indicate the more obvious aspects of such a process. In Joyce's case there are several that can be indicated. In a conversation with one of his language students in Zurich in 1917, the late Georges Borach, he briefly explained one of the reasons for the inception of this work: "The most beautiful and embracing subject is that of Ulysses. It is more human than Hamlet, Don Quixote, Dante or Faust. It embodies everything. The rejuvenation of old Faustus is distasteful to me. The most beautiful human traits and emotions are found in Ulysses. I was twelve years old when I studied the Trojan War but the story of Ulysses alone remained in my recollection. It was the mysticism that pleased me. When I wrote 'Dubliners' I was tempted to give it the title of 'Ulysses at Dublin' but I changed my mind. In Rome when I had written about half of the novel, 'A Portrait of the Artist as a Young Man,' I comprehended that 'Ulysses' could well furnish the sequel."

But there was much more to it than that. Joyce himself was a lost son and he saw himself as such. He was, figuratively speaking, a Telemachus, a son at odds with his homeland and in search of the real father. His experiences in Dublin in 1912 (and who can say how much nearer they brought *Ulysses?*) had emphasized in his sensitive mind the abyss that widened between him and those from whom he sprang. Of whom was he the spiritual son and where would he find the Mystical Father? Europe, of course, to which his natural father, with a rare perspicacity, had constantly urged him to go. With his love of the myth and his identification of himself as Telemachus it is simple to perceive that Joyce had circumscribed his Idea. There remained to be invented a Ulysses and a Penelope and to chart the wanderings of the hero.

The wanderings had suggested themselves to him eight years before in the contemplated short story he had called "Ulysses." At that time, as has been pointed out, he was not ready for the subject. The personal identification of himself with the theme and the profound mythic substance were essential matters that he had not envisaged clearly enough. But now, in the spring of 1914, he saw the book for what it should be and plunged immediately into the intricate labour of composition that was to last another eight years. All Dublin was his Mediterranean Ocean. Homeric parallels sprang up on every side proving anew the universality of the myth. Was not old Michael Cusack, the Citizen of Barney Kiernan's public house, a veritable Polyphemus in his patriotic rages? Was not the original of Gerty McDowell, that girl who had been in the garden with him when he first heard of Henrik Ibsen's pleasure in his *Fortnightly* article, a second Nausicaa? Was not the Nighttown stretching from Amiens Street Railway Station another Island of Circe where men were changed into swine? Was not Glasnevin cemetery a land of the dead, a Hades, and were there not four waters to cross in order to reach it?

The analogies had piled up in Joyce's mind for many years and now that he had his theme, his æsthetic unification of the whole, he could begin the rigorously-disciplined composition. And as he recognized his theme as universal ("It embodies everything") he complicated his labours still more by planning every section to represent an organ of the human body (except the first three sections), to suggest one of the Arts, to have its own Colour, to have its own appropriate Symbol and to have a particular Technic. All these motifs, planned juxtapositions, analogies, thematic progressions and punctilious character delineations were further complicated by his adaptation and development of the *monologue intérieur,* a form of narration of the running stream of thought of a character that he had chanced upon years before in a forgotten book by George Moore's friend, Edouard Dujardin, *Les Lauriers sont Coupés.*[1]

The first sketches for *Ulysses* were suddenly interrupted by Joyce to permit him to turn to another problem that was revolving in his mind. It was the question of complete spiritual freedom between two people who loved each other, the absence of compulsion on either side, the fear of the intellectual that he bind with his will and desire the intuitive gestures of the beloved. This problem he presented (one cannot say that he solved it) in the three-act drama called *Exiles* which he wrote during the three spring months of 1914. The influence of Henrik Ibsen is obvious in the play and when one considers the period of composition it is almost as though the author, already embarked on a work that would be new and unique in English letters, was paying his final compliment to the old master beneath whose dark reasonable actuality vibrating with symbolic inferences he had so long remained a willing captive.[2] He

[1] Formal criticism of Joyce's work has no part in this book and those readers who desire such examination are referred to Mr. Stuart Gilbert's *James Joyce's Ulysses.*

[2] Although this play may have been a final compliment to Ibsen's influence on Joyce's writing, it, by no means, set a final period to his admiration and interest in the old master of Christiania. As late as April, 1934, he was inspired to one of his finest unpublished poems by the remembrance of a performance he had recently seen in Paris of an Ibsen play. Here it is.

Epilogue to Ibsen's "Ghosts"

Dear quick, whose conscience buried deep
The grim old grouser has been salving,
Permit one spectre more to peep.
I am the ghost of Captain Alving.

Silenced and smothered by my past
Like the lewd knight in dirty linen
I struggle forth to swell the cast
And air a long-suppressed opinion.

For muddling weddings into wakes
No fool could vie with Parson Manders.
I, though a dab at ducks and drakes,
Let gooseys serve or sauce their ganders.

My spouse bore me a blighted boy,
Our slavey pupped a bouncing bitch.
Paternity, thy name is joy
When the wise sire knows which is which.

Both swear I am that self-same man
By whom their infants were begotten.
Explain, fate, if you care and can
Why one is sound and one is rotten.

[Cont. on p. 227]

was saying farewell to the past just as he was stepping across the threshold into a new world of unexplored literary adventure.

*Exiles* completed, he returned to *Ulysses*. The idea was clear in his mind and so was the variegated yet unified technique through which he intended to present it. There would be changes, developments, enlargements, and unremitting revision that would continue up to the very moment when the book was finally free of the press but the protagonists were there, rounded and complete, from the day in 1914 when the author wrote: "Stately, plump Buck Mulligan came from the stairhead, bearing a bowl of lather on which a mirror and a razor lay crossed." The Idea was there. The Myth was there. The years of labour stretched indefinitely ahead. And the

> Olaf may plod his stony path
> And live as chastely as Susanna
> Yet pick up in some Turkish bath
> His *quantum est* of *Pox Romana*.
>
> While Haakon hikes up primrose way,
> Spreeing and gleeing while he goes,
> To smirk upon his latter day
> Without a pimple on his nose.
>
> I gave it up I am afraid
> But if I loafed and found it fun
> Remember how a coyclad maid
> Knows how to take it out of one.
>
> The more I dither on and drink
> My midnight bowl of spirit punch
> The firmlier I feel and think
> Friend Manders came too oft to lunch.
>
> Since scuttling ship Vikings like me
> Reck not to whom the blame is laid,
> Y.M.C.A., V.D., T.B.
> Or Harbourmaster of Port-Said.
>
> Blame all and none and take to task
> The harlot's lure, the swain's desire.
> Heal by all means but hardly ask
> Did this man sin or did his sire.
>
> The shack's ablaze. That canting scamp,
> The carpenter, has dished the parson.
> Now had they kept their powder damp
> Like me there would have been no arson.
>
> Nay more, were I not all I was,
> Weak, wanton, waster out and out,
> There would have been no world's applause
> And damn all to write home about.

smiling summer, with good weather everywhere, seemed an auspicious season to plunge into the work.

But the Time-Spirit, aided and abetted by the conniving politicians of Europe, had other plans for the unsuspecting world. In June Princip shot down the Archduke Franz Ferdinand of Austria and his morganatic wife at Sarajevo and the Chancelleries of the great powers began their deathly game of chess, a game that ended in a stalemate, an overturned chessboard and the mobilization of armed forces. War broke out early in August and Joyce suddenly found himself a free prisoner in Trieste, a citizen of an enemy state in the hands of Austria. It was an unpleasant and nerve-racking situation. It is true that he was not obliged to cease teaching in the Commercial Academy but many of his private students—either for reasons of patriotism or because the Austrian armies swallowed them up—forsook him. Stanislaus, who had been vacationing in the Carso hills, was interned and sent to the camp at Katzenau. Joyce, isolated, viewed by the Triestines with that mob suspicion that accompanies all wars and deprived of a great part of his livelihood, was completely disorientated. The war had nothing to do with him; he was an Irishman, not an Englishman; he was fond of the Triestines and the old ramshackle Austro-Hungarian Empire; all his mind was concentred in his art: yet the war had plunged ruthlessly into his private life and destroyed that tranquillity of mind that was so necessary to him. Silvio Benco, writing of him at this period, declares: "One would meet him in the street walking, with his hasty step, but lost in meditation, his lips tight together in a hard horizontal line. He would bow and look at one fixedly, and avoided stopping or exchanging a few words. The official position of the Irishman at war with England was now that of a British citizen at war with Austria. It was not easy to accept and less easy to deny."

It was at this hard instant of time, when Joyce did not know which way to turn, that unexpected and generous aid arrived from Ireland. Mr. Michael Healy, His Majesty's Inspector of Customs in Galway and uncle to Nora Joyce, with whom Joyce, it will be remembered, passed so pleasant a time in 1912, came nobly to the rescue. Through the double intermediaries of a Belfast Irishman resident in Switzerland and a Triestine family with extensive English relations he contrived to forward to Joyce a monthly remittance of ten pounds. It was this act of spontaneous generosity that kept the harassed writer and his family afloat upon the agitated waves of war-convulsed Trieste during the dark early days of the conflict. It was the sort of unlooked-for manna that was to descend more than once upon Joyce during the crucial moments of his life.

As the months marched on to the increasing thunder of guns and it became evident that Italy would cast in her lot with the Allies the nervous tension in Trieste tautened until it became practically impossible to do any work there. One seemed to be existing on live wires. The natural sympathies of a great part of the Triestines were Italian but their business interests were firmly planted in Austria. Thus they were torn between two powerful and conflicting factors, the emotions of the heart and the sovereignty of the pocketbook. Joyce viewed the situation with a grim irony and after Italy, making her belated choice, had joined in the struggle on the side of the nations "making the world safe for democracy" he remarked dryly to a friend (recalling that the Emperor Franz Josef had lost his voice and that Victor Emmanuel was extremely short): "It is a difference of opinion between an old gentleman who is inaudible at twenty paces and a young gentleman who is invisible at the same distance." It amused him, too, to observe the Triestines sitting on the mole and listening to the distant thunder of the great guns and shouting, *"Avanti, Cagoia!"* ("Forward, caterpillars!") in mockery of the Italian *"Avanti, Savoia!"* But he could not work with any degree of peace and this was of more importance to him than the suicide of dynasties. Like most of the intellectuals of his time in the countries at war, he had lost his bearings.

It was then that two of his students, both Greeks and both of noble birth, Baron Ambrogio Ralli and Count Francesco Sordina,[1] came to his aid. Through their influence, and after giving his parole

[1] Sordina was one of the greatest swordsmen in Europe and during the brief transition period of Triestine severance from Austria before its attachment to Italy was first and last Chief Magistrate of the once Immediate City. Both Ralli and Sordina are now dead but till the times of their deaths, which took place in the last few years, they regularly received (and replied) at Christmas and the New Year messages of grateful remembrance from the writer whose life they had possibly saved.

not to take any part in the conflict, the Austrian military authorities gave him and his family permission to leave Trieste and go to the neutral country of Switzerland. It was a welcome release for Joyce. Though he was forced to leave his furniture behind him and though the future before him in Switzerland was nebulous and uncertain it was better than remaining a free prisoner in enemy territory and within sound of the guns. He had reached that point in *Ulysses* that reads: "A choir gives back menace and echo, assisting about the altar's horns, the snorted Latin of jackpriests moving burly in their albs, tonsured and oiled and gelded, fat with the fat of kidneys of wheat." In Switzerland he could go on from there.

Late in the sixth month, some time after he had acted as witness at the marriage of his sister Eileen to Frantisek Shaurek of Prague, he and his family started for Lausanne but they got no farther than Zurich.

# Eight

JOYCE and his family arrived in Zurich on June 21, 1915 (St. Aloysius' Day), and immediately secured temporary quarters at the same Gasthaus where they had spent their honeymoon. It was not the same Zurich that he had lived in eleven years before. That relatively-calm little city with its practical-minded German-Swiss inhabitants had been submerged in the great backwash of the war. True enough, the topographical aspects were what they had been: there was still the placid lake with its wooded fringe and its fine houses on the farther shore; the Bahnhofstrasse was as broad and glittering as ever; the Limmat and the Sihl ran as usual under their little bridges and the old town with its climbing and turning streets reached towards the sky as it had reached in the days when the first guildsmen raced about the bonfire on Sechseläuten to intimidate that indigenous winter-demon called the Bögg. But that was all. The stage was the same but the actors had changed.

A flood of foreigners driven in by the warring nations jabbered a dozen tongues in the streets. Refugees, people expelled from enemy territory, war profiteers, spies, deserters, interned soldiers, personalities of pacific or artistic temperament who desired to avoid a world gone mad, shady fellows with shifty eyes seeking questionable adventures, all these sought the haven of neutrality that was Switzerland and concentred on Zurich. The Bahnhofstrasse was nicknamed the Balkanstrasse because of its motley aspect. Glum Zurich burghers observed with disfavour the Jewish profiteers, the *Schieber,* who gathered and gesticulated about the steps of Leu's bank every morning, winning and losing fortunes in the exchange fluctuations. There were Jews from Poland, from Russia, from Rumania, from Austria, from Holland, from Spain and from Italy, some dressed in the height of fashion, others looking like old-clothesmen and still others in attire that was almost mediæval. A large number of Greeks swarmed through the city, too. Every warring nation had its own propaganda bureau, sometimes discreetly disguised, and an illimitable flood of persuasive and generally fallacious argument issued from them. Curiously enough, the British and the Germans generally sought each other's society and despised their allies. Everybody detested the Swiss, and the Zurichers in turn detested all the foreigners without exception. It is interesting to note that during Carnival time there is a students' ball which invariably ends with a free fight between the Swiss and the foreigners. During the first year of the war many people wondered what would happen at this affair, if, for instance, one body of the divided foreigners would side with the Swiss or whether the battle would degenerate into a three-cornered tussle. When the time came Britisher, German, Frenchman and Austrian fought stoutly shoulder to shoulder against the Swiss.

Joyce was not long in adjusting himself to this hectic scene. He found many Triestine friends among the refugees and made new ones, principally among the Jews and Greeks. One of his first gestures was to advertise in the daily newspapers for English students and within a few months he had secured sufficient to carry on his precarious existence. It was a hard, miserably-paid labour but it was all that he could do. He took no side in the war and confined himself to a regret that France and Germany, the two cultural forces of Europe, were at each other's throats. As an Irishman he considered himself a neutral, as neutral, in fact, as a Swiss should be. He was content to stand aside and observe with some irony the Gilbertian antics of the heterogeneous society that plotted, conspired, argued and propagandized all around him. His only passion was the completion of *Ulysses* and this he immediately attacked as soon as he had settled himself, carrying on from that portion of the third section called "Proteus" that he had finished in Trieste. He worked under difficulties, for his eyes were troubling him again and he was soon consulting the Zurich doctors. During the four years that he lived in Zurich he went in turn for treatment to Weber, Haab *fils,* Gamper, Stehli and Siedler. Tall, thin, nervous, harassed but always moved to humour by the grotesque and the absurd inconsistencies of his environment, he soon became a notable figure in a city that fairly overflowed with unusual personalities.

Matters went miserably at first. He could barely cover his daily expenses from the fees he received for teaching the English language and the two books he had published brought him in practically nothing. News of his difficult struggle reached London and the energetic Ezra Pound decided to do something about it. He went to W. B. Yeats, George Moore and Edmund Gosse and explained the predicament of the Dubliner in Zurich. This resulted in these three literary figures appealing to the then Prime Minister, Mr. Asquith, and some time after Joyce received the sum of one hundred pounds from the Privy Purse. It was a welcome windfall and Joyce was properly grateful for it. But even so it did not destroy his attitude of neutrality. He continued to be neither a pro-Englander nor an anti-Englander, although it is to be surmised that the gesture on the part of the English Government was propagandist in intent. Joyce remained what he had been for years, a Dubliner alienated by the paralysis and cruel inconsistency of the city of his birth.

As 1915 crept into 1916 a group of companions gradually attached themselves to Joyce. Among the earliest (all language students) were Edmund Brauchbar, Georges Borach and Victor Sax. Still later, when he had settled upon the Pfauen Restaurant as a favourite nightly resort, others came to him, among them Frank Budgen, Paul Suter, Paul Wiederkehr, a wine merchant, Mario Lenaci and, less often, Claud W. Sykes and Paul Ruggiero. All of them played some part, large or small, in his life. Their interests were variegated and with them he could discuss many things, music, painting, the theatre, even politics when he so desired, although the desire seems to have been seldom active. Not all of these friends were encountered during his first year in Zurich but as a whole they form a composite of his contacts during the period he passed in the Swiss city, a composite of men who were intelligent and aware of the unique genius of Joyce. It is, perhaps, to anticipate to allude to the Pfauen Restaurant but the friends of Joyce at this period seem to remember him best seated in that restaurant before a carafe of Fendant de Sion, that pale greenish-amber wine which he called *Erzherzogin,* the Archduchess, and talking dryly of art and letters.

Meanwhile the war roared on outside of that neutral terrain

that was Switzerland, great battles were won and lost and the countries standing aside from the conflict were flooded with propaganda. In Ireland matters were approaching a climax which culminated in the Easter Week Rebellion of 1916. Joyce continued to follow affairs in Ireland (as well as he could from his distance) but he had little to say about them. His political attitude, if the opinions of a man immersed in a vast literary endeavour to the practical exclusion of all else may be so dignified, was not simple to grasp. It may be divined, perhaps, through two statements of his. When leaving Trieste in 1915 he had to apply for a passport to the United States Consul there who had charge of British interests. Apparently this official, who seems to have been officious as well, was nonplussed by Joyce's bored replies and finally remarked that he himself was proud to feel that he was acting for the British Consul, "the representative of the King of England." Joyce said, "The British Consul is not the representative of the King of England. He is an official paid by my father for the protection of my person." The other remark was made in connection with the struggle for Irish independence when a questioner asked him if he did not look forward to the emergence of an independent Ireland. Joyce is reported to have counterqueried, "So that I might declare myself its first enemy?" There is reason to believe, however, that Joyce was convinced from the first that the cause of Irish independence would be eventually won. He knew the temper of his own people. But he was very guarded in expressing his opinions except to his intimate friends. He knew too well the hysterical spy mania that was as rampant in Zurich as it was in the great capitals of the world. Even when the *Journal de Genève* offered him a large fee to write an article on the Irish situation he refused, explaining that he never wrote for newspapers. This was not strictly true for he had written on Ireland for the *Piccolo della Sera* and even in Zurich he augmented his scanty funds by translating articles for a local journal but he distrusted the English temperament in wartime. "Horn of a bull, hoof of a horse, smile of a Saxon." The distrust was bred in the bone and reached back even to the dark mythos that impregnated the soil of Ireland.

The year 1916 was marked by three events important to Joyce as a writer seeking a public. An American publisher, Ben W.

Huebsch, imported sheets of *Dubliners* from Grant Richards and published the book in New York. The volume, bound in blue-green cloth with the title stamped on the side and back in green ink, was received by the American critics with praise, although the public, dazed by the flood of conflicting war propaganda, neglected it and turned instead to such productions as Arthur Guy Empey's *Over the Top*. The firm of Huebsch even went further than importing the sheets of *Dubliners*. It accepted the manuscript of *A Portrait of the Artist as a Young Man* as well and published the book in this very same year. The appearance of the dark-blue volume proved to be a tremendous stride into fame for Joyce. Discerning critics immediately placed him in the forerank of English-writing authors. A new and unique power had arrived and a small intelligent audience was aware of it. In spite of the hurly-burly of British war propaganda that was steadily inflaming the American mind against the Central Powers there yet remained enough reasoning individuals to recognize literature when they saw it. The fact that they were few was of small importance. It had always been so.

The Egoist Press had intended to publish *A Portrait of the Artist as a Young Man* in London this year also but Joyce's old enemy, the Moral British Printer, intervened again. The editors of the Egoist Press tried printer after printer but the result was always the same, a demand for deletions or a simple refusal to print the book. It is of interest to note that English printers were writing in the Year of Our Lord 1916 in this vein:

> We return the manuscript which you left with us and beg to say that we could not for one moment entertain any idea of printing such a production. We are convinced that you would run a very great risk in putting such a book on the market, and would advise, if you still think of publishing it, to have it gone over carefully, and all objectionable passages expunged. (From a provincial firm)

> We beg to return the manuscript of *A Portrait of the Artist as a Young Man* as it contains objectionable matter which we could not print. (From a well-known London firm of printers)

> At the present time labour troubles here make it difficult for us to undertake any new business, but in the case of the novel submitted we

regret that we cannot see our way to produce it without some adjustment even of the part sent to us.

(From an Edinburgh firm of printers)

I had a few minutes leisure last night and dipped very superficially into this story. It may be true to life but there are expressions therein which, to record in print, seems to me to serve no useful purpose and which I could not agree to produce. I herewith beg to return the manuscript.

(From a prominent London firm of printers)

In accordance to our conversation over the telephone yesterday we are returning the book to you and regret that we cannot proceed with same unless the passages marked in blue pencil are modified or removed.

(From a London firm whose estimate had been accepted and who had already started on the setting up of the type. Thirty-nine passages were blue-pencilled)

Our reader has carefully gone through same and has drawn our attention to several paragraphs which we regret we do not see our way to pass. If you could get the author to delete or modify these paragraphs we shall be only too pleased to submit you an estimate, as we shall esteem it a pleasure to resume our old business relations.

(From the branch of a firm that had at one time printed the *Egoist*)

We are pleased to receive your enquiry . . . but our acceptance of the work will probably be subject to the same conditions as required by your other printers. Our standing is such that we are very particular as to what we put our name to, and we would not knowingly undertake any work of a doubtful character even though it may be a classic. We should be glad if you would point out the particular passages to which the other printers have taken exception, and we shall then be better able to say whether or no we will consider the matter. . . . We thank you for so kindly giving us a sight of the complete story, but regret we do not feel inclined to undertake the printing of this unless you exclude some of the paragraphs which others have taken exceptions to.

(From a well-known provincial firm)

It was the same old story again and eventually the Egoist Press was compelled to import sheets from America into England where the book was published the following year.

Despite the sheepheadedness of the Moral British Printer the eighteen months that Joyce passed in Zurich (if we bring him to the end of 1916) include the most rapid growth in public esteem that he had ever experienced within such a limited period. His fame had reached America and it had also spread in England. Zurich recognized him as a figure of importance. New friends were continually gathering about him and some of them already had heard portions of *Ulysses*. Dublin might continue to scoff but the opinion of Dublin was becoming increasingly inconsequential. Joyce's oyster was the world now and the shell was beginning to open. At the same time he was still plodding away at his English lessons, for the question of money never ceased to be an harassing problem. He had changed his address several times, removing from the Gartenstrasse to 10, Kreuzstrasse and later to 73, Seefeldstrasse where he shared a flat with Philip Jarnach, Busoni's secretary and assistant *Kapellmeister* at the Stadttheater. Still later he and his family divided this flat with Charlotte Sauermann, one of the leading sopranos of the Zurich opera. And, to settle once for all with these addresses, during the last year or so of his sojourn in Zurich he lived respectively at 38, Universitäts-Strasse and at 29, Universitäts-Strasse.

It was through the good offices of Charlotte Sauermann that Joyce's financial difficulties were partially ameliorated. She heard him singing one day and, surprised at the quality of his voice, became interested in him and his future. It was a simple matter to perceive that Joyce's lack of money forced him to give up the precious time he should be working at his book to the drudgery of language teaching. Madame Sauermann decided to do something about it. She visited Mrs. Harold McCormick, only daughter of the late John D. Rockefeller, Sr., then living in Zurich and the centre about which the psychoanalytical group revolved, and spoke to her about the Irish writer who contending with the difficulties of eye troubles and onerous language teaching was struggling to complete a vast work. The result of this kindly interference was that Joyce received a notification from Mrs. McCormick's legal representative that hereafter he would receive the sum of a thousand Swiss francs each month. It seemed like manna from heaven to Joyce for it meant that he could relieve himself from some part of his arduous teaching and devote this freed time to the formidable problems of *Ulysses*. This he did and each month until shortly before his return to Trieste after the war was over he received the pension. How it was stopped is a story to be told in its place.

Things now ran somewhat smoother for Joyce. He experienced a feeling of partial freedom from hateful routine, a feeling that he had never experienced before, and the thousand and one bits of paper upon which he was writing *Ulysses* grew to an imposing mass. It was his habit to carry constantly about with him tiny writing blocks which fitted into his waistcoat pocket and many of his companions in Zurich saw him suddenly withdraw one of these blocks and scribble a few words upon it. This might happen in the street or in a restaurant or while he was in the midst of a conversation in his own flat. How he ever assembled these multitudinous notes was a puzzle for his complicated and apparently haphazard method of cross-indexing seemed impossible for a writer with such bad eyesight. There was, of course, the magnifying glass which he always carried about with him, but one of his Zurich friends declares that the handwriting was so bad, sometimes a mere smear of pencil with, perhaps, a single letter recognizable, that even the best eyes could not make it out. Yet the notes, the phrases, the adumbrations of numberless motifs, continued to fall like little mosaics into the narrative and section after section of *Ulysses* was completed and turned over to some friend to be copied on the typewriter.

There is no better description of the way in which Joyce found his material than that set down by Mr. Frank Budgen (who met the author a year or so after the period here considered) and it may be quoted:

Joyce's method of composition always seemed to me to be that of a poet rather than that of a prose writer. The words he wrote were far advanced in his mind before they found shape on paper. He was constantly and indefatigably in pursuit of the solution to some problem of homeric correspondence or technical expression or trait of character in Bloom or another personage of 'Ulysses'; or some physiological fact was necessary to give him the key to some part of his epic of the human body. Sculptor or painter, daylight worker, having laid aside the tools of his trade for the day, would relax, but Joyce's preoccupation with his book was never ending. He was always looking and listening for the necessary fact or word; and he was a great believer in his luck. What he needed would come to him. That which he collected would prove useful in its time and place. And as, in a sense, the theme of 'Ulysses' is the whole of life, there was no end to the variety of material that went into its building. Of the time detail of 1904 was none around him, but what he saw and heard in 1918 or 1919 would do just as well, for the shapes of life remain constant: only the dress and manners change. I have seen him collect in the space of a few hours the oddest assortment of material: a parody on the 'House that Jack Built,' the name and action of a poison, the method of caning boys on training ships, the wobbly cessation of a tired unfinished sentence, the nervous trick of a convive turning his glass in inward-turning circles, a Swiss music-hall joke turning on a pun in Swiss dialect, a description of the Fitzsimmons shift.[1]

To this strenuous endeavour, then, Joyce's existence ran parallel with the Great War. And because he could work anywhere, because his material might be sought and recognized in all places and at all times, he was to be seen often in the streets and restaurants of Zurich, sitting in the Pfauen or the Augustinerhof, walking around the lake with, perhaps, a Greek friend, say, Nicholas Santos[2] of Corfu who used to recite bits of the *Odyssey* to him, or Antonio Chalas or Pavlos Phocas, discoursing with Felix Beran the Austrian poet who years later translated *Pomes Penyeach* into German, attending the opera (he never missed a performance of *Die Meistersinger*), listening to some German play in the theatre, talking of Trieste with the sad, brown-eyed, bristly-moustached Simeone Levi who had complained after he read *A Portrait of the Artist as a Young Man,* "But I don't never understand it," or mounting to the Observatory with his son to see the stars and listen to the old Austrian astronomer Siegmund Feilbogen, the pacifist, say, "How can people look at them and say there is no God?"

He encountered many of the foreign writers who had found in Zurich a haven during the madness that obsessed the rest of the

[1] *James Joyce and the Making of Ulysses,* by Frank Budgen. Grayson and Grayson, London.

[2] Nicholas Santos was a very ignorant Corfiote in spite of his familiarity with Homer. Another person who often came to talk with Joyce when the condition of his eyes kept him immured in a dark room was Umberto Moggi, father of one of Giorgio's playmates. He was a splendid type of Tuscan peasant, black-bearded, with eyes which Dante calls "gli occhi onesti ed tardi." He was a green-grocer and could neither read nor write nor even sign his name. Joyce never met anybody who had Moggi's command of the Italian language.

world. Among those whom he met before he left the Swiss city in 1919 was Carl Bleibtreu who had written a book called *Die Lösung der Shakespeare Frage,* a work attempting to demonstrate that Roger Manners, Earl of Rutland, had written the plays commonly ascribed to one William Shakespeare. Joyce passed an entire afternoon discussing the Rutland theory with this author. Whether or not he took any stock in it is a mystery. He was sufficiently impressed, however, to introduce it in *Ulysses:* "Herr Bleibtreu, the man Piper met in Berlin, who is working up that Rutland theory, believes that the secret is hidden in the Stratford monument. He is going to visit the present duke, Piper says, and prove to him that his ancestor wrote the plays. It will come as a surprise to his grace. But he believes his theory." Joyce met, too, Réné Schickerlé, the Alsatian writer, and Schickerlé wanted him to translate his play *Hans in dem Schnakenloch.* Nothing came of it. Frank Wedekind, the celebrated German dramatist, was in Zurich during the greater part of 1917 and performed in his own plays. Joyce met him and was interested enough to go and see the performances. Stefan Zweig was there and his play, *Jeremias,* was acted at the Stadttheater. Nicolai Lenin, already planning to shake the world, frequented a café, the Odéon, to which Joyce often went. And Romain Rolland was among the refugees who sought in Zurich a place of peace. All of these personalities give an idea of what a little international metropolis Zurich became during the four years of the war. Their presence, and the presence of the countless host of others who belonged not in Switzerland but in far-lying places beyond the high borders, afford some conception of the clashing atmosphere that sparkled as though filled with electricity above the placid lake.

It was the largest conglomeration of expatriates, refugees, adventurers and propagandists, probably, that had ever been assembled together in one small city. Through it all Joyce continued to maintain his aloof and somewhat scornful neutrality towards the outcome of the struggle. When he did express himself it was in a humorous vein, a vein of parody, as in the words he put to the old music-hall song of "Mr. Dooley":

> Who is the funny fellow who declines to go to church
> Since pope and priest and parson left the poor man in the lurch

And taught their flocks the only way to save all human souls
Was piercing human bodies through with dum-dum bullet holes?
It's Mr. Dooley, it's Mr. Dooley,
The wisest wight our country ever knew.
Who will release us
From Jingo Jesus,
Prays Mr. Dooley—ooley—ooley—oo.

He abhorred war because it was a settlement of nothing, merely a brute exhibition of who was the strongest in physique and material paraphernalia. It was reason that won always, not the fact that one person or nation possessed more strength or wealth than another. Questions settled by force were never settled for him. They were merely brutally silenced for the moment. Tomorrow the same question would be asked again. It was not Jeanne d'Arc who was vanquished at Rouen; it was the entire English conception. Neither was it Pearse, MacDonagh, Joseph Mary Plunkett and James Connolly who lost their argument before the firing squad in Kilmainham; it was again the English conception. Joyce had no patience with stupid force.

So we see him at this midmoment of the war, existing in a city that was fearfully like a boiling cauldron and with the *brouhaha* of mad days about him but walking through it with his mind intent upon an olive-faced man whom he had created and set peregrinating through the streets of the Dublin of 1904. What was the war to him?—no more than an argument between stupid men who could settle nothing by reason. There was not even a cause to be admired. There was nothing but rapaciousness and the complicated duels of commercial supremacies. If the conflict had arisen because of a persecuted people he might have sympathized, but who could say that Great Britain, France, Germany, Austria, Russia and the United States were persecuted peoples? For God's sake, let things be finished and let men think of the arts again. He had already reached a point in his uncompleted book where he had set down the lines, "Perfume of embraces all him assailed. With hungered flesh obscurely, he mutely craved to adore." He had paused for a long time after that, pondering the rhythm and unusual juxtaposition of words. There was something new, something more important than a won battle, in the fall of those words and the suggestion that they gave to him. And knowing this he knew that *Ulysses* was of much more importance to him than the Great War. He was marching into a new terrain of literature where no man had ever marched before.

He had always been sure of himself but now he was surer than ever. His tenacity of purpose was being vindicated. There was a satisfaction here, for his family was growing up. Giorgio had passed his eleventh year and was a sturdy boy, an amazingly good swimmer, and Lucia, approaching her ninth birthday, was developing into a dark-haired, blue-eyed girl of graceful slender figure. As he watched them moving about the flat, speaking in the Zuridütsch dialect they had picked up so quickly but just as often in the Triestine dialect that was, after all, their mother tongue, he experienced a mingled sense of pleasure and power. The flight from the North Wall in Dublin, the flight of more than twelve years before, had not been in vain. What he had then seen mistily he now saw clearly. The dæmon that had pushed him on had been a true dæmon and he was both its slave and its master. Where it would continue to push him he did not know but he did know that he could control the impulses which it aroused in him. It was an Irish dæmon. It sprang out of the dark soil of Ireland. It rose from the gnostic mythos. It curled like a smoke above the grave-mound of Queen Buan and the secret place where the Anna Liffey had her birth. And as it had pushed him into a myth of waking life so might it push him towards a myth of sleeping life. It would be a natural step, for already he was delving deep into the subconscious of his characters in *Ulysses*.

II

The progress he was making towards a broad recognition in the English-speaking countries became accelerated in 1917. In America Ben W. Huebsch, observing the near-exhaustion of his edition of the English-printed sheets of *Dubliners,* ordered an American edition to be set up. And in England the Egoist Press finally found a printer who consented to put into type *A Portrait of the Artist as a Young Man* in its entirety and without swooning in modest moral shame. Most important, perhaps, of all to Joyce was the review of *A Portrait of the Artist as a Young Man* that H. G. Wells contributed to the February twenty-fourth number of the *Nation*. It contained astonishing praise from a powerful commentator. It also contained blame (Wells, for instance, gagged at what he called the cloacal obsession of the Irish writer), but the blame was forgotten in the face of such statements as "Its claim to be literature is as good as the claim of the last book of 'Gulliver's Travels'" and "One conversation in the book is a superb success, the one in which Mr. Dedalus carves the Christmas turkey; I write with all due deliberation that Sterne himself could not have done it better." Joyce, in spite of his precarious financial state, could not but feel that time was changing and a fair wind favouring him.

There were great activities, too, in Zurich (which had become the most important city in Switzerland) and these must have greatly exhilarated the mind of Joyce. An electric feverish atmosphere pulsated through the town and though there was a shortage of food there was a plethora of intellectual and artistic fare. All the belligerents adopted the tactics of trying to justify themselves and their causes by intensive cultural and artistic propaganda. During this year, 1917, for instance, the Zurich municipal theatre received visits from Max Reinhardt's dramatic company, the Comédie-Française, the Burgtheater, the Theater an der Wien, and the Milan Scala. Other companies from France, Germany and Austria visited the town. Celebrated conductors, including Nikisch and Weingartner, came with their orchestras. At the Kunsthaus were exhibitions of French, German, Austrian and Italian paintings. With art, music, the opera, great artists and a horde of intellectuals fleeing from the war-torn countries Zurich became, in a measure, the æsthetic centre of Europe. It was a kindly fate, after all, that had led Joyce to this effervescing town, the fittest place, perhaps, in the world for him to dwell and labour upon the great structure of *Ulysses*.

There were humorous characters to be encountered too, the flotsam and jetsam of half a dozen countries, and one at least among them had a brief indirect influence on Joyce's career. Joyce knew him first under the name of Joe Martin. It was not his real name but for various reasons that must be suppressed. Joe Martin, then, waited upon the Irish writer one day in the spring of 1917 and made the astonishing proposal that Joyce write a cinema scenario for him, its title to be *Wine, Women and Song*. "We'll get wealthy women into it," explained Martin, "women in fur pelts. We'll teach them how to walk and then charge them a fee for being in the film." Later Joyce discovered that the astute Mr. Martin proposed to shoot his picture without any film at all in the camera; in other words, the project was a barefaced swindle to be based on the vanity of the "women in fur pelts." But at the moment Joyce listened with some tolerance. Prices in Zurich were rising weekly and everybody in the overcrowded town was struggling desperately to make ends meet. Joyce was no exception. He had a family to support and a windfall was a windfall. Therefore he half-consented to occupy himself with *Wine, Women and Song*.

Some time later (still in the springtime) Joe Martin sent to Joyce as an assistant in the preparation of the scenario Mr. Claud W. Sykes, an actor who had played in the company of Sir Herbert Beerbohm Tree. It was because he was the connecting link, so to speak, between Joyce and Mr. Sykes that Joe Martin was of indirect influence on the Irish writer's career in Zurich. This we shall see in another section. As for *Wine, Women and Song*, this sly scheme of the slippery Mr. Martin came to nothing. Perhaps the "women in pelts" did not materialize or, more probably, Joyce and Sykes realized the ridiculousness of the venture and withdrew from it, leaving Joe Martin without scenario writers. Joe also conceived the idea of producing Joyce's *Exiles*. He had, in fact, played in New York in *The Yellow Ticket* and he proposed himself to play the part of Robert Hand in the Joyce play. He affirmed that he knew in the Hôtel Baur au Lac a woman who could play the part of Bertha Rowan to perfection, pointing out that she was splendidly developed, had swell dresses and plenty of furs and diamonds. Joyce apparently agreed to the proposal which the vicissitudes of Joe's career never permitted to materialize.

The ambitious Joe, however, did not vanish from Joyce's life for a long time after that. It is, perhaps, permissible to run ahead of chronology here and briefly note the various *rencontres* the Dublin writer had with this bizarre individual for they give a fair picture of the strange and shifty characters that infested Zurich during the war years, characters that always amused Joyce and whose eccentricities he ticketed away in his mind. For instance, Joyce was instrumental in getting Joe out of prison and into hospital at one time. Joe, properly grateful, turned up at Joyce's dwelling and presented him with a parcel. "It is a gift for you," he said. "I made it in prison." When the parcel was opened the gift was revealed as a wooden box shaped like a family Bible with "My First Success. By James Joyes" neatly printed on the back of it. "When you make money," explained Joe, "you can conceal it in the box. Everybody will think it's a book." Another time Joyce and Mrs. Joyce encountered Joe on the Bahnhofstrasse. The adventurer had undergone a marvellous transformation. He was wearing the latest extravagant cut in suits, beige gaiters, a gaudy tie and canary-coloured gloves. In his lapel was a large flower, in his hand a malacca stick, and in his mouth a huge cigar. It was eleven o'clock in the morning but Joe insisted that Joyce have some champagne with him. They went into Huguemin's. "Do you want any shirtwaists?" Joe asked. "Or artificial pearls?" Joyce was dubious about either but the next day Joe showed up with both shirtwaists and pearls and jumped on the pearls to prove that they were unbreakable. A week later he was in the Zurich prison. From this he was extricated by the Dutch Consul in Zurich to whom Joyce had gone. It was at this time that Joyce discovered, by receiving a letter of profuse gratitude from Joe's aged father in Amsterdam and thanking him for his efforts on behalf of the "black sheep of my family," that Joe was in reality the son of a well-known gynæcologist in a large European city. From the prison Joe-Jules-Judas was transferred to the hospital. "This time I am all in," he wrote to Joyce. But he wasn't. For a brief period he acted as prompter for the English players. Then he disappeared. Six years or so later Joyce ran across him in Ostend. He was in good health, well-dressed and the owner of a large motorcar and a house in Brussels. And from there he disappears out of Joyce's life. Rumour, however, has it that he has reformed and is now a pillar of respectability.

During this spring and summer of 1917 Joyce laboured assiduously at *Ulysses*. He was hampered by the objectionable language lessons so necessary if he was to pay his rent and eat and the increasing troubles with his eyes. Still the pile of notes grew and the opening sections developed into a form of completeness, rounded links in the great undertaking that were ready for typing. The war thundered on beyond the borders of Switzerland but Ulysses proceeded on his inevitable odyssey unconscious of battles won, drawn or defeated. Joyce, wrapped in his æsthetic problems, could not be bothered by the senseless struggle into which the United States had just entered.

It was at this dolorous period of time that he received an unexpected aid that was to free him during the ensuing years from all language teaching and make it possible for him to devote all his energies to his writing. Miss Harriet Weaver, the editor in succession to Miss Dora Marsden of the *Egoist,* had been for some time a devoted admirer of Joyce's work and the difficulties against which he struggled in order to express himself aroused a great concern in her mind. She was convinced that something should be done for the Irish writer and as no one else appeared likely to do it she did it herself. Joyce's reception of her first gesture has been communicated by Felix Beran, who edited the periodical for which the Dubliner did various translations. "At that time," he writes, "Joyce was already bothered by trouble with his eyes and was often hindered at work. Once I found him in his house alone in an artificially-darkened room. The impression was depressing. In spite of that I have retained an extraordinarily beautiful remembrance of that meeting. While we were chatting there was a ring at the front door. Joyce was not allowed to leave the dark room and so I sent out and took the mail from the mailman. It was a registered letter from an English bank and Joyce begged me to open and read it aloud. The bank wrote that an admirer of Joyce, who did not want to be named, had commissioned it to pay him five hundred Swiss francs each month, including the past three months. At that time Joyce was in sore financial straits and here came real help in need."

These payments continued for some time and then Miss Weaver, anonymous no longer so far as Joyce was concerned, made a second and greater gesture. She transferred outright to Joyce a substantial sum of money so that he could draw the interest on his own investments and not depend on the uncertainty of a monthly payment that might be withdrawn at any moment as the whim of the patron dictated. The interest on this gift, added to Mrs. McCormick's aid, made it possible for Joyce to live modestly and devote all his time to his writing. It is impossible to overpraise the unique gesture of Miss Weaver. Such acts of generosity are so rare in a world where the artist is generally neglected for the sake of more obvious spectacles of philanthropy that it should be dwelt upon for a moment. The rich man usually desires to give his money to foundations that will bear his name or with which his name will be associated. However, it is impossible to do that with the individual artist. John Jones cannot subsidize James Joyce on the condition that James Joyce sign his books thereafter The John Jones Foundation. But Miss Weaver, during a period of war when nobody was thinking of artists, discreetly and with a complete withdrawal of herself, made it possible for Joyce to achieve his artistic goal in comparative comfort. Lorenzo de' Medici did no more.

Freed at last from the drudgery of teaching (and what must his emotions have been at that happy liberation?), Joyce decided to avoid the danger to his eyes of the foehn wind of Zurich and go to Locarno where the climate was better and he could labour in peace. By the autumn of 1917 he was settled there in the Pension Villa Rossa, later moving to the Pension Daheim. *Ulysses* progressed rapidly. Miss Weaver had agreed to publish certain episodes in the *Egoist* (certain episodes because the printer refused to set up the entire work) and an American monthly, the *Little Review,* edited by Miss Margaret Anderson and Miss Jane Heap (to whom Joyce had been introduced by mail by Ezra Pound—now corresponding constantly with the exiled writer), decided to attempt the serialization of the entire work in the following year. It became necessary, therefore, that the manuscript be properly typed. Joyce searched about him for someone who would be willing to undertake this labour (no easy one, at all) and eventually settled upon Mr. Claud Sykes who had been introduced to him by the marvellous Joe Martin. Sykes had been of a sympathetic nature; he had proved intelligent; there had been a number of meetings between the two men, some in Joyce's flat and others in Sykes' *pension* in the Plattenstrasse, and the conversations had ranged from the Greek analogies of *Ulysses* to the probabilities of Mrs. Bandman Palmer playing *Leah, the Forsaken* in Dublin in 1904.

Mr. Sykes, although in Zurich, was quite willing to do the typing. The only thing he lacked was a typewriter. And because it gives another picture of the Gilbertian aspects of Zurich in war-time the story of the acquisition of the machine may be set down here. Joyce suggested that Sykes go to a certain Goldschmidt and beg the loan of a typewriter from him. Now Goldschmidt was an Austrian Jew who worked along with a number of able-bodied compatriots in the Oesterreich-Ungarisches-Hilfsverein, a society established to assist subjects of the Dual Monarchy. Their work exempted them from army service and therefore they took care to make it seem as arduous as possible. Unauthorized individuals were not welcome in their office, the reason being that some spy might get in and see that the personnel of the Oesterreich-Ungarisches-Hilfsverein was really doing nothing but sitting with their feet on the desks, all distressed Austrians and Hungarians having been expatriated long before. Being warned of the state of affairs Sykes took no notice of the clerk in the outer office who clamoured that Herr Goldschmidt was not there and even if he was there he would be far too busy to see anyone. The visitor simply walked past the clerk and into the inner office where he found Herr Goldschmidt dreamily examining the ceiling. "Ah, Herr Sykes," exclaimed the Austrian Jew, "come in and have a cigarette. We have nothing to do today." The typewriter (there being no use for typewriters in the Hilfsverein) was willingly and instantly loaned. When Sykes reported the incident to Joyce it moved him to compose a verse to the tune of the "Amorous Goldfish" in *The Geisha*.

> A Goldschmidt swam in a Kriegsverein
> As wise little Goldschmidts do,
> And he loved every scion of the Habsburg line,
> Each Archduke proud, the whole jimbang crowd,
> And he felt that they loved him, too.
> Herr Rosenbaum and Rosenfeld
> And every other Feld except Schlachtfeld
> All worked like niggers, totting rows of crazy figures,
> To save Kaiser Karl and Goldschmidt, too.
>
> Chorus:
> For he said it is bet—bet—better
> To stick stamps on some God-damned letter
> Than be shot in a trench

Amid shells and stench,
Jesus Gott, Donnerwet—wet—wetter.

Sykes immediately started typing the first three books (The Telemachia) of *Ulysses* and envelopes of copy passed regularly between Locarno and Zurich. Sometimes Joyce would slip a limerick in for the amusement of the typist, a literary sin (if sin it be) for which he had had a weakness since his early Dublin days. As for instance:

There's a George of the Georges named David
With whose words we are now night and day fed.
    He cries: I'll give small rations
    To all the small nations.
Bully God made this world—but I'll save it.

Among others written just before or during this period three may be quoted.

There's a donor of lavish largesse
Who once bought a play in MS.
    He found out what it all meant
    By the final instalment
But poor Scriptor was left in a mess.

(The subject of the above was the late Mr. John Quinn, the Irish-American lawyer and bibliophile resident in New York whom Ezra Pound had introduced to Joyce by mail and who had purchased the manuscript of *Exiles*.)

There's a hairy-faced Moslem named Simon
Whose tones are not those of a shy man
    When with cast-iron lungs
    He howls twenty-five tongues—
But he's not at all easy to rhyme on.

(Simeone Levi has been mentioned before as one of the characters who infested Zurich during the war years.)

There is a clean climber called Sykes
Who goes scrambling through ditches and dykes.
    To skate on his scalp
    Down the side of an Alp
Is the kind of diversion he likes.

The winter closed in on Locarno and Joyce's lightheartedness became tempered by the illness of Nora Joyce. On January 2, 1918, he was writing to Sykes: "Please convey my wife's excuses for her taciturnity both to Mrs. Sykes and Mrs. Bleibtreu from whom she had a card today. She has been constantly ill and has even had a very bad nervous breakdown here so that I really do not know what to do—whether to go to Zurich on the offchance of finding a flat or leaving this pension and looking for a flat here. Instead of doing her good the stay here has made her much worse." However, the flat was found in Zurich and early in the new year he was back in the feverishly-pulsing little city. He brought with him the news that Sturge Moore of the London Stage Society was contemplating a production of *Exiles*. Because of the difficulties of casting this performance never took place. The idea of the stage, nevertheless, was fresh in Joyce's mind and caused him to enter willingly into a project that occupied most of his spare time (and some of the time he should have confined to his book as well) during 1918.

III

This year was the period of Joyce's activities on behalf of the English Players and the troublesome lawsuits that followed the first production. For some time pro-Englanders had asked why it was that Great Britain took no part in the vast flood of propaganda that was deluging Zurich. Surely there was something that could be done to impress on the swollen population of the city the artistic importance of the English people. And what could better represent the land of Shakespeare than the drama? The play was the thing. Sykes, being an experienced actor, was often approached on this subject. The idea of acting again was agreeable enough to him and early in the spring he discussed the possibilities of a theatrical production with Joyce, a production that might lead to others and the formation of a regular company. Both decided that in view of the grandiose scale on which the warring powers launched their propaganda it would be futile to attempt anything unless it could be done most excellently on the small scale available to them. The chief difficulty would be to find players really capable of the principal rôles; the minor parts, of course, could be entrusted to amateurs from the English colony. Joyce himself caught at the idea with alacrity. He had been interested in the stage since he had played as a boy in Dublin; the abandoned production of *Exiles* was still fresh in his mind; and, furthermore, it was conveyed to him unofficially but pretty plainly that he should officially do something in return for what had been done for him—*i.e.,* the gift from the King's Privy Purse.

Sykes finally decided that Oscar Wilde's *The Importance of Being Earnest* would be the safest venture for a first production, and Joyce, pleased with the selection, volunteered to be the English actor's joint partner and carry half the expenses. The English Consulate in Zurich, being informed of the idea, promised its moral support, although it would guarantee nothing towards the costs. Joyce undertook the business arrangements and Sykes assumed responsibility for the direction and production of the play.

The first problem was to find actors suitable to the various rôles. Zurich was combed and the result appeared to be encouraging except for one part. Mr. Tristan Rawson, an opera singer at the Cologne municipal theatre before the war, rather diffidently agreed to attempt the rôle of John Worthing, J.P. It would be the first time he had ever appeared in legitimate drama. Margaret Matthews, an American actress, was cast as Lady Bracknall. An English actress, Evelyn Cotton, accepted the part of the Honourable Gwendolen Fairfax. Sykes himself undertook to play the Reverend Canon Chasuble, D.D., and his wife, Daisy Race, an experienced actress, was cast as Cicely Cardew. The minor rôles of Merriman, the butler, Lane, the manservant, and Miss Prism, the governess, were assigned respectively to Charles Fleming (who also acted as stage manager), Cecil Palmer and Ethel Turner. But the important rôle of Algernon Moncrieff proved to be a worrisome problem. For a time it appeared as though the venture would fail because no person suitable to the part could be found. Finally somebody thought of a young man named Henry Carr, employed at the British Consulate, who was right for the rôle in voice, manner and appearance. If he could be trained and his inexperience covered by the professional players he might be possible. Sykes approached Carr and the young man consented to play the part,

though under the pseudonym of M. A. Ford, the British Consulate
refusing to permit him to act under his own name.

Rehearsals commenced and everything went smoothly at first.
The players seemed well suited to their parts and Carr, the only
amateur in an important rôle, worked so diligently that it appeared certain the professionals would be able to swing him along
easily into the rhythm of the comedy. Then, gradually, vague troubles began to appear. It became noticeable to the entire company
that Carr's behaviour toward Joyce was one of veiled indefinable
hostility, an insolence unreasonable and unwarrantable in a younger
man of no particular talents towards one who was older and far
more experienced in life and certainly of greater and more recognized achievement. Of course, the Easter Week Rebellion in Dublin was still fresh in the minds of English Tories and there were
many who abominated the Irish because of it; but Carr's home was
in Canada and few people could attribute this political hatred to
him. The other members of the cast finally (and kindly) ascribed
Carr's peculiar behaviour to his war experiences. He had been
wounded and afterward a prisoner in Germany, coming to Zurich
under the scheme for the exchange of prisoners then in force. In
spite of Carr, however, outward harmony was preserved till after
the first performance, Joyce, as usual, taking no particular heed
of those who disliked him.

This first performance took place at the Theater zur Kaufleuten, a hall at 18, Pelikanstrasse, on the evening of April twenty-
ninth before a full house that seemed well-pleased with the production. Joyce, who was looking after the front of the theatre,
spoke to Bennett, the British Consul, during the interval and the
latter congratulated him on the performance. For the moment
everything seemed to go well. The audience, reading their programmes, discovered that the English Players proposed to present,
as circumstances would permit, a list of plays including *She Stoops
to Conquer, Pippa Passes, The Pigeon, The Heather Field, Riders
to the Sea, The Dark Lady of the Sonnets* and *Exiles*. It is easy to
see Joyce's hand in this selection for out of the seven plays announced five were by Irishmen.

After the comedy had reached its conclusion to generous applause Joyce invited all the players to a supper that he had arranged. To the surprise of everybody Carr declined to attend, offering some trivial excuse for his absence. Trouble seemed to be brewing now but just what it was no one could guess. The next day, however, Sykes knew. He was called upon by Carr and Rawson and it was revealed that Carr considered himself decidedly insulted by the financial arrangements of the English Players. It will be remembered that Joyce was business manager, and perhaps it is necessary here to enlarge somewhat on the plan of salaries which he had a hand in arranging. It was obvious from the first that the players could not be remunerated adequately from the limited proceeds of one performance for the hours they sacrificed to rehearsals. As a matter of fact, these hours so sacrificed were not calculated to involve any financial hardships on the players for all of them were engaged at other occupations and the rehearsals were so scheduled as to suit their free time. It was Joyce and Sykes alone who stood to lose by the venture for the thousand and one details of the production did take them away from their own work and the final expenses (theatre rent, printing of tickets, programmes, etc.) devolved on them. Therefore, the two managers drew up a salary list in which they allotted as much as they could to the professional players and themselves and gave to the amateurs small sums, mere token payments, to show their good will. This scheme was explained to the members of the cast at the beginning of the rehearsals and all of them seemed to understand and acquiesce in the arrangement. Carr, for instance, declared that he would prefer to have no payment at all but Sykes insisted that something should be given to uphold the principle that every player should receive money. It was hoped to increase the payments if further performances proved successful.

Carr, however, had an angry bee in his bonnet. He was insulted by the small sum he received and declared it to be no more than a tip. He had expended much more than that, he expostulated, on the new trousers he had secured for the rôle of Algy. Sykes, and then Rawson, argued in a friendly fashion with the indignant young man and eventually Carr appeared to be pacified. At the same time he expressed a deal of resentment against Joyce whom he seemed to blame for some mysterious humiliation. When he left Sykes, however, he seemed to be in a more reasonable mood and even willing to take part in any future performances of the English Players.

But this was a false lull. Two days later when Joyce went to the British Consulate to collect some money for sold tickets from Carr the affair flared up again. The young consular employee (in the presence of two other employees named Smith and Gann) refused to turn over the money and demanded instead a sum out of all proportion for the new trousers he had purchased. When Joyce refused this all the pent-up rage against the Irish writer that had been swelling in Carr's mind burst forth in choice Billingsgate. He called Joyce opprobrious names and threatened to "wring his bloody neck and chuck him down the stairs." Joyce, always cool when attacked, merely remarked that that was not the language to use in a government office and left the Consulate. Carr, of course, immediately withdrew from the English Players and as Sykes could not find a substitute at the moment a projected performance in Basle had to be cancelled.

It will be consistent here to put aside for the moment the further history of the English Players and follow the Joyce-Carr imbroglio to its conclusion. First of all, the British Consulate withdrew its moral support (there had never been any financial support) from the English Players and endeavoured to thrust obstacles in the way of any future performances. Hints reached Sykes that the boycott would be removed if Joyce were thrown over but Sykes preferred to stand by his business manager. This boycott made itself especially felt when Sykes attempted to produce G. K. Chesterton's *Magic* as a second offering. Two promising newcomers, one an American and the other an Englishman, abruptly withdrew from the cast after a couple of rehearsals, expressing regret and admitting that influence had been brought to bear on them.

As for Joyce, he was harassed by the British Consulate in every possible way. Among other things, the minor representatives of His Majesty's Government dispatched a letter to him requesting him to volunteer for service in the British army. He replied immediately: "James Joyce presents his compliments to the B.M. Consul General and returns a document addressed to him in error."

This request for military service was a ridiculous and brutal gesture, for the Consulate was perfectly aware that Joyce's defective eyesight prevented him from serving in any army and that he was living in Zurich as a freed prisoner who had given his parole to reside in a neutral country for the duration of the war. Joyce, on his part, protested strongly to the British Consulate about Carr's behaviour but, naturally, received no response. He then laid his case before Sir Horace Rumbold, the British Minister in Berne. The gesture is revelatory of Joyce's character and tenacity when he is convinced he is in the right. As at Clongowes when, a small boy, he had ventured into the sacred precincts of the Reverend John S. Conmee, S.J., to protest against injustice and as in 1911 he had written directly to King George V concerning the disputed passage in *Dubliners,* so now did he turn to the highest British authority in Switzerland with a demand for fair dealing. He met, as he probably expected, with a flat refusal to take any steps in the matter. He thereupon brought two actions against Carr, one for threats of violence and the other for the price of three unpaid-for tickets to the performance of *The Importance of Being Earnest.* Carr immediately countersuited for nineteen pounds fifteen shillings, alternatively twelve pounds, for the price of garments specially purchased for the play.

Two of the actions came up before the Bezirksgericht Zurich on the fifteenth of October, 1918. Judge Billeter presided. Carr was represented by the Norwegian Vice-Consul, Wettstein. In the matter of the action for the price of three unpaid-for tickets Joyce was awarded one pound plus interest at five per cent from May 3, 1918; and Carr's action for nineteen pounds fifteen shillings, alternatively twelve pounds, was disallowed. The costs in both cases were declared against Carr and the consular employee was further ordered to pay Joyce two pounds ten shillings damages. All this may sound a little like Gilbert and Sullivan; therefore, it should be pointed out that Joyce, despite his indignation and insistence on justice, did not fail to extract some humour from it. For example, he celebrated the legal verdicts by composing several verses to the tune of "Tipperary." The C.G., of course, is the Consul-General.

### The C.G. is Not Literary

Up to rheumy Zurich came an Irishman one day,
And as the town was rather dull he thought he'd give a play,
So that the German propagandists might be rightly riled,
But the bully British Philistine once more drove Oscar Wilde.

> Chorus: Oh, the C.G. is not literary,
> And his handymen are rogues.
> The C.G.'s about as literary
> As an Irish kish of brogues.
> We have paid up all expenses
> As the good Swiss public knows,
> But we'll be damned well damned before we pay for
> Private Carr's swank hose.

When the play was over Carr with rage began to dance,
Saying I want twenty quid for them there dandy pants,
So fork us out the tin or Comrade Bennett here and me,
We're going to wring your bloody necks, we're out for liberty.

> Chorus: As before.

They found a Norse solicitor to prove that white was black,
That one can boss in Switzerland beneath the Union Jack;
They went off to the Gerichtshof, but came back like Jack and Jill
For the pants came tumbling after, and the judge is laughing still.

> Chorus: Oh, the C.G. is not literary,
> And his handymen are rogues.
> The C.G.'s about as literary
> As an Irish kish of brogues.
> So farewell, Bruiser Bennett,
> And goodbye, Chummy Carr;
> If you put a beggar up on horseback,
> Why 'e dunno where 'e are.

There was still a third case to be heard, however, that in which
Joyce sued Carr for threats of violence. Owing to the law's delays
this was postponed until long after the Armistice and when it did
come up Carr had quit Switzerland for Canada. Joyce was badly
let down by his lawyer, who first advised him to withdraw and
then failed to put in an appearance in court on the day the action
was called for hearing. Was this another case of the 'hidden hand'?

Whatever it was, Joyce put up a determined fight against the consular lawyer, Wettstein; but the action fell to the ground when Smith and Gann, who had been present when the insult was given, blandly declared they had heard and seen nothing. Joyce was ordered to pay one hundred and twenty Swiss francs (then about four pounds sixteen shillings) as court costs. This ended the great Joyce-Carr feud.

It has been described at some length here because distorted rumours of Joyce's activities during the Great War and before it have been spread abroad by inaccurate and malicious commentators. For instance, according to a nondescript and untruthful biographical article on the writer that appeared some years ago in an American Roman Catholic monthly Joyce made his money by selling all his information about Austria to the British authorities in Rome (!) after his release from Trieste, and, further, he gave every assistance to the British and was engaged in their propaganda office. The effect of this on the Irish-American public can be imagined. The truth was that Joyce was in litigation with the British authorities in Switzerland during his last years in Zurich and was, without a doubt, the best-hated British subject (by British bureaucrats, of course) in the country. Perhaps that was because he was not a fag or the son of a fag or the grandson of a fag. Joyce did not meddle in politics in any way. He was above the conflict as were all the wise unimpassioned minds of the time and his entire devotion and travail were concentrated on the development and perfection of his own art.

Here one must return to the history of the English Players. G. K. Chesterton's *Magic* being abandoned by Sykes because of consular interference, a programme of three one-act plays was put in rehearsal. They were J. M. Barrie's *The Twelve Pound Look,* John M. Synge's *Riders to the Sea,* and George Bernard Shaw's *The Dark Lady of the Sonnets.* The Joyce influence was pronounced in Synge's playlet. He was called in to teach the actors the genuine Irish *caoine* and Nora Joyce played excellently the rôle of Kathleen. It is interesting to note how often this play entered Joyce's life. He read it in manuscript in 1902, he translated it into Italian in Trieste years later, and now he was supervising its first production in Zurich. This première, with the other two playlets, was performed on June 17, 1918, at the Pfauentheater and Joyce wrote for the printed programme a set of notes describing the plays that deserves to be rescued.

### The Twelve Pound Look
### by J. M. Barrie.

One Sims is about to be knighted: possibly, as the name would suggest, for having patented a hairgrower. He is discovered rehearsing his part with his wife whose portrait we see on the wall, painted by a Royal Academician, also knighted, presumably for having painted the label for the hairgrower. A typist is announced. This typist is his runaway wife of some fourteen years before. From their conversation we learn that she left him not for another man but to work out her salvation by typewriting. She had saved twelve pounds and bought a typewriter. The twelve pound look, she says, is that look of independence in a wife's eye which every husband should beware of. The new knight's new wife, "noted for her wit"—chary of it, too—seems likely to acquire the look if given time. Typewriters, however, are rather scarce at present.

### Riders to the Sea
### By John M. Synge.

Synge's first play, written in Paris in 1902 out of his memories of Aran. The play shows a mother and her dead son, her last, the *anagke* being the inexorable sea which claims all her sons, Seumas and Patch and Stephen and Shaun. Whether a brief tragedy be possible or not (a point on which Aristotle had some doubts) the ear and the heart mislead one gravely if this brief scene from "poor Aran" be not the work of a tragic poet.

### The Dark Lady of the Sonnets
### By G. B. Shaw

Mr. Shaw here presents three orthodox figures—a virgin queen, a Shakespeare sober at midnight and a free giver of gold and the dark-haired maid of honour, Mary Fitton, discovered in the eighties by Thomas Tyler and Mr. Harris. Shakespeare comes to Whitehall to meet her and learns from a well-languaged beefeater that Mr. W. H. has forestalled him. The poet vents his spleen on the first woman who passes. It is the queen and she seems not loth to be accosted. She orders the maid of honour out of the way. When Shakespeare, however, begs her to endow his theatre she refers him with fine cruelty to her lord treasurer and leaves him. The most regicide of playwrights prays God to save her and goes home weighing against a lightened purse, love's treason, an old queen's leer and the evil eye of a government official, a horror still to come.

During the summer the English Players took *The Importance of Being Earnest* on tour through Western Switzerland, the part of Algy being played by Charles Pussy, a professional actor living in Vevey. The towns visited were Lausanne, Geneva, Montreux and Interlaken. The great influenza epidemic broke out shortly before the beginning of the tour and because of this the audiences (excepting the one at Geneva) were very sparse. The agent of the company was Mr. Arnold Meckel, a young Russian who died recently in Paris. He became afterward one of the best known impresarios in Europe, acting for Argentina, the Sakharovs, Udey Shankar, etc. The tour resulted in a financial loss which was borne by Joyce and Sykes. Joyce travelled only as far as Lausanne. Being the father of two children he considered it more prudent to return to Zurich which was comparatively free of the epidemic. A second reason brought him back too, and that was the pathological condition of his eyes. He had been suffering for some time (always acute attacks of iritis) but the tragic climax occurred on August eighteenth, the birthday of Franz Joseph of Austria. On the evening of this day he was strolling down the broad bustling Bahnhofstrasse with Nora Joyce when a sudden and unexpected eye attack halted him in his tracks. It was not iritis. For twenty minutes he was unable to move and he was carried to a near-by bench. Around the arc lamps he saw spinning rainbows. Almost immediately he realized that he had that dreaded ailment, glaucoma. He was helped to his flat and a week or so later iridectomy (cutting a triangular piece out of the afflicted right eye) was performed on him by Professor Siedler. It was discovered that the circulation of the eye was impeded and for several weeks Joyce remained a practically-blind convalescent in a darkened room unable to write or read.

Yet upon the return of the English Players from their unsuccessful tour he was ready and willing to exert himself on their behalf. A new play, George Bernard Shaw's *Mrs. Warren's Profession,* was put into rehearsal and produced on September thir-

tieth at the Pfauentheater. Such a production was an adventure at
the time for the theme of Shaw's play was so delicate that most
managers shied away from publicly presenting it. In London it
had been given by the Stage Society before a special audience of
members and friends. In Zurich it was well attended and though
it aroused comment it was not attacked. Perhaps the motley colony resident in the Swiss centre had seen and heard too much in
the past four years to be particularly shocked by Shaw's subject.

Between this performance and the next production of the
English Players a number of momentous events occurred. There
was, of course, the hearing of the actions between Joyce and Carr.
But more startling than this were the final agonies of the war.
Stanley Houghton's *Hindle Wakes* was the play selected, and the
rehearsals progressed under extreme difficulties. The influenza epidemic had spread to Zurich and this caused several postponements.
Then, too, came the climax of the war in November when the Central Powers collapsed. Revolution broke out in Germany and had
its immediate repercussion in Zurich in the form of a general
strike fomented by the radical agitators. For about ten days no
passenger trains left the city, no trams ran, no post functioned
and no newspapers appeared. Cavalry units patrolled the thoroughfares and about the only other moving traffic were the funeral
hearses carrying the victims of the influenza epidemic to the ceme-
teries. The city was divided into sections and if one desired to cross
from one section to another one had to explain one's business to
a soldier with a fixed bayonet. On November eleventh, a day
wildly celebrated in London, Paris, Rome and New York, the
Zurichers did not know whether the world was at peace or war.
One fed upon nothing but rumours. All that the perturbed Zurichers knew was that a personal war of their own was being waged
in the streets of the city. Joyce and Sykes held several anxious con-
sultations and eventually decided to carry on with the play. This
was not easy. During the general strike the company was rehearsing almost every evening in a hall more than two miles from the
district where most of them lived. Therefore, each day the players
gathered together at a chosen rendezvous and trudged *en masse*
through the patrolled streets to their goal, hearing, perhaps, the
spatter of rifle fire in the side lanes and seeing the lines of women

carrying bread cards waiting before the bakeries. To add to the difficulties Bernard Glenning, who was rehearsing the part of Alan Jeffcote, suddenly died of influenza a few days before the date scheduled for the performance. Charles Fleming, who had been with the company since its inception, substituted in the rôle. It was on the second of December, some time after the collapse of the general strike and when Zurich was again assuming a normal appearance, that *Hindle Wakes* was finally presented at the Theater zur Kaufleuten, the modest hall in the Pelikanstrasse.

Eight days later (on December eleventh) an Anglo-French-Italian program of one-act plays was given in the same hall. They were *Il Cantico dei Cantici* by Felice Cavallotti, acted by Italian amateurs assembled and coached by Joyce; *Le Baiser* by Théodore de Banville, played by two actors from the Théâtre-Français de Zurich; and Robert Browning's *In a Balcony,* performed by members of the English Players. Joyce assisted this last poetical play by singing an Italian song behind the scene immediately after the rise of the curtain. It was "Amante Tradito" from the collection of "affetti amorosi" by Giovanni Stefani (1621).

With this triple production Joyce withdrew from any active participation in the business or artistic details of the English Players. The organization continued, nevertheless, until 1920 and gave a number of excellent performances. Joyce attended every one of them as long as he remained in Zurich. The reasons for his withdrawal are not far to seek. *Ulysses* claimed most of his time. The precarious state of his eyes required him to use them as little as possible. With the peace his mind began to turn back to Trieste where his furniture had been stored for four years. And the boycott of the English Players by the British Consulate was proving to be a serious disadvantage to the struggling actors. Joyce knew that this would be lifted if he severed his official connection with the company. For many reasons, then, it was wiser for him to withdraw. Yet some months after the friendly rupture he reappeared in the guise of an 'angel.' An American admirer, Mr. Schofield Thayer, belatedly hearing of his difficulties with Carr and the British Consulate from Mr. and Mrs. Padraic Colum, gave him a thousand dollars to assist his cause and Joyce, his litigation at an end, immediately turned over the greater part of this money to the English Players.

At the same time, as a sort of ironical commentary on the people who had been his antagonists in the lawsuits and amongst British officialdom, he carefully embedded certain names in *Ulysses*. Thus we find Private Carr knocking down Stephen Dedalus in the great phantasmagoria called "Circe." Sir Horace Rumbold becomes H. Rumbold,[1] the barber-hangman, and Messrs. Smith and Gann are mentioned under the names of Joe Gann and Toad Smith, victims of the hangman. The British Consul at Zurich is pictured as Battling Bennett, the bruiser, and the consular lawyer, named as Ole Pfotts Wettstein, becomes his second. Still later, when Sir Horace Rumbold was transferred to Warsaw, Joyce dashed off eight lines which he sent to Sykes; "for your next production of 'Pippa Passes.'"

The Right Man in the Wrong Place

> The pig's in the barley,
> The fat's in the fire:
> Old Europe can hardly
> Find twopence to buy her.
> Jack Spratt's in his office,
> Puffed, powdered and curled:
> Rumbold's in Warsaw—
> All's right with the world.

IV

During this long period of activities on behalf of the English Players, a period tragically broken into by the malady of his eyes, Joyce had not ceased to work at *Ulysses*. That astonishing composition seemed to go on at all hours of the day or night and wherever he happened to be at the moment. Neither was his presentation to the world halted. During 1918 Ben W. Huebsch published in America editions of *Chamber Music* and *Exiles*. In England Grant Richards printed the play. And back in America the Cornhill Com-

[1] This name was also selected on account of the legendary glass of rum associated with capital execution in France.

pany of Boston testified to their admiration of the author by pirating *Chamber Music*. It was the first of several piracies that were to irritate Joyce exceedingly.

The year 1919 appeared to be an auspicious period in the history of the world. The war was over and the representatives of the victorious powers were dictating the impossible peace treaties at Versailles and Saint-Germain-en-Laye. Woodrow Wilson was the new saviour of the world and there was great enthusiasm over the League of Nations. Everything, including art, had been made safe for democracy. Joyce was not so sure of all this and more than once he inquired of his friends "Who won this war?" an inquiry as earnest as it may seem ironical. Frank Budgen once replied, "We shall know when the mass-production goods come pouring in." The first to be seen were stacks of tins of Japanese salmon in a shop window on the Limmat Quai.

The summer of 1919 passed swiftly to the resumption of normal living after the nightmare of the war. It was marked by one event of importance to Joyce. *Exiles* was produced in Munich in a German translation. Joyce was disappointed at his inability to secure a visa permitting him to enter Germany and witnessing the performance but he did manage to arrange for the presentation of bouquets to the actresses playing the principal rôles, an attention he has always paid to actresses in his play. The play was not a success, chiefly, it has been stated, because of the bad translation.

The resumption of normal living occasioned a general clearing out in Zurich. Government agencies were closing down; paroled prisoners were joyously returning to their native countries; and the swarming profiteers, pockets bulging with bank notes, were flocking to the capitals of the victorious nations where the 'pickings' would be better. Joyce began to think of Trieste where his furniture was stored and which, after all, he could claim as his adopted home. He had never regarded his long sojourn in Zurich as anything more than a temporary shift necessitated by the war. The fact that Stanislaus, released from his internment camp, was back in Trieste was a second inducement to go. And, perhaps, a third was curiosity. Trieste was now Italian in government as well as in language and manners. What would it be like without the picture of Franz Josef in every tobacco shop?

By the autumn Joyce had arranged his affairs so that he could depart. One of the last things he did was to dispatch the manuscript of that portion of *Ulysses* he had completed (it ran from the beginning to the conclusion of the Cyclops section—somewhat less than half the book) to Mrs. McCormick as a testimonial of his gratitude for her kindness in supplementing his scanty income. The day before his departure for Trieste Joyce was intensely surprised to receive his script back without any explanation for its return. He went immediately to the Hôtel Baur au Lac and demanded to see Mrs. McCormick. She was polite but distinctly cool in her manner towards him. When Joyce explained that he had intended the manuscript to be a gift Mrs. McCormick responded rather shortly, "Oh, you will need the script. You will possibly have to raise money by it sooner or later." Joyce went away mystified. He had thought the income from Miss Weaver's gift plus Mrs. McCormick's monthly payment would assure him a modest living and make it unnecessary for him to sell any more of his manuscripts. The next day he discovered his error. In the first mail he received a note from Mrs. McCormick's representative briefly informing him that the monthly payments were discontinued.

The reasons for this change of attitude on the part of Mrs. McCormick were never elucidated. Joyce's friends in Zurich have offered various explanations but they are no more than surmises. One is that Mrs. McCormick was affronted when Joyce refused to be psychoanalyzed by Dr. Jung, a refusal, by the way, that he made flatly and angrily. Another explanation is that certain expressions in the manuscript shocked Mrs. McCormick's tender sensibilities. Still another is that a certain individual in Zurich, well-known to Joyce from the Trieste days, had gone to Mrs. McCormick and told her that Joyce was wasting his days and nights in riotous living and drinking. It was true that Joyce frequented the Pfauen Restaurant-Café during most evenings when he was not attending the theatre or the opera and it was also true that he drank wine, but these relaxations from a long day's travail could hardly be called riotous living. Whatever the explanation may be the fact remains that Joyce and his family arrived in Trieste during the autumn of 1919 with a decidedly inadequate income.[1]

[1] Several times during Joyce's career this brusque and unexplained attitude of certain admirers of his has taken place. There were at least two instances of it in Dublin—one before he left and one during his last visit there, another in Trieste after he had become famous as we shall see shortly, and it has reappeared in later years also. There is no single explanation so far as these different admirers are concerned that will fit all these cases, but the fact remains that all through his life he seems to have had admiration both in its spiritual and its material form spontaneously and suddenly offered him and subsequently just as suddenly transformed into passive or open hostility.

# Nine

THE chaotic war years had changed Trieste as much as they had changed the rest of the world. What had been formerly an Austro-Hungarian dependency was now an integral portion of the Italian kingdom and Joyce was not long in discovering that the new flag carried with it a psychological transformation demolishing almost completely the gay leisurely old milieu that he had known. In the deplorable progression of fantastic events more had been destroyed than buildings and lives and traditions and national frontiers; an era with all its peculiar impulses had been mercilessly assassinated as well. This had not been so perceptible to Joyce in Zurich, for there he had existed from the first in the spinning midst of a frantic period of abnormal activities that permitted no thoughtful comparison with the past. It was different in Trieste. The long years he had lived there before the war furnished him with an exact picture to place beside this new Trieste for which, among other things, Italy had gone to war. True enough, the general scene was the same but where was the spirit that had flavoured all under the ramshackle empire of the Habsburgs? It was gone, vanished in the great wind that had blown a slower-tempoed civilization into oblivion.

As Joyce and his family settled temporarily with his Czech brother-in-law, Frantisek Shaureck, his sister Eileen and his brother Stanislaus in congested quarters at Via Sanità, 2, he could observe this new spirit of things with a little more leisure than he had ever enjoyed in Trieste before. The hard necessity of constant teaching was removed by his modest income. He could occupy his time now with the composition of *Ulysses* and an indulgence (limited, to be sure) in that easy social companionship that brightened his evenings. There were old friends at hand and he lost no time in seeking them out. He seemed older to these acquaintances, almost worn out in appearance, and manifestly troubled by his eyesight. However, it was but the surface that had been marked by time; within, the mind and creative will, more fertile than ever, functioned with amazing clarity and discipline. Silvio Benco, risen to editorship of a newspaper and among the first to encounter Joyce, recalls that "his tall and exceedingly thin figure was covered by one of those monastic habits with military belts which were being used as overcoats. It was too short for him and gave him rather strange proportions." Francini-Bruni was living in Trieste in a fourth-floor apartment and to it went Joyce and his family nearly every week. These were gay evenings, partial recaptures of the past, when the wine flowed (that enlivening white Chianti) and Tuscan dishes smoked on the table and the writer, exhilarated by good fellowship, returned to his second love, music, and sang until long after midnight. Occupants of the apartment house, comfortably tucked in their beds, could hear the slow careful footsteps of Joyce as he descended the four flights of stairs after one of these evenings.[1] There was the Restaurant Bonavia where one might eat and smoke and drink and converse as writers and philosophers have done time out of mind. Joyce loved this carefree life but he did not let it interfere too much with *Ulysses*.

That great work steadily marched on toward its conclusion. In another year, he hoped, it would be finished. With a sort of methodical disorderliness that might confuse others but was as plain as a precise army map to him he prepared the material for each episode, making his notes for composition, assembling his enormous masses of quotations, references, ideas and essays in various styles. He was like a charioteer driving a score of restless horses before him and keeping each one in its proper place. Those friends who heard him read aloud from his manuscript or the numbers of the *Little Review* in which sections of *Ulysses* were appearing

[1] Alas for the lasting fidelities of friendship! Some years after Joyce's departure from Trieste for Paris Francini-Bruni delivered a lecture in Trieste containing his reminiscences of Joyce. A large number of former pupils and friends of Joyce, including his brother Stanislaus, were present. The lecture, according to Stanislaus, was a very curious evening's entertainment because a great many in the audience, after having expressed their disapproval of various passages of a lecture which they had supposed was going to be a friendly tribute from a colleague, got up one after another and left the hall. Francini-Bruni afterward published this lecture in pamphlet form under the title "Joyce Spogliato in Pazza" (Joyce Stripped in Public). This remarkable effort ended with a prayer to the Most High that the dissolute evil-liver might be touched by Grace and see the error of his ways.

(seven issues in 1918, ten issues in 1919, and six issues in 1920[1])
were impressed by the gigantic architecture of the work, although
they were sometimes puzzled by a technique that was absolutely
new to them. During the year that Joyce lived in Trieste he completed the tenth and eleventh sections of the book, those now
known as "Nausikaa" and "The Oxen of the Sun," and then
started simultaneously sections twelve and thirteen, "Circe" and
"Eumæus," work on thirteen being a sort of relief from the ex-
hausting and painful creation of twelve. The vast enterprise was
now well in hand and Joyce realized that he was accomplishing
with complete success the difficult æsthetic task he had set himself five years before. Not even a World War had been able to
halt it.

As a matter of fact, he was at a point of time that was as important for him as it was for the rest of the world. The era of new
ways and values had dawned, that post-war world born out of the
terrible peace that the Allies imposed upon the Central Powers
and which, alas, would be the breeding place for possible cataclysms
as violent and far-reaching as that of 1914. For the time being, however, it continued to be the Victory Year and the birth date of an
amazing period that was as iconoclastic in literary movements and
æsthetic experimentations as it was in revised social concepts and
distorted national traditions. It was not alone that the politicians
of Versailles were changing the map of the earth; a new breed of
thinkers, released from the despotism of an old way of life, were
changing the mind of humanity as well. Young men (and sometimes older men, too) turned their backs in arrogant dissatisfaction
and scorn on what appeared to them as the outworn and exhausted
æsthetics of the past and attempted to create a new æsthetic for a
new time, a post-war art for a post-war world. Painters, composers,
sculptors, novelists, having put the war of guns behind them,
turned to the war of ideas.

This was opportune for Joyce and *Ulysses,* for he, the arch-
iconoclast of them all, naturally became the spearhead of the new
attack on the old tradition in literature. Already young men in
the studios of London and Paris and New York knew his name

[1] See "Biographical Notes on James Joyce's 'Ulysses,' " by R. F. Roberts in the
*Colophon: New Series,* No. 4, Vol. I.

and acclaimed the potentialities of his leadership. Without an effort on his part he had been tacitly accepted by many an energetic youthful writer as the literary Moses who would lead the post-war procession into the Promised Land. This was unusual because Joyce was comparatively far from the mêlée and took no part in its vigorous dialectics. It was his work alone that spoke for him and the voices of a few who had epistolary contact with him. Without deviating at all from the path he had mapped for himself fifteen years before he suddenly found himself in the vanguard of the creative explorers of the post-war era. Perhaps a cataclysm had been necessary for the rest of the world to catch up with him. Perhaps an earth-shaking explosion had been necessary to blow down the moss-grown walls of tradition and make possible a perspective of the vast plain of time where art might venture without the heavy archaic armour of the past. Whatever it was, the moment was propitious for Joyce and Joyce was ready for the moment.

By the spring of 1920 the conviction that he was badly placed in Trieste was firmly fixed in the mind of the Dubliner. His father, John Stanislaus, had arrived at this conclusion ten years before and had never ceased to write to him on this subject. It was a conviction that Joyce had arrived at by slow stages and, perhaps, had fought at first. He owed an emotional duty to the city where he had passed so many of the precarious years of his life, the city, indeed, where his children had been born, where *The Portrait of the Artist as a Young Man* and *Exiles* had been written and where Ulysses-Bloom had first begun his great odyssey through the streets of Dublin, but he owed an even greater duty to his reason and to his future. It was not alone that he was cabined, cribbed and confined in the congested quarters on the Via Sanità that he shared with his brother-in-law and brother and that the crowded city did not seem to possess a single free apartment suitable for him and his family; no, there was more to it than that. He had loved the old Trieste and it is possible that his increasing familiarity with the new Trieste, that Trieste of Victor Emmanuel, was revealing to him the deplorable lack of an ancient atmosphere violently desired. But important as this disillusionment was there was another reason even more important. The Time Spirit was calling. The new post-war world was beckoning. Intellectually, he was comparatively isolated in Trieste (there was not even the motley assemblage of diverse personalities he had known and enjoyed at Zurich) and he was too far from the spinning centre of things. He was very conscious of what was happening in the rest of the world and he was quite aware that Trieste could never be an international capital of the creative arts. Friends and well-wishers, the Egoist group among others, were apprising him of this fact. It was time, too, to think of a publisher for *Ulysses* and his sad experience in dealing with publishers by correspondence in the past had not been forgotten. A number of things, then, began to draw him away from Trieste while a hesitancy (encouraged, perhaps, by habitude and affection) vainly battled against them. He needed a final fillip of urging from some assertive personality who was in the very midst of the new movement in arts and letters. In due course it came.

For some years, now, Joyce had been corresponding with Ezra Pound, a correspondence very formal on Joyce's part, and it was the culminating point in this exchange of letters that finally convinced the Dubliner he should leave Trieste. Pound asked Joyce to meet him at Desenzano during the early summer of 1920 and to that beautiful Italian town Joyce went, accompanied by his son. The conversation that ensued convinced Joyce that the wise thing to do would be to venture on Paris again, settle there in the heart of the boiling post-war art movements and finish *Ulysses* in the city that had first called to him in 1902. Many seasons and tremendous changes had shifted the visage of life since he had last strolled the streets of the city by the Seine. It would be as fascinating as it was prudent to renew his acquaintance with what, after all, was the everlasting capital of all the arts.

His decision once made, there followed a period of preparation. There was clothing to be assembled and books to be packed and placed in the hands of a forwarding agency. A few farewell dinners. Good-byes to Svevo and Benco and Francini-Bruni and Silvestri and a few others. A last look at the Città Vecchia. And then, on a June day in 1920, the Joyce ménage was again on its travels. It was so that exiles lived, pausing here or there for a longer or a shorter sojourn and then moving on again at the behest of the Time Spirit and knowing always that there were no permanencies of place when the mind was roving through all space. Leaving Trieste and a somewhat gloomy Stanislaus behind him,[1] Joyce (and his family) paused first at Venice. After two days in the city of the Doges he moved on to Milan. He passed through Switzerland without stopping. Perhaps his memories of the four war years that he had passed in that high country were too close for him to stop and renew the flavour of them. The frontiers of France were passed and a night was spent in Dijon where the cooking is so perfect and the wines are so fine. And so on June 23, 1920, Joyce arrived at the Gare de Lyon and passed out into the flash and sparkle of the streets of Paris. The trip had been costly and his wallet was practically empty.

## II

One must pause and regard Joyce at this moment. He is tall, thin, and grave in demeanour. There are grey streaks in his hair and his strong chin is tufted with a small beard. His moustache does not conceal his thin firm lips. Behind his glasses his eyes peer somewhat myopically. He is thirty-eight years old. And this Paris through which he travels to 9, Rue de l'Université on the Left Bank where quarters have been engaged for him? It is a new and vital Paris, a City of Victory, of bustle and confusion, of music and art galleries and crowded cafés and argumentative writers and rich war profiteers. It is also the Eternal Paris, that 'lamp for lovers lit in the wood of the world' where the wide boulevards and the little ancient streets are coloured at twilight by a warm enchanted glow that is to be found in no other city in the world. It is, as it always has been, the veritable heart of all good things where civilization achieves a finesse that is denied to London and New York and Rome and Berlin. It possesses something charming for everybody from the sleepiest *clochard* under the Seine bridge to the gravest member of the Institute pausing on the quay before the

---

[1] The relations between the two brothers practically end here. Stanislaus had little sympathy with *Ulysses* and none at all with *Finnegans Wake*. The two men have met three times since: once in Paris, once in Salzburg where Stanislaus had come with his newly-married wife, and once in Zurich where Joyce had gone in an unsuccessful effort to obtain a position as teacher for his brother in that canton when owing to the strained relations between Italy and Great Britain the latter had been temporarily deprived of his position in Trieste which he has since reacquired.

ironical smile of Voltaire. Joyce, as he unpacked his manuscripts
and notebooks in his quarters at 9, Rue de l'Université, must have
wondered regretfully why he had stayed away from it for so long.
However, he could comfort himself with the thought that it had
been a forced absence. The *deus ex machina* who had directed his
days had been a dishonest employment agency that had sent him
on a wild-goose chase to Zurich sixteen years before. After that,
chance and hard necessity had ordained his dwelling places. And
perhaps chance and hard necessity knew what they were about.
At least, he was in Paris now even if the journey had taken a devil
of a long time.

And Ezra Pound was in Paris, too. The fantastic American
poet, leader and smasher of movements, always half a mile ahead
of the vanguard—any vanguard at all, hardest swearing æsthete
of them all, was a large bundle of unpredictable electricity. To
Joyce he seemed a miracle of ebulliency, gusto and help. He immediately took the Irish writer in hand and proceeded to introduce him to Paris and Paris to him. He presented Joyce with a suit
of clothes (the coat was too small) and Joyce encountered his first
acquaintances in Paris clad in these garments, a sort of sheep, so
to speak, in wolf's clothing. Pound was kind, assiduous, and one
never knew what he would do next. He took Joyce from salon to
salon, exhibited him with the pride of an expert showman, and
brought to his quarters such astonishingly unsuspected fish as
Lincoln Steffens. Through Pound the Dubliner encountered nearly
all the French writers of the moment, among them Reinach, Spire,
Soupault, Eluard and Aragon. Pound was a dynamo with a laugh
like the triumphant bray of a jackass and Joyce, who was of a
much more reserved temperament and tentatively feeling his way
in this lively new milieu, was as encouraged as he was bewildered
by the flamboyancy of the self-confident American. He suspected
that Pound had been disappointed in him at their first meeting and
considered him pretty much of a hopeless bourgeois. Pound, of
course, was an æsthete, perhaps the most vehement æsthete in
Paris. His beard, his open collar, his earring, the lopsided table he
had made for himself, the coats he wore, his aggressive manner-
isms, all these things proclaimed to the world in the most militant
way that he was continuously either lashing or thumbing his nose

at the Philistines. Joyce with his family pictures, his penchant for old-fashioned furniture—square tables, for instance, neckties and subdued clothing, courtly manners, general quietude, and sound bourgeois restaurants was quite the reverse. Still, the two men got along together very well (though Pound was ever ready for an argument) and Joyce has always been quite frank in acknowledging his indebtedness to Pound during these first seasons in Paris.

One of the first things that Joyce noticed in this new Paris was an extraordinary interest in Homer. It seemed like a good omen for *Ulysses*. (It is too bad that he didn't know that Ezra Pound's father's first name was Homer!) To Stanislaus he wrote late in July: "Odyssey very much in the air here. Anatole France is writing *Le Cyclope*. G. Fauré, the musician, an opera, *Penelope*. Giraudoux has written *Elpenor* (Paddy Dignam). Guillaume Apollinaire, *Les Mamelles de Tiresias*." As for *Ulysses,* it did not march very fast during Joyce's first few weeks in Paris. There were too many people to see and too many places to go. But by the time he had settled in a flat at 5, Rue de l'Assomption in the Passy quarter (it had been loaned to him for a period of three months by Ludmila Savitzky, Madame Bloch), and this was some time in July, he was again hard at work. To Stanislaus he wrote on July twenty-fifth: "Madame Circe advances regally towards her completion, after which I hope to join a tennis club."

He was in high spirits at this time for the world appeared to be opening auspiciously before him. He was being accorded a recognition such as he had never received before and he seemed to be in the very heart of the things that mattered. It had been a wise move, to leave Trieste and all its pleasant memories behind. The indefatigable Pound had opened doors right and left for him and the quick recognition of what he had to give kept them open. Translators had approached him. Madame Bloch was busy at a French version of *A Portrait of the Artist as a Young Man*.[1] Three others were at work on the short stories in *Dubliners,*[2] and a Swiss review was considering the publication of some of them. Another translator had turned the play *Exiles* into French, and Lugné-Poe,

[1] *"Dedalus"—Portrait de l'artiste jeune par lui-même.* Traduit par Ludmila Savitzky. It was published by La Sirène in 1924.
[2] *Gens de Dublin.* Traduit par Yva Fernandez, Hélène du Pasquier, et Jacques-Paul Reynaud. Préface de Valery Larbaud. It was published by Plon in 1926.

former director of the Théâtre de l'Odéon and now of the Théâtre de l'Œuvre, was seriously considering a production of it. All of this was like manna to Joyce and as he laboured mightily at the great Circe phantasmagoria that was the transfiguration and mingling of all the multitudinous threads of *Ulysses* he experienced the thrilling realization that he was achieving his proper place in time.

He maintained his steady interest in Irish affairs (there had never been a time throughout the long years when he had neglected them) and he followed with ironic curiosity the political divagations of that passion-rocked island. Toward the end of August he wrote to Stanislaus:

> I enclose cutting of Lord French's latest speech—delivered in Dublin. He has left Ireland, which, being an Irishman, he refuses to annihilate. Sir Horace Rumbold has been unanimously chosen as First Emperor of Ireland. Please hang the Union Jack out of the scullery window at the exact instant when he ascends his ancestral throne of alabaster. If a man named Buckley [1] calls, asking to see His Majesty, he is on no account to be admitted.
>
> By Order
> James
> (Heb. Vat. Terg. Ex. Lut. Hosp. Litt. Angl. Pon. Max.).

Recollection of Sir Horace Rumbold, who had done so badly by him in Zurich during the war years, aroused him to a new version of an old squib and a day or two later he forwarded to Stanislaus "The Right Heart in the Wrong Place."

> Of spinach and gammon
> Bull's full to the crupper,
> White lice and black famine
> Are the Mayor of Cork's supper;
> But the pride of old Ireland
> Must be damnably humbled
> If a Joyce is found cleaning
> The boots of a Rumbold.

August was an extremely important month for Joyce. In the first place, Miss Harriet Weaver made another generous gift of

---

[1] The name Buckley refers to the grotesque story "How Buckley Shot the Russian General," second of the three stories (or four if the summaries are counted) which occur in various forms through *Finnegans Wake*. See page 338 *et seq.* in Joyce's work.

money (her second) to the writer and this eased measurably the difficulties of living in what was then one of the highest-priced cities in the world. To enlarge again upon this generosity would be redundant, but, at the risk of repetition, it should be emphasized that without Miss Weaver's extraordinary and unexpected largess the path of Joyce through the post-war world would have been one of stark despair and ignoble grind without much chance for creative writing. The summer was lightened, too, by the social aspect of things. Although Joyce went not at all into what is called society with a capital S he did meet many people. T. S. Eliot and his wife and Wyndham Lewis kept moving between London, Paris and the country, and dinners and lunches became a pleasant habit. Old friends appeared on the scene from the Zurich days, Frank Budgen, for instance, and Mr. and Mrs. Claud W. Sykes. An American officer, the late William Aspenwall Bradley, an enthusiastic admirer of Joyce, presented him with an army overcoat. John Quinn, in America, was developing an intensive interest in the Irish writer and testifying to it by gifts of money and advice. This was pleasing enough but there was a fly in the ointment that began to irritate Joyce. Who was to be the publisher of *Ulysses?*

It was a question that could not, as yet, be definitely answered. Late in August Joyce informed Stanislaus: "Huebsch is crying off 'Ulysses.' Miss Weaver writes nobody will permit it. So it will be published, it seems, in Paris and bear Mr. John Rodker's imprint as English printer." There was one obvious reason that militated against the publication of *Ulysses* by the average commercial publisher and that was its unabashed frankness of language. Then, too, certain natural functions heretofore carefully ignored by novelists were described by the author in terms that were neither oblique nor veiled. Now it is only the exceptional publisher who is courageous (or, as the publisher himself might say, mad) enough to risk conflict with official authorities for the sake of art. That was not business. It is so much more easy to compromise, to suppress a slice here or there, to fall back on innocuous euphemisms, to castrate, as it were, so that the Moral English Printer, the snuffling censors, the pulpit pounders, the governmental watchdogs and the smug Philistines might not be shocked. In that way it was only the conscience of the author that suffered, and who in the devil cared about the conscience of the author? Certainly not the publisher. Joyce knew all this for he had undergone humiliating experiences in the past (as we have seen) and he had no illusions about the difficulties attending the publication of his new work. At the same time, he *knew* that the book would be set before the public (or a portion of the public) in some way. The spirit of the times (however sluggish it might seem to be) was with him and the old order of things would have to give way before it. In America, for the moment, the old order appeared to be strongly entrenched. Already three issues of the *Little Review* had been seized by officials of the United States Post Office because of alleged obscenity.[1] Naturally enough, B. W. Huebsch, who had published all of Joyce's previous books in America, was viewing the prospect and consequences of the publication of an unexpurgated *Ulysses* with some uneasiness. It was this problem of a publisher, then, that began to occupy Joyce's mind increasingly as the summer of 1920 paled into the autumn and the huge manuscript marched steadily towards its conclusion.

His tenancy of Ludmila Savitzky's flat in the Rue de l'Assomption coming to a close, Joyce removed to 5, Boulevard Raspail where he lived until the French writer, Valery Larbaud, offered him his quarters at 71, Rue Cardinal Lemoine. Larbaud, then at the peak of his fame and wielding considerable authority in French literary circles, proved to be an earnest and powerful pleader for Joyce and it may be affirmed that it was mainly due to his efforts that the Irish writer became widely known among French writers and critics.[2] It was Larbaud who, riding one day around the Arc de Triomphe with Joyce, pointed to the Eternal Flame and asked, "How long do you think that will burn?" Joyce replied dryly, "Until the Unknown Soldier gets up in disgust and blows it out." Once settled in the Larbaud flat Joyce's labours on *Ulysses* were complicated by a recurrence of his eye troubles. The constant attacks of iritis culminated in one so painful that he rolled on the floor in extreme agony. Dr. Louis Borsch was called in and treated the unhappy victim. The attack passed away but the effects of it

[1] These were the issues for January and June 1919 and January 1920.

[2] Other good and willing friends to Joyce at this time were Léon-Paul Fargue, the French poet and prose-writer, and George Antheil, the American composer, then resident in Paris. Antheil was to make an opera out of *Ulysses* but composed only the few pages that were published as a supplement to the now-defunct magazine, *This Quarter*.

and the fears of what might follow were perceptible from this time on in Joyce's changed demeanour. Indeed, for the next ten years (during which he underwent nine operations) his life was literally darkened by his eye troubles and the consequent fear of complete blindness. It was a terrible predicament for a writer (especially one who based so much of his work on careful observation and extraordinary documentation) and one should bear this in mind when those years are considered. Joyce's life, it will be observed, was a constant struggle against horrific odds, prejudices, mob smugness, poverty and physical disability.

In October arrived the disturbing news of another seizure of the *Little Review* by the authorities in New York. This time it was more serious for the seizure was instigated and made by John S. Sumner, New York agent for the Society for the Suppression of Vice and court proceedings were instituted. The defendants, Miss Margaret C. Anderson and Miss Jane Heap, editors of the *Little Review* who had been substituted for Mrs. Josephine Bell Arens, proprietor of the bookshop from which issues of the July-August 1920 number of the magazine had been purchased by John S. Sumner, were charged with the publication of a periodical alleged to represent and to be descriptive of certain scenes of lewdness and obscenity. The pages enumerated in the affidavit contained portions of the chapter in *Ulysses* commonly called "Nausikaa" and a portion of an article by Sherwood Anderson entitled "A New Testament." John Quinn immediately took up the defence for Miss Anderson and Miss Heap.

It may be of some interest to preserve for the laughing eyes of posterity the complaint of the pure-minded Mr. Sumner.

> First Division,
> City Magistrate's Court,
> Second District.

CITY AND COUNTY ⎫
OF NEW YORK ⎭ ss.:

JOHN S. SUMNER, Agent of the New York Society for the Suppression of Vice of No. 215 West 22nd Street, aged 44 years, occupation secretary, being duly sworn, deposes and says: that on the 17th day of September 1920 and prior thereto at the City of New York in the County of New York, at No. 27 West 8th Street, Margaret C. Anderson and Jane Heap did unlawfully utter, publish, manufacture and prepare and assist in uttering, publishing, manufacturing and preparing a certain obscene, lewd, lascivious, filthy, indecent and disgusting magazine, which said magazine is hereto entitled by the words following, to wit: "The Little Review" July-August 1920, which said magazine represents and is descriptive of scenes of lewdness and of obscenity, and particularly upon pages 42, 43, 44, 45, 46, 47, 48, 50, 51, 53, 55, 57, 59, 60, and which magazine is so obscene, lewd, lascivious, filthy, indecent and disgusting, that a minute description of the same would be offensive to the Court and improper to be placed upon the record thereof, wherefore a fuller description of the same is not set forth in this complaint, all in violation of Section 1141 of the Penal Law of the State of New York.

Deponent further alleges that on or about September 29th, 1920, he called at 27 West 8th Street, Manhattan Borough, New York City, and there received certain copies of said magazine from Josephine Bell Arens who stated that said magazine was prepared and published by Margaret C. Anderson and another in the upper part of said premises, and that on October 4, 1920, deponent had a conversation with said Margaret C. Anderson and Jane Heap, who stated to deponent that they were the publishers of and had prepared said Magazine and that they gloried in it.

(Signed) JOHN S. SUMNER.

Sworn to before me this
21st day of October, 1920.
(Signed) J. E. Corrigan,
City Magistrate.

Any comment on the tactics of Mr. Sumner and his society are needless here for both now seem to be impertinent and foul-minded curses of the past. The late Mr. John Quinn, primarily because of his interest and respect for Joyce (he had long before ceased to have any interest in the *Little Review*), attempted a campaign of postponements of the trial of the case, the reason being that *Ulysses'* might be published, perhaps in a privately-printed subscribers' edition, in the interim and so bring in to the author a respectable royalty. Quinn failed. The case was set for February 14, 1921, and it was lost. Miss Anderson and Miss Heap, as publishers, were fined a hundred dollars and their fingerprints were taken. Thus the official stamp of obscenity, lewdness, lasciviousness, filthiness, indecency and disgust was placed upon *Ulysses* in the United States of America. Poor Leopold Bloom! Poor Gerty MacDowell!

The immediate result of this case was of aggravating importance to Joyce. The following three letters tell the story as clearly as any summary.

March 24, 1921

Mr. John Quinn,
31 Nassau Street,
New York City.

DEAR MR. QUINN,

Following our telephone conversation on the subject of the publication of James Joyce's "Ulysses," I have to say that the recent criminal proceedings against The Little Review, of which the editors were found guilty on a charge arising out of the publication of a chapter of "Ulysses," makes the publication of a volume containing that chapter a perilous thing, in my opinion as a layman.

My past course with regard to Joyce's works is sufficient to prove my genuine interest and my desire to bring his work before the American public. I still wish to continue to publish him, but as matters stand at present I strongly recommend that Joyce make such alterations in the condemned chapter as will make it conform to the law.

I request that you present this suggestion to Mr. Joyce, unless you are empowered to decline it without consulting him, and that I be apprized of his reply before proceeding with the negotiations relating to the publication of "Ulysses."

Very truly yours,

B. W. HUEBSCH.

March 25, 1921.

Mr. B. W. Huebsch,
116 West 13<sup>th</sup> Street,
New York City.

DEAR MR. HUEBSCH,

I received your letter of March 24th this morning. When I get time to write to Mr. Joyce, which may be in the next month or six weeks, I will send him a copy of your letter to me.

You recommend that he make "such alterations in the condemned chapter as will make it conform to the law," and you request that I present that suggestion to him, unless I am "empowered to decline it without consulting him." While I am not "empowered" to either accept or decline any suggestion regarding Mr. Joyce's publications, I am as certain as I can be of anything that Mr. Joyce would, had the suggestion been made direct to him, reject it unqualifiedly.

I do not know quite what you mean by the last clause of the third paragraph of your letter about your being apprized of his reply "before proceeding with the negotiations relating to the publication of 'Ulysses.'" As I told you, Joyce had practically put the matter of the contract for the American edition in my hands, and we had talked about royalties and so forth. Perhaps you meant "before proceeding *with me* in the negotiations." You may assume that Mr. Joyce would reject unconditionally and unqualifiedly your recommendation that he make the alterations referred to, and I take it that I am to assume in writing to him that you do not desire to publish the book in the form as written. Over and over again Mr. Joyce has written to me that it must be published as written, even with the parts that were cut out of The Little Review restored and with some other parts written in. It would therefore be a waste of ink or of typewriter's time to pass your suggestion on to him.

That being his determination, expressed in advance and repeated many times, I take it that you do not care to consider further the publication of "Ulysses." Will you please confirm this in writing to me so that I may act accordingly?

Yours very truly,

JOHN QUINN.

April 5, 1921.

Mr. John Quinn,
31 Nassau Street,
New York City.

DEAR MR. QUINN,

In accordance with your telephone request I send you this note to confirm my attitude toward Joyce's "Ulysses."

A New York court having held that the publication of a part of this in The Little Review was a violation of the law, I am unwilling to publish the book unless some changes are made in the manuscript as submitted to me by Miss H. C. Weaver who represents Joyce in London.

In view of your statement that Joyce declines absolutely to make any alterations, I must decline to publish it. I repeat, however, that if you or Joyce, or both, conclude that a change of some kind in the manuscript is desirable, I feel that I am entitled to the first offer of the American rights under those circumstances.

At your request I send herewith the manuscript of the book exactly in the shape as it was delivered to me by Miss Weaver in London. My understanding with her was that I should return the book to her if I do not publish it, so strictly speaking, I am violating that understanding by sending it to you. Under the circumstances, I would thank you to send me an acknowledgement which will entirely absolve me, so that I may set myself straight with Miss Weaver.

Very truly yours,

B. W. HUEBSCH.

And so ended the possibility (although Mr. Quinn had some ineffectual dealings with the firm of Boni and Liveright) of the publication of *Ulysses* in the United States. That country, except for bootlegged copies, would have to wait thirteen years for it.

Joyce, as may very well be imagined, was disappointed and hurt. He was labouring mightily during this winter and early spring of 1921 at the book and the difficulties of writing under severe eyestrain were intensified by the dubiousness of a proper publication. He had moved back to 9, Rue de l'Université, where he worked in a bedroom where three slept without a desk and without books. It was an arduous business and even new friends failed to lighten it very much. Sometimes, however, these friends gave him ideas which he incorporated into *Ulysses*. For instance, he called at the Châtillon country home of Mr. and Mrs. Richard Wallace and found Mrs. Wallace sitting in the garden with a young painter. The conversation was long-winded and dull and as Joyce drowsily listened he heard his hostess continually repeating the word "yes." She must have said it a hundred and fifty times and in every possible nuance of voice. And suddenly Joyce realized that he had found the motif word for the end of *Ulysses*. In the final section, that great sleepy soliloquy of Marion Bloom,[1] there are four key words that serve, so to speak, as foci about which circle the thoughts of the reclining woman, "he," "bottom," "woman," and, the last (an affirmation of life), "yes." [2] Joyce, by

[1] There were two models for this great character of Molly Bloom, one a Dubliner and the other an Italian. The war-time correspondence of the Italian passed through Joyce's hands during the period he lived in Zurich. There was nothing political in these letters, whose grammar Joyce corrected, but the Austrian censors must have had more than one sizzling moment while reading them. That, however, did not perturb the full-blooded Italian lady.

[2] Regarding the last word of *Ulysses* see a similar allusion in an article on *Finnegans Wake* in the *Revue de Paris,* September 1st issue, 1939.

the way, was inspired to his technique in this section by the viewing of an astronomical film depicting the starry circling heavens at night.

To continue with the friends, there were the painter, Myron Nutting, and the journalist, William Bird. Between these and others, Joyce managed to find many pleasant evenings when the condition of his eyes permitted. There were plays and operas to see and dinners in favourite restaurants. There were evenings when he read portions of the new book to interested and absorbed listeners and there were evenings when he sang to his guests old Irish songs, "The Brown and the Yellow Ale," for instance, and the new parody of "Molly Brannigan," which he had written in honour of his own Molly Bloom.

Man dear, did you never hear of buxom Molly Bloom at all,
As plump an Irish beauty, sir, as Annie Levy Blumenthal,
If she sat in the vice-regal box Tim Healy'd have no room at all,
    But curl up in a corner at a glance from her eye.
The tale of her ups and downs would aisy fill a handybook
That would cover the whole world across from Gib right on to Sandy
      Hook,
But now that tale is told, ahone, I've lost my daring dandy look
    Since Molly Bloom has gone and left me here for to die.

Man dear, I remember when my roving time was troubling me
We picnicked fine in storm or shine in France and Spain and Hungary,
And she said I'd be her first and last while the wine I poured went bub-
      bling free.
    Now every male she meets with has a finger in her pie.
Man dear, I remember how with all the heart and brain of me
I arrayed her for the bridal, but, oh, she proved the bane of me,
With more puppies sniffing round her than the wooers of Penelope
    She's left me on her doorstep like a dog for to die.

My left eye is wake and his neighbour full of water, man,
I cannot see the lass I limned for Ireland's gamest daughter, man,
When I hear her lovers tumbling in their thousands for to court her,
      man,
    If I were sure I'd not be seen I'd sit down and cry.
May you live, may you love like this gaily spinning earth of ours,

And every morn a gallous sun awake you to fresh wealth of gold,
But if I cling like a child to the clouds that are your petticoats,
  O Molly, handsome Molly, sure you won't let me die? [1]

Friends of this period affirm that the man Joyce was the most astonishing mixture of courtly seriousness and fantastic humour that they had ever encountered. His wit was often dry and ironic and unexpected. From a contemplative silence he would suddenly plunge forward with a quick riposte and then just as abruptly retreat into his silence again. He observed as well as he could observe with his failing eyesight and he was often content to just sit and listen without speaking a word at all. Sometimes there were ample reasons for this silence. As he once told his brother he could never talk to a vacuum and more than one vacuum forced his unwelcome attentions on the Dubliner. It was the late Theodore Roosevelt who once remarked that every new movement had a lunatic fringe and Joyce, who was rapidly assuming the bulk and importance of a movement in himself, was no exception to this statement. About him was gathering a lunatic fringe of half-baked young men and women (although he rarely saw them) who were more attracted by the superficial aspects of his clean and iconoclastic break with tradition than by the profounder reasons for it. They were like the parasites and imitators that the late W. B. Yeats once inveighed against in a little poem; those fools who took his many-coloured cloak and wore it in the world's eye and forced the poet to the decision that it was better to walk naked. Joyce, however, had nothing to do with this lunatic fringe. He was bland and polite . . . and silent. With closer friends he let himself go and one of

[1] Joyce once described to me the dream that led up to the writing of this parody. He saw Molly Bloom on a hillock under a sky full of moonlit clouds rushing overhead. She had just picked up from the grass a child's black coffin and flung it after the figure of a man passing down a side road by the field she was in. It struck his shoulders, and she said, "I've done with you." The man was Bloom seen from behind. There was a shout of laughter from some American journalists in the road opposite, led by Ezra Pound. Joyce was very indignant and vaulted over a gate into the field and strode up to her and delivered the one speech of his life. It was very long, eloquent and full of passion, explaining all the last episode of *Ulysses* to her. She wore a black opera cloak, or *sortie de bal*, had become slightly grey and looked like *la* Duse. She smiled when Joyce ended on an astronomical climax, and then, bending, picked up a tiny snuffbox, in the form of a little black coffin, and tossed it towards him, saying, "And I have done with you, too, Mr. Joyce." Joyce had a snuffbox like the one she tossed to him when he was at Clongowes Wood College. It was given to him by his godfather, Philip McCann, together with a larger one to fill it from.

them has a memory of Joyce in a voluminous cloak skimming like a bat out of hell in a fantastic dance over one of the ancient bridges that crossed the Seine while the midnight stars shone down on Paris.

Curiously enough, even at such infectious moments when his nervous vitality was given full play there remained an uncrossable distance between Joyce and his closest friends. He still belonged completely to himself and, though he might be friendliness and affectionate concern personified, no one in contact with him (his family, perhaps, excepted) remained unaware of this mysterious distance, this remoteness, so to speak, that so subtly cut Joyce apart from those around him. He continued to walk alone in that particular world he had created for himself as far back at 1904. To walk with him one would have to be a part of that world and that, of course, was impossible. He was capable of friendship as many knew and quite willing to go far out of his way and sometimes at great expense to his quietude of mind to testify to that friendship but he was incapable of ever losing himself in the emotional entanglements and compromises of human relationships. In spite of this aloofness of self, this congenital refusal to surrender, he rarely failed to attract admiring and assiduous friends to himself, men of understanding who were solicitous about the difficulties that beset his path and eager to aid him in any way that they could. There were those who would read for him when he could no longer follow the letters on closely-printed pages, those who would assist him in his correspondence and the compilation of his notes and those who would type for him when his manuscripts were ready.

As 1921 moved along Joyce was concerned more and more with the vital question of who was to publish *Ulysses*. He was nearing the end of the book now and that important matter had yet to be settled. Miss Weaver had informed him that there was absolutely no chance at all of publication in England. The Moral British Printer was adamantine in his self-righteous attitude of horror. The *Little Review* case, as we have seen, had permanently destroyed all chances in America. There remained, then, Paris. John Rodker, who had succeeded Ezra Pound as the foreign editor of the *Little Review,* was willing to put his name on the book for

England as publisher for the *Egoist* but not having a private printing press in his pocket and discovering, as Miss Weaver had discovered, that no English printer would dare set up the plates there was nothing that he could do at the moment.

Quite suddenly, however, the problem was solved.

### III

At the home of André Spire, the French writer, Joyce (through Ezra Pound) had encountered a very businesslike young American woman who was conducting a bookshop for English readers in Paris. She was Miss Sylvia Beach, formerly of Princeton, New Jersey, but now of the Rue de l'Odéon, Paris, and her bookshop, two small rooms on the same street, was called Shakespeare and Company. It was an unusual bookshop in that it carried only good books and periodicals or, at least, books and periodicals with good intentions. It was also a lending library. Miss Beach, modernistic in taste and animated by a lively scorn for the standardized fiction of the time and the smugly-safe predilections of the Philistines, saw to it that the chaff of letters did not litter her little shop; but anything that was modern (even frankly experimental) in tendency or that had established itself with some degree of finality as literature was welcome. The result was a bookshop that attracted most of the more serious younger writers of the day who happened to be in Paris. In a way, Shakespeare and Company was rapidly assuming the status of a clearinghouse and clubroom for the youthful leaders and followers of the so-called radical movements in postwar American and English letters. There might be found at various times Ezra Pound, John Rodker, T. S. Eliot, Wyndham Lewis, Robert McAlmon, Mina Loy, Gertrude Stein, Ernest Hemingway, and others even more fantastic in their conceptions of what the New Literature should be.

Across the road from Shakespeare and Company was the French bookshop of Miss Beach's friend, Mademoiselle Adrienne Monnier, La Maison des Amis des Livres. This shop corresponded to Shakespeare and Company in its insistence on what was new, experimental and unconventional in French books and periodicals. Naturally it drew to its rooms a buzzing congregation of the more unfettered Gallic writers. Thus the short block from the Place de l'Odéon, with its memories of Camille Desmoulins and the great historical cataclysms of France, to the Carrefour de l'Odéon, where twenty years before a penniless Joyce had argued mightily in a small café with Canudo, Villona, Routh and the elephantine Däubler, was, to all intents and purposes, a sort of assembling place, a second home, for all that was young and bold and iconoclastic in Paris among English, American and French writers. It was, in a way, the street of the eaglets, although many who were already eagles, Paul Valéry, for example, might be seen often enough treading its pavements towards one of the two unusual and provocative bookshops.

Joyce, then, encountered Miss Sylvia Beach and the relationship that was soon established thereafter between them was of great importance and aid to the Irish writer. In short, it was that of publisher and author. Miss Beach had learned of the difficulties attending the publication of *Ulysses,* how, for instance, the publishers in two great countries were crying off in fear and consternation from the manuscript as though it were a time bomb about to explode (which it was, in a way), and the daring idea occurred to her that she might publish it herself under the ægis of Shakespeare and Company. To think with her was to act, for she was and is an extremely vital personality with great courage and definite convictions, and therefore she broached the subject to Joyce. He, at the end of his rope so far as negotiations with the large established firms of London and New York were concerned, recognized in Miss Beach's offer an immediate solution of his problem and he was glad to acquiesce and place in her capable hands the huge manuscript.

It was necessary, first of all, for Miss Beach to find understanding and meticulous printers, for the book with its thousand and one tricks with the English language, with punctuation and with sentence structure would be a formidable task for even the most erudite of English printers. She found them in the firm of Maurice Darantière. Joyce has written: "These were very scrupulous and understanding French printers in Dijon, the capital of the French printing press." And, indeed, they had to be scrupulous and understanding. They had, perhaps, to follow the most difficult script they had ever encountered in the course of their lives, a script that besides being written in a foreign tongue was also a definite enlargement of that tongue in that it pushed forward the possibilities of the English language and the subtle encircling of thought by a new and daring use and arrangement of English words and grammar. As one reconsiders the difficulties set before these French printers the thought occurs that perhaps it was of some advantage to them that they were working on a foreign language. They, at least, were not bound by the customary assumptions of what the language should be. They could follow, like precise instruments, the words of the manuscript without deviating from the master sheet before them and assuming, as so many printers assume, that what they saw were errors of the coypist that must be corrected by their own omniscient selves. They lacked, also, that habitude of thinking that made sentences fall into the accustomed order. This ignorance, then, of what they were setting up in type was of a distinct advantage to Joyce. They might not know what they were putting into print but, at the same time, their unconscious prejudices were not urging them towards a constant and irritating correction (as an English printer might think) of the script before them.

Yet the difficulties for these ambitious printers in Dijon were enormous. It was not alone the complexities of the script that challenged them; it was also the constant corrections and additions of the author. Joyce, when receiving a batch of proofs, did more than correct them and insist that they follow perfectly the manuscript from which they had worked. He added; he rewrote; he enlarged; he developed. A galley proof to him was, so to speak, a challenge and his constant search for the complete development and realization of what he desired to express meant enormous and painstaking polishing of the text. The precise and amazingly complicated interrelationships of the multitudinous themes had to be perfectly planted and developed and this necessity, as Joyce saw it when the galleys were stretched out before him, meant fastidious and (to the printers, at least) seemingly endless revisions. More than half a dozen complete proofs of *Ulysses* were pulled during the latter half of 1921 and on every one of them were corrections, changes and additions. Joyce knew what he wanted to do and he meant to have it as perfect as possible.

It must be remembered that during this period of the printing of *Ulysses* Joyce's eyes were troubling him greatly and the task of proofreading was laborious. He was aided by various friends but these friends could do nothing (except at second hand) about the revisions and additions. Joyce had to do these himself. He was fortunate in both his publisher and his printers. Miss Beach was of constant and great assistance and her wise conviction of the vast importance of the book she was bringing to life and her increasing admiration and affection for the author of it fortified her determination to see her difficult task through with the utmost degree of success that was possible. The printers, too, were tireless in their endeavours, revising without complaint and doing all that they could from a typographical point of view to send *Ulysses* into the world in a guise that might be worthy of the content.

In the meantime, as the winter of 1921 closed in and the cold winds fled across the Seine and before the closed terraces of the cafés the little braziers of charcoal were set up, Joyce's many friends and acquaintances were doing their share, too. It is difficult, now, to recall the excitement (in a limited circle, to be sure) with which the complete *Ulysses* was awaited during that gentle winter; but one may remember the conversation and the speculation, the announcements and the impatience, the rumours and the expectation that attended the imminent birth of the book. Those who had read a portion of the work (from the beginning to a first instalment of the fourteenth section—with some deletions) in the *Little Review* or heard the author himself read it aloud had some idea of what was coming but the rest of the world had only a vague idea— sharpened, perhaps, by spreading comment—of what the book would be.

Joyce, himself, as may very well be imagined, was working furiously. He was doing something that he had not done in the case of his previous books, actually composing, for his voluminous additions were no less than that, while his manuscript went through the press and came out in the form of galleys and page proofs. At the same time, he was indulging in some degree of social life, seeing his friends, dining (he had now added a number of restaurants to his favourite list), hearing his beloved operas (for his love of music was a love that would not be denied), and following, as best he could, what was happening in the various art worlds of Paris. 1921 melted into 1922 and his fortieth birthday approached. At the same time, the laborious task of proofreading reached an end and he was ready, at last, to sit back and wait for the printed book.

He must have felt empty at that moment. He must have had the feeling that a great and moving period in his life had reached its conclusion. After all, he had started *Ulysses* before the beginning of the World War. He had worked on it in Trieste when Trieste was Austro-Hungarian; he had worked on it in Zurich throughout the most troublous and tragic days that the world had ever seen; he had worked on it again in Trieste when Trieste was Italian; and he had worked on it for more than a year in that post-war Paris that was so bubbling with life and ambitious ventures in letters. It was a long period—seven years—and it seemed even longer because of the hectic era that had been packed into those years. Well, now it was finished and he could sit back and stretch his legs a bit and regard the world at his leisure. But could he? For the moment, perhaps, he did not wonder about it but if he had questioned the subconscious dæmon that was always with him he might have heard another story. It would have told him that he had merely completed one huge venture only to prepare himself for another.

On February 2, 1922, that day on which he had been born in Rathgar and which he always celebrated by a special dinner in the intimacy of his family and a few friends, he was able to display the first printed copy of *Ulysses*. It was ready for the public at last. Miss Beach had published an edition of a thousand copies, all numbered. Numbers 1 to 100 were on Dutch handmade paper and signed by the author; numbers 101 to 250 were on vergé d'Arches paper, unsigned; and numbers 251 to 1,000 were on hand-made paper, also unsigned. It was a fat heavy book in blue covers with a plain matter-of-fact *Ulysses* printed across the front in white,[1] the sort of book, in fact, that enticed one into it for it gave promise of much meat. There are books like that just as there are books

---

[1] Blue and white are the national colours of Greece, land of Ulysses.

that instantly repel the reader. One commentator (the bibliophile, R. F. Roberts, a specialist in books) later remarked that it seemed to him "one of the most appropriate first editions of a book ever published." All this is to the credit and taste of Miss Beach and the firm of Maurice Darantière.

As Joyce held it in his hand on that February evening in 1922 it is quite possible that he wondered what its fortunes would be in the years to come. It requires a section in itself to follow those fortunes.

# Ten

ERE, then, is the biography of a book.

It does not pretend to be an exhaustive biography crammed with facts, figures and anecdotes but rather a running survey with brief pauses at what may be called climactic moments in the astonishing odyssey of a volume that triumphantly survived the relentless attempts of two great countries to suppress it. It won out eventually because it was more durable, being a manifest classic, than the Philistinian wrath that sought to sweep it into oblivion. But for many years its struggle to penetrate the English-reading countries was desperate and, at times, apparently helpless. Laws, prejudices, censors, Holy Church and all the Mrs. Grundys (in petticoats or trousers) of Great Britain and the United States merged into a solid wall to keep the blasphemous and obscene monster of a book from their pure and unpolluted shores. They might just as well have attempted to stem the waters of Victoria Falls. *Ulysses* was too astounding an achievement, too imperative a necessity in a world of crumbling fiction, too momentous a plunging forward into the unexplored possibilities of the written word and the enveloping theme and the potent enlargement of structural technique ever to be destroyed by the frantic ukases and persecutions of the hypocritical and biased guardians of what they themselves ordained should be public morals.

The first printing of *Ulysses* (that thousand copies already mentioned) was practically exhausted within a month of publication. On March 20, 1922, Joyce wrote to his brother Stanislaus, "Nobody of my admirers in Trieste subscribed for 'Ulysses' except Baron Ralli. The first English notice appeared last week, and the day after 148 copies were ordered. The edition, 750 copies at 150 francs, is out of print since Wednesday last. There remain only fifty copies of the de luxe and about eighty of the 250 franc, so the bowsies had better hurry up." Joyce, at this time, was sanguine enough to believe that there would be no particular difficulty about privately-printed English and American editions to be sold by subscription. He was soon to find out that this was not as simple as it seemed. The watchdogs of Anglo-Saxon and American morals were awakening and beginning to growl as the various reviews appeared in newspapers and periodicals. It is interesting (and of some historical significance) to recall how the book was received by the literary critics of the day. Take England first.

Mr. Sisley Huddleston fired the first gun (a very mild discharge of blanks) in the *Observer* for Sunday, March fifth. He opened his column and a fifth by stating:

> No book has ever been more eagerly and curiously awaited by the strange little inner circle of book-lovers and *littérateurs* than James Joyce's "Ulysses." It is folly to be afraid of uttering big words because big words are abused and have become almost empty of meaning in many mouths; and with all my courage I will repeat what a few folk in somewhat precious *cénacles* have been saying—that Mr. James Joyce is a man of genius. I believe the assertion to be strictly justified, though Mr. Joyce must remain, for special reasons, caviare to the general. I confess that I cannot see how the work upon which Mr. Joyce spent seven strenuous years, years of wrestling and of agony, can ever be given to the public.

Mr. Huddleston, it will be observed, was a kindly and well-meaning doubting Thomas. His article sold some two hundred copies and was especially useful at the time it was written. He admired the author tremendously and aspects of his work aroused unqualified praise. "Here is erudition transfigured by imagination." The critic understood the stream-of-consciousness method employed by Joyce but it is to be suspected that the real meaning of *Ulysses,* the theme itself, escaped him. He was appalled by the "gross animality" of the book. "There is one chapter devoted to the revery of a woman, and her *monologue intérieur* is, I imagine—and am bound in all honesty to say—the vilest, according to ordinary standards, in all literature. And yet its very obscenity is somehow beautiful and wrings the soul to pity. Is that not high art?" Mr. Huddleston concluded by suggesting that Joyce had "exaggerated the vulgarity and magnified the madness of mankind and the mysterious materiality of the universe."

Mr. J. Middleton Murry, writing in the *Nation* and the *Athe-*

*naeum,* declared, "The head that is strong enough to read 'Ulysses' will not be turned by it." And then he gave his own conception of the book, writing:

Upon such a head, indeed, the influence of "Ulysses" may be wholly excellent. For the driving impulse of this remarkable book is an immense, an unprecedented, liberation of suppressions. Something utterly different from the childish and futile coprophily of the "Young Girl's Diary" and other Freudian confessions; the liberation of the suppressions of an adult man who has lived under the shadow of the Roman-Catholic Church in a country where that Church is at its least European, and is merely an immense reinforcement of Puritanism. And not only is the effort at liberation much vaster and more significant than the corresponding efforts with which modern literature begins to be strewn, but the mind which undertakes it is indisputably the mind of an artist, abnormally sensitive to the secret individuality of emotions and things, abnormally sensitive also to spiritual beauty. A singular chapter of "The Brothers Karamazov" bears the title "Self-Lacerations." "Ulysses" is, fundamentally (though it is much besides), an immense, a prodigious self-laceration, the tearing-away from himself, by a half-demented man of genius, of inhibitions and limitations which have grown to be flesh of his flesh. And those who read it will profit by the vicarious sacrifice.

This was acute, though in a narrow sense, and it revealed a commentator who saw beyond, far beyond, Mr. Sisley Huddleston. And to make his opinion of the book quite definite (and that required courage in 1922) Mr. Murry, in considering the fifteenth section of *Ulysses* declared: "In this part of 'Ulysses'—let us say it plainly, in order that we may have our share of the contempt or the glory a hundred years hence—a genius of the very highest order, strictly comparable to Goethe's or Dostoevsky's, is evident. This transcendental buffoonery, this sudden uprush of the *vis comica* into a world wherein the tragic incompatibility of the practical and the instinctive is embodied, is a very great achievement. It is the vital centre of Mr. Joyce's book, and the intensity of life which it contains is sufficient to animate the whole of it."

Mr. Arnold Bennett, writing in the *Outlook* for April twenty-ninth, was even more emphatic. He had his strictures to make and he made them, but, serious as they were, it was his praise that most readers remembered. He wrote, in part:

James Joyce is a very astonishing phenomenon in letters. He is some-times dazzlingly original. If he does not see life whole he sees it pierc-ingly. His ingenuity is marvellous. He has wit. He has prodigious hu-mour. He is afraid of naught. And had heaven in its wisdom thought fit not to deprive him of that basic sagacity and the moral self-dominion which alone enable an artist to assemble and control and fully utilize his powers, he would have stood a chance of being one of the greatest novel-ists that ever lived. The best portions of the novel (unfortunately they constitute only a fraction of the whole) are superb. I single out the long orgiastic scene, and the long unspoken monologue of Mrs. Bloom which closes the book. The former will easily bear comparison with Rabelais at his fantastical finest; it leaves Petronius out of sight. It has plenary inspiration. It is the richest stuff, handled with a virtuosity to match the quality of the material. The latter (forty difficult pages, some twenty-five thousand words without any punctuation at all) might in its utterly convincing realism be an actual document, the magical record of inmost thoughts thought by a woman that existed. Talk about understanding "feminine psychology" . . . I have never read anything to surpass it, and I doubt if I have ever read anything to equal it. My blame may have seemed extravagant, and my praise may seem extravagant, but that is how I feel about James Joyce. The book is not pornographic, but it is more indecent, obscene, scatological, and licentious than the majority of professedly pornographical books. . . . For myself I think that in the main it is not justified by results obtained; but I must plainly add, at the risk of opprobrium, that in the finest passages it is in my opinion justified.

And Mr. Holbrook Jackson, the historian of the Yellow Nine-ties, airing his opinion in the June number of *Today,* declared (after petulantly exclaiming " 'Ulysses' is like a country without roads"): "With all its faults, it is the biggest event in the history of the Eng-lish novel since 'Jude.' "

*Ulysses,* then, was launched. It was a work to be discussed in drawing rooms, studios and public-house bars. It was a focal point for furious argument, strenuous opposition and the wildest praise. Almost immediately imitators sprang up from nowhere and the Joycian cult came into the open. The "lunatic fringe" began to flutter in the electrical air. Some of the attacks on the book passed all bounds of coherence and critical calmness and, to balance the picture between praise and recrimination, it may be just to note some of these attacks. In England three stood out, as representative of the others, three from such strange paladins of British virtue as Mr. Alfred Noyes, Mr. James Douglas and the *Pink 'Un*. Mr. Noyes, hurling his papier-mâché thunderbolt in the *Sunday Chronicle* of Manchester, howled: "It is simply the foulest book that has ever found its way into print." He went on to say: "The writing of the book is bad simply as writing and much of it is obscure through sheer disorder of the syntax. But—there is no foulness conceivable to the mind of man that has not been poured forth into its imbecile pages." How different this was to the opinions of Messrs. Arnold Bennett and J. Middleton Murry. Mr. Noyes was aware of this and unerringly placed himself where he belonged when he wrote indignantly: "But what concerns us all and most urgently demands consideration is the appalling fact that our Metropolitan criticism should have been treating such works as those of Mr. Joyce seriously as works of genius at the very moment when journal after journal is helping to depreciate some of the noblest pages in our literary history. The battle that is being waged round the work of Tennyson, for instance, the assault that has been made upon all the great Victorian writers are indications of a destructive spirit which may lead us far along the road to barbarism. . . . The best thing that could happen to English literature," he concluded, "is that a large number of our critics should be taken to a remote place in the country and locked up alone for six months with a volume of Wordsworth."

Mr. James Douglas (in the *Sunday Express* for May twenty-eighth) was equally amazed, shocked, discomfited and appalled. He wrote:

I have read it, and I say deliberately that it is the most infamously obscene book in ancient or modern literature. The obscenity of Rabelais is innocent compared with its leprous and scabrous horrors. All the secret sewers of vice are canalized in its flood of unimaginable thoughts, images and pornographic words. And its unclean lunacies are larded with appalling and revolting blasphemies directed against the Christian religion and against the holy name of Christ—blasphemies hitherto associated with the most degraded orgies of Satanism and the Black Mass.

And here let me say frankly that I have evidence which establishes the fact that the book is already the Bible of beings who are exiles and outcasts in this and in every civilized country. It is also adopted by the Freudians as the supreme glory of their dirty and degraded cult, which masquerades in pseudo-scientific raiment under the name of "Psycho-Analysis."

And in conclusion Douglas, Douglas, tender and true, declared:

This is a libel on Ireland, for if Ireland were to accept the paternity of Joyce and his Dublin Joyceries, which out-rosses the rosseries of the Parisian stews, Ireland would indeed become one of the dying nations, and degenerate into a latrine and a sewer. The England of Milton and Wordsworth at least stands firm in defence of decency, decorum, good manners and good morals.

*The Pink 'Un* (officially known as the *Sporting Times*) was just as vehement. Aramis (whoever he was), writing in the issue for April first, displayed his capabilities as a literary critic by announcing:

James Joyce is a writer of talent, but in "Ulysses" he has ruled out all the elementary decencies of life and dwells appreciatively on things that sniggering louts of schoolboys guffaw about. In addition to this stupid glorification of mere filth, the book suffers from being written in the manner of a demented George Meredith. There are whole chapters of it without any punctuation or other guide to what the writer is really getting at. Two thirds of it is incoherent, and the passages that are plainly written are devoid of wit, displaying only a coarse salacrity [sic] intended for humour.

The conclusion of the erudite *Pink 'Un* was, "The main contents of the book are enough to make a Hottentot sick," the idea evidently being that the "salacrity" of certain passages would upset the stomachs of our Black Brothers from South Africa.

It was Mr. J. Middleton Murry who had first broached the influence of the Roman Catholic Church on Joyce's attitude toward the subtle problems of the heart and mind that he was promulgating in *Ulysses* and it was Mr. Cecil Maitland, writing in the *New Witness* for August fourth, who presented another aspect of this theme. He wrote:

There is an idea prevalent among English Catholic converts, Roman and Anglo, that the Catholic life is one of simple devoutness, tempered by beer, carols and jollity in public houses, with perhaps an occasional good fat sin to be expiated by a thumping penance thrown in. These devout souls will probably gasp incredulously at being told that Aquinas would probably be more at home with Freud than, for instance, Mr. G. K. Chesterton. No one, however, who is acquainted with Catholic education in Catholic countries could fail to recognize the source of Mr. Joyce's "Weltanschauung." He sees the world as theologians showed it to him. His humour is the cloacal humour of the refectory; his contempt is the priests' denigration of the body, and his view of sex has the obscenity of a confessor's manual, reinforced by the profound perception and consequent disgust of a great imaginative writer.

If we consider Mr. Joyce's work from this point of view, it becomes clear that while his study of humanity remains incomplete, the defect is not due to any inherent lack of imagination on his part. Rather it arises from the fact that to a Catholic who no longer believes that he has an immortal soul, fashioned in the image of God, a human being becomes merely a specially cunning animal. I suggest then that Mr. Joyce's failure is not his own, but that of the Catholic system, which has not had the strength to hold him to its transcendentalism, and from whose errors he has not been able to set himself free.

This, of course, was not the Irish idea and in turning to Irish comment on *Ulysses* we have another point of view altogether. A gentleman writing under the pseudonym of "Domini Canis" in the *Dublin Review* gave what seemed to be the orthodox Roman Catholic attitude toward the book. ". . . A fearful travesty on persons, happenings and intimate life of the most morbid and sickening description," he declared, and goes on: "We are prepared to do justice to the power and litheness of the style, when intelligible, to the occasional beauty of a paragraph, and to the adventurous headlong experiments in new literary form, but as a whole we regard it as the screed of one possessed. . . . In this work the spiritually offensive and the physically unclean are united . . . in its reading lies not only the description but the commission of sin against the Holy Ghost. Having tasted and rejected the devilish drench, we most earnestly hope that this book be not only placed on the Index Expurgatorius, but that its reading and communication be made a reserved case. . . . A great Jesuit-trained talent has gone over malignantly and mockingly to the powers of evil . . ."

George W. Russell—A.E.—hoped that *Ulysses* might be "the

*Inferno* with possibilities of a *Purgatorio* and a *Paradiso* yet to come, to make it unquestionably the greatest fiction of the twentieth century." John Eglinton, writing in an American periodical (the *Dial*), was as suave as ever. "The book has been received with enthusiasm by those who provisionally determine literary fame in Ireland," he admitted, but, at the same time, he did not think it "very high class." "I read on," he explained, "with an admiration chiefly of the heroic persistence of the author, of the number of things he knows, notices, remembers, of the unfailing vitality and purity of his phrase, of his superb powers of mimicry and literary impersonation, of the half-kindly and painstaking exactness which mitigates his cruelty. . . . I doubt whether this massive work is of good augury for Irish literature . . ." he concluded. "Mr. Joyce's masterpiece is a violent interruption of what is known as the Irish literary renascence."

This was acute. When we remember the long years that Joyce had set himself against the parochial and romantic aspects of that same Irish Literary Renascence we can easily see why *Ulysses* should be considered "a violent interruption" by a disciple of the movement. Indeed, it was more than an interruption; it was a death blow. Valery Larbaud's emphatic statement, "With this book Ireland makes a sensational re-entrance into high European literature," puts the situation in a nutshell. How could Irish letters be the same after *Ulysses?* They couldn't and a new breed of Irish writers, among them Brinsley MacNamara, Liam O'Flaherty, Sean O'Casey and Samuel Beckett, sprang up to prove it. Gone were the dainty days of A.E.'s brood of goslings.

Mr. Shane Leslie, however, did not think so. Writing in the *Quarterly Review* for October 1922, he stoutly maintained:

> From any Christian point of view this book must be proclaimed anathema, simply because it tries to pour ridicule on the most sacred themes and characters in what has been the religion of Europe for nearly two thousand years. And this is the book which ignorant French critics hail as the proof of Ireland's re-entry into European literature! It contains the literary germs of that fell movement which politically has destroyed the greater part of Slavic Europe. If it is a summons or inspiration to the Celtic end of Europe to do likewise, it would be better for Ireland to sink under the seas and join Atlantis, rather than allow her life of letters to affect the least reconciliation with a book which,

owing to accidents of circumstance, probably only Dubliners can really understand in detail. Certainly, it takes a Dubliner to pick out the familiar names and allusions of twenty years ago, though the references to men who have become as important as Arthur Griffith assume a more universal hearing. And we are sorry to say that it would take a theologian, even Jesuit, to understand all the theological references. At the same time, nobody in his senses would hold Clongowes School responsible for this portent. It was its ill fortune to breed without being able to harness a striking literary genius, who has since yoked himself to the steeds of Comedy and Blasphemy and taken headlong flight, shall we say like the Gadarene swine, into a choking sea of impropriety. If George Moore is right in saying that "blasphemy is the literature of Catholic countries," this is verily literature.

And Mrs. Mary M. Colum, writing in the *Freeman* (an American weekly) for July nineteenth, expressed another fear of what the influence of *Ulysses* might do to creative literature. With sharp intelligence she dismissed the accusations of obscenity, declaring, "But it is doubtful that obscenity in literature ever really corrupted anybody." She expressed her fear when she wrote:

The alarming thing about "Ulysses" is very different; it is that it shows the amazing inroads that science is making on literature. Mr. Joyce's book is of as much interest as science as it is as literature; in some parts it is of purely scientific and non-artistic interest. It seems to me a real and not a fantastic fear that science will oust literature altogether as a part of human expression; and from that point of view "Ulysses" is a dangerous indication. From that point of view, also, I do not consider it as important to literature as "Portrait of the Artist." After "Ulysses" I cannot see how anyone can go on calling books written in the subconscious method, novels. It is as plain as day that a new literary form has appeared, from which the accepted form of the novel has nothing to fear; the novel is as distinct from this form as in his day Samuel Richardson's invention was from the drama.

Perhaps the completest understatement concerning *Ulysses* from an Irish source was that of the *Irish Independent,* "Ulysses has come in for some severe criticisms."

Opinion in the United States may be illustrated through the reviews of three men, Mr. Edmund Wilson, Mr. Gilbert Seldes and Dr. Joseph Collins.

Mr. Wilson, writing in the *New Republic* for July fifth, had plenty of fault to find with the book but never from a moralistic point of view. For one thing he found it too long and dull. "It is almost as if in distending the story to ten times its natural size he had finally managed to burst it and leave it partially deflated." The parallels with Homer displeased the critic, too. ". . . I cannot but feel that Mr. Joyce made a mistake to have the whole plan of his story depend on the structure of the Odyssey rather than on the natural demands of the situation." And Mr. Wilson bogged, also, at what he called the "sterilities and practical jokes" played on the English language and the styles of bygone writers. However, having disposed of his complaints, the reviewer had signal praise to give. He wrote:

Yet, for all its appalling longueurs, Ulysses is a work of high genius. Its importance seems to me to lie, not so much in its opening new doors to knowledge—unless in setting an example to Anglo-Saxon writers of putting down everything without compunction—or in inventing new literary forms—Joyce's formula is really, as I have indicated, nearly seventy-five years old—as in its once more setting the standard of the novel so high that it need not be ashamed to take its place beside poetry and drama. Ulysses has the effect at once of making everything else look brassy. Since I have read it, the texture of other novelists seems intolerably loose and careless; when I come suddenly unawares upon a page that I have written myself I quake like a guilty thing surprised.

Mr. Gilbert Seldes contributed his review to the *Nation* for August thirtieth. He had no fault to find with the book and its impact upon his clean-cut and impartial intelligence produced one of those illuminating articles that really convey to the general reader the substance of the work discussed. It was probably the best review written in the United States. His concluding paragraph deserves to be preserved intact.

I have not the space to discuss the æsthetic questions which the book brings up nor to indicate what its effect upon the novel may be. I have called Joyce formidable because it is already clear that the innovations in method and the developments in structure which he has used with a skill approaching perfection are going to have an incalculable effect upon the writers of the future; he is formidable because his imitators will make use of his freedom without imposing upon themselves the duties and disciplines he has suffered; I cannot see how any novelist will be able (nor why he should altogether want) entirely to escape his influence. The book has literally hundreds of points of interest not even suggested here. One must take for granted the ordinary equipment of the novelist; one must assume also that there are faults, idiosyncrasies, difficulties. More important still are the interests associated with "the uncreated conscience of my race"—the Catholic and Irish. I have written this analysis of "Ulysses" as one not too familiar with either—as an indication that the book can have absolute validity and interest, in the sense that all which is local and private in the "Divine Comedy" does not detract from its interest and validity. But these and other points have been made in the brilliant reviews which "Ulysses" has already evoked. One cannot leave it without noting again that in the change of Stephen Dedalus from his affinity with the old artificer to his kinship with Ulysses-Bloom, Joyce has created an image of contemporary life; nor without testifying that this epic of defeat, in which there is not a scamped page nor a moment of weakness, in which whole chapters are monuments to the power and the glory of the written word, is in itself a victory of the creative intelligence over the chaos of uncreated things and a triumph of devotion, to my mind one of the most significant and beautiful of our time.

In the New York *Times Book Review and Magazine* for May twenty-eighth, Dr. Joseph Collins, a neurologist to whom all authors were case-histories, had more to say about Joyce than *Ulysses* and he said it with that omniscient confidence that is the hallmark of most psychiatrists. Dr. Collins gave the impression that he possessed the peculiar power of taking the author apart to see what made him tick. However, his summation of Joyce (as deduced from *Ulysses* and the earlier books) is not without interest in revealing the reactions of a doctor.

Mr. Joyce [the psychological observer declared] had the good fortune to be born with a quality which the world calls genius. Nature exacts a penalty, a galling income tax from geniuses, and as a rule she co-endows them with unamenability to law and order. Genius and reverence are antipodal, Galileo being the exception to the rule. Mr. Joyce has no reverence for organized religion, for conventional morality, for literary style or form. He has no conception of the word obedience, and he bends the knee neither to God nor man. It is very interesting, and most important to have the revelations of such a personality, to have them first-hand and not dressed up. Heretofore our only avenues of information of such personalities led through the asylums for the insane, for it was there that such revelations as those of Mr. Joyce were made without reserve. Lest anyone should construe this statement to be a subterfuge on my part to impugn the sanity of Mr. Joyce, let me say at once that he is one of the sanest geniuses that I have ever known.

He had the profound misfortune to lose his faith and he cannot rid himself of the obsession that the Jesuits did it for him, and he is trying to get square with them by saying disagreeable things about them and holding their teachings up to scorn and obloquy. He was so unfortunate as to be born without a sense of duty, of service, of conformity to the State, to the community, to society, and he is convinced that he ought to tell about it, just as some who have experienced a surgical operation feel that they must relate minutely all the details of it, particularly at dinner parties and to casual acquaintances.

Finally, I venture a prophecy: Not ten men or women out of a hundred can read "Ulysses" through, and of the ten who succeed in doing so, five of them will do it as *tour de force*. I am probably the only person, aside from the author, that has ever read it twice from beginning to end.[1] I have learned more psychology and psychiatry from it than I did in ten years at the Neurological Institute. There are other angles at which "Ulysses" can be viewed profitably, but they are not many.

Stephen Dedalus in his Parisian tranquillity (if the modern Minos has been given the lethal warm bath) will pretend indifference to the publication of a laudatory study of "Ulysses" a hundred years hence, but he is as sure to get it as Dostoevsky, and surer than Mallarmé.

In France the critical reception of the book was mainly friendly but limited to those commentators who could read English. Valery Larbaud naturally led the van. In *La Nouvelle Revue Française* he declared: *"Je crois que l'audace et la dureté avec lesquelles Joyce décrit et met en scène les instincts réputés les plus bas de la nature humaine lui viennent de l'exemple que lui ont donné les grands casuistes de la Compagnie . . . De ces grands casuistes, Joyce a la froideur intrépide, et à l'égard des faiblesses de la chair la même absence de tout respect humain . . . Quand on songe à la discipline à laquelle l'auteur s'est soumis, on se demande comment a pu sortir, de ce formidable travail d'angencement, une œuvre aussi vivante,*

---

[1] What a monstrous and asinine assumption. Dr. Collins needed attention from a neurologist himself at this moment.

*aussi émouvante, aussi humaine . . . L'auteur n'a jamais perdu de
vue l'humanité de ses personnages, tout ce mélange de qualités et
de défauts, de bassesse et de grandeur dont il sont faites; l'homme,
la créature de chair, parcourant sa petite journée . . ."* Monsieur
Edmond Jaloux, one of the most powerful of French critics, was
particularly kind in the *Revue de Paris*, writing, in part:

*La surprise que l'on éprouve en lisant* Ulysses *provient de ce que
les œuvres littéraires, depuis trois siècles, ont en quelque sorte divisé
l'esprit humain pour mieux régner sur lui. Ces compartiments logiques
établis dans le domain de la vie mentale ont, en effet, aidé puissamment
à la diffusion de la littérature. Mais James Joyce remonte directement
à l'origine de tout, c'est-à-dire à l'homme. Son œuvre, qui ouvre si
brusquement quelques-unes des portes de l'avenir, semble provenir
directement du seizième siècle; on y trouve l'aspect encyclopédique des
grandes œuvres de cette époque, leur souci de connaître la vérité, leur
volonté de pénétrer la vie tout entière et ses sciences au moyen d'un
truchement spirituel, cette horreur de la dissimulation, de l'escamotage
qui sont si sensibles chez un Montaigne, chez un Rabelais. C'est surtout
à celui-ci que James Joyce fait penser—autant qu'un Irlandais de la fin
du dix-neuvième siècle, à la fois réaliste et symboliste peut ressembler à
un Tourangeau de la Renaissance—et alors les audaces, les excès, les
bizarreries apparentes cesserent d'en cacher la vaste et véritable beauté.*

One might go on culling these extracts from the newspapers
and periodicals of half a dozen countries until enough were assembled to make up a respectable-sized book; but it would be merely
piling Pelion on Ossa. Enough has been preserved here to show the
world-wide reception of *Ulysses* during its first year of life between
blue-paper covers; to reveal its resounding impact on the literary
scene of its time, to illustrate its reception by startled, disconcerted,
laudatory or angrily shocked critics, and to emphasize with what
immediacy Joyce leaped into the category of world-known figures.
*Ulysses* was dynamite and when it was flung into the literary scene
of 1922 its consequent effect was the effect of dynamite. There was
an explosion and when the smoke had lifted it was perceptible that
the literary scene was no longer the same. The débris of Time had
been blown away and a new road stretched before those eyes that
could see.

## II

Even before a moiety of these reviews, attacks and disquisitions had appeared in print the great game of smuggling *Ulysses* into countries where it was forbidden had begun. It was transported in all sorts of sly ways and some curious expedients were resorted to by the literary *contrabandistas*. There is one story to the effect that a Dubliner anxious to read the book had his copy enclosed in an empty Guinness stout barrel and so conveyed on a barge across the Irish Sea and up the Liffey. Another would-be reader, an American, persuaded a friend in Paris to tear up the volume and dispatch across the Atlantic Ocean a dozen sheets at a time folded into innocent French newspapers. In the bottom of hat-trunks, snugly folded in lacy lingerie, thrust under the waistcoat and so adding a portly appearance to the traveller, once with a cover of the Bible pasted over it, *Ulysses,* despite those ferrets the customs inspectors, steadily percolated into the English-reading countries. There it was passed from hand to hand, sometimes until it was tattered, and the younger authors and critics of the early nineteen-twenties realized that here, at last, was the Book of their generation and the vast well from which might be drawn the heady waters of a new and necessary movement in world letters. Even with all this increasing smuggling, however, copies were all too scarce to supply the swelling demand. It was not until October 1922 (eight months after the first thousand had been put on sale) that a second printing appeared, this time with a title page announcing that it was published by John Rodker, Paris, for the Egoist Press, London. It was, of course, from the same plates as the first printing and differed in no wise from it in format. There were two thousand copies in this second printing but the United States Post Office authorities seized and burned five hundred of them (a Hitlerian prophecy, so to speak) upon their arrival at the Port of New York. Not deterred by this stupid tragedy, Mr. Rodker assumed responsibility for a third printing (January 1923) of five hundred copies. An even worse tragedy befell it. Four hundred and ninety-nine copies of this printing were confiscated by the English customs authorities at Folkestone and forever disappeared from view. So that was that and Mr. Rodker retired incontinently from the unequal battlefield. The odds against him were too great. It will be observed that during the first year of its life, then, as a published book no more than 2,501 copies of *Ulysses* seem to have got into circulation. This fact is amazing when we consider the tremendous amount of publicity concerning the book that was appearing in England, France and America and already spreading into several other countries.

Perhaps it was this publicity (not all of it healthy or intelligent and a portion of it despicable in intent) that eventually attracted to Shakespeare and Company and other Paris bookshops a growing procession of pleasure-minded tourists, many of them pert young American misses, who considered it a daring thing to procure a copy of *Ulysses* and sneak it back to their homes. What the book was and what it stood for was entirely beyond their conception or powers of comprehension but they had heard that it contained (to quote literally from one of them) "some swell dirty passages." That spicy expectation, for the most part, was their sole reason for desiring it. For these infantile troglodytes the acquisition of *Ulysses* became a vogue. One was not in the fashion if one did not possess it. It was the thing to do, like wasting one's time over crossword puzzles, or, to come closer to their own peculiar reasoning, like having a *Kama-Sutra* or *The Perfumed Garden* or one of Mr. Charles Carrington's lubricious publications. It just showed the folks back home what you could get in that naughty gay Paree. It is to be hoped that a few among this class of book buyers finally realized that what they had purchased was about as removed from pornography as Homer's *Odyssey* or *The Divine Comedy*. However, the vogue had its good side in that it increased mightily the sales of *Ulysses* and thus improved the possibilities of its reaching more serious readers; for, after all, many of the copies so lightly purchased *pour le vogue* found their way into the hands of dealers who had graver-minded clients. The sad part of it was that many of these graver-minded clients, unable to go to Paris, had to pay through the nose for the book while Joyce benefited not at all from the exorbitant prices. Between January 1924 and December 1925 Shakespeare and Company, animated by the raised demand, issued the fourth to the seventh printings of "Ulysses," using the original plates; and between May 1926 and May 1930 the same publisher brought out the eighth to the eleventh printings, these four being from type entirely reset and with a majority of the errors imbedded in the first seven printings corrected. After the eleventh printing Miss Sylvia Beach ceased to be Joyce's publisher. Thus over a period of eight years there was a total of eleven printings (the fate of Mr. Rodker's unfortunate second edition for the Egoist Press really reduces it to ten) but, as only the first three were numbered, it is impossible to give a fair estimate of the complete sales. However, there is no doubt but that *Ulysses,* in spite of all the bans against it and the extra activities of customs inspectors, made an extremely agreeable showing for its author and its publisher. Indeed, the book reached a wider audience than any prohibited work had done before or since.

Naturally, this success (two successes, if you will; one for its extraordinary literary merit and the other a *succès de scandale*) aroused the avaricious attention of those shameless vultures among publishers called book-pirates. Owing to the lamentable fact that Joyce was unable to obtain any copyright protection in the countries where the volume was banned it was open game there for any printer who desired to steal the book, garble it by clumsy bowdlerization, print it and sell it for his own profit. Joyce had no legal recourse whatsoever. It was in the United States of America that advantage was taken of the writer's helplessness to protect his own work.

In July 1926 there appeared in New York the first issue of a periodical called *Two Worlds Monthly*. It was edited by one Samuel Roth, formerly proprietor of a bookshop in Greenwich Village and who had now entered the magazine-publishing field with a will "Devoted to the Increase of the Gaiety of Nations." This first issue of *Two Worlds Monthly* was dedicated "to James Joyce who will probably plead the cause of our time at the bar of posterity," and it included a first instalment of *Ulysses.* Further issues of *Two Worlds Monthly* followed, each one continuing the serialization of Joyce's book albeit considerably pruned, bowdlerized and even changed by the substitution of words designed because of their assonance to suggest deleted words that might have aroused Mr. John S. Sumner and his vice-snuffing bloodhounds. Mr. Roth, it will be observed, was playing safe. It was not long before news of this unauthorized publication reached Paris and Joyce, Miss Beach and various friends protested strenuously against it. Mr. Roth, whose hide was apparently that of a rhinoceros, went merrily on with his serialization. On November 1, 1926, a press story concerning the matter appeared in the New York *Evening Post.*

Serial publication in America of "Ulysses," banned from the United States in novel form in 1931, but now running in the Two Worlds Monthly, was sanctioned by James Joyce, according to statements made to the Evening Post by Samuel Roth, publisher of the magazine.

Rumors were revived late last week with the arrival in New York of several friends and literary colleagues of Joyce, that Joyce had not known of or agreed to the serialization of his masterpiece in America and would obstruct its further printing if he had legal grounds for action.

Roth, however, has denied the growing charges that the novel was "pirated" without the cognizance of its author.

"Arrangements exist between Mr. Joyce and myself in regard to the publication of 'Ulyssess,'" Mr. Roth told an Evening Post reporter. He added that these arrangements were based upon negotiations he had had with the Irish writer before the work was serialized. Asked to reveal the nature of these arrangements, Mr. Roth said that he did not feel at liberty to do so.

"It would place Mr. Joyce in an unfavorable light," he said.

The publisher of the revised and serialized version of the 700 page work, that has been called by some critics as great as the masterpieces of Rabelais, explained that he had paid Joyce $250 for serial publication of five instalments of Joyce's new work, called an "Unnamed Novel." But beyond intimating that he had had negotiations with Joyce for the printing of "Ulysses," Roth declined to reveal the nature of the negotiations, financial or otherwise, in regard to that book.

Serialization of "Ulysses" in unabridged form was begun in the Little Review in New York five years ago, but was banned when court action was started by the Society for the Prevention of Vice. Having been banned, the book was without copyright protection in the United States, so that its reproduction, unless stopped by another ban, could not be legally prevented by Joyce.

Joyce's friends say the author has made most of his money from the private sale of his book in America. Sales up to the first of January, 1924, amounted to $21,144 it was pointed out. The novel sold for as much as $100 a copy, shortly after its first printing, which was done in Paris by Sylvia Beach.

Miss Beach, upon reading this story, cabled the New York *Evening Post* on November sixteenth as follows:

NEW YORK EVENING POST
NEW YORK
REFERENCE YOUR INTERVIEW WITH SAMUEL ROTH FIRST NOVEMBER TWO
WORLDS SERIAL PUBLICATION OF JAMES JOYCE'S ULYSSES IS UNAUTHORIZED
UNPAID FOR AND THE TEXT HAS BEEN ALTERED
                                                    SYLVIA BEACH

She further strengthened this statement by composing an open letter to the American press. It ran:

                                        18th November, 1926.
DEAR SIR,

An American monthly called 'Two Worlds,' with an admitted sale of fifty thousand copies, edited by Mr. Samuel Roth, is publishing serially a version revised by Mr. Roth of ULYSSES. I think your readers ought to know that this edition is unauthorized by Mr. Joyce, unpaid for by Mr. Roth, and that the text has been altered. No negotiations existed or exist between Mr. Roth and Mr. Joyce, whose interests I represent, for this serial publication, and Mr. Roth has not paid any money for the book which he is pirating and mutilating.

Mr. Roth some time ago printed also without permission and without payment in his 'Two Worlds' quarterly fragments of Mr. Joyce's new work which had appeared in European reviews. I wrote to him remonstrating and obtained two hundred dollars and a promise of more which never came.

In No. 4 of 'Two Worlds' quarterly, which, according to Mr. Roth, appears in a limited edition of 450 numbered copies after which the type is distributed, Mr. Roth announces that subscribers will receive their copy "signed by the leading contributor." As Mr. Roth has admitted to Mr. Ernest Hemingway that his sales of this quarterly amount not to 450 but to eight thousand copies and one of these eight thousand copies may be in the possession of a reader of yours I shall be greatly obliged if that reader will let me know immediately by what "leading contributor" his or her copy of 'Two Worlds' quarterly is signed.

                            Yours faithfully,
                            SYLVIA BEACH,
                            Publisher of ULYSSES.

None of these remonstrances halted the hardy Mr. Roth. *Ulysses,* in a crudely-trimmed version, continued to appear in *Two Worlds Monthly.* In fact, it ran until the June (or July) issue of 1927, that being the last number published of this project "Devoted to the Increase of the Gaiety of Nations." Mr. Roth, it appears, had arguments (or, rather, what he considered to be arguments) on his own side. He protested, first of all, that the work had been "auto-matically turned over" to him by Ezra Pound, who indignantly denied it, and that he meant to succeed where "the Chicago ladies" (presumably Miss Margaret C. Anderson and Miss Jane Heap) had failed; namely, to complete a serialization of *Ulysses* in America. Again, he declared that he had posted $2,500 with his lawyer which would not only pay Joyce's expenses to New York to "answer my charges against him for his conduct in the matter of my publication of his 'Ulysses' in Two Worlds Monthly" but would afford him an opportunity to "dine with the Van Dorens, see the Woolworth Building, and get a thousand dollars in cash besides." Never, it would seem, was there such colossal impudence from an oppor-tunist of suspect character than from the amazing Mr. Roth.

Long before this curious gentleman had concluded his illegal partial serialization of *Ulysses* in his magazine a protest against the enterprise, engineered by various friends of Joyce in Paris, had been drawn up and signed by no less than one hundred and sixty-seven famous authors and prominent figures in letters and distributed to the press. It deserves to be preserved if only for the reason that few documents have ever assembled together so many famous names on one page. It was dated "Paris, 2nd. February, 1927" (Joyce's forty-fifth birthday, by the way) and read:

It is a matter of common knowledge that the *Ulysses* of Mr. James Joyce is being republished in the United States, in a magazine edited by Samuel Roth, and that this republication is being made without authoriza-tion by Mr. Joyce; without payment to Mr. Joyce and with alterations which seriously corrupt the text. This appropriation and mutilation of Mr. Joyce's property is made under colour of legal protection in that *Ulysses* which is published in France and which has been excluded from the mails in the United States is not protected by copyright in the United States. The question of justification of that exclusion is not now in issue; similar decisions have been made by government officials with reference to works of art before this. The question in issue is whether the public (including the editors and publishers to whom his advertise-ments are offered) will encourage Mr. Samuel Roth to take advantage of the resultant legal difficulty of the author to deprive him of his prop-erty and to mutilate the creation of his art. The undersigned protest against Mr. Roth's conduct in republishing *Ulysses* and appeal to the American public in the name of that security of works of the intellect

and the imagination without which art cannot live, to oppose to Mr.
Roth's enterprise the full power of honorable and fair opinion.

Lascelles Abercrombie
Richard Aldington
Sherwood Anderson
René Arcos
M. Arcybacheff
Ebba Atterbom
Azorin, *Président de l'Académie Espagnole*
C. du Baissauray
Léon Bazalgette
Jacinto Benavente
Silvio Benco
Julien Benda
Arnold Bennett
Jacques Benoist-Méchin
Konrad Bercovici
J. D. Beresford
Rudolph Binding
Massimo Bontempelli
Jean de Bosschère
Ivan Bounine, *de l'Académie Russe*
Robert Bridges
Eugène Brieux, *de l'Académie Française*
Bryher
Olaf Bull
Mary Butts
Louis Cazamian
Jacques Chenevière
Abel Chevalley
Maurice Constantin-Weyer
Albert Crémieux
Benjamin Crémieux
Benedetto Croce
Ernst Robert Curtius
Francis Dickie
H.D.
Norman Douglas
Charles Du Bos
Georges Duhamel

Edouard Dujardin
Luc Durtain
Albert Einstein
T. S. Eliot
Havelock Ellis
Edouard Estaunié, *de l'Académie Française*
Léon-Paul Fargue
E. M. Forster
François Fosca
Gaston Gallimard
John Galsworthy
Edward Garnett
Giovanni Gentile
Philip Gibbs
André Gide
Bernard Gilbert
Ivan Goll
Ramon Gomez de la Serna
Cora Gordon
Jan Gordon
Georg Goyert
Alice S. Green
Julian Green
Augusta Gregory
Daniel Halévy
Knut Hamsun
Jane Harrison
H. Livingston Hartley
Ernest Hemingway
Yrjo Hirn
Hugo von Hofmannsthal
Sisley Huddleston
Stephen Hudson
George F. Hummel
Bampton Hunt
Bravig Imbs
Holbrook Jackson
Edmond Jaloux
Storm Jameson

Juan Ramon Jimenez
Eugene Jolas
Henry Festing Jones
Georg Kaiser
Hermann Keyserling
Manuel Komroff
A. Kouprine
René Lalou
Pierre de Lanux
Valery Larbaud
D. H. Lawrence
Frédéric Lefèvre
Emile Legouis
Wyndham Lewis
Ludwig Lewisohn
Victor Llona
Mina Loy
Archibald MacLeish
Brinsley MacNamara
Maurice Maeterlinck
Thomas Mann
Antonio Marichalar
Maurice Martin du Gard
Dora Marsden
John Masefield
W. Somerset Maugham
André Maurois
D. Merejkowsky
Régis Michaud
Gabriel Miró
Hope Mirrlees
T. Sturge Moore
Paul Morand
Auguste Morel
Arthur Moss
J. Middleton Murry
Sean O'Casey
Liam O'Flaherty
José Ortega y Gasset
Seumas O'Sullivan
Elliot H. Paul
Jean Paulhan

Arthur Pinero
Luigi Pirandello
Jean Prévost
Marcel Prévost, *de l'Académie
Française*
C. F. Ramuz
Alfonso Reyes
Ernest Rhys
Elmer L. Rice
Dorothy Richardson
Jacques Robertfrance
Lennox Robinson
John Rodker
Romain Rolland
Jules Romains
Bertrand Russell
George W. Russell "A.E."
Ludmilla Savitzky
Jean Schlumberger
May Sinclair
W. L. Smyser
E. OE. Somerville
Philippe Soupault
André Spire
Th. Stephanides
James Stephens
André Suares
Italo Svevo
Frank Swinnerton
Arthur Symons
Marcel Thiébaut
Virgil Thomson
Robert de Traz
C. R. Trevelyan
Miguel de Unamuno
Laurence Vail
Paul Valéry, *de l'Académie
Française*
Fernand Vandérem
Fritz Vanderpyl
Francis Viélé-Griffin
Hugh Walpole

| | |
|---|---|
| Jacob Wassermann | Thornton Wilder |
| H. G. Wells | Robert Wolf |
| Rebecca West | Virginia Woolf |
| Anna Wickham | W. B. Yeats |

It will be noticed that ten Irish writers signed this document. With the final issue of *Two Worlds Monthly* (June, or July, 1927) the unauthorized serialization of *Ulysses* came to an abrupt termination. Mr. Roth had succeeded in publishing fourteen complete (except for his own emendations and cuts) sections of the work. But already Joyce, through the American law firm of Chadbourne, Stanchfield and Levy, had sought for an injunction restraining the astonishing pirate from further using his name and work. Theoretically Joyce might have no legal control of his uncopyrighted book in the United States but he had hope that the American courts would stretch a point and justify him in his endeavours to put an end to such callous thievery. He realized this hope, for more than a year later the following injunction was adjudged and decreed.

INJUNCTION

> At a Special Term, Part 11, of the Supreme Court, held in and for the County of New York, at the Court House thereof in the Borough of Manhattan, New York City, on the 27th day of December 1928.

PRESENT:

HON. RICHARD H. MITCHELL
*Justice*

JAMES JOYCE,
*Plaintiff,*
—against—

SAMUEL ROTH and TWO WORLDS PUBLISHING COMPANY, INC.,
*Defendants.*

Upon the summons, amended complaint and the answers thereto, the deposition of Samuel Roth, subscribed January 10, 1928, the deposition of James Joyce, taken March 8, 1928, the stipulation between the attorneys for the respective parties and consent of defendants thereto, both dated December 19, 1928, and all other proceedings heretofore had herein:

*Now,* on motion of Chadbourne, Stanchfield and Levy, plaintiff's attorneys, it is

*Adjudged and decreed* that the above-named defendants Samuel Roth and Two Worlds Publishing Company, Inc., and each of them, their officers, assistants, agents and servants are hereby enjoined, under the penalty by law prescribed, from using the name of the plaintiff for advertising purposes or for purposes of trade by

(*a*) Publishing, printing, stating or advertising the name of the plaintiff in connection with any magazine, periodical or other publication published by defendants or either of them;

(*b*) Publishing, printing, stating or advertising the name of the plaintiff in connection with any book, writing, manuscript or other work of the plaintiff;

(*c*) Publishing, printing, stating or advertising, or otherwise disseminating the name of the plaintiff in connection with any book, writing, manuscript or other work of the plaintiff, including the book "Ulysses," in any issue of Two Worlds Monthly, Two Worlds Quarterly, or any other magazine, periodical or other publication, heretofore or hereafter published by defendants.

Enter,

R. H. M.

J. S. C.

THOMAS F. FARLEY

*Clerk.*

It was a hollow victory for Joyce, for some time thereafter there appeared in the subterranean book-marts of New York a forged edition of *Ulysses*.[1] Joyce has described this as "a photographic forgery of the Paris edition and which contained the falsification of the Dijon printer's imprint," but Mr. R. F. Roberts, who has studied the matter carefully, differs. He has written in the *Colophon:*

It is evidently the result of instructions from somebody to a printer to "duplicate" the Shakespeare and Company 9th printing, and the result is amusing enough. In general format it is the same book, but five minutes spent in collation will reveal to anyone that it is a fraud. It begins with

---

[1] Rumour has it that the plates were made in France.

"Jonthan" for "Jonathan" on the page showing Cape as one of the other publishers of Joyce, and ends with a bold falsification (as Joyce remarks) of Darantière's name as the printer. The pagination is the same but the type font is perceptibly smaller; the paper is a considerably heavier stock and the book is consequently about one-eighth of an inch thicker.

It is also immediately evident that this edition enjoyed little or no proofreading, for it abounds with all sorts of typographical errors, and in one instance a line is transposed, upside down, eight lines out of place. Apparently the publisher felt that the known peculiarities of the authentic text would cover any deficiencies in this one, and that as long as the book was not bowdlerized, the purchasers would be happy regardless. It is, in fact, admissible that if one were not familiar with the Paris editions, particularly the 8th or 9th printings, he might well believe this to be simply a very bad example of the genuine article.

How many pirated editions were printed and then bootlegged there is, of course, no way of estimating accurately. I daresay they were numerous, but I have not yet succeeded in finding one of the photographic facsimilies mentioned by Joyce, if, indeed, he actually means a facsimile made by a photographic process.

All of this probably makes doleful reading but it is important in so far as it shows what can be done in the United States to an unprotected book. The laws that govern such matters (or, rather, the lack of laws) have long infuriated European publishers and authors.

However, the tide of fortune for Joyce and *Ulysses* began to turn in the year following the injunction against Samuel Roth. In February, 1929, there appeared under the auspices of La Maison des Amis des Livres, Mademoiselle Adrienne Monnier's bookshop across the Rue de l'Odéon from Shakespeare and Company, a French translation of the book. *Ulysse. Traduction française intégrale de M. Auguste Morel, assisté par M. Stuart Gilbert, entièrement revue par M. Valery Larbaud et l'auteur* was a venture of vast importance to Joyce for it gave him a new audience in a new tongue, and, perhaps, the most intelligent and impartial in the world. The translation was a *tour de force* of dexterity and faithfulness to the original.[1]

The last Shakespeare and Company edition (as has been pointed out already) was published in May 1930, and for more than two

[1] Other translations of *Ulysses* now exist, German, Czech, Polish, Spanish, Russian and Japanese, for instance, but it is proposed in this book to confine attention primarily to the fortunes of the work in English with a few indications of French receptivity.

years thereafter *Ulysses* was not printed at all in English. Then, in December 1932, the Odyssey Press of Hamburg-Paris-Bologna issued in two volumes an edition that was surprisingly free from typographical inaccuracies. It carried the statement: "The present edition may be regarded as the definitive standard edition, as it has been specially revised, at the author's request, by Stuart Gilbert." Mr. R. F. Roberts remarks, concerning it: "The Odyssey Press edition no longer appears in the general catalogue of German publications, nor for that matter does the German translation of it. Apparently Mr. Bloom's racial membership furnishes a new reason for suppression of his epic; to the moral ban on it in England, and the religious (and moral) in Ireland, is now joined the socio-political in Germany. I might add that Mirsky, in a critical capacity, has already condemned it in Russia as having no practical message for the worker, and I have no doubt that by this time some Spaniard has voiced objections to the portrait of Mrs. Bloom on the ground that it reflects unfavorably on the character of Spanish womanhood."

One might add to the comments of Mr. Roberts that *Ulysses* does not appear to be on the Index Librorum Prohibitorum of the Vatican. It certainly was not in 1935 when the Rector of a European university went carefully through his copy of this catalogue. Neither was it among the titles burned in the holocaust of books in Berlin at the opening of the present German régime. It is not prohibited in Italy, where it is on sale anywhere. According to reports reaching Paris several years ago, as a result of a Literary Congress in Moscow the Soviet ban on the book was lifted (after fourteen years) and a state edition was published without any remuneration to the author. It does not appear (nor does any other book by Joyce) in the list of prohibited books issued by the government of Eire under the Censorship Act of 1925 coming down to the present day and containing about sixteen hundred volumes including works by George Bernard Shaw, George Moore, Sean O'Casey, Liam O'Flaherty, H. G. Wells, Aldous Huxley, W. Somerset Maugham, Ernest Hemingway, Theodore Dreiser, and Kay Boyle. It is reported that the Japanese Home Office intervened after the publication of the Japanese translation and obliged the Tokyo publisher to bring out further copies with blanks in the place of certain passages. However, this is unverified.

Whatever winds of intolerance were blowing ever more furiously in certain European countries, there was another and more refreshing wind, hurrying old squeamishnesses and archaic taboos before it and vitalizing the cultural atmosphere of the great democracies. In the United States, in particular, this new attitude toward letters, contemporary with the New Deal toward business and workingmen, was evident. Mr. Sumner and his band of moral policemen were being put to rout. They had suffered defeat over a number of books that they sought to suppress: *Mademoiselle de Maupin,* for instance, *The Well of Loneliness,* the birth-control works of Dr. Marie Stopes, *Casanova's Homecoming* and *God's Little Acre.* This gradual shift toward a more liberal reception of works of art naturally pointed towards a reconsideration of *Ulysses* as a possible unmolested publication in the Republic. And there was a publisher in New York City adventurous enough to take the step.

He was Mr. Bennett A. Cerf, of Random House, Inc., and by the spring of 1932 he was actively engaged in clearing the way legally for Joyce's masterpiece. First of all, it was necessary for a copy of "Ulysses" to be imported into the United States without any concealment, for that copy to be seized by government officials and for a test case to be brought in the United States District Court. All this was done. The firm of Messrs. Greenbaum, Wolff and Ernst was retained by the claimant to fight for a decree dismissing the libel and the case passed through those various legal steps that led to a judge's opinion. This opinion was rendered on December 6, 1933, by the Honourable John M. Woolsey and it freed *Ulysses* for unmolested publication in the United States.

It is impossible to overestimate the importance of this opinion. Mr. Morris L. Ernst, who fought with his usual sagacity and determination for the liberation of the book, set forth the reasons for this importance in a brief foreword to the American edition. In part, he declared:

The *Ulysses* case marks a turning point. It is a body-blow for the censors. The necessity for hypocrisy and circumlocution in literature has been eliminated. Writers need no longer seek refuge in euphemisms. They may now describe basic human functions without fear of the law.

The *Ulysses* case has a three-fold significance. The definition and criteria of obscenity have long vexed us. Judge Woolsey has given us a formula which is lucid, rational and practical. In doing so he has not only charted a labyrinthine branch of the law, but has written an opinion which raises him to the level of former Supreme Court Justice Oliver Wendell Holmes as a master of juridical prose. His service to the cause of free letters has been of no less moment. But perhaps his greatest service has been to the community. The precedent he has established will do much to rescue the mental pabulum of the public from the censors who have striven to convert it into treacle, and will help to make it the strong, provocative fare it ought to be.

Certainly this monumental decision deserves to be preserved here in this biographical chapter of *Ulysses.*

UNITED STATES DISTRICT COURT
Southern District of New York

| |
|---|
| United States of America<br>*Libelant*<br><br>v.<br><br>One Book called "Ulysses"<br>Random House, Inc.,<br>*Claimant* |

OPINION

A. 110-59

*On cross motions for a decree in a libel of confiscation, supplemented by a stipulation—hereinafter described—brought by the United States against the book "Ulysses" by James Joyce, under Section 305 of the Tariff Act of 1930, Title 19 United States Code, Section 1305, on the ground that the book is obscene within the meaning of that Section, and, hence, is not importable into the United States, but is subject to seizure, forfeiture and confiscation and destruction.*

United States Attorney—by Samuel C. Coleman, Esq., and Nicholas Atlas, Esq., of counsel—for the United States, in support of motion for a decree of forfeiture, and in opposition to motion for a decree dismissing the libel.

Messrs. Greenbaum, Wolff & Ernst,—by Morris L. Ernst, Esq., and Alexander Lindey, Esq., of counsel—attorneys for claimant Random House, Inc., in support of motion for a dceree dismissing the libel, and in opposition to motion for a decree of forfeiture.

WOOLSEY, J:

The motion for a decree dismissing the libel herein is granted, and, consequently, of course, the Government's motion for a decree of forfeiture and destruction is denied.

Accordingly a decree dismissing the libel without costs may be entered herein.

I. The practice followed in this case is in accordance with the suggestion made by me in the case of *United States v. One Book Entitled "Contraception,"* 51 F. (2d) 525, and is as follows:

After issue was joined by the filing of the claimant's answer to the libel for forfeiture against "Ulysses," a stipulation was made between the United States Attorney's office and the attorneys for the claimant providing:

1. That the book "Ulysses" should be deemed to have been annexed to and to have become part of the libel just as if it had been incorporated in its entirety therein.

2. That the parties waived their right to a trial by jury.

3. That each party agreed to move for decree in its favor.

4. That on such cross motions the Court might decide all the questions of law and fact involved and render a general finding thereon.

5. That on the decision of such motions the decree of the Court might be entered as if it were a decree after trial.

It seems to me that a procedure of this kind is highly appropriate in libels for the confiscation of books such as this. It is an especially advantageous procedure in the instant case because on account of the length of "Ulysses" and the difficulty of reading it, a jury trial would have been an extremely unsatisfactory, if not an almost impossible, method of dealing with it.

II. I have read "Ulysses" once in its entirety and I have read those passages of which the Government particularly complains several times. In fact, for many weeks, my spare time has been devoted to the consideration of the decision which my duty would require me to make in this matter.

"Ulysses" is not an easy book to read or to understand. But there has been much written about it, and in order properly to approach the consideration of it it is advisable to read a number of other books which have now become its satellites. The study of "Ulysses" is, therefore, a heavy task.

III. The reputation of "Ulysses" in the literary world, however, warranted my taking such time as was necessary to enable me to satisfy myself as to the intent with which the book was written, for, of course, in any case where a book is claimed to be obscene it must first be determined, whether the intent with which it was written was what is called, according to the usual phrase, pornographic,—that is, written for the purpose of exploiting obscenity.

If the conclusion is that the book is pornographic that is the end of the inquiry and forfeiture must follow.

But in "Ulysses," in spite of its unusual frankness, I do not detect anywhere the leer of the sensualist. I hold, therefore, that it is not pornographic.

IV. In writing "Ulysses," Joyce sought to make a serious experiment in a new, if not wholly novel, literary genre. He takes persons of the lower middle class living in Dublin in 1904 and seeks not only to describe what they did on a certain day early in June of that year as they went about the City bent on their usual occupations, but also to tell what many of them thought about the while.

Joyce has attempted—it seems to me, with astonishing success—to show how the screen of consciousness with its ever-shifting kaleidoscopic impressions carries, as it were on a plastic palimpsest, not only what is in the focus of each man's observation of the actual things about him, but also in a penumbral zone residua of past impressions, some recent and some drawn up by association from the domain of the subconscious. He shows how each of these impressions affects the life and behavior of the character which he is describing.

What he seeks to get is not unlike the result of a double or, if that is possible, a multiple exposure on a cinema film which would give a clear foreground with a background visible but somewhat blurred and out of focus in varying degrees.

To convey by words an effect which obviously lends itself more appropriately to a graphic technique, accounts, it seems to me, for much of the obscurity which meets a reader of "Ulysses." And it also explains another aspect of the book, which I have further to consider, namely, Joyce's sincerity and his honest effort to show exactly how the minds of his characters operate.

If Joyce did not attempt to be honest in developing the technique which he has adopted in "Ulysses" the result would be psychologically misleading and thus unfaithful to his chosen technique. Such an attitude would be artistically inexcusable.

It is because Joyce has been loyal to his technique and has not funked its necessary implications, but has honestly attempted to tell fully what his characters think about, that he has been the subject of so many attacks and that his purpose has been so often misunderstood and misrepresented. For his attempt sincerely and honestly to realize his objective has required him incidentally to use certain words which are generally considered dirty words and has led at times to what many think is a too poignant preoccupation with sex in the thoughts of his characters.

The words which are criticized as dirty are old Saxon words known to almost all men and, I venture, to many women, and are such words as would be naturally and habitually used, I believe, by the types of folk whose life, physical and mental, Joyce is seeking to describe. In respect of the recurrent emergence of the theme of sex in the minds of his characters, it must always be remembered that his locale was Celtic and his season Spring.

Whether or not one enjoys such a technique as Joyce uses is a matter of taste on which disagreement or argument is futile, but to subject that technique to the standards of some other technique seems to me to be little short of absurd.

Accordingly, I hold that "Ulysses" is a sincere and honest book and I think that the criticisms of it are entirely disposed of by its rationale.

V. Furthermore, "Ulysses" is an amazing *tour de force* when one considers the success which has been in the main achieved with such a difficult objective as Joyce set for himself. As I have stated, "Ulysses" is not an easy book to read. It is brilliant and dull, intelligible and obscure by turns. In many places it seems to me to be disgusting, but although it contains, as I have mentioned above, many words usually considered dirty, I have not found anything that I consider to be dirt for dirt's sake. Each word of the book contributes like a bit of mosaic to the detail of the picture which Joyce is seeking to construct for his readers.

If one does not wish to associate with such folk as Joyce describes, that is one's own choice. In order to avoid indirect contact with them one may not wish to read "Ulysses"; that is quite understandable. But when such a real artist in words, as Joyce undoubtedly is, seeks to draw a true picture of the lower middle class in a European city, ought it to be impossible for the American public legally to see that picture?

To answer this question it is not sufficient merely to find, as I have found above, that Joyce did not write "Ulysses" with what is commonly called pornographic intent, I must endeavor to apply a more objective standard to his book in order to determine its effect in the result, irrespective of the intent with which it was written.

VI. The statute under which the libel is filed only denounces, in so far as we are here concerned, the importation into the United States from any foreign country of "any obscene book." Section 305 of the Tariff Act of 1930, Title 19 United States Code, Section 1305. It does not marshal against books the spectrum of condemnatory adjectives found, commonly, in laws dealing with matters of this kind. I am, therefore, only required to determine whether "Ulysses" is obscene within the legal definition of that word.

The meaning of the word "obscene" as legally defined by the Courts is: tending to stir the sex impulses or to lead to sexually impure and lustful thoughts. *Dunlop* v. *United States,* 165 U. S. 486, 501; *United States* v. *One Book Entitled "Married Love,"* 48 F. (2d) 821, 824; *United States v. One Book Entitled "Contraception,"* 51 F. (2d) 525, 528; and compare *Dysart v. United States,* 272 U. S. 655, 657; *Swearingen v. United States,* 161 U. S. 446, 450; *United States v. Dennett,* 39 F. (2d) 564, 568 (C.C.A.2); *People v. Wendling,* 258 N. Y. 451, 453.

Whether a particular book would tend to excite such impulses and thoughts must be tested by the Court's opinion as to its effect on a person with average sex instincts—what the French would call *l'homme moyen sensuel*—who plays, in this branch of legal inquiry, the same role of hypothetical reagent as does the "reasonable man" in the law of torts and the "man learned in the art" on questions of invention in patent law.

The risk involved in the use of such a reagent arises from the inherent tendency of the trier of facts, however fair he may intend to be, to make his reagent too much subservient to his own idiosyncrasies. Here, I have attempted to avoid this, if possible, and to make my reagent herein more objective than he might otherwise be, by adopting the following course:

After I had made my decision in regard to the aspect of "Ulysses," now under consideration, I checked my impressions with two friends of mine who in my opinion answered to the above stated requirement for my reagent.

These literary assessors—as I might properly describe them—were called on separately, and neither knew that I was consulting the other. They are men whose opinion on literature and on life I value most highly. They had both read "Ulysses," and, of course, were wholly unconnected with this cause.

Without letting either of my assessors know what my decision was, I gave to each of them the legal definition of obscene and asked each whether in his opinion "Ulysses" was obscene within that definition.

I was interested to find that they both agreed with my opinion: that reading "Ulysses" in its entirety, as a book must be read on such a test as this, did not tend to excite sexual impulses or lustful thoughts but that its net effect on them was only that of a somewhat tragic and very powerful commentary on the inner lives of men and women.

It is only with the normal person that the law is concerned. Such a test as I have described, therefore, is the only proper test of obscenity in the case of a book like "Ulysses" which is a sincere and serious attempt to devise a new literary method for the observation and description of mankind.

I am quite aware that owing to some of its scenes "Ulysses" is a rather strong draught to ask some sensitive, though normal, persons to take. But my considered opinion, after long reflection, is that whilst in many places the effect of "Ulysses" on the reader undoubtedly is somewhat emetic, no where does it tend to be an aphrodisiac.

"Ulysses" may, therefore, be admitted into the United States.

*December* 6, 1933

*John M Woolsey*
United States District Judge

Naturally, the forces that were attempting to maintain the suppression of the book did not admit defeat with this great decision. There was another legal body to which they might have recourse and to it they went. There were proceedings before the Court of Appeals, three judges presiding, and though the opposing elements fought with great vigour and acrimony they failed to have Judge Woolsey's decision reversed. The freedom of Joyce's book was maintained.

*Ulysses,* then, under the imprint of Random House, Inc., appeared in February 1934, and its reception by the public was nothing less than sensational. Some thirty-five thousand copies were gobbled up by American readers and a vast bulk of commentary, filling columns and pages, crowded newspapers and magazines. Thus twelve years after its first appearance the book had a second birth, so to speak, and amply proved its lasting vitality and enduring merit. The sales continued and when these pages were written they had approached the fifty thousand mark. One may now glance back at Dr. Joseph Collins's prophecy with an ironic smile. The reasons for the durability of *Ulysses* are only too evident (to the intelligent and impartial reader) and, therefore, it is unnecessary to repeat what has already been indicated in this chapter regarding the virtues of the book. It can all be summed up in the statement: No veritable classic can ever be suppressed.

The success of the Random House, Inc., printing of *Ulysses* aroused the interest of the publishers of fine editions and the next year (November 1935) the Limited Editions Club brought out a beautifully-conceived and numbered printing of the book. This volume, designed by George Macy and printed at the Printing Office of the Limited Editions Club, Westport, Connecticut, was illustrated with hand-printed etchings by Henri Matisse and prefaced with an Introduction by Stuart Gilbert. It was a large book (nine and one-half by eleven and one-half inches) printed in 12-point and 14-point Scotch linotype on toned Worthy rag paper and bound in brown Bancroft buckram with a design stamped and embossed, in bas-relief, in gold. At last *Ulysses,* no longer a furtive wanderer over the face of the globe, was appearing in his proper habiliments as he, a royal personage, deserved to appear. One might say that the storm-tossed traveller had reached Ithaca and home.

And now, with the victory in the United States to show the way, the tide of fortune turned in England. Perhaps it was due to the changed social atmosphere occasioned by a new reign; perhaps again, the Moral British Printer was being subtly transformed by the liberalistic currents of thought and action of the day. Anyway, during 1936 the firm of John Lane: The Bodley Head issued a limited edition of *Ulysses.* One thousand numbered copies (one hundred on mould-made paper, bound in calf vellum and signed by the author, and nine hundred unsigned on Japan vellum paper and bound in linen buckram) made up this printing. The next year (1937) the same firm issued what might be called the first authorized English trade edition. It was a photo-offset reproduction, reduced in size, of the limited edition. A cheaper edition, priced at 12/6, is announced for publication in London this year (1940).

And so this biography of a book (perhaps a helter-skelter one) comes to a victorious conclusion. Composed in three countries, pirated, suppressed, violently attacked and defamed, welcomed first in France and then doggedly winning its uncompromising way in the English-speaking countries, it furnishes as fascinating a history as any book ever written. One wonders what Mr. Sisley Huddleston now thinks of his statement: "I confess that I cannot see how the work upon which Mr. Joyce spent seven strenuous years, years of wrestling and of agony, can ever be given to the public."

# Eleven

A ND now, returning to 1922, the personal story of Joyce must
be resumed.

The fame of *Ulysses,* spreading so rapidly about the
world, naturally concentred attention on the author, and while
Joyce, unlike Byron, did not wake up one morning to find himself
suddenly famous (he was already that in the circles that counted)
he did discover himself to be a focal point of enlarged and intent
interest. Friends he had never dreamt existed sprang up on all
sides and so did malicious rumour-mongers who disseminated libellous accounts of his past that were based on misinformation and pure
fabrication. What he did and what he had to say became "news."
The professional lion-hunters were out to bag him and it was only
by his supreme indifference to them that he preserved himself intact.
He had been through too rigorous a mill to be tempted by the
honey that was proffered him. He continued, as he had done all
his life, to refuse to give interviews or special statements; indeed,
if anything, he became even more chary of expressing opinions on
his contemporaries. Though he might, and did, have definite opinions on most subjects of interest of the day, he preferred to keep
them to himself or share them with a few intimate friends. In a
phrase, he walked alone as he had always walked alone and he
could not help it if a crowd was following him. Indeed, before
the year was out he was so far ahead of the crowd that it ceased
to exist for him.

There is no doubt but that he accepted his just celebrity with
some equanimity, for that, after all, was one of the legitimate rewards
of the successful artist; but he never sought the spotlight or played
histrionically for acclaim as did so many of the modern writers of
his time. Figuratively speaking, he never put rings in his ears. Of
course, those (mostly Dubliners) whose envy and spite because of
his escape from the "Seventh City in Christendom" aroused a ran-

corous detestation of him in their lesser minds sought to prove that this was not so, that he was, in fact, a "joke," and as evidence of this they settled on his seriousness of demeanour. That, to them, was a "preposterous pose." Just how they expected him to act is not quite plain. As a matter of fact, his very existence was a "preposterous pose" to them.

Joyce ignored these attacks as he now ignored all attacks against him, although privately he was irritated by the wanton lengths to which these vilifiers went. With his usual gravity he encountered a host of new acquaintances and some of them, because of their evident sincerity, he tacitly accepted into his small circle of friends. Some strange birds lighted on his doorstep. The Dail Eireann Minister of Publicity was one of them. This gentleman asked him if he intended to return to Ireland at present and Joyce, recalling that "hospitable bog," dryly answered, "Not for the present." Then there was Rita Rasi. This prince, a son of the King of Cambodia, was living in Paris and, desiring to separate himself from the Indo-Chinese reigning house and being vastly attracted to Joyce's book, changed his name to René-Ulysse. He used to send his visiting card under his new style to his adopted literary godfather on the first day of every Annamite year. Joyce and his wife later attended one of these festivities where they met this unusual and apparently very-contented admirer. At last accounts, René-Ulysse was practising in Normandy as a French physician. His cousin, Prince Norrindett-Norrodun, also an admirer of Joyce and a fellow traveller with the writer into the French provinces to hear John Sullivan, the famous Irish tenor, sing in operas seldom heard in Paris,[1] is now in Cambodia where he apparently acts as secretary to his uncle, the present king.

Joyce attended a large number of lunches and dinners during this period of great excitement over *Ulysses*. For instance, he was entertained at lunch by the British and Irish press of Paris, Admiral Sir Edward Heaton-Ellis being in the chair. The writer's straight spare form became familiar to scores of people as he passed slowly along the Rue de l'Odéon on his way to Shakespeare and Company,

[1] The operas that Joyce heard with this Cambodian prince were Halévy's *La Juive,* Reyer's *Sigurd,* and Verdi's *Il Trovatore.*

whose windows blossomed with his books and photographs, or sat with a few friends in one of his favourite restaurants, the Café de la Paix (generally after a visit to the Opéra) or Chez Francis on the Place de l'Alma or Les Trianons opposite the Gare Montparnasse (this eating-place, a centre of regional cooking and a great haunt of his for many years) or Ferrari's Italian restaurant on the Avenue Rapp where the polenta was so good.

But in certain milieus (the popular stamping grounds of many an "emancipated" modernist) he was never seen or seen only as a passing figure. Montmartre, the Butte, terrain of Mimi Pinson, with all its razzle-dazzle of lights and dancings, was one of them and another was the clot of crowded cafés about the intersection of the Boulevard Raspail and the Boulevard Montparnasse where London clerks and Kokomo salesmen and American temporary expatriates gathered to diminish the stocks of Pernod in France. Joyce was never a *flâneur* in any sense of the word, no loiterer on the terraces of neon-lighted cafés. He maintained rigorously his self-imposed régime of never drinking alcoholic beverages during the day. It was only when night fell sprawling on the roofs of Paris and the late dinner hour was at hand that his thoughts (released from the day's discipline of labour) turned to the pleasant bottle or carafe of white wine (he never drank red) that would crown the long hours of literary creation. He was quiet, self-contained, always a little formal in manner, willing to listen while he smoked his cigarettes (*jaunes*) and small cigars (*Voltigeurs*) or lifted in a beringed hand (the one exotic touch about him) his goblet of Riesling or Swiss Neufchâtel. It was only very late in the evening and in the company of extremely close friends that his wit, dry or ironic, came into play and a joyous desire to dance agitated him. Then the afflicted eyes would brighten behind the thick-lensed glasses while a Bacchic fervour would exude from him and enliven the atmosphere.

However, if life seemed to be opening auspiciously before him, Fate, in the form of those same afflicted eyes, almost immediately darkened the horizons of his future. In this year (1922) his left eye suffered a severe attack of glaucoma (it will be remembered that in 1918 it was the right eye that so suffered) and he was treated by Dr. Morax. The attack did not persist but it was an ominous presage of what pathological complications might be expected in the years to come unless brave and desperate efforts were made to avert them. The power of his vision (so important to a writer) was steadily weakening and an actual fear of complete blindness in the near or far future constantly tortured his mind. During the next eight years he was never wholly free from this terrible presentiment and it may be as well to set down here (as a gloomy backdrop to all his other activities) a chronological survey of the drastic steps he took to preserve his dwindling eyesight. Ezra Pound had insisted more than once that a major cause of Joyce's eye troubles was the condition of his teeth. He advised that they be extracted. Therefore, in 1923, the writer, willing to follow any advice that sounded sensible, went to a Parisian dentist and suffered the agony of having most of his teeth drawn out. A number of them turned out to be abscessed. One good result of this multiple operation was the cessation of the attacks of iritis that had annually tortured Joyce for eighteen years. However, the mass-extraction of teeth did nothing to ameliorate the condition of the cataracts that now clouded both eyes. These, especially the soft one on the left eye, presented a grave problem and during the next four years (1923 to 1926) Joyce underwent no less than seven operations on this left eye. The crystalline lens was successfully removed but the exudates following the operations organized themselves in such a way as to result in almost total occlusion of vision in that eye. It was during these years, and, indeed, at irregular intervals for a number of years thereafter, that casual visitors to the restaurants that Joyce frequented observed with interest and much speculation the grave and courtly gentleman with the black triangular patch of cloth completely concealing one eye.

There are many forms of bravery and though Joyce, with a disarming modesty, professes to have no particular physical courage and to fear thunder, dogs and the riotous ocean waters as one fears the devil, the history of his patient courage (the courage of a highly-sensitive man) under the knives of the eye surgeons during these years and the years that followed assuredly proves that he possessed a major form of bravery that should arouse the sincerest admiration. To lie back helplessly and watch the little glittering scalpel descending towards one's eyes not once but ten times through the years and to realize the consequences hanging upon that sliver of steel and still to preserve one's equanimity requires a particular sort of courage that transcends the necessary acquiescence in the trials that must be undergone. The virtues of bravery, after all, are measured by the degree that one suffers in subduing instinctive fear.

In 1925 the right eye began to trouble Joyce again (episcleritis) and in 1926 a severe attack of conjunctivitis materially lowered the power of vision in it. The next year, 1929, this same right eye was again weakened by an attack of blepharitis. We can well imagine Joyce's state of mind by this time. He had tried everything that oculists had devised or suggested, operations, salicylate, scopolamine, atropine, leeches, iodic blood cures and vapor baths and still the pathological condition of his eyes grew steadily worse. A host of eye specialists had treated him (Weber, Ziedler, Haab *fils*, Marina, Gamper and Stehli in Zurich; Morax, Collinson, Hartman and Borsch in Paris; Tolde in Salzburg; Heesch in Munich; Colin in Nice; Brewster, Stewart and James in London) and some of them had alleviated his sufferings or arrested for a period the increasing fogginess of his vision but none of them could boast that he had put a definite stop to it. It was during the next year (1930) that Joyce, through a former language student of his in Zurich, the late Georges Borach, finally met and became a patient of the doctor who was to do more for him than all the others put together. He was Professor Alfred Vogt of Zurich, one of the great eye doctors of the world.

On May 15, 1930, Professor Vogt performed a ninth operation for tertiary cataract on Joyce's left eye. The growth was cut through horizontally but the proposed operation could not be completed as the vitreous body, most of which seemed to have been lost during the last two operations by Dr. Borsch, threatened to collapse completely by emergence or during the acute attack of scopolamine poisoning which immediately followed. The dangers attendant on this ninth operation were successfully avoided as was an excessive hæmorrhage. Ten days after the operation an attack of mechanical iritis, owing to the presence of blood, occurred but this lasted only ten hours and did not leave any exudate. A week later leeches were applied which successfully removed all the blood from the anterior chamber of the eye. On June third it became possible to make a microscopic examination and this revealed that the incision made, contrary to what happened in other operations, had remained open and unclogged by exudate but that blood had entered into the vitreous body, which a much-operated eye would take some months to eliminate. It also revealed that at the last operation the back wall of the capsule of the lens had not been removed, possibly because its removal was too difficult, and that in the period between the eighth and ninth operations (four and a half years) it had been gradually overclouded so that it was now in a condition of almost secondary cataract, thereby occluding practical sight. The right eye did not suffer appreciably in consequence of this operation on the left eye but it presented a complicated cataract.

Professor Vogt advised two more operations, for he was convinced from his careful examination that Joyce's eyes could be saved. The most favourable factor, according to him and previous medical opinions, was the fact that the optic nerve and the periphery of the retina in both eyes functioned perfectly normally and that the macula, also, was normal. Professor Vogt believed, too, and time proved him to be right, that the ninth operation he had performed would produce some amelioration of vision in the left eye, which, before, had a seeing power of 1/800 at 1/1000. On the other hand, he noted that the seeing power of the right eye (estimated some months before at 1/30) was slowly diminishing as the cataract developed. His conclusions were that, if two further operations were made with special instruments and when the eye was in a non-glaucomatous condition, there was every hope of ultimately obtaining a fair measure of clear and practical vision.

Extensive attention has been paid to this operation by Professor Vogt and, of course, at the expense of the others, for two reasons. The first is because it was without doubt the most important operation that Joyce underwent and the second because of the difficulties over which Professor Vogt triumphed.[1] Today, Joyce, ten operations behind him, continues his medical treatments and undergoes many examinations. He has passed through months when he could hardly see his hand before his face and has finally reached a time when his eyesight seems to have achieved a stationary degree of vision. It is poor vision (as vision goes) but it suffices to permit him to stroll about Paris without continually depending on the arm of his companion. He can read with the aid of an enlarging glass; he can attend the theatre, the opera and the cinema; and he can write —although very slowly. This, then, is the painful and often embarrassing predicament through which the latter years of Joyce's life have marched and it should always be kept in mind when we consider his personality or his achievements. It is impossible for him to react to life with the spontaneous unconcern of the man with normal eyesight who barely has to look before he leaps. Joyce must pick his way carefully, making sure that it is on stable ground that he plants his foot, and exert other senses to recompense himself for the partial failure of one. The critic would do well to consider this in any exhaustive attempt to analyse the work of Joyce.

And now to return to 1922 again and pick up the thread of the writer's activities. A number of omniscient scribblers and prophets had confidently asserted that with *Ulysses* Joyce had reached the end of his journey through creative literature, that, in fact, he could advance no further in an æsthetic sense and was in a cul-de-sac. In other words, he had pushed his daring conception of letters as far as it was possible to go and that nothing lay beyond except arbitrary incoherence and wilful mystification. But all of them were wrong. Even his friends who supposed that he would rest for several years from writing were wrong. In the early summer of 1922, *Ulysses* being launched and started on its eventful history, Joyce went to England for a vacation. He passed through London (which he had

---

[1] After performing this difficult operation, which no oculists in London and Paris would undertake, Professor Vogt declined to accept any fee whatsoever. When Giorgio Joyce asked him what his fee was he said he was well-repaid if he had been able to restore a "great literary talent to the world" and would accept nothing but a copy of *Ulysses* inscribed for his daughter, now Mrs. Vogt-Wiederkehr. The same generosity was evinced a year later when the writer of this book, accompanied by Joyce, had his eyes examined by Professor Vogt. The great specialist refused any fee from the friend of the great writer.

not seen for ten years) and eventually settled in Bognor in Sussex. There, while wandering about the pleasant countryside and hearing the Sussex dialect and observing the recurring undulations and sweep of the grassy downs, the conception of a new work, a work that would far outdistance even *Ulysses* in unique plan and substance, flowered in his mind. Who would attempt to say from what particular seed it flowered? Or from how many? These are the mysteries of creation and any discussion of them is always nine parts assumption. Certainly, one of the seeds had been planted in Joyce's conscious and subconscious selves as far back as the Triestine days. Then he had read and digested the work of the Neapolitan, Giambattista Vico (memories of the Vico Road in Dalkey!), especially the treatise on the philosophy of history called the *Scienza Nuova*. He had read, also, as far back as his college days the metaphysical writings of Giordano Bruno of Nola (the 'Nolan' of "The Day of the Rabblement") who had influenced Vico to some degree. From the theories of these two men, then, we may say that certain (and vastly important) aspects of Joyce's new conception had their genesis.

In his treatise Vico had put forward a theory of history in which he contended that human societies originate, develop and reach their end according to fixed laws or rotation, moving, or, rather, rotating in similar cycles. Further, this theory was to be deduced not from a review of chronologically-arranged historical events (inferring them to be unconnected phenomena) but from the lives, actual or legendary, of race heroes, that is, personalities that become in themselves mass-personalities; for what, after all, is the race hero but the visible symbol of the heroic consciousness of the race? Thus, Cæsar, Charlemagne, Napoleon and Wellington become One in the mystic interpretation that dismisses chronology and accepts and views history as a Whole, as a vast fluctuating ocean that is always there but continually shifted by great tides.

Vico, too, had his precise conception of the beginnings of human history, the thunderclap that raised primitive Man's eyes to the heavens, taught him fear and drove him into caves where the idea of the Family began. (That thunderclap—"bababadalgharaghtakamminarronnkonnbronntonnerronntuonnthunntrovarrhounawnskawntoohoohoordenenthurnuk!"—is on the first page of *Finnegans*

*Wake*.[1]) The Thunder created Religion (a result of fear); Religion created Society; Society developed into Monarchy (a despotism); Monarchy becomes the Feudal Idea; the Feudal Idea turns into Democracy; Democracy changes to Anarchy; Anarchy is corrected by heroic will (the strong mass-man) into Monarchy again; then comes interdestruction, the dispersal of the Nations and the Phœnix of Society rising from the ashes. This is a hasty and crude indication of Vico's theory and it leaves out much that is pertinent in the curious philosopher-scientist's conception of the development of the human race, for example, his treatments of Language, Poetry and Myth. Enough, however, has been set down here to give a vague idea of one mighty seed from which Joyce's new work sprang and flowered.

The revolutionary conception had for its *modus operandi* a

[1] The title, of course, is taken from the old Irish comic song, "Finnegan's Wake." There are several versions of this curious effort by an unknown author but here is the one that seems to be the more widely known.

### Finnegan's Wake

> Tim Finnegan lived in Walker Street,
> An Irish gintleman, mighty odd.
> He'd a bit of a brogue, so neat and sweet,
> And to rise in the world Tim carried a hod.
> But Tim had a sort of tippling way;
> With a love of liquor Tim was born,
> And, to help him through his work each day,
> Took a drop of the creature every morn.

Chorus:

> Whack. Hurroo. Now dance to your partners,
> Welt the flure, your trotters shake;
> Isn't it all the truth I've told ye,
> Lots of fun at Finnegan's wake?

> One morning Tim was rather full,
> His head felt heavy and it made him shake.
> He fell from the ladder and broke his skull,
> So they carried him home, his corpse to wake.
> They rolled him up in a nice clean sheet
> And laid him out upon the bed,
> With fourteen candles round his feet
> And a bushel of praties round his head.

Cho.: as before.

> His friends assembled at his wake,
> Missus Finnegan called out for lunch;
> And first they laid in tay and cakes,
> Then pipes and tobaccy and whisky punch.　[Cont. on p. 334]

merging of time and space and race and characters. It would be written in a language that would telescope many meanings into single words by newly-minting those words from the vast slag-heaps of language. An attempt would be made to break the bounds of formal speech and achieve that plane where the word, no longer a much-handled and partially-defaced token to arouse in the reader's mind an approximation of the thing meant, became the thing meant itself. It would be the sort of language that must be seen and heard as well as read. It would sparkle and flow like a river and it would sink heavily into the grey fogs of sleep. A unity that out-Aristotled Aristotle's unities, a unity, as it were, that unified all time, all history and all language, would control and shape the new work. It would have the gigantic dimensions of a Myth and yet it would be contained within the fleeting instants of a dream. It would be a

Miss Biddy O'Neil began to cry:
"Such a purty corpse did yez ever see.
Arrah, Tim mavourneen, and why did ye lave me?"
"Hold your gob," sez Judy Magee.

Cho.: as before.

Then Peggy O'Connor took up the job.
"Arrah, Biddy," sez she, "ye're wrong, in sure."
But Judy gave her a belt in the gob,
And left her sprawling on the flure.
Each side in war did soon engage;
'Twas woman to woman and man to man;
Shillelah law was all the rage
And a bloody ruction soon began.

Cho.: as before.

Micky Malony raised his head,
When a gallon of whisky flew at him;
It missed him, and, hopping on the bed,
The liquor scattered over Tim.
"Och, he revives. See how he raises."
And Timothy, jumping from the bed,
Cried, while he lathered round like blazes,
"Bad luck to your sowls. D'ye think I'm dead?"

Chorus:

Whack. Hurroo. Now dance to your partners,
Welt the flure, your trotters shake;
Isn't it all the truth I've told ye,
Lots of fun at Finnegan's wake?

The rambunctious Finnegan is introduced into Joyce's *Finnegans Wake* as early as page two.

Myth of sleeping life as *Ulysses* had been a Myth of waking life. In this way would the writer give heed to his dæmon and reach the logical journey's end of his difficult wayfaring.

Naturally the new work would be Irish in texture although at the same time its warp and woof would imprison the universal. Dublin would be all cities, the Anna Liffey all rivers and Howth all mountains. As the idea possessed Joyce he began to see it as a work that fell into various parts, each one of them loosely based on an aspect of Vico's theory leavened with the metaphysics of Bruno. Part one would be curdling with the intertwining shadows and phantoms of the past and so corresponding to the Neapolitan's first institution of Religion or Birth; part two, the love games of the children, Marriage or Maturity; part three, the four levels of sleep, Burial or Corruption; and part four, the beginning of the day, Vico's Providence. Through these parts would move figures of mythic proportions, being men and women and yet being more than men and women in that they would be all men and women. Names for these personages slipt suddenly into the creator's mind: Earwicker, an old Sussex name, for the composite protagonist who would move on several levels through the cloudy substance of the work, Humphrey Chimpden Earwicker, no less, whose initials adumbrated Here Comes Everybody; Anna Livia for the river that was all rivers, the Liffey, the dancing babbling 'deloothering' essence of fecundity; Jute and Mutt for protozoic godlike figures watching sluggishly and commenting with heavy thick tongues over time's divagations; Taff and Butt and Chuffy and Glugger and Kersse and Matt Gregory and Marcus Lyons and Luke Tarpey and Johnny MacDougall (Matthew, Mark, Luke and John or the Four Waves or the Four Parts of Ireland) and Shaun the impudent and his brother Shem, a minor host, in fact, whose entities enlarged or diminished, took on new shapes and faces and conducted themselves like the insubstantial yet vivid figures in a dream.[1]

Joyce, full to bursting with his new project, did not actually begin to put down notes and stray phrases for the work until the autumn when he was enjoying the warm skies and Mediterranean sunsets at Nice. Then he began to write again. It is interesting to

[1] It must be emphasized again that in this biographical presentation of James Joyce no attempt will be made to analyse, criticize or exhaustively treat his books. That should be the subject matter for another volume and another writer.

note that he had the title for the book in mind at this time and confided it to his wife. She, a miracle among women, kept the title to herself for seventeen years although many a sly and curious friend attempted to trap her into revealing it. At this time, too, a further word should be added about Nora Joyce. Her mind and her attitude towards life seem to have been essentially practical, in other words, a direct reverse of her husband's mind and attitude towards life. This was a lucky state of affairs for Joyce, perhaps the most impractical man in the world, because it gave a stabilizing influence to the household. Mrs. Joyce was assiduous in guarding her husband from the many hangers-on and victimizers of genius who sought for anything they could get out of the writer and she transformed his home into a place were he could work in peace. If she became impatient at times before situations that seemed to her far from healthy for her husband it was but natural and a testimony to her concern for his welfare. On the whole, her brightness of disposition and roguish Irish humour added a delightful touch to the Joyce household. At this time, too, Giorgio, now a stalwart youth of seventeen with promise of an extraordinarily fine singing voice, and Lucia, in her fifteenth year, a dark vividly-coloured girl with marked artistic inclinations, became personalities in their own right and kindled a new spirit of things beneath the Joyce roof.

Returned from Nice, the writer, intent on his new project, plunged anew into a mingled life of labour and pleasure, often interrupted, alas, by the deplorable condition of his eyes. He continued to be sought' by admirers, fellow writers and mere curiosity hounds but his reserved demeanour kept them all fairly at bay. Joyce was invariably courteous, treating with the same impartial politeness the walrus-moustached chauffeur of his taxicab and Mr. Arnold Bennett or Sir Plutus Porter. He has been observed in one day discussing music with a great tenor of the Paris Opéra and reciting Verlaine to an admiring cab-driver. It was this Joyce, the well-seasoned Joyce, so to speak, that may be said to have reached the end of his long odyssey. With the publication of *Ulysses* and the conception of and first labours at the new work to follow (to be called for so long *Work in Progress* [1]) he had climbed to

---

[1] This provisional title was given to it by the late Ford Madox Ford who published the first fragment of it. He was thus the book's godfather. Joyce, in turn, is the godfather to one of Ford Madox Ford's daughters.

that point of time where fame, freedom from material worries and solid achievement presumably combined to bring an end to the personal and more obvious drama of his wanderings.

It is, therefore, more simple to bulk the years that followed 1922 and treat them as a whole, noting the high lights, of course, and keeping in mind always the two running accompaniments of the vexatious and finally triumphant history of *Ulysses* and the sombre progression of the author's afflicted eyes. Both these stories have been set forth. They are revelatory of the hardships that beset even the most successful writer. Indeed, if the outward drama (always the most obvious) of travel and struggle and uncertainty be ended there still exists an inward struggle that never ends and will never end as long as the artist (in these tempestuous days a stranger in a strange land) pursues his solitary road through time. Joyce, always the artist, had found this out long ago and he continued to encounter the constant difficulties and face them with a *sang-froid* that was as pertinacious and determined as his will to express himself as his dæmon directed. No matter what compromising advice might be offered him, no matter what he might hear from Dublin, no matter what the economic scene might suggest as the safer way for him to go, he would not surrender in any way. The path that he had chosen in 1904 was still the path that he would follow to the end. It was this ironlike indomitability that made him what he was, an Irish writer unlike all other Irish writers. As a matter of fact, he belonged no longer to Ireland except in so far as his work was permeated with the Irish scene. Like Flaubert and Dostoevsky and Proust, he belonged to the international world of letters where national boundaries mean nothing at all.

II

Joyce had been a migratory bird about the various quarters of Paris since his arrival in 1920 and it was not until 1925 that he finally lighted in a comparatively permanent nest of his own. During the five years between those dates he had removed himself, his family and his steadily swelling baggage no less than ten times: from 9, Rue de l'Université to 5, Rue de l'Assomption to 5, Boulevard Raspail to 71, Rue Cardinal-Lemoine to 9, Rue de l'Université to 26, Avenue Charles-Floquet to the Hôtel Victoria-Palace at 6,

Rue Blaise-Desgoffe to 8, Avenue Charles-Floquet to the Hôtel Victoria-Palace again and, finally, to 2, Square Robiac, a cul-de-sac off 192, Rue de Grenelle in one of the oldest and pleasantest quarters of Paris where he settled for five or six years with all his furniture, books and pictures about him. He was in the middle of history. During his walks he constantly passed great gates to cobbled courtyards where crumbling armorial bearings in dark stone spoke mutely of more spacious days. And hardly more than a pebble's toss away crouched the old cannon before the Invalides where the Emperor slept under the gilded dome. Dotting the long slowly-twisting Rue de Grenelle were typical little French shops, cobblers, zinc-bistros, *caves,* cheap restaurants, *merceries* and *épiceries* as well as imposing government buildings flying the tricolour and foreign embassies. Joyce loved this quarter of Paris. Later, to bring the record up to date (for 2, Square Robiac, after all, did not prove to be a permanency), he removed to further Paris halting places: 2, Avenue Saint-Philibert; 42, Rue Galilée; and 7, Rue Edmond-Valentin.

There were various reasons for these thirteen shifts in fifteen years. At the beginning, as we have seen, it was necessity, lack of funds and the kind relief of loaned apartments. Later it was a desire to have done with unsatisfactory furnished places and build up a home of one's own, an ambition that was first achieved at 2, Square Robiac. And, finally, contributory causes for further removals may be found in the marriage of Giorgio Joyce—which made a large apartment no longer necessary—and the extended journeys to Zurich and elsewhere for eye treatment (sometimes lasting for months) which rendered it uneconomical to carry on an empty dwelling in Paris. Joyce, it must be insisted, was never really satisfied with a temporary residence (though his frequent removals may suggest as much); he desired all the familiar things that he possessed about him and in their accustomed places and the "feel" of permanency in the atmosphere of his quarters where, sometimes tying himself up into magnificent knots, he could lounge in his easy chair and set down the notes for his work. Vagabondage of any sort (except as a travelling treat) was obnoxious to him. He is, primarily, a family man, methodical in household ways, enjoying his principal meal at noon (with which he drinks nothing stronger than tea), regular in habits, pleased with his own piano and gramophone and comfortable velvet house-jacket. This may seem paradoxical in view of his far-flung wanderings, but nevertheless it is true. No one has ever seen the real Joyce who has not seen him in the relaxed pleasantness of his own home.

Yet he enjoys travelling, his vacation sprees, the exhilarating experience of exploring new places and partaking of unfamiliar sensations of terrain and habit. During the years that followed the publication of *Ulysses* he visited about all that was worth visiting in Western Europe except Spain. The enumeration of these many places would be tiresome but a representative list may be given to emphasize Joyce's familiarity with the European world he had adopted and to illustrate his cosmopolitanism . . . and it must be remembered that this cosmopolitanism was vastly deepened by his familiarity with the various tongues of the lands he visited. He was never really a stranger anywhere. For example, then: Etretat, Fécamp, Saint-Malo, Mont-Saint-Michel, Arcachon, Le Havre, Dieppe, Strasbourg, Marseilles, Nice, Fontainebleau, Dijon, Lyon, Avignon, Basle, Zurich, Innsbruck, Salzburg, Munich, Wiesbaden, Ostend, The Hague, Amsterdam, London, Torquay, Oxford, Bristol, Llandudno, and even a trip to Denmark. Some of these visits were short in duration but all of them were remarkable for the extent to which Joyce could seize and savour the atmosphere of a place, and this, often enough, when he could barely see a half dozen steps before him. He possesses that virtue of the good traveller, the ability to adapt himself mentally to his surroundings and achieve a historical perspective of the place visited.

Through these years of frequent travel, of tragic eye troubles, of unjustified slander, of precious friendships and of shifting forces in an unstable Europe teetering like a great Humpty-Dumpty on an impossible peace treaty Joyce laboured at the book called *Work in Progress*. The Time-Spirit changed; old literary movements died and new literary movements were born; writing for the sake of one's self or one's art became *démodé* and propaganda and politics sucked up the vital forces of the majority of the younger men; still Joyce laboured—when he was able to labour—at *Work in Progress*. By the 1930's he had lived in five distinct eras of history, every one of them differing from the other. There had been the pre-Boer War period in Ireland where the shadow of Parnell had fallen long across the lintel of Time; there had been the Edwardian Era, smug and stuffy and still smelling faintly of Victorian bombazine; there had been the chaotic and monstrous years of the World War when everything, even human values and eternal verities, seemed to be in a mad state of flux; there had been the post-World War span of seasons, the dancing time of the Lost Generation, the age of jazz and reckless gestures and sudden excitements and deep disappointments; and, last of all, there was the World of the Dictators, of Stalin and Hitler and Mussolini and Franco and the War Chiefs of Japan.[1] One will look in vain to find the thumbprints of these varying stages of history on the work of Joyce. Through all these calm or satisfied or angry or turbulent years he has marched on the undeviating road of his own art, undisturbed by explosions, no matter how world-shaking, and never stepping aside at the frantic beckonings of opportunisms.

Even attack, and he has never ceased to be attacked in certain quarters, moved him not at all. He might bleakly wonder sometimes why he should be the butt of so many scurrilous onslaughts but the idea of striking back in the same poisonous manner never enters his mind. He cannot dissipate his intelligence in such a meaningless way. Even when the attacker is a man of position in the world of letters. During the Centenary Exposition of the *Revue des Deux Mondes* there was exhibited a portion of a letter signed by the late Sir Edmund Gosse. It read as follows:

17 Hanover Terrace,
Regent's Park,
N.W. 1.

June 7, 1924.

MY DEAR MONSIEUR GILLET,

I should very much regret your paying Mr. J. Joyce the compliment of an article in the "Revue des Deux Mondes." You could only expose the worthlessness and impudence of his writings, and surely it would be a mistake to give him the prominence. I have a difficulty in describing to you *in writing* the character of Mr. Joyce's notoriety. It is partly political; it is partly a perfectly cynical appeal to sheer indecency. He is, of course, not entirely without talent, but he is a literary . . .

The rest of the letter was not exposed to view. Louis Gillet, now of the *Académie Française,* luckily knew when to spice Anglo-Saxon advice with a large pinch of salt and the senseless and un-

---

[1] And now, alas, the heart-rending catastrophe of the second world war. Joyce continues to live in France, though not in Paris.

forgivable judgement of the author of "Peach and apple and apricot" bore no weight with the French writer. Monsieur Gillet continues to be one of Joyce's friendliest admirers.

During this same year when Sir Edmund Gosse was attempting to stifle the spread of the Irish writer's fame in France, Joyce attended a dinner given in honour of Valery Larbaud by Paul Morand in the Restaurant Marguery and there he met for the first time the then city editor of the Paris edition of the Chicago *Tribune*. It was an opportune encounter both for the newspaperman, Eugene Jolas, and for Joyce. Jolas, a Lorrainer by birth although educated in the United States, was a young man of distinctly literary inclinations, modernistic in theories and intensely concerned with the experimental development of the word, of language, in the literature of the present and the future. Commanding with facility three languages and blessed with a sensitive, mystic and unique poetical gift, he was admirably equipped to appreciate the extent and value of Joyce's *Work in Progress*. Furthermore, he possessed a cultured, capable, artistic-minded wife, Maria Jolas. Joyce was already familiar with the literary reportage called "Rambles Through Literary Paris" that Jolas conducted each Sunday in the Chicago *Tribune* in addition to his important desk work as city editor, and the Irish writer took the opportunity of this chance encounter to thank the newspaperman for various kindly references to *Ulysses*. In recalling that meeting, Jolas declared of Joyce, "He surprised me by his non-literary attitude. His humanity, if you wish."

It was not for two years that the two men met again and this time Jolas was intent on the project of founding a magazine to be called *transition* and which would offer to a cultured audience the work of the most original literary experimenters of the day. Here, then, was an opportunity for Joyce's *Work in Progress* to appear serially in print, and the writer took advantage of it. One Sunday evening he invited Maria and Eugene Jolas, Elliot Paul, Sylvia Beach and Adrienne Monnier to his apartment where he read the first part of his new book. The first instalment of it appeared in the first issue of *transition* dated April, 1927, five years and three months after *Ulysses* had been ushered into an amazed reading world. Since that period the friendship between Maria and Eugene Jolas and the Joyce family has been constant and a source of vast pleasure to both ménages.

The history of *transition* (interesting enough in itself and certain to be written someday) concerns us here only in so far as it was the vehicle by which a large portion of *Work in Progress* rode into a disputed fame. As the new work appeared, at first monthly and then quarterly and sometimes, indeed, irregularly, a tumult of comment, but little of it of any critical value, greeted the various instalments. They were praised; they were attacked; they were parodied. Old friends of Joyce shook their heads and intimated that he had gone too far this time; new friends became imitators and valiant champions of the new form. Not one in a hundred knew what *Work in Progress* was about and yet at least fifty out of every hundred were curiously disturbed and charmed as one is charmed by an unmistakable music that sounds in the air and yet carries meanings beyond the traditional ear. They saw a new art form before them but could not grasp the key. That would take time and the shedding of many old prejudices and customary approaches to letters.

Yet the new work was a logical progression from the old and those who had followed the development of Joyce's art throughout the years recognized it as such. Some few of his former followers, through either mental incapacity or wilful anger at the lengths to which the writer had gone, fell away or became silent or scornful; but these desertions troubled Joyce not at all. He was impervious to blame, praise, surprise or remonstrance. He had done what he wanted to do in *Ulysses* and he meant to do what he wanted to do in the new work. His audience was the least of his concerns. He had always desired to be heard (as any sensible author desires to be heard) but he had never trimmed his sails to travel with the popular taste. He did not do so now. Being possessed with his subject and knowing perfectly what he was doing he had no time to waste on ill or partially informed criticism or advice. He lived entirely in the strange mythical world he had created, seeing it always from the inside, and, perhaps, vaguely amazed but never irritated at those who could not sense its peculiar essence.

And so he continued to write, to expend, sometimes, a thousand hours of energy on a score of pages, to amass his voluminous notes, to revise and revise until his first draft bore hardly any resemblance to the final copy, to pursue with an ardour and an astonishing tirelessness his unceasing search for the precise expression that would envelop his design, while sicknesses, operations, personal crises, necessary travels and various difficulties obstructed but never halted his creative labours. Time passed; the world changed; certain dates became of moment to him. On December 10, 1930, his son Giorgio, now widely known for his fine baritone voice, married Helen Kastor Fleischmann of New York and Paris. On December 29, 1931, his father, John Stanislaus, died in Dublin after a long illness that had kept the famous old wit bedridden for a number of years. On February 15, 1932, his grandson, Stephen, was born. These were events calculated to impress upon him how long and how far he had travelled through time. With his son gone and his daughter Lucia apart from him for reasons of health,[1] he found himself alone again with his wife as he had been in Pola and Trieste so many years before. The death of his father proved to be a sharp blow, for he had greatly loved his astonishing old parent. His grandson was an endless source of pleasure and pride to him.

*Work in Progress,* to persist in its temporary name, continued to appear serially in *transition*. Excerpts from it also were published in limited editions and in pamphlet form, "Anna Livia Plurabelle," "Tales Told of Shem and Shaun," "Haveth Childers Everywhere," "The Mime of Nick, Mick and the Maggies" and "Storiella as She is Syung." Apropos of the publication of "Anna Livia Plurabelle" and "Haveth Childers Everywhere" in the *Criterion Miscellany* of Faber and Faber, London, Joyce concocted a little rhyme.

> Buy a book in brown paper
> From Faber and Faber
> To hear Annie Liffie trip, tumble and caper.
> Sevensinns in her singthings,
> Plurabells on her prose,
> Sheashell ebb music wayriver she flows.
>
> Humptydump Dublin squeaks through his norse;
> Humptydump Dublin hath a horriple vorse.

---

[1] A facet of Lucia's artistic sensibilities flowered in a series of beautiful illuminated initials that recall the work of medieval monks. Some of them may be seen in the facsimile edition in MSS. of *Pomes Penyeach* (The Obelisk Press, Paris); Chaucer's poem to the Blessed Virgin entitled "A. B. C.," with a Preface by Louis Gillet, of the Académie Française (The Obelisk Press, Paris); and the fragment of the then *Work in Progress* entitled *Storiella as She is Syung* published by Lord Carlow at the Corvinus Press, London.

But for all his kinks english plus his irismanx brogues
Humptydump Dublin's granddada of all rogues.[1]

No, he never forgot his Dublin.

Neither did he forget his poetry. In 1927, the year when *Work
in Progress* first began to appear in *transition,* Shakespeare and
Company published a tiny booklet, *Pomes Penyeach,* containing
thirteen of his poems, the first dating as far back as 1904.[2] Several
of his loveliest verses are to be found in this miniature volume.
They reveal a marked difference from the delicate and precious
contents of *Chamber Music* in that nearly all of them suggest that
they have been inspired by a reality, a person, a loved one or a sight
seen, a boat or light reflected in water at night.

Throughout this period, too, while laboring at *Work in Progress,* Joyce amused himself occasionally by the translation of poetry
either from a foreign tongue into English or from English into a
foreign tongue. His aptitude for such difficult re-creation may be
illustrated by two examples. For one, he sent James Stephens a
translation of that poet's own "Stephen's Green" on the common
birthday that both Irish writers have. Stephens's poem reads as
follows:

> The wind stood up and gave a shout.
> He whistled on his fingers and
>
> Kicked the withered leaves about
> And thumped the branches with his hand
>
> And said he'd kill and kill.
> And so he will and so he will.

Here is Joyce's translation into French.

### Les Verts de Jacques

> Le vent d'un saut lance son cri,
> Se siffle sur les doigts et puis

---

[1] During this period there appeared, also, in the *Nouvelle Revue Française,* a translation of the "Anna Livia Plurabelle" fragment into French (partial) made by Philippe
Soupault, Alfred Perron, Paul Léon, Adrienne Monnier, Samuel Beckett and Joyce. A complete translation into German of this fragment was made by Ivan Goll, Daniel Brody,
Eugene Jolas, Leonard Frank and Joyce. A partial Italian translation, which Joyce considers
the best of the three, was made by Ettore Settanni, Nino Frank and the author himself.

[2] Later set to music by thirteen different composers and published in a deluxe edition
by the Oxford University Press.

Trépigne les feuilles d'automne,
Craque les branches qu'il assomme.

Je tuerai, crie-t-il, holâ!
Et vous verrez s'il le fera!

And, for an example of Joyce translating a foreign poem into English, here is one of the poems in the suite by Gottfried Keller called *Lebendig Begraben,* a suite, by the way, set to music by Keller's fellow Swiss, Othmar Schoeck (regarded by Joyce as easily the first of living composers). First of all, Keller's original poem:

Nun hab' ich gar die Rose aufgefressen
Die sie mir in die starre Hand gegeben.
Das ich nur einmal wuerde Rosen essen
Das haett' ich nie geglaubt in meinem Leben.

Nur moecht' ich wissen ob es eine rote
Od' eine weisse Rose da gewesen.
Gib taeglich uns, O Herr, von Deinem Brote
Und, wenn Du willst, erloes uns von dem Boesen!

And now, Joyce's English version:

Now have I fed and eaten up the rose
Which then she laid within my stiffcold hand.
That I should ever feed upon a rose
I never had believed in liveman's land.

Only I wonder was it white or red
The flower that in this dark my food has been.
Give us, and if Thou give, thy daily bread,
Deliver us from evil, Lord. Amen.

During these years Joyce was greatly assisted in routine and business matters by various friends who made it a point to see that his precarious vision was not overtaxed. These friends read to him, took over most of his correspondence, aided him in correcting proof, attended to commercial details for him, walked with him, and, in a word, made it possible for him to reserve most of his strength for his creative labours.

In addition to the Jolases there should be mentioned, as most valuable of these volunteers, Paul Léon and Stuart Gilbert. Both of them, men of perspicacity, sound sense and artistic comprehension, capably fulfilled what may roughly be defined as secretarial posts. In particular Mr. Léon was (and is) almost the right arm of Joyce so far as business details, the inexhaustible minutiæ of the famed writer's days, were (and are) concerned. He more than any other friend devotes the larger part of his time to Joyce's interests. For the last dozen years, in sickness or health, night and day, he has been an absolutely disinterested and devoted friend and it is very doubtful that Joyce could have done what he has done without Léon's generous help. There is a calmness, a methodical precision and a practicability about this man (who is both legally and artistically minded) that is of immense value to Joyce. Big and dark, with a rolling, ironic eye and a snorting laugh, he is as sympathetic in company as he is capable in grasping business details.

Joyce, on his part, exerted himself strenuously for the advancement of his friends and those whose accomplishments he admired. When he became really interested in the work of some artist (it mattered not what art) his enthusiasm knew no bounds and he was indefatigable in fighting the man's battles. He has waged long and assiduous campaigns, for instance, to advance the literary fame of such forgotten writers as Edouard Dujardin and Italo Suevo. Perhaps the best known of these personal campaigns for another was the one he conducted for several years to spread the fame and advance the fortunes of John Sullivan, the famous Irish tenor. Joyce's dogged insistence, his unwearying persistency and his unwavering determination during these periods were a marvel to his friends. Indeed, some of them protested that he was diverting too much energy from his own work into the battle for his admired singer. Sullivan, who sang at the Paris Opéra and in all the great opera houses throughout the provinces of France and Italy, possessed a full and magnificent tenor voice and with it he could achieve notes impossible to other singers. Joyce once remarked, "I have been through the score of *Guillaume Tell,* and I discover that Sullivan sings 456 G's, 93 A flats, 92 A's, 54 B flats, 15 B's, 19 C's, and 2 C sharps. Nobody else can do it." He desired that all the world should know the virtues of this singer. Therefore, he dispatched letters and telegrams to right and left, bullied important personages, conductors, patrons of opera, into hearing his favourite singer and pulled every string and turned every stone calculated to advance Sullivan's fortunes that he could.

To such activities, then, time passed and finally came the moment when Joyce could announce to his friends that the end of his *Work in Progress* was in sight. The long galley sheets began to come in and while the writer was correcting the first part of his book he was still composing the last part. It was in mid-November, 1938, that the last words were written and at his birthday celebration in the home of his son on February 2, 1939, he displayed the first bound copy and so revealed the title he had guarded, except from his wife, so jealously for seventeen years. The successor to *Ulysses* was *Finnegans Wake.*[1]

### III

One last picture.

Long after the twilight has fallen upon a wintry Paris and the lights flash in the cafés a number of motorcars converge on the brown apartment house where Joyce has his habitation. It is the second day of February and the writer has reached another milestone (or should we call it date-stone?) in his journey through time. It is the evening when his friends gather about him to celebrate and acknowledge his birthday. These friends assemble in the salon, a simple and comfortable room where the most noticeable furnishings are the crammed glass-fronted bookcase (not really his "working" books, for these are crowded two deep on many shelves in his study) and the open piano. There are pictures on the walls, not the treasured portraits of the Joyce forebears, for they now hang in the salon of Helen and Giorgio Joyce, but small charming paintings by Jack B. Yeats and portraits of Nora Joyce. The lights are restful but undimmed, for Joyce detests a sombre room and too many shadows lessen his limited vision; the chairs (unlike the usual stiff-backed French chairs) are comfortable and conducive to lounging; the apéritifs, untouched by Joyce himself, are many

---

[1] *Finnegans Wake* was officially published in both England and the United States on May 4, 1939. It was listed among "Books Received" by a Dublin newspaper as *"Finnegans Wake* by Sean O'Casey"! This mistake, however, brought Joyce two friendly letters, one from Sean O'Casey, who believed it was intentional, and the other from the editor who said it was unintentional.

and excellent; the blue smoke from cigarettes curls about the specially-designed glass chandelier. Tongues wag; there is much laughter and chatter; abstruse problems are instinctively avoided; and the writer, perhaps in his dark-coloured house-jacket, easy slippers and the embroidered waistcoat of his grandfather, sits or, rather, slouches seemingly boneless in his chair and listens or speaks in a low modulated voice to those who cluster about him. There emanates from him none of the pompous kingship so obvious in a number of famous writers. Neither does he appear to take any particular pleasure in talking about his own work. Eventually the glass doors to the dining room are flung open and all troop in to the long table brightly winking with glasses and silver. Though Joyce himself eats most abstemiously, there is always a plethora of food for his guests and a small Niagara Falls of excellent wines. As the serving plates are passed and the wines, always one or two of Swiss vintage, gurgle happily into the goblets it is of historical interest to pick out the faces about the table.

Joyce, ruddy-faced, his thin lips curling in a smile beneath his small moustache, his hair now generously snowed with white, the lenses of his glasses reflecting back the lights of the room, leans to left and right and gently urges the virtues of his Swiss wines on his neighbours while he holds and vaguely flourishes the long Italian Virginia cigars (shaped something like a rat's tail) which he smokes upon these occasions. Nora Joyce, her blue eyes attentively watching over her end of the table, her carefully-coiffed grey hair giving her an almost regal appearance, her poise impeccable and assured, maintains an element of gaiety about her that sometimes arouses the curiosity of her husband. He bends his head across the table and demands, "What did she say now?" He begins to smile before he receives the answer. Between these two sway backward and forward two rows of faces: Giorgio Joyce, dark-haired, eyes guarded by glasses, small-moustached, resembling faintly from a distance the baritone Lawrence Tibbett; Helen Joyce, her features as cleanly cut as those on a Byzantine cameo, dusky-haired, chic as only those women who know all the finesses of their Paris are chic; Paul Léon, large-boned, large-eyed, black-moustached, slightly bowed as though a part of the weight of the world was resting upon his shoulders; Eugene Jolas, square-shouldered, hair flecked with grey, presenting the head and features of a later Roman emperor; Maria Jolas, tall, laughing-eyed, radiating mingled good humour and efficiency; John Sullivan, dark-eyebrowed and bold-featured and burly in build; Stuart Gilbert, quizzical-eyed, quiet and giving no hint that he was once a judge; his wife, a bright little hummingbird of a woman; Marie-Louise Soupault, dark-featured and thoroughly French in manner; Samuel Beckett, tall and lean, eye-glassed, reserved and almost remote in his bearing. There are others that might be mentioned, Georges Pelorson and his wife, Paul-Léon Fargue, Sally and William Bird, Mary and Padraic Colum (if they happen to be in Paris), Peggy Guggenheim, Philippe Soupault, but a composite picture has its limitations.

There are no set speeches at this long table but there is plenty of banter and gusty laughter. After the last course of the dinner is served and dispatched, the birthday cake (generally a huge affair blazing with candles and designed to illustrate some step in the progress of *Finnegans Wake*) is brought in and placed before Joyce. He blows mightily at the candles and cuts the first slice. Champagne corks pop and the writer receives the felicitations of his friends and responds briefly, almost shyly, to their good wishes. The group breaks up and drifts back to the salon.

Music follows. Mrs. Jolas or Mrs. Sullivan or another seats herself at the piano and strikes the first notes. A light of anticipation and pleasure breaks across Joyce's face, for this is the moment for which he has been waiting. Music, and especially the singing voice, will always be his second passion. Luckily, good voices never fail to be present at these birthday festivals. Mrs. Jolas possesses a fine dramatic soprano; John Sullivan, of course, is famed all over Europe; and Giorgio Joyce's well-trained and impressive baritone never fails to provide a happy climax to the evening. There is singing, then, operatic arias, French and Italian and German songs, Irish airs and English ballads. Presently Joyce himself is singing, his fine tenor clouded, perhaps, by the years but his artistry and his obvious enjoyment making up for the inevitable inroads of time. He sings the old songs that he loves and is not allowed to rest until he has rendered "Molly Bloom." That accomplished to the hilarious satisfaction of all, Joyce must have another glass of wine. He evidences some restlessness and his friends know what is imminent. It is the time for dancing.

No one who has not seen Joyce dance can have any idea from a brief description what his terpsichorean talents are like. To enlivening music he breaks into a high fantastic dance all by himself, a dance that is full of quaint antics, high kicks and astonishing figures. He dances with all his body, head, hands and feet and the evolutions through which he goes, eccentric but never losing the beat of the music, are calculated to arouse a suspicion in the beholder that he has no bones at all. Others join in the dances and he weaves wild and original patterns with them. When the music stops he sinks contentedly into his chair. The festival has been a success.

It is after midnight when the moment for parting (delayed as long as possible) comes. Joyce stands by his door bidding good night to his guests, and as they depart down the stairs and into the night they glance back and see standing above them the tall lean figure of a great gentleman and a great writer.

November 15, 1939.

*That is the way I like to remember him and that was the way I hoped to see him again. But it was not to be. The last time I saw James Joyce was in the late autumn of 1938. He was standing on the train platform in the Gare Saint-Lazare, waving his cane violently at my wife and myself as our boat-train for Cherbourg drew slowly out of the station. We both believed that this was a temporary parting, that I would come back to France from the United States within a year; but Fate, in the form of World War II, intervened and completely disrupted the accustomed course of human affairs. What the gigantic catastrophe did to Joyce is unknown, but it is my personal belief that it killed him. His high sensitivity could not surmount it.*

*When the German hordes occupied France, and Paris was shut off from the rest of the world, he was isolated. The royalties from his books could not reach him, and he was reduced to practically existing on a dole from the United States Embassy. Eventually he managed to get out of France and into Switzerland, reaching Zurich where he had lived during World War I. History was repeating itself, but the man was tired, his highly nervous nature could not stand up to this new destruction of all that he held dear. He developed an intestinal affliction and was removed to the Schwesternhaus von Rotenkreuz Hospital. There he was operated upon, and though blood transfusions were given him and for a brief while he seemed to be recovering, the end had come. He died at 2:15 A.M., January 13, 1941. He was nineteen days less than fifty-nine years old. On January 15 his body was laid to rest in the Allmend Fluntern Cemetery on the outskirts of Zurich.*

*He died in a dark hour when there seemed little hope of the survival of the civilization he had known and loved. But he left behind him an accomplishment and an influence that are as valid today as they were when the sun was shining over his beloved Paris of the 1920's.*

*November, 1948.*

# ACKNOWLEDGEMENTS

My acknowledgements for material, hints and suggestions during the writing of this book are many and it is possible that some due have been forgotten or overlooked. To James Joyce himself I am indebted for his patience in answering questions, his calm unconcern for my deductions and assumptions and his permission to print unpublished or rare writings by him. To the graciousness of Mrs. James Joyce I incline an admiring head. In Dublin I acknowledge gratefully aid and suggestions from Seumas O'Sullivan, Jack B. Yeats, Brinsley Macnamara, Liam O'Flaherty, Arthur Koehler, Thomas Pugh, David H. Charles, Alfred Bergan (the "little Alf Bergan" of *Ulysses*), the late "Davy" Byrne and Constantine P. Curran, his wife, and his daughter, Elizabeth. In England my acknowledgements are due to George Joyce (brother to James Joyce), the late Herbert Hughes, Miss Harriet Weaver, T. S. Eliot, Frank Budgen, Claud W. Sykes, John Eglinton (W. K. Magee) and Dr. Jacob Schwartz; in Paris they are tendered to Eugene and Maria Jolas, Paul Léon, Sylvia Beach, John Sullivan, Robert McAlmon, Stuart Gilbert, William S. Bird, George Slocombe, the late Jack B. Kahane, Philippe Soupault, Mademoiselle Madeleine Chabrier, and Mademoiselle Denise Clairouin; in New York to Padraic and Mary Colum, Alfred F. Goldsmith, Miss Nora Mead, Bennett Cerf, J. Francis Byrne and R. F. Roberts; in Zurich to the late Georges Borach, Félix Beran, Paul Ruggiero and Professor Alfred Vogt; and in Trieste to Professor Stanislaus Joyce, who very kindly and at some trouble to himself supplied me with copies of the long series of letters he had received from his brother, James Joyce.

# INDEX